Atlantis Studies in Computing

Volume 2

Series Editors: **Jan A. Bergstra, Michael W. Mislove**

Atlantis Studies in Computing

Series Editors:

Jan A. Bergstra
Informatics Institute
University of Amsterdam
Amsterdam, The Netherlands

Michael W. Mislove
Department of Mathematics
Tulane University
New Orleans, USA

(ISSN: 2212-8565)

Aims and scope of the series

The series aims at publishing books in the areas of computer science, computer and network technology, IT management, information technology and informatics from the technological, managerial, theoretical/fundamental, social or historical perspective.

We welcome books in the following categories:

Technical monographs: these will be reviewed as to timeliness, usefulness, relevance, completeness and clarity of presentation.

Textbooks.

Books of a more speculative nature: these will be reviewed as to relevance and clarity of presentation.

For more information on this series and our other book series, please visit our website at:

www.atlantis-press.com/publications/books

ATLANTIS PRESS

AMSTERDAM – PARIS – BEIJING

Instruction Sequences for Computer Science

Jan A. Bergstra and Cornelis A. Middelburg

Institute of Informatics, Faculty of Science, University of Amsterdam
Amsterdam, the Netherlands

ATLANTIS PRESS

AMSTERDAM – PARIS – BEIJING

Atlantis Press

8, square des Bouleaux
75019 Paris, France

For information on all Atlantis Press publications, visit our website at: *www.atlantis-press.com*

Atlantis Studies in Computing

Volume 1: Code Generation with Templates - B.J. Arnoldus, M.G.J. Van den Brand, A. Serebrenik

ISBNs
Print: 978-94-6239-049-2
E-Book: 978-94-91216-65-7
ISSN: 2212-8565

Preface

The concept of an instruction sequence is a key concept in practice, but strangely enough it has as yet not come prominently into the picture in theoretical circles. In much work on computer architecture, instruction sequences are under discussion. In spite of this, the notion of an instruction sequence has never been subjected to systematic and precise analysis. Moreover, in work on computer architecture, the viewpoint is usually taken that a program is in essence an instruction sequence. By contrast, in the theory of computation, different viewpoints on what is a program are usually taken. This state of affairs brought us to define a general notion of an instruction sequence, to subject it to a systematic and precise analysis, and to provide evidence for the hypothesis that the notion of an instruction sequence is relevant to diverse subjects from the theory of computation and the area of computer architecture. Many results of the work in question are brought together in this book with the aim to bring instruction sequences as a theme in computer science better into the picture.

To put it otherwise, this book concerns instruction sequences, the behaviours produced by instruction sequences under execution, the interaction between these behaviours and components of the execution environment concerning the processing of instructions, the expressiveness of instruction sequences, and various issues relating to well-known subjects from computer science where we found that the notion of an instruction sequence is relevant. Most of the issues in question are of a computation-theoretic or computer-architectural kind. They relate to subjects such as the halting problem, non-uniform computational complexity, instruction sequence performance and instruction set architecture. Some of the issues considered are somehow related to process algebra, namely remote instruction processing and instruction sequence producible processes. Some variations on instruction sequences of the usual kind, such as instruction sequences without a directional bias and probabilistic instruction sequences, are also considered.

This book is primarily intended for researchers in computer science interested in instruction sequences as a theme in computer science. It is also meant to be suitable as supplementary reading in courses for graduate students and advanced undergraduate students in computer science. Chapters 5 and 6 may as much appeal to those who are primarily interested in the subjects from the theory of computation and the area of computer architecture, respectively, that come up in these chapters. Chapter 7 may as much appeal to those who are primarily interested in process algebra.

Throughout the book, some familiarity with equational logic, universal algebra, and elementary set theory is assumed. In Sect. 5.2, some familiarity with non-uniform computational complexity is assumed. In Sect. 5.1, Sect. 6.2 and Chap. 7, some familiarity with computability, instruction set architectures and process algebra, respectively, would be helpful. Chapter 2 is a prerequisite for Chap. 3, and both chapters are prerequisites for all subsequent chapters.

Chapter 2 introduces an algebraic theory SPISA of single-pass instruction sequences and an algebraic theory BTA of mathematical objects that represent in a direct way the behaviours produced by instruction sequences under execution. The objects concerned are called threads. It is made precise in the setting of the latter theory which behaviours are produced by the instruction sequences considered in the former theory. The instruction sequences in question include both finite and infinite ones, but the theory provides a notation by means of which all of them can be represented finitely. This chapter also introduces alternative notations ISNR and ISNA by means of which all these instruction sequences can be represented finitely as well, but which are closer to existing assembly languages.

Chapter 3 introduces so-called services, which represent the behaviours exhibited by the components of an execution environment that are capable of processing particular instructions and doing so independently, and extends BTA with an operator meant for the composition of families of named services and operators that have a direct bearing on the processing of instructions by services from such service families. In addition, the concept of a functional unit, which is an abstract model of a machine, is introduced. In the frequently occurring case that the behaviours represented by services can be viewed as the behaviours of a machine in its different states, the services concerned are completely determined by a functional unit. Some extensions of ISNR and ISNA with additional instructions are explained with the help of some simple functional units.

Chapter 4 gives answers to basic expressiveness issues regarding SPISA. In this case, expressiveness is basically about which behaviours can be produced by instruction sequences under execution, which instructions can be removed without reducing the class of behaviours that can be produced by instruction sequences under execution, how to enlarge the class of behaviours that can be produced by instruction sequences under execution, et cetera. This chapter is also concerned with some issues that arise from the investigation of expressiveness issues regarding SPISA. For example, it is shown that a finite-state execution mechanism for a set of instruction sequences that by itself can produce each finite-state behaviour from an instruction sequence belonging to the set of instruction sequences in question is unfeasible.

Chapter 5 concerns two subjects from the theory of computation, namely the halting problem and non-uniform computational complexity. Positioning Turing's result regarding the undecidability of the halting problem as a result about programs rather than machines, and taking single-pass instruction sequences as considered in SPISA as programs, the autosolvability requirement that a program of a certain kind must solve the halting problem for all programs of that kind is analysed. Thinking in terms of single-pass instruction sequences as considered in SPISA, counterparts of the classical non-uniform complexity classes P/poly and $\mathrm{NP}/\mathrm{poly}$ are defined, a notion of completeness for the counterpart of $\mathrm{NP}/\mathrm{poly}$ is introduced, several complexity hypotheses are formulated, and it is shown that a problem closely related to 3SAT is NP-complete as well as complete for the counterpart of $\mathrm{NP}/\mathrm{poly}$.

Chapter 6 concerns two subjects from the area of computer architecture, namely instruction sequence performance and instruction set architectures. We study the effect of eliminating indirect jump instructions from instruction sequences with direct and indirect jump instructions on the interactive performance of instruction sequences. A strict version of the concept of a load/store instruction set architecture is proposed for theoretical work relevant to the design of instruction set architectures, and it is studied how the transformations on the states of the main memory of a strict load/store instruction set architecture that can be achieved by executing instruction sequences on it depend on the parameters involved.

Chapter 7 concerns two subjects related to process algebra, namely protocols to deal with remote instruction processing and instruction sequence producible processes. If instruction processing takes place remotely, this means that a stream of instructions to be processed arises at one place and the processing of that stream of instructions is handled at another place. Process algebra is used to describe two protocols to deal with this phenomenon. Because process algebra is considered relevant to computer science, there must be programmed systems whose behaviours are taken for processes as considered in process algebra. It is shown that all finite-state processes can be produced by single-pass instruction sequences as considered in SPISA, provided that the cluster fair abstraction rule known from the algebraic theory of processes called ACP is valid.

Chapter 8 introduces three variations of instruction sequences as considered in SPISA, namely polyadic instruction sequences, instruction sequences without a directional bias, and probabilistic instruction sequences. A polyadic instruction sequence is a possibly parameterized instruction sequence fragment that can produce a joint behaviour together with other such fragments because the fragment being executed can switch over execution to another. Instruction sequences without a directional bias require that for each instruction whose effect involves that execution proceeds in the forward direction, there is a counterpart whose effect involves that execution proceeds in the backward direction. Probabilistic instruction sequences are instruction sequences that contain instructions that are themselves probabilistic by nature.

There are also four appendices. In Appendix A, five challenges for the point of view from which the approach to semantics followed in Chaps. 2 and 3 originates are sketched. In Appendix B, some results about functional units for natural numbers are given, which are except one computability results that are not directly related to existing results that we know of. In Appendix C, the usefulness of the dynamically instantiated instructions introduced in Chap. 3 is illustrated by means of an example. In Appendix D, a model of a hypothetical execution environment for instruction sequences, designed for the purpose of explaining how instruction sequences as considered in SPISA may be executed, is discussed.

A glossary of the notations introduced in this book and the general mathematical notations used in this book can be found from page 221 onward. At this point, one further remark about notation may be useful: bold-faced italic letters, with or without decorations, will be used as syntactical variables in this book.

Acknowledgements

This book brings together and streamlines work done by a group of people which includes, in addition to the authors, Inge Bethke, Marijke Loots, Alban Ponse and Mark van der Zwaag. The work in question was partly carried out in the framework of projects funded by the Netherlands Organisation for Scientific Research (NWO).

Amsterdam, April 2012 *J. A. Bergstra and C. A. Middelburg*

Contents

List of Tables

Chapter 1

Introduction

The concept of an instruction sequence is a very primitive concept in computing. It has always been relevant to computing because of the fact that execution of instruction sequences underlies virtually all past and current generations of computers. It happens that, given a precise definition of the concept of an instruction sequence, many issues in computer science can be clearly explained in terms of instruction sequences, from issues of a computer-architectural kind to issues of a computation-theoretic kind. A simple yet interesting example is that a program can be defined as a text that denotes an instruction sequence. Such a definition corresponds to an empirical perspective found among practitioners.

In theoretical computer science, the meaning of programs usually plays a prominent part in the explanation of many issues concerning programs. Moreover, what is taken for the meaning of programs is mathematical by nature. On the other hand, it is customary that practitioners do not fall back on the mathematical meaning of programs in case explanation of issues concerning programs is needed. They phrase their explanations from an empirical perspective. An empirical perspective that we consider appealing is the perspective that a program is in essence an instruction sequence and an instruction sequence under execution produces a behaviour that is controlled by its execution environment in the sense that each step performed actuates the processing of an instruction by the execution environment and a reply returned at completion of the processing determines how the behaviour proceeds.

The work brought together in this book started with an attempt to approach the semantics of programming languages from the perspective mentioned above. The first published paper on this approach is [Bergstra and Loots (2000)]. That paper is superseded by [Bergstra and Loots (2002)] with regard to the groundwork for the approach: an algebraic theory of single-pass instruction sequences and an algebraic theory of mathematical objects that represent in a direct way the behaviours produced by instruction sequences under execution. The main advantages of the approach is that it does not require a lot of mathematical background and that it is more appealing to practitioners than the main approaches to programming language semantics: the operational approach, the denotational approach and the axiomatic approach. For an overview of these approaches, see e.g. [Mosses (2006)].

As a continuation of the work on the above-mentioned approach to programming language semantics, the notion of an instruction sequence was subjected to systematic and precise analysis using the groundwork laid earlier. This led among other things to expressiveness results about the instruction sequences considered and variations of the instruction sequences considered. Instruction sequences are under discussion for many years in diverse work on computer architecture, as witnessed by e.g. [Lunde (1977); Patterson and Ditzel (1980); Hennessy *et al.* (1982); Baker (1991); Xia and Torrellas (1996); Brock and Hunt (1997); Nair and Hopkins (1997); Ofelt and Hennessy (2000); Tennenhouse and Wetherall (2007)], but the notion of an instruction sequence has never been subjected to any precise analysis before.

As another continuation of the work on the above-mentioned approach to programming language semantics, selected issues relating to well-known subjects from the theory of computation and the area of computer architecture were rigorously investigated thinking in terms of instruction sequences. The subjects from the theory of computation, namely the halting problem and non-uniform computational complexity, are usually investigated thinking in terms of a common model of computation such as Turing machines and Boolean circuits. The subjects from the area of computer architecture, namely instruction sequence performance, instruction set architectures and remote instruction processing, are usually not investigated in a rigorous way at all.

A lot of the above-mentioned work is brought together in this book with the aim to bring instruction sequences as a theme in computer science better into the picture. In our opinion, the book demonstrates that the concept of an instruction sequence offers a novel and useful viewpoint on issues relating to diverse subjects. In view of the very primitive nature of this concept, it is in fact rather surprising that instruction sequences have never been a theme in computer science. Looking ahead, we expect that a theoretical understanding of issues in terms of instruction sequences will become increasingly more important to a growing number of developments in computer science. Among them are for instance the developments with respect to techniques for high-performance program execution on classical or non-classical computers and techniques for estimating execution times of hard real-time systems. For these and other such developments, the abstractions usually made do not allow for all relevant details to be considered.

This book brings together and streamlines work presented before in peer-reviewed articles in journals or conference proceedings and preprints archived on the arXiv. The sources of the different chapters are as follows:

- Chap. 2 originates mainly from [Bergstra and Loots (2002); Bergstra and Middelburg (2010c, 2012a)];
- Chap. 3 originates mainly from [Bergstra and Middelburg (2007a, 2009b, 2012a)];
- Chap. 4 originates mainly from [Ponse and van der Zwaag (2006); Bergstra and Middelburg (2008b, 2012b)];
- Chap. 5 originates mainly from [Bergstra and Middelburg (2010a, 2012a)];
- Chap. 6 originates mainly from [Bergstra and Middelburg (2010b, 2011a)];
- Chap. 7 originates mainly from [Bergstra and Middelburg (2011c)];
- Chap. 8 originates mainly from [Bergstra and Ponse (2009); Bergstra and Middelburg (2009a, 2011d)];
- Appendix A originates mainly from [Bergstra and Middelburg (2009a)];
- Appendix B originates mainly from [Bergstra and Middelburg (2012a)];
- Appendix C originates mainly from [Bergstra and Middelburg (2009b)];
- Appendix D originates mainly from [Bergstra and Ponse (2007)].

Chapter 2

Instruction Sequences

This chapter concerns instruction sequences and the behaviours produced by instruction sequences under execution. An instruction sequence under execution is considered to produce a behaviour that is controlled by its execution environment in the sense that each step performed actuates the processing of an instruction by the execution environment and a reply returned at completion of the processing determines how the behaviour proceeds.

We introduce an algebraic theory of single-pass instruction sequences and an algebraic theory of mathematical objects that represent in a direct way the behaviours produced by instruction sequences under execution. We make precise in the setting of the latter theory which behaviours are produced by the instruction sequences considered in the former theory. The instruction sequences in question include both finite and infinite ones, but the theory provides a notation by means of which all of them can be represented finitely. However, this notation is not intended for actual programming. We also devise several alternative notations by means of which all these instruction sequences can be represented finitely as well, but which are closer to existing assembly languages.

This chapter is not concerned with the interaction between instruction sequences under execution and components of their execution environment concerning the processing of instructions. Chapter 3 is devoted to this kind of interaction.

2.1 Single Pass Instruction Sequence Algebra

In this section, we present SPISA (Single Pass Instruction Sequence Algebra). As suggested by the name, SPISA is an algebraic theory of single-pass instruction sequences. The starting-point of this theory is the simple and appealing perception of a sequential program as a single-pass instruction sequence, i.e. a finite or infinite sequence of instructions of which each instruction is executed at most once and can be dropped after it has been executed or jumped over.

The concepts underlying the primitives of SPISA are common in programming, but the particular form of the primitives is not common. The predominant concern in the design of the theory has been to achieve simple syntax and semantics, while maintaining the expressive power of arbitrary finite control. The delivery of a Boolean value at termination of the execution of an instruction sequence is supported to deal naturally with instruction sequences that implement some test.

2.1.1 *Primitive instructions*

In SPISA, it is assumed that a fixed but arbitrary set $\mathfrak{A}$ of *basic instructions* has been given. The intuition is that the execution of a basic instruction modifies in many instances a state and produces in all instances a reply at its completion. The possible replies are $\mathtt{t}$ (standing for true) and $\mathtt{f}$ (standing for false), and the actual reply is in most instances state-dependent. Therefore, successive executions of the same basic instruction may produce different replies. The set $\mathfrak{A}$ is the basis for the set of instructions that may appear in the instruction sequences considered in SPISA. These instructions are called primitive instructions.

SPISA has the following *primitive instructions*:

- for each $\boldsymbol{a} \in \mathfrak{A}$, a *plain basic instruction* $\boldsymbol{a}$;
- for each $\boldsymbol{a} \in \mathfrak{A}$, a *positive test instruction* $+\boldsymbol{a}$;
- for each $\boldsymbol{a} \in \mathfrak{A}$, a *negative test instruction* $-\boldsymbol{a}$;
- for each $l \in \mathbb{N}$, a *forward jump instruction* $\#l$;
- a *plain termination instruction* $!$;
- a *positive termination instruction* $!\mathtt{t}$;
- a *negative termination instruction* $!\mathtt{f}$.

We write $\mathfrak{I}$ for the set of all primitive instructions of SPISA. On execution of an instruction sequence, these primitive instructions have the following effects:

- the effect of a positive test instruction $+\boldsymbol{a}$ is that basic instruction $\boldsymbol{a}$ is executed and execution proceeds with the next primitive instruction if $\mathtt{t}$ is produced and otherwise the next primitive instruction is skipped and execution proceeds with the primitive instruction following the skipped one — if there is no primitive instruction to proceed with, inaction occurs;
- the effect of a negative test instruction $-\boldsymbol{a}$ is the same as the effect of $+\boldsymbol{a}$, but with the

role of the value produced reversed;

- the effect of a plain basic instruction a is the same as the effect of $+a$, but execution always proceeds as if t is produced;
- the effect of a forward jump instruction $\#l$ is that execution proceeds with the lth next primitive instruction of the instruction sequence concerned — if l equals 0 or there is no primitive instruction to proceed with, inaction occurs;
- the effect of the plain termination instruction ! is that execution terminates without delivery of a Boolean value;
- the effect of the positive termination instruction !t is that execution terminates with delivery of the Boolean value t;
- the effect of the negative termination instruction !f is that execution terminates with delivery of the Boolean value f.

2.1.2 *Constants, operators and equational axioms*

SPISA has one sort: the sort **IS** of *instruction sequences*. We make this sort explicit to anticipate the need for many-sortedness in Sect. 2.2.5. To build terms of sort **IS**, SPISA has the following constants and operators:

- for each $u \in \mathfrak{I}$, the *instruction* constant $u : \to \mathbf{IS}$;
- the binary *concatenation* operator $\_ \,;\, \_ : \mathbf{IS} \times \mathbf{IS} \to \mathbf{IS}$;
- the unary *repetition* operator $\_^{\omega} : \mathbf{IS} \to \mathbf{IS}$.

We assume that there are infinitely many variables of sort **IS**, including X, Y, Z. SPISA terms are built as usual. We use infix notation for concatenation and postfix notation for repetition.

A closed SPISA term is considered to denote a non-empty, finite or eventually periodic infinite sequence of primitive instructions.[1] The instruction sequence denoted by a closed term of the form $t \,;\, t'$ is the instruction sequence denoted by t concatenated with the instruction sequence denoted by t'. The instruction sequence denoted by a closed term of the form t^{ω} is the instruction sequence denoted by t concatenated infinitely many times with itself. Some simple examples of closed SPISA terms are

$$\mathtt{a} \,;\, \mathtt{b} \,;\, \mathtt{c}\,, \qquad +\mathtt{a} \,;\, \#2 \,;\, \#3 \,;\, \mathtt{b} \,;\, !\mathtt{t}\,, \qquad \mathtt{a} \,;\, (\mathtt{b} \,;\, \mathtt{c})^{\omega}\,.$$

[1] An eventually periodic infinite sequence is an infinite sequence with only finitely many distinct suffixes.

Table 2.1 Axioms of SPISA

$(X ; Y) ; Z = X ; (Y ; Z)$	SPISA1
$(X^n)^\omega = X^\omega$	SPISA2
$X^\omega ; Y = X^\omega$	SPISA3
$(X ; Y)^\omega = X ; (Y ; X)^\omega$	SPISA4

On execution of the instruction sequence denoted by the first term, the basic instructions a, b and c are executed in that order and after that inaction occurs. On execution of the instruction sequence denoted by the second term, the basic instruction a is executed first, if the execution of a produces the reply t, the basic instruction b is executed next and after that execution terminates with delivery of the value t, and if the execution of a produces the reply f, inaction occurs. On execution of the instruction sequence denoted by the third term, the basic instruction a is executed first, and after that the basic instructions b and c are executed in that order repeatedly forever. In Sect. 3.1.4, we will give examples of instruction sequences for which the delivery of a Boolean value at termination of their execution is natural.

Closed SPISA terms are considered equal if they represent the same instruction sequence. The axioms for instruction sequence equivalence are given in Table 2.1. In this table, n stands for an arbitrary positive natural number. The term t^n, where t is a SPISA term, is defined by induction on n as follows: $t^1 = t$ and $t^{n+1} = t ; t^n$.

The *unfolding* equation $X^\omega = X ; X^\omega$ is derivable.

Lemma 2.1. *The equation $X^\omega = X ; X^\omega$ is derivable from the axioms of* SPISA.

Proof. This equation is derived as follows:

$$\begin{aligned} X^\omega &= (X ; X)^\omega && \text{by SPISA2} \\ &= X ; (X ; X)^\omega && \text{by SPISA4} \\ &= X ; X^\omega && \text{by SPISA2 .} \end{aligned}$$

□

Definition 2.1. A closed SPISA term is in *first canonical form* if it is of the form t or $t ; t'^\omega$, where t and t' are closed SPISA terms in which the repetition operator does not occur.

Each closed SPISA term is derivably equal to a closed SPISA term in first canonical form.

Lemma 2.2. *For all closed* SPISA *terms t, there exists a closed* SPISA *term t' in first canonical form such that $t = t'$ is derivable from the axioms of* SPISA.

Proof. This is proved by induction on the structure of t. The case $t \equiv u$ is trivial. In the case $t \equiv t_1 \,;\, t_2$, by the induction hypothesis, there exist closed SPISA terms t_1' and t_2' in first canonical form such that $t_1 = t_1'$ and $t_2 = t_2'$ are derivable. That $t_1' \,;\, t_2'$ is derivably equal to a closed SPISA term in first canonical form is easily proved by case distinction on the two possible forms of t_1'. In the case $t \equiv {t_1}^{\omega}$, by the induction hypothesis, there exists a closed SPISA term t_1' in first canonical form such that $t_1 = t_1'$ is derivable. That ${t_1'}^{\omega}$ is derivably equal to a closed SPISA term in first canonical form is easily proved by case distinction on the two possible forms of t_1', using Lemma 2.1. □

For example:

$$(\mathtt{a}\,;\mathtt{b})^{\omega}\,;\mathtt{c}\,;\,! = \mathtt{a}\,;(\mathtt{b}\,;\mathtt{a})^{\omega}\,,$$
$$+\mathtt{a}\,;(\#4\,;\mathtt{b}\,;(-\mathtt{c}\,;\#5\,;\,!)^{\omega})^{\omega} = +\mathtt{a}\,;\#4\,;\mathtt{b}\,;(-\mathtt{c}\,;\#5\,;\,!)^{\omega}\,.$$

Lemma 2.2 will be used several times in subsequent chapters.

2.1.3 *The initial model*

A typical model of SPISA is the model in which:

- the domain is the set of all finite and eventually periodic infinite sequences over the set $\mathfrak{I}$ of primitive instructions;
- the operation associated with ; is concatenation;
- the operation associated with $^{\omega}$ is the operation $\underline{^{\omega}}$ defined as follows:
  - if U is a finite sequence over $\mathfrak{I}$, then $U^{\underline{\omega}}$ is the unique eventually periodic infinite sequence U' such that U concatenated n times with itself is a proper prefix of U' for each $n \in \mathbb{N}$;
  - if U is an eventually periodic infinite sequence over $\mathfrak{I}$, then $U^{\underline{\omega}}$ is U.

The elements of the domain of this model are called SPISA *instruction sequences*.

The model of SPISA described above is an initial model of SPISA. If we speak about *the* initial model of SPISA, we have this model in mind. However, if we speak about the

Table 2.2 Axioms for the structural congruence predicate

$\#n{+}1 ; \boldsymbol{u}_1 ; \ldots ; \boldsymbol{u}_n ; \#0 \cong_{\mathrm{s}} \#0 ; \boldsymbol{u}_1 ; \ldots ; \boldsymbol{u}_n ; \#0$	SC1
$\#n{+}1 ; \boldsymbol{u}_1 ; \ldots ; \boldsymbol{u}_n ; \#l \cong_{\mathrm{s}} \#l{+}n{+}1 ; \boldsymbol{u}_1 ; \ldots ; \boldsymbol{u}_n ; \#l$	SC2
$(\#l{+}n{+}1 ; \boldsymbol{u}_1 ; \ldots ; \boldsymbol{u}_n)^\omega \cong_{\mathrm{s}} (\#l ; \boldsymbol{u}_1 ; \ldots ; \boldsymbol{u}_n)^\omega$	SC3
$\#l{+}n{+}n'{+}2 ; \boldsymbol{u}_1 ; \ldots ; \boldsymbol{u}_n ; (\boldsymbol{v}_1 ; \ldots ; \boldsymbol{v}_{n'+1})^\omega \cong_{\mathrm{s}}$ $\#l{+}n{+}1 ; \boldsymbol{u}_1 ; \ldots ; \boldsymbol{u}_n ; (\boldsymbol{v}_1 ; \ldots ; \boldsymbol{v}_{n'+1})^\omega$	SC4
$X = Y \Rightarrow X \cong_{\mathrm{s}} Y$	SC5
$X \cong_{\mathrm{s}} X$	SC6
$X \cong_{\mathrm{s}} Y \Rightarrow Y \cong_{\mathrm{s}} X$	SC7
$X \cong_{\mathrm{s}} Y \wedge Y \cong_{\mathrm{s}} Z \Rightarrow X \cong_{\mathrm{s}} Z$	SC8
$\boldsymbol{X} \cong_{\mathrm{s}} \boldsymbol{Y} \Rightarrow \boldsymbol{t}\,[\boldsymbol{X}/\boldsymbol{Z}] \cong_{\mathrm{s}} \boldsymbol{t}\,[\boldsymbol{Y}/\boldsymbol{Z}]$	SC9

initial model of another algebraic theory, we have the quotient algebra of the closed term algebra modulo derivable equality in mind.

2.1.4 *Structural congruence*

SPISA instruction sequences are considered structurally the same if they are the same after changing all chained jumps into single jumps and making all jumps into the repeating part as short as possible if they are eventually periodic infinite sequences.

We introduce the *structural congruence* predicate $\_ \cong_{\mathrm{s}} \_ : \mathbf{IS} \times \mathbf{IS}$. A formula of the form $\boldsymbol{t} \cong_{\mathrm{s}} \boldsymbol{t}'$ is true if the instruction sequences denoted by $\boldsymbol{t}$ and $\boldsymbol{t}'$ are structurally the same. The axioms for the structural congruence predicate are given in Table 2.2.[2] In this table, $\boldsymbol{u}_1, \ldots, \boldsymbol{u}_n, \boldsymbol{v}_1, \ldots, \boldsymbol{v}_{n'+1}$ stand for arbitrary primitive instructions from $\mathfrak{I}$, $\boldsymbol{X}, \boldsymbol{Y}, \boldsymbol{Z}$ stand for arbitrary variables, $\boldsymbol{t}$ stands for an arbitrary SPISA term, and n, n', l stand for arbitrary natural numbers.

We write SPISA+SC for SPISA extended with the predicate $\cong_{\mathrm{s}}$ and the axioms SC1–SC9.

Each closed SPISA term is structurally congruent to one in first canonical form that does not have chained jumps and has shortest possible jumps into the repeating part if it has a repeating part.

[2]We write $\boldsymbol{t}\,[\boldsymbol{t}'/\boldsymbol{X}]$ for the result of substituting term $\boldsymbol{t}'$ for variable $\boldsymbol{X}$ in term $\boldsymbol{t}$.

Definition 2.2. A closed SPISA term t *has chained jumps* if there exists a closed SPISA term t' such that $t = t'$ and t' contains a subterm of the form $\#n{+}1 ; u_1 ; \ldots ; u_n ; \#l$. A closed SPISA term t *has a repeating part* if it is of the form $u_1 ; \ldots ; u_m ; (v_1 ; \ldots ; v_k)^\omega$. A closed SPISA term t of the form $u_1 ; \ldots ; u_m ; (v_1 ; \ldots ; v_k)^\omega$ *has shortest possible jumps into the repeating part* if: (i) for each $i \in [1, m]$ for which u_i is of the form $\#l$, $l \leq k + m - i$; (ii) for each $j \in [1, k]$ for which v_j is of the form $\#l$, $l \leq k - 1$.

Definition 2.3. A closed SPISA term is in *second canonical form* if it is in first canonical form, does not have chained jumps, and has shortest possible jumps into the repeating part if it has a repeating part.

Each closed SPISA term is derivably structurally congruent to a term in second canonical form.

Lemma 2.3. *For all closed* SPISA *terms* t, *there exists a closed* SPISA *terms* t' *in second canonical form such that* $t \cong_{\mathrm{s}} t'$ *is derivable from the axioms of* SPISA+SC.

Proof. By Lemma 2.2, there exists a closed SPISA terms t'' in first canonical form such that $t \cong_{\mathrm{s}} t''$ is derivable from the axioms of SPISA. If t'' has chained jumps, it can be transformed into a closed SPISA term that does not have chained jumps by repeated applications of SC1–SC3, alternated with applications of SC9 and $(X ; Y)^\omega \cong_{\mathrm{s}} X ; (Y ; X)^\omega$ (which follows immediately from SPISA4 and SC5). If t'' does not have shortest possible jumps into the repeating part, it can be transformed into a closed SPISA term that has shortest possible jumps into the repeating part by repeated applications of SC3 (for $l > 0$) and SC4, alternated with applications of SC9. □

For example:

$$+\mathtt{a} ; \#10 ; \mathtt{b} ; (-\mathtt{c} ; \#3)^\omega \cong_{\mathrm{s}} +\mathtt{a} ; \#2 ; \mathtt{b} ; (-\mathtt{c} ; \#1)^\omega ,$$
$$+\mathtt{a} ; \#2 ; (\mathtt{b} ; \#2 ; \mathtt{c} ; \#2)^\omega \cong_{\mathrm{s}} +\mathtt{a} ; \#0 ; (\mathtt{b} ; \#0 ; \mathtt{c} ; \#0)^\omega .$$

Lemma 2.3 will be used several times in subsequent chapters.

In Sect. 2.2.5, we will make precise which behaviours are produced by SPISA instruction sequences. There, use is made of structural congruence to deal with the case where there is an infinite chain of jumps. In Sect. 2.2.6, we will introduce behavioural congruence. Structural congruence implies behavioural congruence.

2.2 Basic Thread Algebra

In this section, we present BTA (Basic Thread Algebra). BTA is an algebraic theory of mathematical objects which represent in a direct way the behaviours produced by instruction sequences under execution: upon each action performed by such an object, a reply from an execution environment, which takes the action as an instruction to be processed, determines how the object proceeds. The objects concerned are called threads. We also introduce an operator meant for the extraction of the threads that represents the behaviours produced by SPISA instruction sequences under execution from the SPISA instruction sequences, and discuss the behavioural equivalence on SPISA instruction sequences induced by this operator.

In [Bergstra and Loots (2002)], BPPA (Basic Polarized Process Algebra) was introduced as a setting for the description and analysis of the behaviours produced by instruction sequences under execution. Later BPPA has been renamed to BTA. In this book, however, the name BTA is used for BPPA extended with two constants for termination with delivery of a Boolean value.

2.2.1 *Constants, operators and equational axioms*

In BTA, it is assumed that a fixed but arbitrary set $\mathcal{A}$ of *basic actions*, with $\mathsf{tau} \notin \mathcal{A}$, has been given. We write $\mathcal{A}_{\mathsf{tau}}$ for $\mathcal{A} \cup \{\mathsf{tau}\}$. The members of $\mathcal{A}_{\mathsf{tau}}$ are referred to as *actions*.

A thread is a behaviour which consists of performing actions in a sequential fashion. Upon each basic action performed, a reply from an execution environment determines how the thread proceeds. The possible replies are the Boolean values t and f. Performing the action tau will always lead to the reply t.

BTA has one sort: the sort $\mathbf{T}$ of *threads*. We make this sort explicit to anticipate the need for many-sortedness in Sects. 2.2.5 and 3.1.2. To build terms of sort $\mathbf{T}$, BTA has the following constants and operators:

- the *inaction* constant $\mathsf{D} : \to \mathbf{T}$;
- the *plain termination* constant $\mathsf{S} : \to \mathbf{T}$;
- the *positive termination* constant $\mathsf{S{+}} : \to \mathbf{T}$;
- the *negative termination* constant $\mathsf{S{-}} : \to \mathbf{T}$;
- for each $a \in \mathcal{A}_{\mathsf{tau}}$, the binary *postconditional composition* operator $\_ \trianglelefteq a \trianglerighteq \_ : \mathbf{T} \times \mathbf{T} \to \mathbf{T}$.

We assume that there are infinitely many variables of sort $\mathbf{T}$, including x, y. BTA terms are built as usual. We use infix notation for postconditional composition. We introduce *action prefixing* as an abbreviation: $\boldsymbol{a} \circ \boldsymbol{t}$, where $\boldsymbol{a} \in \mathcal{A}_{\mathsf{tau}}$ and $\boldsymbol{t}$ is a term of sort $\mathbf{T}$, abbreviates $\boldsymbol{t} \trianglelefteq \boldsymbol{a} \trianglerighteq \boldsymbol{t}$.

The thread denoted by a closed term of the form $\boldsymbol{t} \trianglelefteq \boldsymbol{a} \trianglerighteq \boldsymbol{t}'$ will first perform $\boldsymbol{a}$, and then proceed as the thread denoted by $\boldsymbol{t}$ if the reply from the execution environment is t and proceed as the thread denoted by $\boldsymbol{t}'$ if the reply from the execution environment is f. The thread denoted by D will become inactive, the thread denoted by S will terminate without delivery of a Boolean value, and the threads denoted by $\mathsf{S+}$ and $\mathsf{S-}$ will terminate with delivery of the Boolean values t and f, respectively.

The action prefixing abbreviation is quite useful. For example, the abbreviated closed BTA term

$$\mathsf{a} \circ \mathsf{b} \circ \mathsf{c} \circ \mathsf{D}$$

abbreviates the closed BTA term

$$((\mathsf{D} \trianglelefteq \mathsf{c} \trianglerighteq \mathsf{D}) \trianglelefteq \mathsf{b} \trianglerighteq (\mathsf{D} \trianglelefteq \mathsf{c} \trianglerighteq \mathsf{D})) \trianglelefteq \mathsf{a} \trianglerighteq ((\mathsf{D} \trianglelefteq \mathsf{c} \trianglerighteq \mathsf{D}) \trianglelefteq \mathsf{b} \trianglerighteq (\mathsf{D} \trianglelefteq \mathsf{c} \trianglerighteq \mathsf{D}))\;.$$

This term denotes the thread that, irrespective of the replies from the execution environment, performs basic actions a, b and c in that order and next becomes inactive. Other examples of abbreviated closed BTA terms are

$$\mathsf{a} \circ (\mathsf{S} \trianglelefteq \mathsf{b} \trianglerighteq \mathsf{D})\;, \qquad (\mathsf{b} \circ \mathsf{S}) \trianglelefteq \mathsf{a} \trianglerighteq \mathsf{D}\;.$$

The first abbreviated term denotes the thread that first performs basic action a, next performs basic action b, if the reply from the execution environment on performing b is t, after that terminates without delivery of a Boolean value, and if the reply from the execution environment on performing b is f, after that becomes inactive. The second abbreviated term denotes the thread that first performs basic action a, if the reply from the execution environment on performing a is t, next performs the basic action b and after that terminates without delivery of a Boolean value, and if the reply from the execution environment on performing a is f, next becomes inactive.

We will also sometimes use the notation $\boldsymbol{a}^n \circ \boldsymbol{t}$ for n times repeated action prefixing. The term $\boldsymbol{a}^n \circ \boldsymbol{t}$ is defined by induction on n as follows: $\boldsymbol{a}^0 \circ \boldsymbol{t} = \boldsymbol{t}$ and $\boldsymbol{a}^{n+1} \circ \boldsymbol{t} = \boldsymbol{a} \circ (\boldsymbol{a}^n \circ \boldsymbol{t})$. In the sequel, we identify expressions of the form $\boldsymbol{a} \circ \boldsymbol{t}$ and $\boldsymbol{a}^n \circ \boldsymbol{t}$ with the BTA term they stand for.

BTA has only one axiom. This axiom is given in Table 2.3.

Table 2.3 Axiom of BTA

$x \trianglelefteq \mathsf{tau} \trianglerighteq y = x \trianglelefteq \mathsf{tau} \trianglerighteq x$	T1

2.2.2 *Recursion*

Each closed BTA term denotes a finite thread, i.e. a thread with a finite upper bound to the number of actions that it can perform. Infinite threads, i.e. threads without a finite upper bound to the number of actions that it can perform, can be described by guarded recursion.

Definition 2.4. A *guarded recursive specification* over BTA is a set of recursion equations $\{x = t_x \mid x \in \mathcal{V}\}$, where $\mathcal{V}$ is a set of variables (of sort $\mathbf{T}$) and each t_x is a BTA term of the form D, S, S+, S− or $t \trianglelefteq a \trianglerighteq t'$ with t and t' that contain only variables from $\mathcal{V}$.

We are only interested in models of BTA in which guarded recursive specifications have unique solutions, such as the projective limit model that will be presented in Sect. 2.2.4.

A simple example of a guarded recursive specification is the one consisting of following two equations:

$$x = x \trianglelefteq \mathsf{a} \trianglerighteq y\ , \qquad y = y \trianglelefteq \mathsf{b} \trianglerighteq \mathsf{S}\ .$$

The x-component of the solution of this guarded recursive specification is the thread that first performs basic action a repeatedly until the reply from the execution environment on performing a is f, next performs basic action b repeatedly until the reply from the execution environment on performing b is f, and after that terminates without delivery of a Boolean value.

We write $\mathrm{V}(E)$, where E is a guarded recursive specification over BTA, for the set of all variables that occur in E.

For each guarded recursive specification E over BTA and each $x \in \mathrm{V}(E)$, we introduce a constant $\langle x|E\rangle$ of sort $\mathbf{T}$ standing for the x-component of the unique solution of E. We write $\langle t|E\rangle$ for t with, for all $y \in \mathrm{V}(E)$, all occurrences of y in t replaced by $\langle y|E\rangle$. The axioms for the constants standing for the components of the unique solutions of guarded recursive specifications over BTA are RDP (Recursive Definition Principle) and RSP (Recursive Specification Principle), which are given in Table 2.4. In this table, x stands for an arbitrary variable, t_x stands for an arbitrary BTA term, and E stands for an arbitrary guarded recursive specification over BTA. Side conditions are added to restrict

Table 2.4 Axioms for guarded recursion

$\langle \boldsymbol{x} \vert \boldsymbol{E} \rangle = \langle \boldsymbol{t_x} \vert \boldsymbol{E} \rangle$	if $\boldsymbol{x} = \boldsymbol{t_x} \in \boldsymbol{E}$	RDP
$\boldsymbol{E} \Rightarrow \boldsymbol{x} = \langle \boldsymbol{x} \vert \boldsymbol{E} \rangle$	if $\boldsymbol{x} \in \mathrm{V}(\boldsymbol{E})$	RSP

Table 2.5 AIP and axioms for the projection operators

$\bigwedge_{n \geq 0} \pi_n(x) = \pi_n(y) \Rightarrow x = y$	AIP
$\pi_0(x) = \mathsf{D}$	P1
$\pi_{n+1}(\mathsf{S+}) = \mathsf{S+}$	P2
$\pi_{n+1}(\mathsf{S-}) = \mathsf{S-}$	P3
$\pi_{n+1}(\mathsf{S}) = \mathsf{S}$	P4
$\pi_{n+1}(\mathsf{D}) = \mathsf{D}$	P5
$\pi_{n+1}(x \unlhd \boldsymbol{a} \unrhd y) = \pi_n(x) \unlhd \boldsymbol{a} \unrhd \pi_n(y)$	P6

what $\boldsymbol{x}$, $\boldsymbol{t_x}$ and $\boldsymbol{E}$ stand for.

RDP and RSP are means to prove closed terms that denote the same infinite thread equal. We introduce AIP (Approximation Induction Principle) as an additional means to prove closed terms that denote the same infinite thread equal. AIP is based on the view that two threads are identical if their approximations up to any finite depth are identical. The approximation up to depth n of a thread is obtained by cutting it off after it has performed n actions. In AIP, the approximation up to depth n is phrased in terms of the unary *projection* operator $\pi_n{:}\mathbf{T} \to \mathbf{T}$. AIP and the axioms for the projection operators are given in Table 2.5. In this table, $\boldsymbol{a}$ stands for an arbitrary basic action from $\mathcal{A}_{\mathsf{tau}}$ and n stands for an arbitrary natural number.

The usefulness of AIP is mainly a result of the fact that the projections of solutions of guarded recursive specifications over BTA are representable by closed BTA terms.

Lemma 2.4. *Let $\boldsymbol{E}$ be a guarded recursive specification over* BTA, *and let $\boldsymbol{x}$ be a variable occurring in $\boldsymbol{E}$. Then, for all $n \in \mathbb{N}$, there exists a closed* BTA *term $\boldsymbol{t}$ such that $\boldsymbol{E} \Rightarrow \pi_n(\boldsymbol{x}) = \boldsymbol{t}$ is derivable from the axioms* P1–P6.

Proof. After replacing n times ($n \geq 0$) all occurrences of each $\boldsymbol{y} \in \mathrm{V}(\boldsymbol{E})$ in the right-hand sides of the equations in $\boldsymbol{E}$ by the right-hand side of the equation for $\boldsymbol{y}$ in $\boldsymbol{E}$, all occurrences of variables in the right-hand sides of the equations are at least at depth $n+1$. We write $\boldsymbol{E}^{(n)}$ for the guarded recursive specification obtained in this way, and we write $\boldsymbol{t}_{\boldsymbol{x}}^{(n)}$ for the right-hand side of the equation for $\boldsymbol{x}$ in $\boldsymbol{E}^{(n)}$. Because all occurrences of variables in $\boldsymbol{t}_{\boldsymbol{x}}^{(n)}$ are at least at depth $n+1$, $\pi_n(\boldsymbol{t}_{\boldsymbol{x}}^{(n)})$ equals a closed BTA term. Now assume $\boldsymbol{E}$ and take an arbitrary $n \geq 0$. Then $\boldsymbol{E}^{(n)}$ and in particular $\boldsymbol{x} = \boldsymbol{t}_{\boldsymbol{x}}^{(n)}$. From this, it follows immediately that $\pi_n(\boldsymbol{x}) = \pi_n(\boldsymbol{t}_{\boldsymbol{x}}^{(n)})$. Hence, $\boldsymbol{E} \Rightarrow \pi_n(\boldsymbol{x}) = \pi_n(\boldsymbol{t}_{\boldsymbol{x}}^{(n)})$. With this the proof is done because $\pi_n(\boldsymbol{t}_{\boldsymbol{x}}^{(n)})$ equals a closed BTA term. □

For example, let $\boldsymbol{E}$ be the guarded recursive specification consisting of the equation $x = x \trianglelefteq \mathsf{a} \trianglerighteq \mathsf{S}$ only. Then the projections of x are as follows:

$$
\begin{aligned}
\pi_0(x) &= \mathsf{D}\,, \\
\pi_1(x) &= \mathsf{D} \trianglelefteq \mathsf{a} \trianglerighteq \mathsf{S}\,, \\
\pi_2(x) &= (\mathsf{D} \trianglelefteq \mathsf{a} \trianglerighteq \mathsf{S}) \trianglelefteq \mathsf{a} \trianglerighteq \mathsf{S}\,, \\
\pi_3(x) &= ((\mathsf{D} \trianglelefteq \mathsf{a} \trianglerighteq \mathsf{S}) \trianglelefteq \mathsf{a} \trianglerighteq \mathsf{S}) \trianglelefteq \mathsf{a} \trianglerighteq \mathsf{S}\,, \\
&\;\;\vdots
\end{aligned}
$$

As a corollary of the proof of Lemma 2.4, we have that RSP follows from axioms P1–P6, RDP and AIP.

Corollary 2.1. *Let $\boldsymbol{E}$ be a guarded recursive specification over* BTA, *and let $\boldsymbol{x}$ be a variable occurring in $\boldsymbol{E}$. Then $\boldsymbol{E} \Rightarrow \boldsymbol{x} = \langle \boldsymbol{x} | \boldsymbol{E} \rangle$ is derivable from the axioms* P1–P6, RDP *and* AIP.

We write BTA+REC for BTA extended with the constants $\langle \boldsymbol{x} | \boldsymbol{E} \rangle$ and the axioms RDP and RSP, and we write BTA+REC+AIP for BTA+REC extended with the operators π_n and the axioms AIP and P1–P6.

2.2.3 *Regular threads*

This section is concerned with an important class of threads, namely the class of regular threads. The threads from this class are threads that can only be in a finite number of states (in the sense made precise below).

We assume that a model $\mathcal{M}$ of BTA in which all guarded recursive specifications have unique solutions has been given.

To express definitions more concisely, the interpretations of the sorts, constants and operators of BTA or some extension thereof in models of the theory concerned will in this book be denoted by the sorts, constants and operators themselves. The ambiguity thus introduced could be obviated by decorating the symbols, with different decorations for different models, when they are used to denote their interpretation in some model. However, it will always be immediately clear from the context how the symbols are used. Moreover, we believe that the decorations are more often than not distracting. Therefore, we leave it to the reader to mentally decorate the symbols wherever appropriate.

Throughout this book, we use the term *thread* for the elements of the interpretation of the sort $\mathbf{T}$ in a certain model of BTA or an extension thereof. Thus, we use the term thread in this section for the elements of the interpretation of the sort $\mathbf{T}$ in $\boldsymbol{\mathcal{M}}$.

Definition 2.5. Let t be a thread. Then the set of *states* or *residual threads* of t, written $Res(t)$, is inductively defined as follows:

- $t \in Res(t)$;
- if $t' \trianglelefteq \boldsymbol{a} \trianglerighteq t'' \in Res(t)$, then $t' \in Res(t)$ and $t'' \in Res(t)$.

Definition 2.6. Let t be a thread and let $\mathcal{A}' \subseteq \mathcal{A}_{\mathsf{tau}}$. Then t is *regular over* $\mathcal{A}'$ if the following conditions are satisfied:

- $Res(t)$ is finite;
- for all $t', t'' \in Res(t)$ and $\boldsymbol{a} \in \mathcal{A}_{\mathsf{tau}}$, $t' \trianglelefteq \boldsymbol{a} \trianglerighteq t'' \in Res(t)$ implies $\boldsymbol{a} \in \mathcal{A}'$.

We say that t is *regular* if t is regular over $\mathcal{A}_{\mathsf{tau}}$.

For example, the solution of the guarded recursive specification consisting of the following two equations:

$$x = \mathsf{a} \circ y \ , \qquad y = (\mathsf{c} \circ y) \trianglelefteq \mathsf{b} \trianglerighteq (x \trianglelefteq \mathsf{d} \trianglerighteq \mathsf{S})$$

has five states and is regular over any $\mathcal{A}' \subseteq \mathcal{A}_{\mathsf{tau}}$ for which $\{\mathsf{a}, \mathsf{b}, \mathsf{c}, \mathsf{d}\} \subseteq \mathcal{A}'$.

In the sequel, we will sometimes make use of the fact that being a regular thread coincides with being the solution of a finite guarded recursive specification in which the right-hand sides of the recursion equations are of a restricted form.

Definition 2.7. A *linear recursive specification* over BTA is a guarded recursive specification $\{\boldsymbol{x} = \boldsymbol{t_x} \mid \boldsymbol{x} \in \mathcal{V}\}$ over BTA, where each $\boldsymbol{t_x}$ is a term of the form D, S, $\mathsf{S+}$, $\mathsf{S-}$ or $\boldsymbol{y} \trianglelefteq \boldsymbol{a} \trianglerighteq \boldsymbol{z}$ with $\boldsymbol{y}, \boldsymbol{z} \in \mathcal{V}$.

Proposition 2.1. *Let t be a thread and let $\mathcal{A}' \subseteq \mathcal{A}_{\mathsf{tau}}$. Then t is regular over $\mathcal{A}'$ iff there exists a finite linear recursive specification $\boldsymbol{E}$ over* BTA *in which only basic actions from $\mathcal{A}'$ occur such that t is a component of the solution of $\boldsymbol{E}$.*

Proof. The implication from left to right is proved as follows. Because t is regular, $Res(t)$ is finite. Hence, there are finitely many threads $t_1, \ldots, t_n$, with $t = t_1$, such that $Res(t) = \{t_1, \ldots, t_n\}$. Now t is the x_1-component of the solution of the linear recursive specification consisting of the following equations:

$$x_i = \begin{cases} \mathsf{S+} & \text{if } t_i = \mathsf{S+} \\ \mathsf{S-} & \text{if } t_i = \mathsf{S-} \\ \mathsf{S} & \text{if } t_i = \mathsf{S} \\ \mathsf{D} & \text{if } t_i = \mathsf{D} \\ x_j \trianglelefteq \boldsymbol{a} \trianglerighteq x_k & \text{if } t_i = t_j \trianglelefteq \boldsymbol{a} \trianglerighteq t_k \end{cases} \qquad \text{for all } i \in [1, n] .$$

Because t is regular over $\mathcal{A}'$, only basic actions from $\mathcal{A}'$ occur in the linear recursive specification constructed in this way.

The implication from right to left is proved as follows. Thread t is a component of the unique solution of a finite linear specification in which only basic actions from $\mathcal{A}'$ occur. This means that there are finitely many threads $t_1, \ldots, t_n$, with $t = t_1$, such that for every $i \in [1, n]$, $t_i = \mathsf{S+}$, $t_i = \mathsf{S-}$, $t_i = \mathsf{S}$, $t_i = \mathsf{D}$ or $t_i = t_j \trianglelefteq \boldsymbol{a} \trianglerighteq t_k$ for some $j, k \in [1, n]$ and $\boldsymbol{a} \in \mathcal{A}'$. Consequently, $t' \in Res(t)$ iff $t' = t_i$ for some $i \in [1, n]$ and moreover $t' \trianglelefteq \boldsymbol{a} \trianglerighteq t'' \in Res(t)$ only if $\boldsymbol{a} \in \mathcal{A}'$. Hence, $Res(t)$ is finite and t is regular over $\mathcal{A}'$. □

2.2.4 *The projective limit model*

In this section, we construct a projective limit model for BTA. In this model, which covers finite and infinite threads, threads are represented by infinite sequences of finite approximations. All guarded recursive specifications over BTA have unique solutions in this model. Recall that we denote the interpretations of constants and operators in models of BTA by the constants and operators themselves.

We will write $\boldsymbol{\mathcal{I}}(\mathrm{BTA})$ for the initial model of BTA and $\boldsymbol{T}(\mathrm{BTA})$ for the domain of $\boldsymbol{\mathcal{I}}(\mathrm{BTA})$.[3] $\boldsymbol{T}(\mathrm{BTA})$ consists of the equivalence classes of closed BTA terms with respect to derivable equality. In other words, modulo derivable equality, $\boldsymbol{T}(\mathrm{BTA})$ is the set of all closed BTA terms. Henceforth, we will identify closed BTA terms with their equivalence class where elements of $\boldsymbol{T}(\mathrm{BTA})$ are concerned.

[3] In the single-sorted case, the interpretation of a sort in a certain model is also called the domain of that model.

Each element of $\boldsymbol{T}(\text{BTA})$ represents a finite thread, i.e. a thread with a finite upper bound to the number of actions that it can perform. Below, we will construct a model that covers infinite threads as well. In preparation for that, we define for all n a function that cuts off threads from $\boldsymbol{T}(\text{BTA})$ after n actions have been performed.

For all $n \in \mathbb{N}$, we have the *projection* function $\pi_n : \boldsymbol{T}(\text{BTA}) \to \boldsymbol{T}(\text{BTA})$, inductively defined by

$$\begin{aligned}
&\pi_0(t) = \mathsf{D}\,, \\
&\pi_{n+1}(\mathsf{S+}) = \mathsf{S+}\,, \\
&\pi_{n+1}(\mathsf{S-}) = \mathsf{S-}\,, \\
&\pi_{n+1}(\mathsf{S}) = \mathsf{S}\,, \\
&\pi_{n+1}(\mathsf{D}) = \mathsf{D}\,, \\
&\pi_{n+1}(t \trianglelefteq \boldsymbol{a} \trianglerighteq t') = \pi_n(t) \trianglelefteq \boldsymbol{a} \trianglerighteq \pi_n(t')\,.
\end{aligned}$$

For $t \in \boldsymbol{T}(\text{BTA})$, $\pi_n(t)$ is called the nth projection of t. It can be thought of as an approximation of t. If $\pi_n(t) \neq t$, then $\pi_{n+1}(t)$ can be thought of as the closest better approximation of t. If $\pi_n(t) = t$, then $\pi_{n+1}(t) = t$ as well. For all $n \in \mathbb{N}$, we will write $\boldsymbol{T}^n(\text{BTA})$ for $\{\pi_n(t) \mid t \in \boldsymbol{T}(\text{BTA})\}$.

The semantic equations given above to define the projection functions have the same shape as the axioms for the projection operators introduced in Sect. 2.2.2.

The property of the projection functions stated in the following lemma will be used below.

Lemma 2.5. *For all $t \in \boldsymbol{T}(\text{BTA})$ and $n, m \in \mathbb{N}$, we have that $\pi_n(\pi_m(t)) = \pi_{\min\{n,m\}}(t)$.*

Proof. This is easily proved by induction on the structure of t. □

In the projective limit model, which covers both finite and infinite threads, threads are represented by *projective sequences*, i.e. infinite sequences $(t_n)_{n\in\mathbb{N}}$ of elements of $\boldsymbol{T}(\text{BTA})$ such that $t_n \in \boldsymbol{T}^n(\text{BTA})$ and $t_n = \pi_n(t_{n+1})$ for all $n \in \mathbb{N}$. In other words, a projective sequence is a sequence of which successive components are successive projections of the same thread. The idea is that any infinite thread is fully characterized by the infinite sequence of all its finite approximations. We will write $\boldsymbol{T}^\infty(\text{BTA})$ for the set of all projective sequences over $\boldsymbol{T}(\text{BTA})$, i.e. the set

$$\left\{(t_n)_{n\in\mathbb{N}} \mid \textstyle\bigwedge_{n\in\mathbb{N}}(t_n \in \boldsymbol{T}^n(\text{BTA}) \land t_n = \pi_n(t_{n+1}))\right\}\,.$$

A simple example of a projective sequence is the sequence

$$(\mathsf{D}, \mathsf{a} \circ \mathsf{D}, \mathsf{a} \circ \mathsf{a} \circ \mathsf{D}, \mathsf{a} \circ \mathsf{a} \circ \mathsf{a} \circ \mathsf{D}, \ldots)\,.$$

In the projective limit model of BTA described below, this projective sequence is the solution of the guarded recursive specification consisting of the single equation $x = \mathsf{a} \circ x$.

Definition 2.8. The *projective limit model* $\mathcal{I}^\infty$(BTA) of BTA consists of the following:

- the set $\boldsymbol{T}^\infty$(BTA), the domain of the projective limit model;
- an element of $\boldsymbol{T}^\infty$(BTA) for each constant of BTA;
- an operation on $\boldsymbol{T}^\infty$(BTA) for each operator of BTA;

where those elements of $\boldsymbol{T}^\infty$(BTA) and operations on $\boldsymbol{T}^\infty$(BTA) are defined as follows:

$$
\begin{aligned}
\mathsf{S+} &= (\pi_n(\mathsf{S+}))_{n\in\mathbb{N}} \,, \\
\mathsf{S-} &= (\pi_n(\mathsf{S-}))_{n\in\mathbb{N}} \,, \\
\mathsf{S} &= (\pi_n(\mathsf{S}))_{n\in\mathbb{N}} \,, \\
\mathsf{D} &= (\pi_n(\mathsf{D}))_{n\in\mathbb{N}} \,, \\
(t_n)_{n\in\mathbb{N}} \trianglelefteq \boldsymbol{a} \trianglerighteq (t'_n)_{n\in\mathbb{N}} &= (\pi_n(t_n \trianglelefteq \boldsymbol{a} \trianglerighteq t'_n))_{n\in\mathbb{N}} \,.
\end{aligned}
$$

Using Lemma 2.5, we easily prove for $(t_n)_{n\in\mathbb{N}}, (t'_n)_{n\in\mathbb{N}} \in \boldsymbol{T}^\infty$(BTA):

$$
\begin{aligned}
&\pi_n(\pi_{n+1}(\mathsf{S+})) = \pi_n(\mathsf{S+}) \,, \\
&\pi_n(\pi_{n+1}(\mathsf{S-})) = \pi_n(\mathsf{S-}) \,, \\
&\pi_n(\pi_{n+1}(\mathsf{S})) = \pi_n(\mathsf{S}) \,, \\
&\pi_n(\pi_{n+1}(\mathsf{D})) = \pi_n(\mathsf{D}) \,, \\
&\pi_n(\pi_{n+1}(t_{n+1} \trianglelefteq \boldsymbol{a} \trianglerighteq t'_{n+1})) = \pi_n(t_n \trianglelefteq \boldsymbol{a} \trianglerighteq t'_n) \,.
\end{aligned}
$$

From this, it follows immediately that the constants and operations defined above are well-defined, i.e. the constants are elements of $\boldsymbol{T}^\infty$(BTA) and the operations always yield elements of $\boldsymbol{T}^\infty$(BTA).

It follows immediately from the construction of the projective limit model of BTA that the axiom of BTA forms a complete axiomatization of this model for equations between closed terms.

The following theorem concerns the uniqueness of solutions of guarded recursive specification.

Theorem 2.1. *Every guarded recursive specification over* BTA *has a unique solution in the projective limit model of* BTA.

Proof. We give a very brief outline of the proof, because the details are outside the scope of this book. In the same way as in [Bergstra and Middelburg (2010c)], we can make $\boldsymbol{T}^\infty$(BTA) into a complete metric space in which all operations of the projective limit model are non-expansive and the postconditional composition operations are contractive and show that the right-hand sides of guarded recursive specifications represent contractive operations in this complete metric space. From this we can establish along the same lines as in [Kranakis (1987)], using Banach's fixed point theorem, that every guarded recursive specification has a unique solution in the projective limit model. □

Definition 2.9. The projective limit model $\mathcal{I}^\infty(\text{BTA+REC})$ of BTA+REC is $\mathcal{I}^\infty(\text{BTA})$ expanded with the elements of $\boldsymbol{T}^\infty(\text{BTA})$ defined by

$$\langle \boldsymbol{x} \,|\, \boldsymbol{E} \rangle = \text{the } \boldsymbol{x}\text{-component of the unique solution of } \boldsymbol{E} \text{ in } \mathcal{I}^\infty(\text{BTA})$$

as interpretations of the additional constants of BTA+REC. The projective limit model $\mathcal{I}^\infty(\text{BTA+REC+AIP})$ of BTA+REC+AIP is $\mathcal{I}^\infty(\text{BTA+REC})$ expanded with the operations on $\boldsymbol{T}^\infty(\text{BTA})$ defined by

$$\pi_k((t_n)_{n \in \mathrm{N}}) = (\pi_n(t_k))_{n \in \mathrm{N}}$$

as interpretations of the additional operators of BTA+REC+AIP.

The initial model $\mathcal{I}(\text{BTA})$ can be embedded in a natural way in the projective limit model $\mathcal{I}^\infty(\text{BTA})$: each $t \in \boldsymbol{T}(\text{BTA})$ corresponds to $(\pi_n(t))_{n \in \mathrm{N}} \in \boldsymbol{T}^\infty(\text{BTA})$. Projection on $\boldsymbol{T}^\infty(\text{BTA})$ is defined such that $\pi_k((t_n)_{n \in \mathrm{N}})$ is t_k embedded in $\boldsymbol{T}^\infty(\text{BTA})$ as described above.

Remark 2.1. The projective limit construction is known as the inverse limit construction in domain theory, the theory underlying the approach of denotational semantics for programming languages (see e.g. [Schmidt (1986)]). In process algebra, this construction has been applied for the first time in [Bergstra and Klop (1984)].

2.2.5 *Thread extraction for instruction sequences*

In this section, we make precise in the setting of BTA which behaviours are produced by SPISA instruction sequences under execution. For that purpose, we combine SPISA+SC with BTA+REC+AIP and extend the combination with an operator meant for the extraction of the threads that represent the behaviours produced by SPISA instruction sequences under execution from the SPISA instruction sequences. In the resulting theory, it is assumed that $\mathcal{A} = \mathfrak{A}$.

The resulting theory has the sorts, constants, operators of both SPISA+SC and BTA+REC+AIP, the predicate $\cong_s$ of SPISA+SC and in addition the following operator:

Table 2.6 Axioms for the thread extraction operator

$\lvert a \rvert = a \circ \mathsf{D}$	TE1	$\lvert \#l{+}2 \,;\, u \rvert = \mathsf{D}$	TE10
$\lvert a \,;\, X \rvert = a \circ \lvert X \rvert$	TE2	$\lvert \#l{+}2 \,;\, u \,;\, X \rvert = \lvert \#l{+}1 \,;\, X \rvert$	TE11
$\lvert {+}a \rvert = a \circ \mathsf{D}$	TE3	$\lvert ! \rvert = \mathsf{S}$	TE12
$\lvert {+}a \,;\, X \rvert = \lvert X \rvert \trianglelefteq a \trianglerighteq \lvert \#2 \,;\, X \rvert$	TE4	$\lvert ! \,;\, X \rvert = \mathsf{S}$	TE13
$\lvert {-}a \rvert = a \circ \mathsf{D}$	TE5	$\lvert !\mathsf{t} \rvert = \mathsf{S}{+}$	TE14
$\lvert {-}a \,;\, X \rvert = \lvert \#2 \,;\, X \rvert \trianglelefteq a \trianglerighteq \lvert X \rvert$	TE6	$\lvert !\mathsf{t} \,;\, X \rvert = \mathsf{S}{+}$	TE15
$\lvert \#l \rvert = \mathsf{D}$	TE7	$\lvert !\mathsf{f} \rvert = \mathsf{S}{-}$	TE16
$\lvert \#0 \,;\, X \rvert = \mathsf{D}$	TE8	$\lvert !\mathsf{f} \,;\, X \rvert = \mathsf{S}{-}$	TE17
$\lvert \#1 \,;\, X \rvert = \lvert X \rvert$	TE9	$X \cong_{\mathrm{s}} \#0 \,;\, Y \;\Rightarrow\; \lvert X \rvert = \mathsf{D}$	TE18

- the *thread extraction* operator $\lvert\_\rvert : \mathbf{IS} \to \mathbf{T}$.

The axioms of the resulting theory are the axioms of both SPISA+SC and BTA+REC+AIP and in addition the axioms for the thread extraction operator given in Table 2.6. In this table, a stands for an arbitrary basic instruction from $\mathfrak{A}$, u stands for an arbitrary primitive instruction from $\mathfrak{I}$, and l stands for an arbitrary natural number.

Axioms TE1–TE17 do not cover the case where there is an infinite chain of jumps. Recall that SPISA instruction sequences are structurally the same if they are the same after changing all chained jumps into single jumps and making all jumps into the repeating part as short as possible if they have repeating parts. Because an infinite chain of forward jumps corresponds to $\#0$, axiom TE18 from Table 2.6 can be read as follows: if X starts with an infinite chain of forward jumps, then $\lvert X \rvert$ equals D.

Note that, in the theory put together above, no difference is made between a basic instruction and the basic action that takes place when it is executed.

Let t and t' be closed terms of sort **IS** and sort **T**, respectively. Then we loosely say that *instruction sequence* t *produces thread* t' if $\lvert t \rvert = t'$.

For example,

$$
\begin{array}{lll}
\mathtt{a} \,;\, \mathtt{b} \,;\, \mathtt{c} & \text{produces} & \mathtt{a} \circ \mathtt{b} \circ \mathtt{c} \circ \mathsf{D}\,, \\
{+}\mathtt{a} \,;\, \#2 \,;\, \#3 \,;\, \mathtt{b} \,;\, !\mathtt{t} & \text{produces} & (\mathtt{b} \circ \mathsf{S}{+}) \trianglelefteq \mathtt{a} \trianglerighteq \mathsf{D}\,, \\
{+}\mathtt{a} \,;\, {-}\mathtt{b} \,;\, \mathtt{c} \,;\, ! & \text{produces} & (\mathsf{S} \trianglelefteq \mathtt{b} \trianglerighteq (\mathtt{c} \circ \mathsf{S})) \trianglelefteq \mathtt{a} \trianglerighteq (\mathtt{c} \circ \mathsf{S})\,, \\
{+}\mathtt{a} \,;\, \#2 \,;\, (\mathtt{b} \,;\, \#2 \,;\, \mathtt{c} \,;\, \#2)^{\omega} & \text{produces} & \mathsf{D} \trianglelefteq \mathtt{a} \trianglerighteq (\mathtt{b} \circ \mathsf{D})\,.
\end{array}
$$

In the case of instruction sequences that are not finite, the produced threads can be described as the solution of a guarded recursive specification. For example, the infinite instruction sequence

$$(\mathtt{a}\,;\,+\mathtt{b})^\omega$$

produces the x-component of the solution of the guarded recursive specification consisting of following two equations:

$$x = \mathtt{a} \circ y\,, \qquad y = x \trianglelefteq \mathtt{b} \trianglerighteq y$$

and the infinite instruction sequence

$$\mathtt{a}\,;\,(+\mathtt{b}\,;\,\#2\,;\,\#3\,;\,\mathtt{c}\,;\,\#4\,;\,-\mathtt{d}\,;\,!\,;\,\mathtt{a})^\omega$$

produces the x-component of the solution of the guarded recursive specification consisting of following two equations:

$$x = \mathtt{a} \circ y\,, \qquad y = (\mathtt{c} \circ y) \trianglelefteq \mathtt{b} \trianglerighteq (x \trianglelefteq \mathtt{d} \trianglerighteq \mathsf{S})\,.$$

2.2.6 *Behavioural equivalence of instruction sequences*

Instruction sequences are behaviourally equivalent if they produce the same behaviour.

Definition 2.10. Let t and t' be closed SPISA terms. Then t and t' are *behaviourally equivalent*, written $t \equiv_{\mathrm{b}} t'$, if $|t| = |t'|$.

Some examples of behavioural equivalence are

$$\begin{aligned}
&-\mathtt{a}\,;\,\mathtt{b}\,;\,\mathtt{c}\,;\,! \equiv_{\mathrm{b}} +\mathtt{a}\,;\,\#2\,;\,\mathtt{b}\,;\,\mathtt{c}\,;\,!\,,\\
&\mathtt{a}\,;\,\mathtt{b}\,;\,\mathtt{c}\,;\,! \equiv_{\mathrm{b}} +\mathtt{a}\,;\,\#2\,;\,\#1\,;\,\mathtt{b}\,;\,\mathtt{c}\,;\,!\,,\\
&\mathtt{a}\,;\,\#2\,;\,\#0\,;\,\mathtt{b}\,;\,\mathtt{c}\,;\,! \equiv_{\mathrm{b}} \mathtt{a}\,;\,\mathtt{b}\,;\,\mathtt{c}\,;\,!\,,\\
&+\mathtt{a}\,;\,\#4\,;\,\mathtt{b}\,;\,(-\mathtt{c}\,;\,\#2\,;\,!)^\omega \equiv_{\mathrm{b}} +\mathtt{a}\,;\,!\,;\,\mathtt{b}\,;\,(-\mathtt{c}\,;\,\#2\,;\,!)^\omega\,.
\end{aligned}$$

Behavioural equivalence is not a congruence. For example,

$$\begin{aligned}
&+\mathtt{a} \equiv_{\mathrm{b}} \mathtt{a}\,,\ \text{ but } +\mathtt{a}\,;\,\mathtt{b} \not\equiv_{\mathrm{b}} \mathtt{a}\,;\,\mathtt{b}\,,\\
&\#2\,;\,\mathtt{a}\,;\,\mathtt{c}\,;\,! \equiv_{\mathrm{b}} \#2\,;\,\mathtt{b}\,;\,\mathtt{c}\,;\,!\,,\ \text{ but } \#2\,;\,\#2\,;\,\mathtt{a}\,;\,\mathtt{c}\,;\,! \not\equiv_{\mathrm{b}} \#2\,;\,\#2\,;\,\mathtt{b}\,;\,\mathtt{c}\,;\,!\,.
\end{aligned}$$

Instruction sequences are behaviourally congruent if they produce the same behaviour irrespective of the way they are entered and the way they are left.

Definition 2.11. Let t and t' be closed SPISA terms. Then t and t' are *behaviourally congruent*, written $t \cong_{\mathrm{b}} t'$, if $\#l\,;\,t\,;\,!^n \equiv_{\mathrm{b}} \#l\,;\,t'\,;\,!^n$ for all $l, n \in \mathbb{N}$.

Behavioural congruence is the largest congruence contained in behavioural equivalence. Structural congruence implies behavioural congruence.

Proposition 2.2. *For all closed* SPISA *terms* t *and* t', $t \cong_s t'$ *implies* $t \cong_b t'$.

Proof. Because $\cong_s$ and $\cong_b$ are congruences, it is sufficient to prove the counterparts of axioms SC1–SC5 in which $\cong_s$ is replaced by $\cong_b$.
SC1: We have to prove that, for all $k, l, n \in \mathbb{N}$:

$$|\#l \,;\, \#n{+}1 \,;\, u_1 \,;\, \ldots \,;\, u_n \,;\, \#0 \,;\, !^k| = |\#l \,;\, \#0 \,;\, u_1 \,;\, \ldots \,;\, u_n \,;\, \#0 \,;\, !^k| \,.$$

This is proved by case distinction between $l = 0$, $l = 1$, and $l > 1$. The cases $l = 0$ and $l > 1$ are trivial, and the case $l = 1$ is easily proved by induction on n.
SC2: This case proved in the same way as the previous one.
SC3: By axiom SPISA3, it is sufficient to prove that, for all $l, l', n \in \mathbb{N}$:

$$|\#l \,;\, (\#l'{+}n{+}1 \,;\, u_1 \,;\, \ldots \,;\, u_n)^\omega| = |\#l \,;\, (\#l' \,;\, u_1 \,;\, \ldots \,;\, u_n)^\omega| \,.$$

This is proved by case distinction between $l = 0$, $l = 1$, $1 < l \leq n + 1$, and $l > n + 1$. The case $l = 0$ is trivial. If we have proved the claim

$$|(\#l'{+}n{+}1 \,;\, u_1 \,;\, \ldots \,;\, u_n)^\omega| = |(\#l' \,;\, u_1 \,;\, \ldots \,;\, u_n)^\omega| \,,$$

then the case $l = 1$ becomes trivial and the case $1 < l \leq n{+}1$ is easily proved by induction on n. The case $l > n + 1$ can be reduced to one of the other three cases after applying the unfolding equation $l/(n + 1)$ times. To prove the claim, it is sufficient, by RSP, to prove that $|(\#l'{+}n{+}1 \,;\, u_1 \,;\, \ldots \,;\, u_n)^\omega|$ and $|(\#l' \,;\, u_1 \,;\, \ldots \,;\, u_n)^\omega|$ are solutions of the same guarded recursive specification. This is easily proved by induction on l', after applying the unfolding equation $l'/(n + 1)$ times.
SC4: This case is proved in a similar way as the previous one.
SC5: This case is trivial. □

Conversely, behavioural congruence does not implies structural congruence. For example,

$$+\mathtt{a} \,;\, ! \,;\, ! \cong_b -\mathtt{a} \,;\, ! \,;\, ! \,, \text{ but } +\mathtt{a} \,;\, ! \,;\, ! \not\cong_s -\mathtt{a} \,;\, ! \,;\, ! \,.$$

Each closed SPISA term is behaviourally equivalent to a term of the form t^ω, where t is a closed SPISA term in which the repetition operator does not occur.

Lemma 2.6. *For all closed* SPISA *terms* t*, there exists a closed* SPISA *term* t' *without occurrences of the repetition operator such that* $t \equiv_b t'^\omega$ *is derivable from the axioms of the theory put together in Sect. 2.2.5.*

Proof. It is easy to check the fact that, for all closed SPISA terms t, $t \equiv_{\mathrm{b}} t \,;\, (\#0)^{\omega}$ is derivable. By Lemma 2.3, Proposition 2.2 and this fact, it follows that for all closed SPISA terms t, there exists a closed SPISA term of the form $t' \,;\, t''^{\omega}$ in second canonical form such that $t \equiv_{\mathrm{b}} t' \,;\, t''^{\omega}$ is derivable. This means that it is sufficient to consider only closed SPISA terms t of the form

$$u_1 \,;\, \ldots \,;\, u_m \,;\, (v_1 \,;\, \ldots \,;\, v_k)^{\omega}$$

that do not have chained jumps, and have shortest possible jumps into the repeating part. Let t' be

$$(u_1 \,;\, \ldots \,;\, u_m \,;\, v'_1 \,;\, \ldots \,;\, v'_k \,;\, \#m{+}2 \,;\, \#m{+}2)^{\omega}\;,$$

where

$$v'_i = \begin{cases} \#l{+}m{+}2 & \text{if } v_i \equiv \#l \wedge i + l > k \\ v_i & \text{if } v_i \not\equiv \#l \vee i + l \leq k\;. \end{cases}$$

Then it easy to check that $t \equiv_{\mathrm{b}} t'^{\omega}$ is derivable. □

For example:

$$+\mathtt{a} \,;\, \#4 \,;\, \mathtt{b} \,;\, (-\mathtt{c} \,;\, \#2 \,;\, !)^{\omega} \equiv_{\mathrm{b}} (+\mathtt{a} \,;\, \#4 \,;\, \mathtt{b} \,;\, -\mathtt{c} \,;\, \#5 \,;\, !)^{\omega}\;,$$
$$+\mathtt{a} \,;\, \#2 \,;\, \mathtt{b} \,;\, (-\mathtt{c} \,;\, \#1)^{\omega} \equiv_{\mathrm{b}} (+\mathtt{a} \,;\, \#2 \,;\, \mathtt{b} \,;\, -\mathtt{c} \,;\, \#5 \,;\, \#4)^{\omega}\;.$$

It will be shown in Sect. 4.1 that long jump are necessary. This can be formulated in terms of behavioural equivalence as follows: for each $n > 0$, there exists a closed SPISA term t for which there does not exist a closed SPISA term t' without occurrences of jump instructions $\#l$ with $l > n$ such that $t \equiv_{\mathrm{b}} t'$.

2.3 Instruction Sequence Notations

The SPISA instruction sequences include both finite and infinite ones, but all of them can be represented finitely by closed SPISA terms. However, these terms are not intended for actual programming. In this section, we present several alternative notations by means of which all SPISA instruction sequences can be represented finitely as well. The ones that are called ISNR and ISNA will be frequently used in the rest of the book. They are about the closest things to existing assembly languages. The only difference between them is that the former has relative jump instructions and the latter has absolute jump instructions. We show that ISNR and ISNA can easily be translated into each other.

2.3.1 *The instruction sequence notation* ISNR

In this section, we introduce the instruction sequence notation ISNR (Instruction Sequence Notation with Relative jumps).

In ISNR, like in SPISA, it is assumed that a fixed but arbitrary set $\mathfrak{A}$ of basic instructions has been given.

ISNR has the primitive instructions of SPISA and in addition:

- for each $l \in \mathbb{N}$, a *backward jump instruction* $\backslash\#l$.

ISNR instruction sequences are expressions of the form $u_1 ; \ldots ; u_k$, where $u_1, \ldots, u_k$ are primitive instructions of ISNR.

On execution of an ISNR instruction sequence, the effects of the plain basic instructions, the positive test instructions, the negative test instructions, the forward jump instructions, and the termination instructions are as in SPISA. The effect of a backward jump instruction $\backslash\#l$ is that execution proceeds with the lth previous primitive instruction of the instruction sequence concerned. If l equals 0 or there is no primitive instruction to proceed with, inaction occurs.

We define the meaning of ISNR instruction sequences by means of a function `isnr2spisa` from the set of all ISNR instruction sequences to the set of all closed SPISA terms. This function is defined by

$$\texttt{isnr2spisa}(u_1 ; \ldots ; u_k) = (\psi_1(u_1) ; \ldots ; \psi_k(u_k) ; \#0 ; \#0)^\omega ,$$

where the auxiliary functions ψ_j from the set of all primitive instructions of ISNR to the set of all primitive instructions of SPISA are defined as follows ($1 \leq j \leq k$):

$$\begin{aligned}
\psi_j(\#l) &= \#l && \text{if } j + l \leq k , \\
\psi_j(\#l) &= \#0 && \text{if } j + l > k , \\
\psi_j(\backslash\#l) &= \#k{+}2{-}l && \text{if } l < j , \\
\psi_j(\backslash\#l) &= \#0 && \text{if } l \geq j , \\
\psi_j(u) &= u && \text{if } u \text{ is not a jump instruction} .
\end{aligned}$$

The idea is that each backward jump can be replaced by a forward jump if the entire instruction sequence is repeated. To enforce that inaction occurs after execution of the last instruction of the instruction sequence if the last instruction is a plain basic instruction, a positive test instruction or a negative test instruction, $\#0 ; \#0$ is appended to $\psi_1(u_1) ; \ldots ; \psi_k(u_k)$.

Let p be an ISNR instruction sequence. Then $\texttt{isnr2spisa}(p)$ represents the meaning of p as a SPISA instruction sequence. For example, the meaning of the ISNR instruction sequence

$$+\mathtt{a}\,;\#4\,;\mathtt{b}\,;\mathtt{c}\,;\backslash\#2$$

is represented by the closed SPISA term

$$(+\mathtt{a}\,;\#0\,;\mathtt{b}\,;\mathtt{c}\,;\#5\,;\#0\,;\#0)^\omega\;.$$

We use the phrase *projection semantics* to refer to the approach to semantics followed above. Meaning functions like isnr2spisa are called *projections*. The main advantage of projection semantics is that it does not require a lot of mathematical background. Found challenges for the point of view from which projection semantics originates are sketched in Appendix A.

The intended behaviour of an ISNR instruction sequence p under execution is the behaviour of the SPISA instruction sequence represented by $\mathtt{isnr2spisa}(p)$ under execution. That is, the behaviour of p under execution, written $|p|_{\mathrm{ISNR}}$, is $|\mathtt{isnr2spisa}(p)|$.

We have that $|u_1\,;\ldots;u_k|_{\mathrm{ISNR}} = |1,u_1\,;\ldots;u_k|$, where $|\_,\_|$ is defined by the following equations:

$$\begin{array}{ll}
|i,u_1\,;\ldots;u_k| = \mathsf{D} & \text{if } i=0 \lor i>k\\
|i,u_1\,;\ldots;u_k| = a\circ|i+1,u_1\,;\ldots;u_k| & \text{if } u_i = a\\
|i,u_1\,;\ldots;u_k| = |i+1,u_1\,;\ldots;u_k| \trianglelefteq a \trianglerighteq |i+2,u_1\,;\ldots;u_k| & \text{if } u_i = +a\\
|i,u_1\,;\ldots;u_k| = |i+2,u_1\,;\ldots;u_k| \trianglelefteq a \trianglerighteq |i+1,u_1\,;\ldots;u_k| & \text{if } u_i = -a\\
|i,u_1\,;\ldots;u_k| = |i+l,u_1\,;\ldots;u_k| & \text{if } u_i = \#l\\
|i,u_1\,;\ldots;u_k| = |i\dot{-}l,u_1\,;\ldots;u_k| & \text{if } u_i = \backslash\#l\\
|i,u_1\,;\ldots;u_k| = \mathsf{S} & \text{if } u_i = !\\
|i,u_1\,;\ldots;u_k| = \mathsf{S+} & \text{if } u_i = !\mathsf{t}\\
|i,u_1\,;\ldots;u_k| = \mathsf{S-} & \text{if } u_i = !\mathsf{f}
\end{array}$$

and the rule that $|i,u_1\,;\ldots;u_k| = \mathsf{D}$ if u_i is the beginning of an infinite jump chain (we refrain from formalizing the condition of this rule).

If $1 \le i \le k$, $|i,u_1\,;\ldots;u_k|$ can be read as the behaviour produced by the ISNR instruction sequence $u_1\,;\ldots;u_k$ if execution starts at the ith primitive instruction. By default, execution starts at the first primitive instruction.

For example, the ISNR instruction sequence

$$\mathsf{a}\,;+\mathsf{b}\,;\#2\,;\#3\,;\mathsf{c}\,;\backslash\#4\,;+\mathsf{d}\,;!\mathsf{t}\,;!\mathsf{f}$$

produces the x-component of the solution of the guarded recursive specification consisting of the following two equations:

$$x = \mathtt{a} \circ y\ , \qquad y = (\mathtt{c} \circ y) \unlhd \mathtt{b} \unrhd (\mathsf{S{+}} \unlhd \mathtt{d} \unrhd \mathsf{S{-}})\ .$$

In this book, we will sometimes use a restricted version of ISNR, called ISNR^{s} (ISNR with strict Boolean termination). The primitive instructions of ISNR^{s} are the primitive instructions of SPISA with the exception of the plain termination instruction. Thus, ISNR^{s} instruction sequences are ISNR instruction sequences in which the plain termination instruction does not occur.

Let *ISN* be either ISNR or ISNR^{s}. Then we will write $;_{i=1}^{n} \boldsymbol{p}_i$, where $\boldsymbol{p}_1, \ldots, \boldsymbol{p}_n$ are *ISN* instruction sequences, for the *ISN* instruction sequence $\boldsymbol{p}_1 \,;\, \ldots \,;\, \boldsymbol{p}_n$.

2.3.2 *The instruction sequence notation* ISNA

In this section, we introduce the instruction sequence notation ISNA (Instruction Sequence Notation with Absolute jumps).

In ISNA, like in SPISA, it is assumed that a fixed but arbitrary set $\mathfrak{A}$ of basic instructions has been given.

ISNA has the primitive instructions of SPISA except the forward jump instructions and in addition:

- for each $l \in \mathbb{N}$, an *absolute jump instruction* $\#\#l$.

ISNA instruction sequences are expressions of the form $\boldsymbol{u}_1 \,;\ldots;\, \boldsymbol{u}_k$, where $\boldsymbol{u}_1, \ldots, \boldsymbol{u}_k$ are primitive instructions of ISNA.

On execution of an ISNA instruction sequence, the effects of the plain basic instructions, the positive test instructions, the negative test instructions, and the termination instructions are as in SPISA. The effect of an absolute jump instruction $\#\#l$ is that execution proceeds with the lth primitive instruction of the instruction sequence concerned. If $\#\#l$ is itself the lth instruction or there is no primitive instruction to proceed with, inaction occurs.

We define the meaning of ISNA instruction sequences by means of a projection `isna2spisa` from the set of all ISNA instruction sequences to the set of all closed SPISA terms. This function is defined by

$$\mathtt{isna2spisa}(\boldsymbol{u}_1 \,;\ldots;\, \boldsymbol{u}_k) = (\varphi_1(\boldsymbol{u}_1) \,;\ldots;\, \varphi_k(\boldsymbol{u}_k) \,;\, \#0 \,;\, \#0)^{\omega}\ ,$$

where the auxiliary functions φ_j from the set of all primitive instructions of ISNA to the set of all primitive instructions of SPISA are defined as follows ($1 \leq j \leq k$):

$$\begin{array}{lll}
\varphi_j(\#\#l) &= \#l{-}j & \text{if } j \leq l \leq k\ , \\
\varphi_j(\#\#l) &= \#k{+}2{-}(j{-}l) & \text{if } 0 < l < j\ , \\
\varphi_j(\#\#l) &= \#0 & \text{if } l = 0 \vee l > k\ , \\
\varphi_j(\boldsymbol{u}) &= \boldsymbol{u} & \text{if } \boldsymbol{u} \text{ is not a jump instruction}\ .
\end{array}$$

Let $\boldsymbol{p}$ be an ISNA instruction sequence. Then $\texttt{isna2spisa}(\boldsymbol{p})$ represents the meaning of $\boldsymbol{p}$ as a SPISA instruction sequence. For example, the meaning of the ISNA instruction sequence

$$+\mathsf{a}\,;\,\#\#6\,;\,\mathsf{b}\,;\,\mathsf{c}\,;\,\#\#3$$

is represented by the closed SPISA term

$$(+\mathsf{a}\,;\,\#0\,;\,\mathsf{b}\,;\,\mathsf{c}\,;\,\#5\,;\,\#0\,;\,\#0)^{\omega}\ .$$

The intended behaviour of an ISNA instruction sequence $\boldsymbol{p}$ under execution is the behaviour of the SPISA instruction sequence represented by $\texttt{isna2spisa}(\boldsymbol{p})$ under execution. That is, the behaviour of $\boldsymbol{p}$ under execution, written $|\boldsymbol{p}|_{\text{ISNA}}$, is $|\texttt{isna2spisa}(\boldsymbol{p})|$.

We have that $|\boldsymbol{u}_1\,;\,\ldots\,;\,\boldsymbol{u}_k|_{\text{ISNA}} = |1, \boldsymbol{u}_1\,;\,\ldots\,;\,\boldsymbol{u}_k|$, where $|\_,\_|$ is defined by the following equations:

$$\begin{array}{ll}
|i, \boldsymbol{u}_1\,;\ldots;\boldsymbol{u}_k| = \mathsf{D} & \text{if } i = 0 \vee i > k \\
|i, \boldsymbol{u}_1\,;\ldots;\boldsymbol{u}_k| = \boldsymbol{a} \circ |i+1, \boldsymbol{u}_1\,;\ldots;\boldsymbol{u}_k| & \text{if } \boldsymbol{u}_i = \boldsymbol{a} \\
|i, \boldsymbol{u}_1\,;\ldots;\boldsymbol{u}_k| = |i+1, \boldsymbol{u}_1\,;\ldots;\boldsymbol{u}_k| \unlhd \boldsymbol{a} \unrhd |i+2, \boldsymbol{u}_1\,;\ldots;\boldsymbol{u}_k| & \text{if } \boldsymbol{u}_i = +\boldsymbol{a} \\
|i, \boldsymbol{u}_1\,;\ldots;\boldsymbol{u}_k| = |i+2, \boldsymbol{u}_1\,;\ldots;\boldsymbol{u}_k| \unlhd \boldsymbol{a} \unrhd |i+1, \boldsymbol{u}_1\,;\ldots;\boldsymbol{u}_k| & \text{if } \boldsymbol{u}_i = -\boldsymbol{a} \\
|i, \boldsymbol{u}_1\,;\ldots;\boldsymbol{u}_k| = |l, \boldsymbol{u}_1\,;\ldots;\boldsymbol{u}_k| & \text{if } \boldsymbol{u}_i = \#\#l \\
|i, \boldsymbol{u}_1\,;\ldots;\boldsymbol{u}_k| = \mathsf{S} & \text{if } \boldsymbol{u}_i = \,! \\
|i, \boldsymbol{u}_1\,;\ldots;\boldsymbol{u}_k| = \mathsf{S{+}} & \text{if } \boldsymbol{u}_i = \,!\mathsf{t} \\
|i, \boldsymbol{u}_1\,;\ldots;\boldsymbol{u}_k| = \mathsf{S{-}} & \text{if } \boldsymbol{u}_i = \,!\mathsf{f}
\end{array}$$

and the rule that $|i, \boldsymbol{u}_1\,;\ldots;\boldsymbol{u}_k| = \mathsf{D}$ if $\boldsymbol{u}_i$ is the beginning of an infinite jump chain.

For example, the ISNA instruction sequence

$$\mathsf{a}\,;\,+\mathsf{b}\,;\,\#\#5\,;\,\#\#7\,;\,\mathsf{c}\,;\,\#\#2\,;\,+\mathsf{d}\,;\,!\mathsf{t}\,;\,!\mathsf{f}$$

produces the x-component of the solution of the guarded recursive specification consisting of the following two equations:

$$x = \mathsf{a} \circ y\ , \qquad y = (\mathsf{c} \circ y) \unlhd \mathsf{b} \unrhd (\mathsf{S{+}} \unlhd \mathsf{d} \unrhd \mathsf{S{-}})\ .$$

2.3.3 *Inter-translatability of* ISNR *and* ISNA

ISNR instruction sequences and ISNA instruction sequences are translatable into each other by the functions `isnr2isna` and `isna2isnr`, respectively. These functions are defined by

$$\mathtt{isnr2isna}(\boldsymbol{u}_1 ; \ldots ; \boldsymbol{u}_k) = \psi_1(\boldsymbol{u}_1) ; \ldots ; \psi_k(\boldsymbol{u}_k) \,,$$

where the auxiliary functions ψ_j from the set of all primitive instructions of ISNR to the set of all primitive instructions of ISNA are defined as follows ($1 \leq j \leq k$):

$$\begin{aligned} \psi_j(\#l) &= \#\#l{+}j \,, \\ \psi_j(\backslash\#l) &= \#\#j{-}l && \text{if } l < j \,, \\ \psi_j(\backslash\#l) &= \#\#0 && \text{if } l \geq j \,, \\ \psi_j(\boldsymbol{u}) &= \boldsymbol{u} && \text{if } \boldsymbol{u} \text{ is not a jump instruction} \,, \end{aligned}$$

and

$$\mathtt{isna2isnr}(\boldsymbol{u}_1 ; \ldots ; \boldsymbol{u}_k) = \varphi_1(\boldsymbol{u}_1) ; \ldots ; \varphi_k(\boldsymbol{u}_k) \,,$$

where the auxiliary functions φ_j from the set of all primitive instructions of ISNA to the set of all primitive instructions of ISNR are defined as follows ($1 \leq j \leq k$):

$$\begin{aligned} \varphi_j(\#\#l) &= \#l{-}j && \text{if } l \geq j \,, \\ \varphi_j(\#\#l) &= \backslash\#j{-}l && \text{if } l < j \,, \\ \varphi_j(\boldsymbol{u}) &= \boldsymbol{u} && \text{if } \boldsymbol{u} \text{ is not a jump instruction} \,. \end{aligned}$$

A simple example of the inter-translatability is:

$$\begin{aligned} &\mathtt{isnr2isna}({+}\mathtt{a} ; \#4 ; \mathtt{b} ; \mathtt{c} ; \backslash\#2) = {+}\mathtt{a} ; \#\#6 ; \mathtt{b} ; \mathtt{c} ; \#\#3 \,, \\ &\mathtt{isna2isnr}({+}\mathtt{a} ; \#\#6 ; \mathtt{b} ; \mathtt{c} ; \#\#3) = {+}\mathtt{a} ; \#4 ; \mathtt{b} ; \mathtt{c} ; \backslash\#2 \,. \end{aligned}$$

We have that the composition of `isnr2isna` and `isna2isnr` in either order is an identity function up to behavioural equivalence.

Proposition 2.3.

(1) For all ISNR *instruction sequences* $\boldsymbol{p}$, $|\mathtt{isna2isnr}(\mathtt{isnr2isna}(\boldsymbol{p}))|_{\mathrm{ISNR}} = |\boldsymbol{p}|_{\mathrm{ISNR}}$.
(2) For all ISNA *instruction sequences* $\boldsymbol{p}$, $|\mathtt{isnr2isna}(\mathtt{isna2isnr}(\boldsymbol{p}))|_{\mathrm{ISNA}} = |\boldsymbol{p}|_{\mathrm{ISNA}}$.

Proof. The proof is trivial. □

2.3.4 *Additional instruction sequence notations*

ISNR and ISNA have the explicit termination instructions from SPISA. ISNRI and ISNAI, which will be presented below, have the implicit termination convention commonly used in assembly languages instead. That is, if there is no primitive instruction to proceed with then termination occurs. Thus, ISNRI and ISNAI are really the closest thing to existing assembly languages. However, they are strictly weaker than SPISA: because the explicit termination instructions from SPISA are not available, termination with a Boolean value is not possible.

ISNRI and ISNAI have the primitive instructions of ISNR and ISNA, respectively, with the exception of the plain, positive and negative termination instructions. ISNRI instruction sequences and ISNAI instruction sequences are expressions of the form $u_1 ; \ldots ; u_k$, where $u_1, \ldots, u_k$ are primitive instructions of ISNRI and ISNAI, respectively.

We define meaning of ISNRI instruction sequences and ISNAI instruction sequences by means of projections `isnri2isnr` from ISNRI instruction sequences to ISNR instruction sequences and `isnai2isna` from ISNAI instruction sequences to ISNA instruction sequences, respectively. These functions are defined by

$$\mathtt{isnri2isnr}(u_1 ; \ldots ; u_k) = \psi_1(u_1) ; \ldots ; \psi_k(u_k) ; ! ; ! ,$$

where the auxiliary functions ψ_j from the set of all primitive instructions of ISNRI to the set of all primitive instructions of ISNR are defined as follows ($1 \leq j \leq k$):

$$\begin{aligned}
\psi_j(\#l) &= ! && \text{if } j + l > k , \\
\psi_j(\#l) &= \#l && \text{if } j + l \leq k , \\
\psi_j(\backslash\#l) &= ! && \text{if } l \geq j , \\
\psi_j(\backslash\#l) &= \backslash\#l && \text{if } l < j , \\
\psi_j(u) &= u && \text{if } u \text{ is not a jump instruction}
\end{aligned}$$

and

$$\mathtt{isnai2isna}(u_1 ; \ldots ; u_k) = \varphi(u_1) ; \ldots ; \varphi(u_k) ; ! ; ! ,$$

where the auxiliary function φ from the set of all primitive instructions of ISNAI to the set of all primitive instructions of ISNA is defined as follows:

$$\begin{aligned}
\varphi(\#\#l) &= ! && \text{if } l = 0 \lor l > k , \\
\varphi(\#\#l) &= \#\#l && \text{if } 0 < l \leq k , \\
\varphi(u) &= u && \text{if } u \text{ is not a jump instruction} .
\end{aligned}$$

Let p be an ISNRI instruction sequence. Then $\mathtt{isnri2isnr}(p)$ is the meaning of p as an ISNR instruction sequence. For example, the meaning of the ISNRI instruction sequence

$$+\mathsf{a} ; \#10 ; \backslash\#1 ; -\mathsf{b} ; \#2 ; +\mathsf{c}$$

is the ISNR instruction sequence

$$\texttt{+a ; ! ; \#1 ; -b ; ! ; +c ; ! ; ! .}$$

Notice that the ISNRI instruction sequence can be considered an ISNR instruction sequence as well. However, execution as ISNR instruction sequence will lead to inaction in all cases where execution as ISNRI instruction sequence will lead to termination. Similar remarks apply to ISNAI instruction sequences.

In [Bergstra and Loots (2002)], a version of SPISA with a somewhat restricted set of primitive instructions is presented. The primitive instructions of this version, which is called PGA, are the primitive instructions of SPISA with the exception of the positive and negative termination instructions. Thus, PGA instruction sequences are SPISA instruction sequences in which the positive and negative termination instructions do not occur.

A hierarchy of instruction sequence notations rooted in PGA is presented in [Bergstra and Loots (2002)] as well. The instruction sequence notation that is the highest in the hierarchy, named PGLS, supports structured programming by offering a rendering of conditional and loop constructs instead of (unstructured) jump instructions. For each of the instruction sequence notations that appear in the hierarchy, except the lowest one, a function is given by means of which each instruction sequence from that instruction sequence notation is translated into an instruction sequence from the first instruction sequence notation lower in the hierarchy that produces the same behaviour on execution. In the case of the lowest one, each instruction sequence is translated into a closed PGA term. Clearly, this way of giving semantics constitutes a further elaboration of projection semantics. ISNRI and ISNAI occur in this hierarchy under the names PGLC and PGLD, respectively.

A PGA tool set is available from `http://www.science.uva.nl/research/prog/projects/pga/toolset`. This tool set includes, for most instruction sequence notations in the above-mentioned hierarchy, a translator to the first instruction sequence notation lower in the hierarchy, a syntax checker, and a simulator of the behaviours produced by instruction sequences under execution (see also [Diertens (2003)]).

Chapter 3

Instruction Processing

This chapter concerns the interaction between instruction sequences under execution and components of their execution environment concerning the processing of instructions. The idea is that an execution environment provides a family of named components of which each is responsible for the processing of particular instructions. The attention is restricted to the components that are capable of processing the instructions concerned independently. With this, we mean that no interaction with external parties is needed by the components to accomplish the processing. Components that are capable of processing instructions for storing and fetching data of an auxiliary nature are typical examples of components that do not need interaction with external parties, but components that are capable of processing instructions for reading input data or showing output data need interaction with external parties.

We introduce so-called services, which represent the behaviours exhibited by the components of an execution environment that are capable of processing particular instructions and doing so independently, and extend the algebraic theory of threads, which represent the behaviours produced by instruction sequences under execution, with an operator meant for the composition of families of named services and operators that have a direct bearing on the processing of instructions by services from such service families.

We also introduce the concept of a functional unit. This concept is useful in the current setting because a functional unit is an abstract model of a machine. In the frequently occurring case where the behaviours exhibited by a component of an execution environment that is capable of processing particular instructions and doing so independently can be viewed as the behaviours of a machine in its different states, the services concerned are completely determined by a functional unit. Some results about functional units for natural numbers are given in Appendix B.

This chapter is also concerned with instruction sequence notations with programming features not found in ISNR or ISNA. We devise instruction sequence notations with indirect jump instructions, returning jump instructions and an accompanying return instruction, and dynamically instantiated instructions and explain these notations with the help of some simple functional units. Dynamic instruction instantiation is a genuine and useful programming feature which is not suggested by existing programming practice. An application of dynamic instruction instantiation is given in Appendix C.

In Appendix D, an analytic execution architecture, i.e. a model of a hypothetical execution environment for instruction sequences, is given. This execution architecture has been designed for the purpose of explaining how an instruction sequence may be executed, and makes explicit the interaction of an instruction sequence under execution with the components of its execution environment.

3.1 Basics of Instruction Processing

In this section, we extend BTA with an operator meant for the composition of families of named services and operators that have a direct bearing on the processing of instructions by services from such service families. The extension in question is based on assumptions with respect to services which characterize them just sufficiently for the purpose of the extension. As a consequence, services represent a rather abstract view on the behaviours exhibited by the components of an execution environment that are capable of processing particular instructions and doing so independently.

A more concrete view on these behaviours, namely as the behaviours of a machines in its different states, is often more comprehensible. Section 3.2 is devoted to this more concrete view.

3.1.1 *Services and service families*

Below, we introduce service families and a composition operator for service families. However, preceding that we will go into some details of services.

It is assumed that a fixed but arbitrary set $\mathcal{M}$ of *methods* has been given. A service is able to process certain methods. The processing of a method may involve a change of the service. At completion of the processing of a method, the service produces a reply value. The possible replies are t, f and d (standing for divergent).

For example, a service may be able to process methods for pushing a natural number on a stack ($\mathtt{push}{:}n$), testing whether the top of the stack equals a natural number ($\mathtt{topeq}{:}n$), and popping the top element from the stack (pop). Processing of a pushing method or a popping method changes the service, because it changes the stack with which it deals, and produces the reply value t if no stack overflow or stack underflow occurs and f otherwise. Processing of a testing method does not change the service, because it does not changes the stack with which it deals, and produces the reply value t if the test succeeds and f otherwise. Attempted processing of a method that the service is not able to process changes the service into one that is not able to process any method and produces the reply d. A precise description of services of this kind will be given in Sect. 3.2.4.

In SFA, the algebraic theory of service families introduced below, the following is assumed with respect to services:

- a signature $\Sigma_{\mathcal{S}}$ has been given that includes the following sorts:
  - the sort $\mathbf{S}$ of *services*;
  - the sort $\mathbf{R}$ of *replies*;

  and the following constants and operators:
  - the *empty service* constant $\delta : \to \mathbf{S}$;
  - the *reply* constants $\mathsf{t}, \mathsf{f}, \mathsf{d}, \mathsf{m} : \to \mathbf{R}$;
  - for each $m \in \mathcal{M}$, the *derived service* operator $\frac{\partial}{\partial m} : \mathbf{S} \to \mathbf{S}$;
  - for each $m \in \mathcal{M}$, the *service reply* operator $\varrho_m : \mathbf{S} \to \mathbf{R}$;
- a minimal $\Sigma_{\mathcal{S}}$-algebra $\boldsymbol{S}$ has been given in which t, f, d and m are mutually different, and
  - $\bigwedge_{m \in \mathcal{M}} \frac{\partial}{\partial m}(z) = z \wedge \varrho_m(z) = \mathsf{d} \Rightarrow z = \delta$ holds;
  - for each $m \in \mathcal{M}$, $\frac{\partial}{\partial m}(z) = \delta \Leftrightarrow \varrho_m(z) = \mathsf{d}$ holds;
  - for each $m \in \mathcal{M}$, $\varrho_m(z) \neq \mathsf{m}$ holds.

The intuition concerning $\frac{\partial}{\partial m}$ and ϱ_m is that on a request to service s to process method m:

- if $\varrho_m(s) \neq \mathsf{d}$, s processes m, produces the reply $\varrho_m(s)$, and then proceeds as $\frac{\partial}{\partial m}(s)$;
- if $\varrho_m(s) = \mathsf{d}$, s is not able to process method m and proceeds as δ.

The empty service δ itself is unable to process any method.

In the sequel, we will restrict ourselves to the case where $\Sigma_{\mathcal{S}}$ consists of the sorts, constants and operators that are mentioned above and a constant of sort $\mathbf{S}$ for each element of the interpretation of the sort $\mathbf{S}$. In that case, any $\Sigma_{\mathcal{S}}$-algebra that can be taken as $\boldsymbol{S}$ is fully determined by the following:

- the interpretation of the sort $\mathbf{S}$;
- the interpretation of each constant of sort $\mathbf{S}$;
- for each $m \in \mathcal{M}$, the interpretation of the operators $\frac{\partial}{\partial m}$ and ϱ_m.

If we characterize a $\Sigma_{\mathcal{S}}$-algebra that can be taken as $\boldsymbol{S}$ in this way, we will refer to the interpretation of the sort $\mathbf{S}$ as the set $\mathcal{S}$ of services.

It is also assumed that a fixed but arbitrary set $\mathcal{F}$ of *foci* has been given. An execution environment is viewed as a set of named components where each name occurs only once. Foci play the role of names of the components of an execution environment. The name of a component of an execution environment is considered to be inherited by the behaviour exhibited by the component. This way, the service family provided by an execution environment is a set of named services where each name occurs only once. Moreover, the names of services in a service family are foci.

SFA has the sorts, constants and operators from $\Sigma_{\mathcal{S}}$ and in addition the following sort:

- the sort $\mathbf{SF}$ of *service families*;

and the following constant and operators:

- the *empty service family* constant $\emptyset : \to \mathbf{SF}$;
- for each $f \in \mathcal{F}$, the unary *singleton service family* operator $f.\_ : \mathbf{S} \to \mathbf{SF}$;
- the binary *service family composition* operator $\_ \oplus \_ : \mathbf{SF} \times \mathbf{SF} \to \mathbf{SF}$;
- for each $F \subseteq \mathcal{F}$, the unary *encapsulation* operator $\partial_F : \mathbf{SF} \to \mathbf{SF}$.

We assume that there are infinitely many variables of sort $\mathbf{S}$, including z, and infinitely many variables of sort $\mathbf{SF}$, including u, v, w. Terms are built as usual in the many-sorted case (see e.g. [Wirsing (1990); Sannella and Tarlecki (1999)]). We use prefix notation for the singleton service family operators and infix notation for the service family composition operator.

The service family denoted by $\emptyset$ is the empty service family. The service family denoted by a closed term of the form $f.t$, where t is a closed term of sort $\mathbf{S}$, consists of one named service only, the service concerned is the service denoted by t, and the name of this service is f. The service family denoted by a closed term of the form $t \oplus t'$, where t and t' are closed terms of sort $\mathbf{SF}$, consists of all named services that belong to either the service family denoted by t or the service family denoted by t'. In the case where a named service from the service family denoted by t and a named service from the service family denoted by t' have the same name, they collapse to an empty service with the name concerned. The

Table 3.1 Axioms of SFA

$u \oplus \emptyset = u$	SFC1	$\partial_{\boldsymbol{F}}(\emptyset) = \emptyset$	SFE1
$u \oplus v = v \oplus u$	SFC2	$\partial_{\boldsymbol{F}}(\boldsymbol{f}.z) = \emptyset \quad \text{if } \boldsymbol{f} \in \boldsymbol{F}$	SFE2
$(u \oplus v) \oplus w = u \oplus (v \oplus w)$	SFC3	$\partial_{\boldsymbol{F}}(\boldsymbol{f}.z) = \boldsymbol{f}.z \;\; \text{if } \boldsymbol{f} \notin \boldsymbol{F}$	SFE3
$\boldsymbol{f}.z \oplus \boldsymbol{f}.z' = \boldsymbol{f}.\delta$	SFC4	$\partial_{\boldsymbol{F}}(u \oplus v) = \partial_{\boldsymbol{F}}(u) \oplus \partial_{\boldsymbol{F}}(v)$	SFE4

service family denoted by a closed term of the form $\partial_{\boldsymbol{F}}(\boldsymbol{t})$, where $\boldsymbol{t}$ is a closed term of sort **SF**, consists of all named services with a name not in $\boldsymbol{F}$ that belong to the service family denoted by $\boldsymbol{t}$.

Let $\boldsymbol{f}$ be a focus, $\boldsymbol{t}$ be a closed term of sort **S** and $\boldsymbol{t}'$ be a closed term of sort **SF**. Then there are no services that collapse to an empty service in the service family composition of the service families denoted by $\boldsymbol{f}.\boldsymbol{t}$ and $\partial_{\{\boldsymbol{f}\}}(\boldsymbol{t}')$. In other words, it is certain that the service denoted by $\boldsymbol{t}$ belongs to the service family denoted by $\boldsymbol{f}.\boldsymbol{t} \oplus \partial_{\{\boldsymbol{f}\}}(\boldsymbol{t}')$. By contrast, it is not certain that the service denoted by $\boldsymbol{t}$ belongs to the service family denoted by $\boldsymbol{f}.\boldsymbol{t} \oplus \boldsymbol{t}'$.

Using the singleton service family operators and the service family composition operator, any finite number of possibly identical services can be brought together in a service family provided that the services concerned are given different names. In Sect. 3.1.4, we will give an example of the use of the singleton service family operators and the service family composition operator. The empty service family constant and the encapsulation operators are primarily meant to axiomatize the operators that are introduced in Sect. 3.1.2.

Remark 3.1. The service family composition operator takes the place of the non-interfering combination operator from [Bergstra and Ponse (2002)]. As suggested by the name, service family composition is composition of service families. Non-interfering combination is composition of services. The non-interfering combination of services can process all methods that can be processed by only one of the services. This has the disadvantage that its usefulness is rather limited without an additional renaming mechanism. For example, a finite number of identical services cannot be brought together in a service by means of non-interfering combination.

The axioms of SFA are given in Table 3.1. In this table, $\boldsymbol{f}$ stands for an arbitrary focus from $\mathcal{F}$ and $\boldsymbol{F}$ stands for an arbitrary subset of $\mathcal{F}$. The axioms of SFA simply formalize the informal explanation given above.

We can prove that each closed SFA term of sort $\mathbf{SF}$ can be reduced to one in which encapsulation operators do not occur.

Lemma 3.1. *For all closed* SFA *terms* t *of sort* $\mathbf{SF}$*, there exists a closed* SFA *term* t' *of sort* $\mathbf{SF}$ *in which encapsulation operators do not occur such that* $t = t'$ *is derivable from the axioms of* SFA.

Proof. This is proved by induction on the structure of t. The cases $t \equiv \emptyset$ and $t \equiv f.t_1$ are trivial, and the case $t \equiv t_1 \oplus t_2$ follows immediately from the induction hypothesis. The case $t \equiv \partial_F(t_1)$ is somewhat more involved. By the induction hypothesis, there exists a closed SFA term t_1' of sort $\mathbf{SF}$ in which encapsulation operators do not occur such that $t_1 = t_1'$. This means that we are done with this case if we have proved the following claim:

> Let t_1' be a closed SFA term of sort $\mathbf{SF}$ in which encapsulation operators do not occur. Then there exists a closed SFA term t' of sort $\mathbf{SF}$ in which encapsulation operators do not occur such that $\partial_F(t_1') = t'$ is derivable from the axioms of SFA.

This claim is easily proved by induction on the structure of t_1'. □

We will write $\bigoplus_{i=1}^{n} t_i$, where $t_1, \ldots, t_n$ are terms of sort $\mathbf{SF}$, for the term $t_1 \oplus \ldots \oplus t_n$.

A typical model of SFA is the free SFA-extension of $\mathcal{S}$. This model will be used in Sect. 3.1.8 to construct a projective limit model for the extension of BTA combined with SFA that will be introduced in Sect. 3.1.2.

3.1.2 *Use, apply and reply*

A thread may interact with the named services from the service family provided by an execution environment. That is, a thread may perform a basic action for the purpose of requesting a named service to process a method and to return a reply at completion of the processing of the method. In this section, we combine BTA with SFA and extend this combination with three operators that relate to this kind of interaction between threads and services. The resulting algebraic theory is called BTA+TSI (BTA with Thread-Service Interaction).

The operators in question are called the use operator, the apply operator, and the reply operator. The difference between the use operator and the apply operator is a matter of perspective: the use operator is concerned with the effects of service families on threads and therefore produces threads, whereas the apply operator is concerned with the effects of threads on service families and therefore produces service families. The reply operator is concerned with the effects of service families on the Boolean values that threads possibly deliver at their termination.

The reply operator produces special values in the case where no Boolean value is delivered at termination or no termination takes place. Thus, it is accomplished that all terms with occurrences of the reply operator denote something. We prefer to use the reply operator only if it is known that termination with delivery of a Boolean value takes place (see also Sect. 3.1.7).

In BTA, it is assumed that a fixed but arbitrary set $\mathcal{A}$ of basic actions has been given. In BTA+TSI, the following additional assumptions relating to $\mathcal{A}$ are made:

- a fixed but arbitrary set $\mathcal{F}$ of foci has been given;
- a fixed but arbitrary set $\mathcal{M}$ of methods has been given;
- $\mathcal{A} = \{f.m \mid f \in \mathcal{F} \wedge m \in \mathcal{M}\}$.

These additional assumptions are made to be able to deal with the kind of interaction between threads and services being considered in BTA+TSI. All three operators mentioned above are concerned with the processing of methods by services from a service family in pursuance of basic actions performed by a thread. Therefore, a method forms a part of each basic action. The service involved in the processing of a method is the service whose name is the focus that forms a part of the basic action in question.

BTA+TSI has the sorts, constants and operators of both BTA and SFA and in addition the following constants and operators:

- the binary *use* operator $\_ \,/\, \_ : \mathbf{T} \times \mathbf{SF} \to \mathbf{T}$;
- the binary *apply* operator $\_ \bullet \_ : \mathbf{T} \times \mathbf{SF} \to \mathbf{SF}$;
- the binary *reply* operator $\_ \,!\, \_ : \mathbf{T} \times \mathbf{SF} \to \mathbf{R}$.

We use infix notation for the use, apply and reply operators.

The thread denoted by a closed term of the form $t \,/\, t'$ and the service family denoted by a closed term of the form $t \bullet t'$ are the thread and service family, respectively, that result from processing the method of each basic action performed by the thread denoted by t by the service in the service family denoted by t' with the focus of the basic action as its name if such a service exists. When the method of a basic action performed by a thread is processed by a service, the service changes in accordance with the method concerned, and affects the thread as follows: the basic action turns into the internal action tau and the two

Table 3.2 Axioms for the use operator

$\mathsf{S{+}} \,/\, u = \mathsf{S{+}}$		U1
$\mathsf{S{-}} \,/\, u = \mathsf{S{-}}$		U2
$\mathsf{S} \,/\, u = \mathsf{S}$		U3
$\mathsf{D} \,/\, u = \mathsf{D}$		U4
$(\mathsf{tau} \circ x) \,/\, u = \mathsf{tau} \circ (x \,/\, u)$		U5
$(x \trianglelefteq \boldsymbol{f}.\boldsymbol{m} \trianglerighteq y) \,/\, \partial_{\{f\}}(u) = (x \,/\, \partial_{\{f\}}(u)) \trianglelefteq \boldsymbol{f}.\boldsymbol{m} \trianglerighteq (y \,/\, \partial_{\{f\}}(u))$		U6
$(x \trianglelefteq \boldsymbol{f}.\boldsymbol{m} \trianglerighteq y) \,/\, (\boldsymbol{f}.\boldsymbol{t} \oplus \partial_{\{f\}}(u)) = \mathsf{tau} \circ (x \,/\, (\boldsymbol{f}.\frac{\partial}{\partial m}\boldsymbol{t} \oplus \partial_{\{f\}}(u)))$	if $\varrho_m(\boldsymbol{t}) = \mathsf{t}$	U7
$(x \trianglelefteq \boldsymbol{f}.\boldsymbol{m} \trianglerighteq y) \,/\, (\boldsymbol{f}.\boldsymbol{t} \oplus \partial_{\{f\}}(u)) = \mathsf{tau} \circ (y \,/\, (\boldsymbol{f}.\frac{\partial}{\partial m}\boldsymbol{t} \oplus \partial_{\{f\}}(u)))$	if $\varrho_m(\boldsymbol{t}) = \mathsf{f}$	U8
$(x \trianglelefteq \boldsymbol{f}.\boldsymbol{m} \trianglerighteq y) \,/\, (\boldsymbol{f}.\boldsymbol{t} \oplus \partial_{\{f\}}(u)) = \mathsf{D}$	if $\varrho_m(\boldsymbol{t}) = \mathsf{d}$	U9

ways to proceed reduce to one on the basis of the reply value produced by the service. The value denoted by a closed term of the form $\boldsymbol{t} \,!\, \boldsymbol{t}'$ is the Boolean value that the thread denoted by $\boldsymbol{t} \,/\, \boldsymbol{t}'$ delivers at its termination if the thread terminates and delivers a Boolean value at termination, the value m (standing for meaningless) if the thread terminates and does not deliver a Boolean value at termination, and the value d if the thread does not terminate.[1]

A simple example of the application of the use operator, the apply operator and the reply operator is

$$((\mathtt{nns.pop} \circ \mathsf{S{+}}) \trianglelefteq \mathtt{nns.topeq{:}0} \trianglerighteq \mathsf{S{-}}) \,/\, \mathtt{nns}.\mathit{NNS}(0\sigma)\ ,$$
$$((\mathtt{nns.pop} \circ \mathsf{S{+}}) \trianglelefteq \mathtt{nns.topeq{:}0} \trianglerighteq \mathsf{S{-}}) \bullet \mathtt{nns}.\mathit{NNS}(0\sigma)\ ,$$
$$((\mathtt{nns.pop} \circ \mathsf{S{+}}) \trianglelefteq \mathtt{nns.topeq{:}0} \trianglerighteq \mathsf{S{-}}) \,!\, \mathtt{nns}.\mathit{NNS}(0\sigma)\ ,$$

where $\mathit{NNS}(\sigma)$ denotes a stack service as described in Sect. 3.1.1 dealing with a stack whose content is represented by the sequence σ. A precise description of stack services will be given in Sect. 3.2.4. The first term denotes the thread that performs tau twice and then terminates with delivery of the Boolean value t. The second term denotes the stack service dealing with a stack whose content is σ, i.e. the content of the stack at termination of the thread denoted by the first term, and the third term denotes the reply value t, i.e. the reply value delivered at termination of the thread denoted by the first term.

The axioms of BTA+TSI are the axioms of BTA, the axioms of SFA, and the axioms given in Tables 3.2, 3.3 and 3.4. In these tables, $\boldsymbol{f}$ stands for an arbitrary focus from $\mathcal{F}$, $\boldsymbol{m}$

[1] A service never produces the value m. The value m was already introduced in Sect. 3.1.1 in order to circumvent

Table 3.3 Axioms for the apply operator

$\mathsf{S{+}} \bullet u = u$	A1
$\mathsf{S{-}} \bullet u = u$	A2
$\mathsf{S} \bullet u = u$	A3
$\mathsf{D} \bullet u = \emptyset$	A4
$(\mathsf{tau} \circ x) \bullet u = x \bullet u$	A5
$(x \trianglelefteq \boldsymbol{f.m} \trianglerighteq y) \bullet \partial_{\{f\}}(u) = \emptyset$	A6
$(x \trianglelefteq \boldsymbol{f.m} \trianglerighteq y) \bullet (\boldsymbol{f.t} \oplus \partial_{\{f\}}(u)) = x \bullet (\boldsymbol{f}.\frac{\partial}{\partial m}\boldsymbol{t} \oplus \partial_{\{f\}}(u))$ if $\varrho_m(\boldsymbol{t}) = \mathsf{t}$	A7
$(x \trianglelefteq \boldsymbol{f.m} \trianglerighteq y) \bullet (\boldsymbol{f.t} \oplus \partial_{\{f\}}(u)) = y \bullet (\boldsymbol{f}.\frac{\partial}{\partial m}\boldsymbol{t} \oplus \partial_{\{f\}}(u))$ if $\varrho_m(\boldsymbol{t}) = \mathsf{f}$	A8
$(x \trianglelefteq \boldsymbol{f.m} \trianglerighteq y) \bullet (\boldsymbol{f.t} \oplus \partial_{\{f\}}(u)) = \emptyset$ if $\varrho_m(\boldsymbol{t}) = \mathsf{d}$	A9

Table 3.4 Axioms for the reply operator

$\mathsf{S{+}} \;!\; u = \mathsf{t}$	R1
$\mathsf{S{-}} \;!\; u = \mathsf{f}$	R2
$\mathsf{S} \;!\; u = \mathsf{m}$	R3
$\mathsf{D} \;!\; u = \mathsf{d}$	R4
$(\mathsf{tau} \circ x) \;!\; u = x \;!\; u$	R5
$(x \trianglelefteq \boldsymbol{f.m} \trianglerighteq y) \;!\; \partial_{\{f\}}(u) = \mathsf{d}$	R6
$(x \trianglelefteq \boldsymbol{f.m} \trianglerighteq y) \;!\; (\boldsymbol{f.t} \oplus \partial_{\{f\}}(u)) = x \;!\; (\boldsymbol{f}.\frac{\partial}{\partial m}\boldsymbol{t} \oplus \partial_{\{f\}}(u))$ if $\varrho_m(\boldsymbol{t}) = \mathsf{t}$	R7
$(x \trianglelefteq \boldsymbol{f.m} \trianglerighteq y) \;!\; (\boldsymbol{f.t} \oplus \partial_{\{f\}}(u)) = y \;!\; (\boldsymbol{f}.\frac{\partial}{\partial m}\boldsymbol{t} \oplus \partial_{\{f\}}(u))$ if $\varrho_m(\boldsymbol{t}) = \mathsf{f}$	R8
$(x \trianglelefteq \boldsymbol{f.m} \trianglerighteq y) \;!\; (\boldsymbol{f.t} \oplus \partial_{\{f\}}(u)) = \mathsf{d}$ if $\varrho_m(\boldsymbol{t}) = \mathsf{d}$	R9

stands for an arbitrary method from $\mathcal{M}$, and $\boldsymbol{t}$ stands for an arbitrary term of sort **S**. The axioms simply formalize the informal explanation given above and in addition stipulate what is the result of use, apply and reply if inappropriate foci or methods are involved.

The following equations are examples of equations that are derivable in the case where

---

the introduction of two sorts of reply values.

the size of σ is less than the maximal stack size:

$$
\begin{aligned}
&(\texttt{nns.push:}n \circ x) \;/\; \texttt{nns}.\mathit{NNS}(\sigma) = \mathsf{tau} \circ (x \;/\; \texttt{nns}.\mathit{NNS}(n\sigma))\;, \\
&(x \unlhd \texttt{nns.pop} \unrhd \mathsf{S}) \;/\; \texttt{nns}.\mathit{NNS}(\epsilon) = \mathsf{tau} \circ \mathsf{S}\;, \\
&(x \unlhd \texttt{nns.pop} \unrhd \mathsf{S}) \;/\; \texttt{nns}.\mathit{NNS}(n\sigma) = \mathsf{tau} \circ (x \;/\; \texttt{nns}.\mathit{NNS}(\sigma))\;, \\
&(\texttt{nns.push:}n \circ x) \bullet \texttt{nns}.\mathit{NNS}(\sigma) = x \bullet \texttt{nns}.\mathit{NNS}(n\sigma)\;, \\
&(x \unlhd \texttt{nns.pop} \unrhd \mathsf{S}) \bullet \texttt{nns}.\mathit{NNS}(\epsilon) = \texttt{nns}.\mathit{NNS}(\epsilon)\;, \\
&(x \unlhd \texttt{nns.pop} \unrhd \mathsf{S}) \bullet \texttt{nns}.\mathit{NNS}(n\sigma) = x \bullet \texttt{nns}.\mathit{NNS}(\sigma)\;, \\
&(\mathsf{S+} \unlhd \texttt{nns.topeq:}n \unrhd \mathsf{S-}) \;!\; \texttt{nns}.\mathit{NNS}(\epsilon) = \mathsf{f}\;, \\
&(\mathsf{S+} \unlhd \texttt{nns.topeq:}n \unrhd \mathsf{S-}) \;!\; \texttt{nns}.\mathit{NNS}(n'\sigma) = \mathsf{f} \text{ if } n \neq n'\;, \\
&(\mathsf{S+} \unlhd \texttt{nns.topeq:}n \unrhd \mathsf{S-}) \;!\; \texttt{nns}.\mathit{NNS}(n'\sigma) = \mathsf{t} \text{ if } n = n'\;.
\end{aligned}
$$

Remark 3.2. The use operator and the apply operator introduced in this section are mainly adaptations of the use operators introduced earlier in [Bergstra and Middelburg (2008b)] and the apply operators introduced earlier in [Bergstra and Ponse (2002)] to service families. The abstracting use operator that will be introduced in Sect. 3.1.9 is an adaptation of the use operators introduced in [Bergstra and Ponse (2002)] to service families. The reply operator has no counterpart in earlier work. The use operators introduced in [Bergstra and Middelburg (2008b)], the apply operators introduced in [Bergstra and Ponse (2002)], and similar counterparts of the reply operator can be introduced as abbreviations. For terms t of sort $\mathbf{T}$ and terms t' of sort $\mathbf{S}$:

$$
\begin{aligned}
&t \;/_f\; t' \text{ abbreviates } t \;/\; f.t'\;, \\
&t \bullet_f t' \text{ abbreviates } t \bullet f.t'\;, \\
&t \;!_f\; t' \text{ abbreviates } t \;!\; f.t'\;.
\end{aligned}
$$

3.1.3 *Recursion*

To deal with infinite threads, we extend BTA+TSI roughly like BTA was extended in Sect. 2.2.2. The notion of a guarded recursive specification is somewhat adapted, and there are additional axioms for reasoning about infinite threads in the contexts of use, apply and reply.

Definition 3.1. A *guarded recursive specification* over BTA+TSI is a set of recursion equations $\{x = t_x \mid x \in \mathcal{V}\}$, where $\mathcal{V}$ is a set of variables of sort $\mathbf{T}$ and each t_x is a BTA+TSI term of sort $\mathbf{T}$ that can be rewritten, using the axioms of BTA+TSI, to a BTA term of the form D, S, S+, S− or $t \unlhd a \unrhd t'$ with t and t' that contain only variables from $\mathcal{V}$.

Table 3.5 Additional axioms for infinite threads

$\pi_n(x \,/\, u) = \pi_n(x) \,/\, u$	U10
$\bigwedge_{k \geq n} t_1\,[\pi_k(\boldsymbol{x})/\boldsymbol{z}] = t_2\,[\pi_k(\boldsymbol{y})/\boldsymbol{z}] \Rightarrow t_1\,[\boldsymbol{x}/\boldsymbol{z}] = t_2\,[\boldsymbol{y}/\boldsymbol{z}]$	A10
$\bigwedge_{k \geq n} t'_1\,[\pi_k(\boldsymbol{x})/\boldsymbol{z}] = t'_2\,[\pi_k(\boldsymbol{y})/\boldsymbol{z}] \Rightarrow t'_1\,[\boldsymbol{x}/\boldsymbol{z}] = t'_2\,[\boldsymbol{y}/\boldsymbol{z}]$	R10

The additional axioms for reasoning about infinite threads in the contexts of use, apply and reply are given in Table 3.5.[2] In this table, $\boldsymbol{x}, \boldsymbol{y}, \boldsymbol{z}$ stand for arbitrary variables of sort $\mathbf{T}$, t_1, t_2 stand for arbitrary terms of sort $\mathbf{SF}$, t'_1, t'_2 stand for arbitrary terms of sort $\mathbf{R}$, and n stands for an arbitrary natural number.

Axioms U10, A10 and R10 allow for reasoning about infinite threads in the contexts of use, apply and reply, respectively. The conditional equation

$$\bigwedge_{k \geq 0} \pi_k(x) \,/\, u = \pi_k(y) \,/\, v \Rightarrow x \,/\, u = y \,/\, v$$

follows immediately from AIP and U10. The conditional equations

$$\bigwedge_{k \geq n} \pi_k(x) \bullet u = \pi_k(y) \bullet v \Rightarrow x \bullet u = y \bullet v\,,$$
$$\bigwedge_{k \geq n} \pi_k(x) \;!\; u = \pi_k(y) \;!\; v \Rightarrow x \;!\; u = y \;!\; v$$

are instances of A10 and R10, respectively.

We write BTA+TSI+REC for BTA+TSI extended with the constants $\langle \boldsymbol{x} | \boldsymbol{E} \rangle$ and the axioms RDP and RSP, and we write BTA+TSI+REC+AIP for BTA+TSI+REC extended with the operators π_n and the axioms AIP, P1–P6, U10, A10 and R10.

Because the use operator, apply operator and reply operator are primarily intended to be used to describe and analyse instruction sequence processing, they are called *instruction sequence processing operators*. Using the combination of SPISA+SC with BTA+TSI+REC+AIP extended with the thread extraction operator and axioms TE1–TE18, we can introduce the instruction sequence processing operators in the settings of ISNR and ISNA. Let *ISN* be either ISNR or ISNA. Then the use operator, apply operator and reply operator are defined on *ISN* instruction sequences as follows:

$$\boldsymbol{p} \,/\, \boldsymbol{t} = |\boldsymbol{p}|_{ISN} \,/\, \boldsymbol{t}\,,$$
$$\boldsymbol{p} \bullet \boldsymbol{t} = |\boldsymbol{p}|_{ISN} \bullet \boldsymbol{t}\,,$$
$$\boldsymbol{p} \;!\; \boldsymbol{t} = |\boldsymbol{p}|_{ISN} \;!\; \boldsymbol{t}$$

[2]We write $t\,[t'/x]$ for the result of substituting term t' for variable x in term t.

for all *ISN* instruction sequences p and all SFA terms t of sort $\mathbf{SF}$.

3.1.4 *Example*

In this section, we use an implementation of a bounded counter by means of a number of Boolean registers as an example to show that it is easy to bring a number of services together in a service family by means of the service family composition operator. Accomplishing something resemblant with the non-interfering service combination operation from [Bergstra and Ponse (2002)] is quite involved. We also show in this example that there are cases in which the delivery of a Boolean value at termination of the execution of an instruction sequence is quite natural.

First, we describe services that make up Boolean registers. The Boolean register services are able to process the following methods:

- the *set to true method* $\mathtt{set{:}t}$;
- the *set to false method* $\mathtt{set{:}f}$;
- the *get method* $\mathtt{get}$.

It is assumed that $\mathtt{set{:}t}, \mathtt{set{:}f}, \mathtt{get} \in \mathcal{M}$.

The methods that Boolean register services are able to process can be explained as follows:

- $\mathtt{set{:}t}$: the contents of the Boolean register becomes t and the reply is t;
- $\mathtt{set{:}f}$: the contents of the Boolean register becomes f and the reply is f;
- $\mathtt{get}$: nothing changes and the reply is the contents of the Boolean register.

For the set $\mathcal{S}$ of services, we take the set $\{BR_\mathsf{t}, BR_\mathsf{f}, \delta\}$ of *Boolean register services*. For each $m \in \mathcal{M}$, we take the functions $\frac{\partial}{\partial m}$ and ϱ_m such that:

$$
\begin{array}{lll}
\frac{\partial}{\partial \mathtt{set{:}t}}(BR_b) = BR_\mathsf{t}\;, & \frac{\partial}{\partial \mathtt{get}}(BR_b) = BR_b\;, & \\
\frac{\partial}{\partial \mathtt{set{:}f}}(BR_b) = BR_\mathsf{f}\;, & \frac{\partial}{\partial m}(BR_b) = \delta & \text{if } m \notin \{\mathtt{set{:}t}, \mathtt{set{:}f}, \mathtt{get}\}\;, \\[1em]
\varrho_{\mathtt{set{:}t}}(BR_b) = \mathsf{t}\;, & \varrho_{\mathtt{get}}(BR_b) = b\;, & \\
\varrho_{\mathtt{set{:}f}}(BR_b) = \mathsf{f}\;, & \varrho_m(BR_b) = \mathsf{d} & \text{if } m \notin \{\mathtt{set{:}t}, \mathtt{set{:}f}, \mathtt{get}\}\;.
\end{array}
$$

Moreover, we take the names BR_t and BR_f used above to denote services from $\mathcal{S}$ for constants of sort $\mathbf{S}$.

We continue with the implementation of a bounded counter by means of a number of Boolean registers. We consider a counter that can contain a natural number in the interval

$[0, 2^n - 1]$ for some $n > 0$. To implement the counter, we represent its content in binary using a collection of n Boolean registers named $\mathtt{br}{:}0, \ldots, \mathtt{br}{:}n{-}1$. We take t for 0 and f for 1, and we take the bit represented by the content of the Boolean register named $\mathtt{br}{:}i$ for a less significant bit than the bit represented by the content of the Boolean register named $\mathtt{br}{:}j$ if $i < j$.

The following ISNR instruction sequences implement set to zero, increment by one, decrement by one, and test on zero, respectively:

$$
\begin{aligned}
\mathit{SETZERO} &= \mathop{;}_{i=0}^{n-1} (\mathtt{br}{:}i.\mathtt{set{:}t}) \mathbin{;} \mathsf{!t} , \\
\mathit{SUCC} &= \mathop{;}_{i=0}^{n-1} ({-}\mathtt{br}{:}i.\mathtt{get} \mathbin{;} \#3 \mathbin{;} \mathtt{br}{:}i.\mathtt{set{:}f} \mathbin{;} \mathsf{!t} \mathbin{;} \mathtt{br}{:}i.\mathtt{set{:}t}) \mathbin{;} \mathsf{!f} , \\
\mathit{PRED} &= \mathop{;}_{i=0}^{n-1} ({+}\mathtt{br}{:}i.\mathtt{get} \mathbin{;} \#3 \mathbin{;} \mathtt{br}{:}i.\mathtt{set{:}t} \mathbin{;} \mathsf{!t} \mathbin{;} \mathtt{br}{:}i.\mathtt{set{:}f}) \mathbin{;} \mathsf{!f} , \\
\mathit{ISZERO} &= \mathop{;}_{i=0}^{n-1} ({-}\mathtt{br}{:}i.\mathtt{get} \mathbin{;} \mathsf{!f}) \mathbin{;} \mathsf{!t} .
\end{aligned}
$$

Concerning the Boolean values delivered at termination of executions of these instruction sequences, we have that:

$$
\begin{aligned}
\mathit{SETZERO} \mathbin{!} \left(\bigoplus_{i=0}^{n-1} \mathtt{br}{:}i.\mathit{BR}_{c_i}\right) &= \mathsf{t} , \\
\mathit{SUCC} \mathbin{!} \left(\bigoplus_{i=0}^{n-1} \mathtt{br}{:}i.\mathit{BR}_{c_i}\right) &= \begin{cases} \mathsf{t} & \text{if } \bigvee_{i=0}^{n-1} c_i = \mathsf{t} \\ \mathsf{f} & \text{if } \bigwedge_{i=0}^{n-1} c_i = \mathsf{f} , \end{cases} \\
\mathit{PRED} \mathbin{!} \left(\bigoplus_{i=0}^{n-1} \mathtt{br}{:}i.\mathit{BR}_{c_i}\right) &= \begin{cases} \mathsf{t} & \text{if } \bigvee_{i=0}^{n-1} c_i = \mathsf{f} \\ \mathsf{f} & \text{if } \bigwedge_{i=0}^{n-1} c_i = \mathsf{t} , \end{cases} \\
\mathit{ISZERO} \mathbin{!} \left(\bigoplus_{i=0}^{n-1} \mathtt{br}{:}i.\mathit{BR}_{c_i}\right) &= \begin{cases} \mathsf{t} & \text{if } \bigwedge_{i=0}^{n-1} c_i = \mathsf{t} \\ \mathsf{f} & \text{if } \bigvee_{i=0}^{n-1} c_i = \mathsf{f} . \end{cases}
\end{aligned}
$$

It is obvious that t is delivered at termination of an execution of $\mathit{SETZERO}$ and that t or f is delivered at termination of an execution of ISZERO depending on whether the content of the counter is zero or not. Increment by one and decrement by one are both modulo 2^n. For that reason, t or f is delivered at termination of an execution of SUCC or PRED depending on whether the content of the counter is really incremented or decremented by one or not.

3.1.5 *Elimination*

We can prove that in BTA+TSI each closed BTA+TSI term of sort **T** can be reduced to a closed BTA term and each closed BTA+TSI term of sort **SF** or **R** can be reduced to a closed SFA term.

The following lemma will be used in the proof of this elimination result.

Lemma 3.2. *Let* $f \in \mathcal{F}$. *Then for all closed* BTA+TSI *terms* t *of sort* $\mathbf{SF}$, *either* $t = \partial_{\{f\}}(t)$ *is derivable from the axioms of* BTA+TSI *or there exists a closed* BTA+TSI *term* t' *of sort* $\mathbf{S}$ *such that* $t = f.t' \oplus \partial_{\{f\}}(t)$ *is derivable from the axioms of* BTA+TSI.

Proof. This is proved by induction on the structure of t. The cases $t \equiv \emptyset$ and $t \equiv f.t_1$ are trivial, the case $t \equiv t_1 \oplus t_2$ follows easily by case distinction on the possible forms of the equations that are derivable for t_1 and t_2 according to the induction hypothesis, and the case $t \equiv \partial_F(t_1)$ follows easily by case distinction on the possible forms of the equation that is derivable for t_1 according to the induction hypothesis. The case $t \equiv t_1 \bullet t_2$ follows easily by induction on the structure of t_1, making case distinctions on the possible forms of the equation that is derivable for t_2 according to the induction hypothesis. □

We continue with the elimination result.

Theorem 3.1.

(1) For all closed BTA+TSI *terms* t *of sort* $\mathbf{T}$, *there exists a closed* BTA *term* t' *of sort* $\mathbf{T}$ *such that* $t = t'$ *is derivable from the axioms of* BTA+TSI.

(2) For all closed BTA+TSI *terms* t *of sort* $\mathbf{SF}$, *there exists a closed* SFA *term* t' *of sort* $\mathbf{SF}$ *such that* $t = t'$ *is derivable from the axioms of* BTA+TSI.

(3) For all closed BTA+TSI *terms* t *of sort* $\mathbf{R}$, *there exists a closed* SFA *term* t' *of sort* $\mathbf{R}$ *such that* $t = t'$ *is derivable from the axioms of* BTA+TSI.

Proof. Property 1 is proved by induction on the structure of t. The cases $t \equiv \mathsf{S+}$, $t \equiv \mathsf{S-}$, $t \equiv \mathsf{S}$ and $t \equiv \mathsf{D}$ are trivial. The cases $t \equiv \mathsf{tau} \circ t_1$ and $t \equiv t_1 \trianglelefteq f.m \trianglerighteq t_2$ follow immediately from the induction hypothesis. The case $t \equiv t_1 \;/\; t_2$ is more involved. By the induction hypothesis, there exists a closed BTA term t_1' such that $t_1 = t_1'$. This means that we are done with this case if we have proved the following claim:

> Let t_1' be a closed BTA term of sort $\mathbf{T}$. Then, for all closed BTA+TSI terms t_2' of sort $\mathbf{SF}$, there exists a closed BTA term t' of sort $\mathbf{T}$ such that $t_1' \;/\; t_2' = t'$ is derivable from the axioms of BTA+TSI.

This claim is easily proved by induction on the structure of t_1' and in the case $t_1' \equiv t_1'' \trianglelefteq f.m \trianglerighteq t_2''$ by case distinction on the possible forms of the equation that is derivable for t_2' according to Lemma 3.2.

Property 2 is proved by induction on the structure of t. The cases $t \equiv \emptyset$ and $t \equiv f.t_1$ are trivial. The cases $t \equiv t_1 \oplus t_2$ and $t \equiv \partial_F(t_1)$ follow immediately from the induction hypothesis. The case $t \equiv t_1 \bullet t_2$ is more involved. By Property 1, there exists a closed BTA term t_1' of sort $\mathbf{T}$ such that $t_1 = t_1'$. By the induction hypothesis, there exists a closed SFA term t_2' of sort $\mathbf{SF}$ such that $t_2 = t_2'$. This means that we are done with this case if we have proved the following claim:

> Let t_2' be a closed SFA term of sort $\mathbf{SF}$. Then, for all closed BTA terms t_1' of sort $\mathbf{T}$, there exists a closed SFA term t' of sort $\mathbf{SF}$ such that $t_1' \bullet t_2' = t'$ is derivable from the axioms of BTA+TSI.

This claim is easily proved by induction on the structure of t_1' and in the case $t_1' \equiv t_1'' \trianglelefteq f.m \trianglerighteq t_2''$ by case distinction on the possible forms of the equation that is derivable for t_2' according to Lemma 3.2.

Property 3 is proved in the same way as Property 2. □

3.1.6 *Properties*

We assume that a minimal model $\mathcal{M}$ of BTA+TSI+REC+AIP has been given. Recall that we denote the interpretations of sorts, constants and operators in $\mathcal{M}$ by the sorts, constants and operators themselves. We write $[\![t]\!]$, where t is a closed term, for the interpretation of t in $\mathcal{M}$.

Below, we will formulate a proposition about the use, apply and reply operators using the *foci* operation foci defined by the following equations ($f \in \mathcal{F}$):

$$\begin{aligned} \mathsf{foci}(\emptyset) &= \emptyset\ , \\ \mathsf{foci}(f.s) &= \{f\}\ , \\ \mathsf{foci}(S \oplus S') &= \mathsf{foci}(S) \cup \mathsf{foci}(S')\ . \end{aligned}$$

The operation foci gives, for each service family, the set of all foci that serve as names of named services belonging to the service family. We will make use of the following properties of foci in the proof of the proposition:

(1) $\mathsf{foci}(S) \cap \mathsf{foci}(S') = \emptyset$ iff $f \notin \mathsf{foci}(S)$ or $f \notin \mathsf{foci}(S')$ for all $f \in \mathcal{F}$;
(2) $f \notin \mathsf{foci}(S)$ iff $\partial_{\{f\}}(S) = S$.

We will write $\mathsf{foci}(t)$, where t is a closed BTA+TSI+REC+AIP term of sort $\mathbf{SF}$, for $\mathsf{foci}([\![t]\!])$.

Proposition 3.1. *For all closed* BTA+TSI+REC *terms* t *of sort* $\mathbf{T}$ *and all closed* BTA+TSI *terms* t' *and* t'' *of sort* **SF** *for which* $\mathsf{foci}(t') \cap \mathsf{foci}(t'') = \emptyset$*, the following holds:*

(1) $t \,/\, (t' \oplus t'') = (t \,/\, t') \,/\, t''$*;*
(2) $t \,!\, (t' \oplus t'') = (t \,/\, t') \,!\, t''$*;*
(3) $\partial_{\mathsf{foci}(t')}(t \bullet (t' \oplus t'')) = (t \,/\, t') \bullet t''$*.*

Proof. By Lemma 2.4, axioms RSP, AIP, U10, A10 and R10, and Theorem 3.1, it is sufficient to prove the proposition for all closed BTA terms t of sort $\mathbf{T}$ and all closed SFA terms t' and t'' of sort **SF** for which $\mathsf{foci}(t') \cap \mathsf{foci}(t'') = \emptyset$. This is straightforward by induction on the structure of t, using the above-mentioned properties of foci. □

In the sequel, we will use relations indicating, for each thread and service family, whether the thread converges on the service family, the thread converges on the service family with a Boolean reply and the thread diverges on the service family.

Definition 3.2. The *convergence* relation $\downarrow \subseteq \mathbf{T} \times \mathbf{SF}$ is inductively defined by the following clauses:

(1) $\mathsf{S} \downarrow S$;
(2) $\mathsf{S{+}} \downarrow S$ and $\mathsf{S{-}} \downarrow S$;
(3) if $t \downarrow S$, then $(\mathsf{tau} \circ t) \downarrow S$;
(4) if $t \downarrow (f.\frac{\partial}{\partial m} s \oplus \partial_{\{f\}}(S))$ and $\varrho_m(s) = \mathsf{t}$, then $(t \trianglelefteq f.m \trianglerighteq t') \downarrow (f.s \oplus \partial_{\{f\}}(S))$;
(5) if $t \downarrow (f.\frac{\partial}{\partial m} s \oplus \partial_{\{f\}}(S))$ and $\varrho_m(s) = \mathsf{f}$, then $(t' \trianglelefteq f.m \trianglerighteq t) \downarrow (f.s \oplus \partial_{\{f\}}(S))$;
(6) if $\pi_n(t) \downarrow S$, then $t \downarrow S$.

The *convergence with Boolean reply* relation $\downarrow_{\mathbb{B}} \subseteq \mathbf{T} \times \mathbf{SF}$ is inductively defined by the clauses $2, \ldots, 6$ for $\downarrow$ with everywhere $\downarrow$ replaced by $\downarrow_{\mathbb{B}}$. The *divergence* relation $\uparrow \subseteq \mathbf{T} \times \mathbf{SF}$ is defined by $t \uparrow S$ iff not $t \downarrow S$.

We will write $t \downarrow t'$, $t \downarrow_{\mathbb{B}} t'$ and $t \uparrow t'$, where t is a closed BTA+TSI+REC+AIP term of sort $\mathbf{T}$ and t' is a closed BTA+TSI+REC+AIP term of sort **SF**, for $[\![t]\!] \downarrow [\![t']\!]$, $[\![t]\!] \downarrow_{\mathbb{B}} [\![t']\!]$ and $[\![t]\!] \uparrow [\![t']\!]$, respectively.

The following two propositions concern the connection between convergence and the reply operator.

Proposition 3.2. *For all closed* BTA+TSI *terms* t *of sort* $\mathbf{T}$ *and closed* BTA+TSI *terms* t' *of sort* **SF** *for which* $t \downarrow t'$*:*

(1) if $\mathsf{S{+}}$ *occurs in* t *and neither* $\mathsf{S{-}}$ *nor* S *occurs in* t*, then* $t \,!\, t' = \mathsf{t}$ *holds;*

(2) *if* $\mathsf{S}-$ *occurs in* t *and neither* $\mathsf{S}+$ *nor* S *occurs in* t*, then* $t\ !\ t' = \mathsf{f}$ *holds;*
(3) *if* S *occurs in* t *and neither* $\mathsf{S}+$ *nor* $\mathsf{S}-$ *occurs in* t*, then* $t\ !\ t' = \mathsf{m}$ *holds.*

Proof. By Theorem 3.1, it is sufficient to prove the proposition for all closed BTA terms t of sort $\mathbf{T}$ and closed SFA terms t' of sort $\mathbf{SF}$ for which $t \downarrow t'$. This is straightforward by induction on the structure of t. □

Proposition 3.3. *For all closed* BTA+TSI+REC *terms* t *of sort* $\mathbf{T}$ *and closed* BTA+TSI *terms* t' *of sort* $\mathbf{SF}$*,* $t \downarrow t'$ *iff* $t\ !\ t' = \mathsf{t}$ *or* $t\ !\ t' = \mathsf{f}$ *or* $t\ !\ t' = \mathsf{m}$ *holds.*

Proof. By Lemma 2.4, axioms RSP and R10, the last clause of the inductive definition of $\downarrow$ given above, the easy to prove fact that $\pi_n(t) \downarrow t'$ implies $\pi_{n+1}(t) \downarrow t'$, and Theorem 3.1, it is sufficient to prove the proposition for all closed BTA terms t of sort $\mathbf{T}$ and closed SFA terms t' of sort $\mathbf{SF}$. This is straightforward by induction on the structure of t. □

We can introduce convergence in the settings of ISNR and ISNA as well. Let *ISN* be either ISNR or ISNA. Then convergence is defined on *ISN* instruction sequences as follows:

$$p \downarrow t = |p|_{ISN} \downarrow t$$

for all *ISN* instruction sequences p and all SFA terms t of sort $\mathbf{SF}$.

3.1.7 *Relevant use conventions*

In the setting of service families, sets of foci play the role of interfaces. The set of all foci that serve as names of named services in a service family is regarded as the interface of that service family. There are cases in which processing does not terminate or, even worse (because it is statically detectable), interfaces of services families do not match. In the case of non-termination, there is nothing that we intend to denote by a term of the form $t \bullet t'$ or $t\ !\ t'$. In the case of non-matching interfaces, there is nothing that we intend to denote by a term of the form $t' \oplus t''$. Moreover, in the case of termination without a Boolean reply, there is also nothing that we intend to denote by a term of the form $t\ !\ t'$.

We propose to comply with the following *relevant use conventions*:

- $t \bullet t'$ is only used if it is known that $t \downarrow t'$;
- $t\ !\ t'$ is only used if it is known that $t \downarrow_{\mathbb{B}} t'$;
- $t' \oplus t''$ is only used if it is known that $\mathsf{foci}(t') \cap \mathsf{foci}(t'') = \emptyset$.

The condition found in the first convention is justified by the fact that in the projective limit model of BTA+TSI+REC+AIP presented in Sect. 3.1.8, $t \bullet t' = \emptyset$ if $t \uparrow t'$. We do not have $t \bullet t' = \emptyset$ only if $t \uparrow t'$. For instance, $\mathsf{S+} \bullet \emptyset = \emptyset$ whereas $\mathsf{S+} \downarrow \emptyset$. Similar remarks apply to the condition found in the second convention.

The idea of relevant use conventions is taken from [Bergstra and Middelburg (2011b)], where it plays a central role in an account of the way in which mathematicians usually deal with division by zero in mathematical texts. According to [Bergstra and Middelburg (2011b)], mathematicians deal with this issue by complying with the convention that p/q is only used if it is known that $q \neq 0$. This approach is justified by the fact that there is nothing that mathematicians intend to denote by p/q if $q = 0$. It yields simpler mathematical texts than the popular approach in theoretical computer science, which is characterized by complete formality in definitions, statements and proofs. In this computer science approach, division is considered a partial function and some logic of partial functions is used. In [Bergstra and Tucker (2007)], deviating from this, division is considered a total function whose value is zero in all cases of division by zero. It may be imagined that this notion of division is the one with which mathematicians make themselves familiar before they start to read and write mathematical texts professionally.

We think that the idea to comply with conventions that exclude the use of terms that are not really intended to denote anything is not only of importance in mathematics, but also in theoretical computer science. For example, the consequence of adapting Proposition 3.1 to comply with the relevant use conventions described above, by adding appropriate conditions to the three properties, is that we do not have to consider in the proof of the proposition the equality of terms by which we do not intend to denote anything.

In the sequel, we will comply with the relevant use conventions described above unless convergence forms a part of the real matter that we are concerned with.

3.1.8 *The extended projective limit model*

Let $\mathcal{I}(\mathrm{SFA})$ be the free SFA-extension of $\mathcal{S}$ and $\mathcal{I}(\mathrm{BTA{+}TSI})$ be the free BTA+TSI-extension of $\mathcal{S}$. From the fact that the signatures of $\mathcal{I}^\infty(\mathrm{BTA})$ and $\mathcal{I}(\mathrm{SFA})$ are disjoint, it follows, by the amalgamation result about expansions presented as Theorem 6.1.1 in [Hodges (1993)] (adapted to the many-sorted case), that there exists a model of BTA combined with SFA such that the restriction to the signature of BTA is $\mathcal{I}^\infty(\mathrm{BTA})$ and the restriction to the signature of SFA is $\mathcal{I}(\mathrm{SFA})$.

Definition 3.3. Let $\mathcal{I}^\infty(\mathrm{BTA{+}SFA})$ be the model of BTA combined with SFA referred to above. Then the *projective limit model* $\mathcal{I}^\infty(\text{BTA+TSI})$ of BTA+TSI is $\mathcal{I}^\infty(\text{BTA+SFA})$ expanded with the operations defined by

$$(t_n)_{n\in\mathbb{N}} \mathbin{/} S = (\pi_n(t_n \mathbin{/} S))_{n\in\mathbb{N}} ,$$
$$(t_n)_{n\in\mathbb{N}} \bullet S = \lim_{k\to\infty}(t_k \bullet S) ,$$
$$(t_n)_{n\in\mathbb{N}} \;!\; S = \lim_{k\to\infty}(t_k \;!\; S)$$

as interpretations of the additional operators of BTA+TSI. On the right-hand side of these equations, the symbols $/$, $\bullet$ and $!$ denote the interpretation of the operators $/$, $\bullet$ and $!$ in $\mathcal{I}(\text{BTA+TSI})$. In the last two equations, the limits are the limits with respect to the discrete topology on the domains associated with the sorts **SF** and **R**, respectively.[3]

The projective limit model $\mathcal{I}^\infty(\text{BTA+TSI})$ of BTA+TSI is expanded to projective limit models $\mathcal{I}^\infty(\text{BTA+TSI+REC})$ and $\mathcal{I}^\infty(\text{BTA+TSI+REC+AIP})$ of BTA+TSI+REC and BTA+TSI+REC+AIP, respectively, in exactly the same way as $\mathcal{I}^\infty(\text{BTA})$ is expanded to $\mathcal{I}^\infty(\text{BTA+REC})$ and $\mathcal{I}^\infty(\text{BTA+REC+AIP})$ in Sect. 2.2.4.

3.1.9 *Abstraction*

With the use operator introduced in Sect. 3.1.2, the action tau is left as a trace of a basic action that has led to the processing of a method, like with the use operators on services introduced in e.g. [Bergstra and Middelburg (2008b)]. However, with the use operators on services introduced in [Bergstra and Ponse (2002)], nothing is left as a trace of a basic action that has led to the processing of a method. Thus, these use operators abstract fully from internal activity. In other words, they are abstracting use operators. In this section, we introduce an abstracting variant of the use operator introduced in Sect. 3.1.2, as well as a general operator for the abstraction from tau.

That is, we introduce the following additional operators:

- the binary *abstracting use* operator $\_ \mathbin{/\!/} \_ : \mathbf{T} \times \mathbf{SF} \to \mathbf{T}$;
- the unary *abstraction* operator $\tau_{\mathsf{tau}} : \mathbf{T} \to \mathbf{T}$.

We use infix notation for the abstracting use operator.

An example of a term in which the abstracting use operator occurs is

$$\langle x|E\rangle \mathbin{/\!/} \mathtt{nnc}.\mathit{NNC}(0) ,$$

[3] In the many-sorted case, the interpretation of a sort in a certain model will also be called the domain associated with the sort in that model.

where E is the guarded recursive specification consisting of the following two equations:

$$x = (\mathtt{nnc.succ} \circ x) \trianglelefteq \mathsf{a} \trianglerighteq (\mathtt{nnc.succ} \circ y)\,, \qquad y = (\mathsf{b} \circ y) \trianglelefteq \mathtt{nnc.pred} \trianglerighteq \mathsf{S}\,.$$

and $NNC(\sigma)$ denotes an unbounded counter service dealing with a counter whose content is σ. An unbounded counter service is able to process methods for setting the content of a counter to zero (`setzero`), incrementing the content of the counter by one (`succ`), decrementing the content of the counter by one (`pred`), and testing whether the content of a counter is zero (`iszero`). Processing of an incrementing method always produces the reply value t and processing of a decrementing method produces the reply value t if the content of the counter is not zero and f otherwise. A precise description of unbounded counter services will be given in Sect. 3.2.5. Using the axioms for the abstracting use operator introduced below, we can prove that $\langle x|E\rangle \mathbin{/\!/} \mathtt{nnc}.NNC(0)$ denotes the x_0-component of the solution of the guarded recursive specification consisting of the following equations:

$$\begin{aligned} x_n &= x_{n+1} \trianglelefteq \mathsf{a} \trianglerighteq y_{n+1} && \text{for all } n \in \mathbb{N}\,, \\ y_0 &= \mathsf{S}\,, \\ y_{n+1} &= \mathsf{b} \circ y_n && \text{for all } n \in \mathbb{N}\,. \end{aligned}$$

This means that the thread denoted by $\langle x|E\rangle \mathbin{/\!/} \mathtt{nnc}.NNC(0)$ can, for each $n \in \mathbb{N}$, first perform $n+1$ times a, next perform $n+1$ times b, and after that terminate. This behaviour cannot be described by a finite linear recursive specification. So $\langle x|E\rangle \mathbin{/\!/} \mathtt{nnc}.NNC(0)$ does not denote a regular thread, whereas $\langle x|E\rangle$ denotes a regular thread.

The abstraction operator is an alternative to the abstracting use operator which looks to be a better choice in the presence of an interleaving operator for multi-threading (see e.g. [Bergstra and Middelburg (2007c)]).

The axioms for the abstracting use operator and the abstraction operator are given in Tables 3.6 and 3.7, respectively. In these tables, f stands for an arbitrary focus from $\mathcal{F}$, m stands for an arbitrary method from $\mathcal{M}$, a stands for an arbitrary basic action from $\mathcal{A}$, and t stands for an arbitrary term of sort **S**.

The additional axioms for reasoning about infinite threads in the contexts of abstracting use and abstraction are given in Table 3.8. Notice that, due to the possible concealment of actions by abstracting use, $\pi_n(x \mathbin{/\!/} u) = \pi_n(x) \mathbin{/\!/} u$ is not a plausible axiom.

It should be mentioned that, for all closed terms t and t' of sort $\mathbf{T}$, $t \mathbin{/\!/} t' = \tau_{\mathsf{tau}}(t \mathbin{/} t')$ if $t = \tau_{\mathsf{tau}}(t)$.

We write BTA+TSI+ABSTR and BTA+TSI+REC+ABSTR for BTA+TSI and BTA+TSI+REC, respectively, extended with the operators $/\!/$ and τ_{tau} and the axioms AU1–

Table 3.6 Axioms for the abstracting use operator

$\mathsf{S+} \mathbin{/\!/} u = \mathsf{S+}$		AU1
$\mathsf{S-} \mathbin{/\!/} u = \mathsf{S-}$		AU2
$\mathsf{S} \mathbin{/\!/} u = \mathsf{S}$		AU3
$\mathsf{D} \mathbin{/\!/} u = \mathsf{D}$		AU4
$(\mathsf{tau} \circ x) \mathbin{/\!/} u = \mathsf{tau} \circ (x \mathbin{/\!/} u)$		AU5
$(x \trianglelefteq \boldsymbol{f}.\boldsymbol{m} \trianglerighteq y) \mathbin{/\!/} \partial_{\{f\}}(u) = (x \mathbin{/\!/} \partial_{\{f\}}(u)) \trianglelefteq \boldsymbol{f}.\boldsymbol{m} \trianglerighteq (y \mathbin{/\!/} \partial_{\{f\}}(u))$		AU6
$(x \trianglelefteq \boldsymbol{f}.\boldsymbol{m} \trianglerighteq y) \mathbin{/\!/} (\boldsymbol{f}.\boldsymbol{t} \oplus \partial_{\{f\}}(u)) = x \mathbin{/\!/} (\boldsymbol{f}.\frac{\partial}{\partial m}\boldsymbol{t} \oplus \partial_{\{f\}}(u))$	if $\varrho_m(\boldsymbol{t}) = \mathsf{t}$	AU7
$(x \trianglelefteq \boldsymbol{f}.\boldsymbol{m} \trianglerighteq y) \mathbin{/\!/} (\boldsymbol{f}.\boldsymbol{t} \oplus \partial_{\{f\}}(u)) = y \mathbin{/\!/} (\boldsymbol{f}.\frac{\partial}{\partial m}\boldsymbol{t} \oplus \partial_{\{f\}}(u))$	if $\varrho_m(\boldsymbol{t}) = \mathsf{f}$	AU8
$(x \trianglelefteq \boldsymbol{f}.\boldsymbol{m} \trianglerighteq y) \mathbin{/\!/} (\boldsymbol{f}.\boldsymbol{t} \oplus \partial_{\{f\}}(u)) = \mathsf{D}$	if $\varrho_m(\boldsymbol{t}) = \mathsf{d}$	AU9

Table 3.7 Axioms for the abstraction operator

$\tau_{\mathsf{tau}}(\mathsf{S}) = \mathsf{S}$	TT1
$\tau_{\mathsf{tau}}(\mathsf{D}) = \mathsf{D}$	TT2
$\tau_{\mathsf{tau}}(\mathsf{tau} \circ x) = \tau_{\mathsf{tau}}(x)$	TT3
$\tau_{\mathsf{tau}}(x \trianglelefteq \boldsymbol{a} \trianglerighteq y) = \tau_{\mathsf{tau}}(x) \trianglelefteq \boldsymbol{a} \trianglerighteq \tau_{\mathsf{tau}}(y)$	TT4

Table 3.8 Additional axioms for infinite threads

$\bigwedge_{n \geq 0} \pi_n(x) \mathbin{/\!/} u = \pi_n(y) \mathbin{/\!/} v \Rightarrow x \mathbin{/\!/} u = y \mathbin{/\!/} v$	AU10
$\bigwedge_{n \geq 0} \tau_{\mathsf{tau}}(\pi_n(x)) = \tau_{\mathsf{tau}}(\pi_n(y)) \Rightarrow \tau_{\mathsf{tau}}(x) = \tau_{\mathsf{tau}}(y)$	TT5

AU9 and TT1–TT4. Moreover, we write BTA+TSI+REC+AIP+ABSTR for BTA+TSI+REC+AIP extended with the operators $/\!/$ and τ_{tau} and the axioms AU1–AU10 and TT1–TT5.

The *projective limit model* $\mathcal{I}^{\infty}$(BTA+TSI) of BTA+TSI can be expanded with the operations defined by

$$\begin{aligned}(t_n)_{n \in \mathbb{N}} \mathbin{/\!/} S &= (\lim_{k \to \infty} \pi_n(t_k \mathbin{/\!/} S))_{n \in \mathbb{N}} \,, \\ \tau_{\mathsf{tau}}((t_n)_{n \in \mathbb{N}}) &= (\lim_{k \to \infty} \pi_n(\tau_{\mathsf{tau}}(t_k)))_{n \in \mathbb{N}}\end{aligned}$$

as interpretations of the abstracting use operator and abstraction operator. On the right-hand side of these equations, the symbol $/\!/$ and τ_{tau} denote the interpretations of the operators $/\!/$ and τ_{tau} in the free BTA+TSI+ABSTR-extension of $\boldsymbol{\mathcal{S}}$. The limits are the limits with respect to the discrete topology on the domain associated with the sort $\mathbf{T}$.

Perhaps contrary to expectations, the interpretations of the operators $/\!/$ and τ_{tau} are not defined by the equations $(t_n)_{n \in \mathbb{N}} \mathbin{/\!/} S = (\pi_n(t_n \mathbin{/\!/} S))_{n \in \mathbb{N}}$ and $\tau_{\mathsf{tau}}((t_n)_{n \in \mathbb{N}}) = (\pi_n(\tau_{\mathsf{tau}}(t_n)))_{n \in \mathbb{N}}$, respectively. Because the depth of the approximations may decrease, this would lead to operations that would not always yield projective sequences. It is easy to see that the operations as defined above always yield projective sequences. The definitions concerned are justified by the following lemma.

Lemma 3.3. *The following holds in the free* BTA+TSI+ABSTR*-extension of* $\boldsymbol{\mathcal{S}}$*:*

$$\begin{aligned}\pi_n(t \mathbin{/\!/} S) &= \lim_{k \to \infty} \pi_n(\pi_k(t) \mathbin{/\!/} S) \,, \\ \pi_n(\tau_{\mathsf{tau}}(t)) &= \lim_{k \to \infty} \pi_n(\tau_{\mathsf{tau}}(\pi_k(t))) \,.\end{aligned}$$

Proof. The proof is easy by induction on the structure of t. □

3.2 Functional Units and Services

This section is concerned with functional units. Services represent a rather abstract view on the behaviours exhibited by the components of an execution environment that are capable of processing particular instructions and doing so independently. A functional unit belongs to a more concrete view on these behaviours, namely as the behaviours of a machine in its different states. If this view is usable, the services concerned are completely determined by a functional unit. We give a precise definition of the concept of a functional unit and introduce four functional units that are used in the rest of the book, namely a Boolean register functional unit, a natural number register functional unit, a natural number stack functional unit and a natural number counter functional unit.

3.2.1 *The concept of a functional unit*

In this section, we introduce the concept of a functional unit and some related concepts.

It is assumed that a non-empty set Σ of *states* has been given. As before, it is assumed that a set $\mathcal{M}$ of methods has been given. However, in the setting of functional units, methods serve as names of operations on a state space. For that reason, the members of $\mathcal{M}$ are called *method names* in the setting of functional units.

Definition 3.4. A *method operation* on Σ is a total function from Σ to $\mathbb{B} \times \Sigma$. A *partial method operation* on Σ is a partial function from Σ to $\mathbb{B} \times \Sigma$.

We write $\mathcal{MO}(\Sigma)$ for the set of all method operations on Σ. We write M^{r} and M^{e}, where $M \in \mathcal{MO}(\Sigma)$, for the unique functions $R : \Sigma \to \mathbb{B}$ and $E : \Sigma \to \Sigma$, respectively, such that $M(\sigma) = (R(\sigma), E(\sigma))$ for all $\sigma \in \Sigma$.

Definition 3.5. A *functional unit* for Σ is a finite subset U of $\mathcal{M} \times \mathcal{MO}(\Sigma)$ such that $(m, M) \in U$ and $(m, M') \in U$ implies $M = M'$.

We write $\mathcal{FU}(\Sigma)$ for the set of all functional units for Σ. We write $\mathcal{I}(U)$, where $U \in \mathcal{FU}(\Sigma)$, for the set $\{m \in \mathcal{M} \mid \exists M \in \mathcal{MO}(\Sigma) \bullet (m, M) \in U\}$. We write m_U, where $U \in \mathcal{FU}(\Sigma)$ and $m \in \mathcal{I}(U)$, for the unique $M \in \mathcal{MO}(\Sigma)$ such that $(m, M) \in U$.

We look upon the set $\mathcal{I}(U)$, where $U \in \mathcal{FU}(\Sigma)$, as the interface of U. It looks to be convenient to have a notation for the restriction of a functional unit to a subset of its interface. We write (I, U), where $U \in \mathcal{FU}(\Sigma)$ and $I \subseteq \mathcal{I}(U)$, for the functional unit $\{(m, M) \in U \mid m \in I\}$.

Definition 3.6. Let $U \in \mathcal{FU}(\Sigma)$. Then an *extension* of U is a $U' \in \mathcal{FU}(\Sigma)$ such that $U \subseteq U'$.

The following is a simple illustration of the use of functional units. An unbounded counter can be modelled by a functional unit for $\mathbb{N}$ with method operations for set to zero, increment by one, decrement by one, and test on zero.

According to the definition of a functional unit given above, $\emptyset \in \mathcal{FU}(\Sigma)$. By that we have a unique functional unit with an empty interface, which is not very interesting in itself. However, when considering services that behave according to functional units, $\emptyset$ is exactly the functional unit according to which the empty service δ (the service that is not able to process any method) behaves.

The method names attached to method operations in functional units should not be confused with the names used to denote specific method operations in describing functional units. Therefore, we will comply with the convention to use names beginning with a lower-case letter in the former case and names beginning with an upper-case letter in the latter case.

We will use ISNR^{s} instruction sequences to derive partial method operations from the method operations of a functional unit. We write $\mathcal{L}(\mathtt{f}.I)$, where $I \subseteq \mathcal{M}$, for the set of all ISNR^{s} instruction sequences, taking the set $\{\mathtt{f}.m \mid m \in I\}$ as the set $\mathfrak{A}$ of basic instructions.

The derivation of partial method operations from the method operations of a functional unit involves services whose processing of methods amounts to replies and service changes according to corresponding method operations of the functional unit concerned. These services can be viewed as the behaviours of a machine, on which the processing in question takes place, in its different states.

We take the set $\mathcal{FU}(\Sigma) \times \Sigma$ as the set $\mathcal{S}$ of services. We write $U(\sigma)$, where $U \in \mathcal{FU}(\Sigma)$ and $\sigma \in \Sigma$, for the service (U, σ). The operations $\frac{\partial}{\partial m}$ and ϱ_m are defined as follows:

$$\frac{\partial}{\partial m}(U(\sigma)) = \begin{cases} U(m^{\mathrm{e}}_U(\sigma)) & \text{if } m \in \mathcal{I}(U) \\ \emptyset(\sigma') & \text{if } m \notin \mathcal{I}(U)\,, \end{cases}$$

$$\varrho_m(U(\sigma)) = \begin{cases} m^{\mathrm{r}}_U(\sigma) & \text{if } m \in \mathcal{I}(U) \\ \mathsf{d} & \text{if } m \notin \mathcal{I}(U)\,, \end{cases}$$

where σ' is a fixed but arbitrary state in Σ.[4]

In order to be able to make use of the axioms for the apply operator and the reply operator from Sect. 3.1.2 hereafter, we want to use these operators for the services being considered here when making the idea of deriving a partial method operation by means of an instruction sequence precise. Therefore, we assume that there is a constant of sort **S** for each $U(\sigma) \in \mathcal{S}$.[5] In this connection, we use the following notational convention: for each $U(\sigma) \in \mathcal{S}$, we write $U(\sigma)$ for the constant of sort **S** whose interpretation is $U(\sigma)$. Note that the service $\emptyset(\sigma')$ is the interpretation of the empty service constant δ.

Definition 3.7. Let $U \in \mathcal{FU}(\Sigma)$, and let $I \subseteq \mathcal{I}(U)$. Then an instruction sequence $p \in \mathcal{L}(\mathtt{f}.I)$ produces a partial method operation $|p|_U$ as follows:

$$\begin{aligned} &|p|_U(\sigma) = (|p|^{\mathrm{r}}_U(\sigma), |p|^{\mathrm{e}}_U(\sigma)) && \text{if } |p|^{\mathrm{r}}_U(\sigma) = \mathsf{t} \lor |p|^{\mathrm{r}}_U(\sigma) = \mathsf{f}\,, \\ &|p|_U(\sigma) \text{ is undefined} && \text{if } |p|^{\mathrm{r}}_U(\sigma) = \mathsf{d}\,, \end{aligned}$$

[4] In contexts where functional units for several state spaces are involved, we would take the union of the corresponding sets of services as the set $\mathcal{S}$ and σ' would be a fixed but arbitrary state from the union of the state spaces concerned.

[5] This may lead to an uncountable number of constants, which is unproblematic and quite normal in model theory.

where

$$|p|^{\mathrm{r}}_U(\sigma) = p \mathbin{!} \mathtt{f}.U(\sigma)\;,$$
$$|p|^{\mathrm{e}}_U(\sigma) = \text{the unique } \sigma' \in \Sigma \text{ such that } p \bullet \mathtt{f}.U(\sigma) = \mathtt{f}.U(\sigma')\;.$$

If $|p|_U$ is total, then it is called a *derived method operation* of U.

Definition 3.8. The binary relation $\leq$ on $\mathcal{FU}(\Sigma)$ is defined by $U \leq U'$ iff for all $(m, M) \in U$, M is a derived method operation of U'. The binary relation $\equiv$ on $\mathcal{FU}(\Sigma)$ is defined by $U \equiv U'$ iff $U \leq U'$ and $U' \leq U$.

Theorem 3.2.

(1) $\leq$ is transitive;

(2) $\equiv$ is an equivalence relation.

Proof. Property 1 is proved by showing that $U \leq U'$ and $U' \leq U''$ implies $U \leq U''$. It is sufficient to show that we can obtain instruction sequences in $\mathcal{L}(\mathtt{f}.\mathcal{I}(U''))$ that produce the method operations of U from the instruction sequences in $\mathcal{L}(\mathtt{f}.\mathcal{I}(U'))$ that produce the method operations of U and the instruction sequences in $\mathcal{L}(\mathtt{f}.\mathcal{I}(U''))$ that produce the method operations of U'. Without loss of generality, we may assume that all instruction sequences are of the form $u_1 \,;\, \ldots \,;\, u_k \,;\, !\mathrm{t} \,;\, !\mathrm{f}$, where, for each $i \in [1, k]$, u_i is a positive test instruction, a forward jump instruction or a backward jump instruction. Let $m \in \mathcal{I}(U)$, and let $p_m \in \mathcal{L}(\mathtt{f}.\mathcal{I}(U'))$ be such that $m_U = |p_m|_{U'}$. Suppose that $\mathcal{I}(U') = \{m'_1, \ldots, m'_n\}$. For each $i \in [1, n]$, let $p_{m'_i} = u^i_1 \,;\ldots;\, u^i_{k_i} \,;\, !\mathrm{t} \,;\, !\mathrm{f} \in \mathcal{L}(\mathtt{f}.\mathcal{I}(U''))$ be such that ${m'_i}_{U'} = |p_{m'_i}|_{U''}$. Consider the $p'_m \in \mathcal{L}(\mathtt{f}.\mathcal{I}(U''))$ obtained from p_m as follows: for each $i \in [1, n]$, (i) first increase the length of each jump over the leftmost occurrence of $+\mathtt{f}.m'_i$ in p_m with $k_i + 1$, and next replace this occurrence of $+\mathtt{f}.m'_i$ by $u^i_1 \,;\, \ldots \,;\, u^i_{k_i}$; (ii) repeat the previous step as long as there are occurrences of $+\mathtt{f}.m'_i$. It is easy to see that $m_U = |p'_m|_{U''}$.

Property 2 follows quite simply. It follows immediately from the definition of $\equiv$ that $\equiv$ is symmetric and from the definition of $\leq$ that $\leq$ is reflexive. From these properties, Property 1 and the definition of $\equiv$, it follows immediately that $\equiv$ is symmetric, reflexive and transitive. □

Definition 3.9. The members of the quotient set $\mathcal{FU}(\Sigma)/{\equiv}$ are called *functional unit degrees*. Let $U \in \mathcal{FU}(\Sigma)$ and $\mathcal{D} \in \mathcal{FU}(\Sigma)/{\equiv}$. Then $\mathcal{D}$ is a *functional unit degree below* U if there exists an $U' \in \mathcal{D}$ such that $U' \leq U$.

Two functional units U and U' belong to the same functional unit degree if and only if U and U' have the same derived method operations. A functional unit degree $\mathcal{D}$ is below a functional unit U if and only if all derived method operations of some member of $\mathcal{D}$ are derived method operations of U.

The binary relation $\leq$ on $\mathcal{FU}(\Sigma)$ is reminiscent of the relative computability relation $\leq$ on algebras introduced in [Lynch and Blum (1981)] because functional units can be looked upon as algebras of a special kind. In the definition of this relative computability relation on algebras, the role of instruction sequences is filled by flow charts. Another difference is that the relation allows for algebras with different domains to be related. This corresponds to a relation on functional units that allows for the states from one state space to be represented by the states from another state space. To the best of our knowledge, the work presented in [Lynch and Blum (1981)] and a few preceding papers of the same authors is the only work on computability that is concerned with a relation comparable to the relation $\leq$ on $\mathcal{FU}(\Sigma)$ defined above.

3.2.2 *A Boolean register functional unit*

In this section, we define a functional unit in $\mathcal{FU}(\mathbb{B})$ that is a register whose possible contents are the Boolean values t and f. This functional unit will often be used in the rest of this book.

The functional unit in question is defined as follows:

$$BR = \{(\texttt{set}{:}b, \mathit{Set}{:}b) \mid b \in \mathbb{B}\} \cup \{(\texttt{get}, \mathit{Get})\} ,$$

where the method operations are defined as follows:

$$\begin{aligned} \mathit{Set}{:}b(\sigma) &= (b, b) , \\ \mathit{Get}(\sigma) &= (\sigma, \sigma) . \end{aligned}$$

The interface $\mathcal{I}(BR)$ of BR can be explained as follows:

- set:b: the content of the register becomes b and the reply is b;
- get: nothing changes and the reply is the content of the register.

For $b \in \mathbb{B}$, the service $BR(b)$ and the service BR_b from Sect. 3.1.4 are the same.

Using Boolean registers, total and partial functions from $\mathbb{B}^n$ to $\mathbb{B}$ ($n \in \mathbb{N}$) can be computed by instruction sequences. In [Bergstra and Bethke (2012)], the following facts are established about the class of all total functions from $\mathbb{B}^*$ to $\mathbb{B}$ whose restriction to $\mathbb{B}^n$

can be computed by an ISNR^{s} instruction sequence without occurrences of backward jump instructions whose length is polynomial in n for each $n \in \mathbb{N}$:

- this class coincides with the complexity class P/poly;
- this class is a proper subclass of the class of all total functions from $\mathbb{B}^*$ to $\mathbb{B}$ whose restriction to $\mathbb{B}^n$ can be computed by an ISNR^{s} instruction sequence whose length is polynomial in n for each $n \in \mathbb{N}$, provided that the well-known complexity-theoretic conjecture $\mathrm{NP} \not\subseteq \mathrm{P}/\mathrm{poly}$ is right.

The latter fact indicates that there are problems for which the instruction sequences solving them can be significantly shorter if backward jump instructions are used.

3.2.3 *A natural number register functional unit*

In this section, we define a functional unit in $\mathcal{FU}([0, n_{\max}])$ ($n_{\max} \in \mathbb{N}$) that is a register whose possible contents are the natural numbers in the interval $[0, n_{\max}]$. This functional unit will among other things be used in Sections 3.3.1–3.3.3 to describe the behaviour of instruction sequences under execution in variants of ISNR and ISNA with indirect jump instructions.

The functional unit in question is defined as follows:

$$\mathit{NNR} = \{(\mathtt{set}{:}n, \mathit{Set}{:}n) \mid n \in [0, n_{\max}]\} \cup \{(\mathtt{eq}{:}n, \mathit{Eq}{:}n) \mid n \in [0, n_{\max}]\} ,$$

where the method operations are defined as follows:

$$\begin{aligned} \mathit{Set}{:}n(\sigma) &= (\mathsf{t}, n) , \\ \mathit{Eq}{:}n(\sigma) &= \begin{cases} (\mathsf{t}, \sigma) & \text{if } n = \sigma \\ (\mathsf{f}, \sigma) & \text{if } n \neq \sigma . \end{cases} \end{aligned}$$

The interface $\mathcal{I}(\mathit{NNR})$ of NNR can be explained as follows:

- $\mathtt{set}{:}n$: the contents of the register becomes n and the reply is t;
- $\mathtt{eq}{:}n$: if the contents of the register equals n, then nothing changes and the reply is t; otherwise nothing changes and the reply is f.

3.2.4 *A natural number stack functional unit*

In this section, we define a functional unit in $\mathcal{FU}(\{\sigma \in [0, n_{\max}]^* \mid \mathrm{len}(\sigma) \leq l_{\max}\})$ ($n_{\max}, l_{\max} \in \mathbb{N}$) that is a bounded stack whose elements can contain the natural numbers in the interval $[0, n_{\max}]$. This functional unit will be used in Sect. 3.3.4 to describe the behaviour of instruction sequences under execution in a variant of ISNA with returning jump instructions and an accompanying return instruction.

The functional unit in question is defined as follows:

$$\begin{aligned} \mathit{NNS} = {} & \{(\texttt{push}{:}n, \mathit{Push}{:}n) \mid n \in [0, n_{\max}]\} \cup \{(\texttt{pop}, \mathit{Pop})\} \\ \cup {} & \{(\texttt{topeq}{:}n, \mathit{Topeq}{:}n) \mid n \in [0, n_{\max}]\} \,, \end{aligned}$$

where the method operations are defined as follows:

$$\begin{aligned} \mathit{Push}{:}n(\sigma) &= \begin{cases} (\mathsf{t}, n\sigma) & \text{if } \mathrm{len}(\sigma) < l_{\max} \\ (\mathsf{f}, \sigma) & \text{if } \mathrm{len}(\sigma) \geq l_{\max} \,, \end{cases} \\ \mathit{Pop}(n'\sigma) &= (\mathsf{t}, \sigma) \,, \\ \mathit{Pop}(\epsilon) &= (\mathsf{f}, \epsilon) \,, \\ \mathit{Topeq}{:}n(n'\sigma) &= \begin{cases} (\mathsf{t}, n'\sigma) & \text{if } n = n' \\ (\mathsf{f}, n'\sigma) & \text{if } n \neq n' \,, \end{cases} \\ \mathit{Topeq}{:}n(\epsilon) &= (\mathsf{f}, \epsilon) \,. \end{aligned}$$

The interface $\mathcal{I}(\mathit{NNS})$ of *NNS* can be explained as follows:

- $\texttt{push}{:}n$: if the length of the stack is less than $l_{\max}$, then the number n is put on top of the stack and the reply is t; otherwise nothing changes and the reply is f;
- $\texttt{pop}$: if the stack is not empty, then the number on top of the stack is removed from the stack and the reply is t; otherwise nothing changes and the reply is f;
- $\texttt{topeq}{:}n$: if the stack is not empty and the number on top of the stack is n, then nothing changes and the reply is t; otherwise nothing changes and the reply is f.

3.2.5 *A natural number counter functional unit*

In this section, we define a functional unit in $\mathcal{FU}(\mathbb{N})$ that is an unbounded counter. This functional unit will be used several times in the rest of this book.

The functional unit in question is defined as follows:

$$\mathit{NNC} = \{(\texttt{setzero}, \mathit{Setzero}), (\texttt{succ}, \mathit{Succ}), (\texttt{pred}, \mathit{Pred}), (\texttt{iszero}, \mathit{Iszero})\} \,.$$

where the method operations are defined as follows:

$$\begin{aligned}
Setzero(\sigma) &= (\mathsf{t}, 0)\ , \\
Succ(\sigma) &= (\mathsf{t}, \sigma + 1)\ , \\
Pred(\sigma) &= \begin{cases} (\mathsf{t}, \sigma - 1) & \text{if } \sigma > 0\ , \\ (\mathsf{f}, \sigma) & \text{if } \sigma = 0\ , \end{cases} \\
Iszero(\sigma) &= \begin{cases} (\mathsf{t}, \sigma) & \text{if } \sigma = 0\ , \\ (\mathsf{f}, \sigma) & \text{if } \sigma > 0\ . \end{cases}
\end{aligned}$$

The interface $\mathcal{I}(NNC)$ of NNC can be explained as follows:

- `setzero`: the content of the counter is set to zero and the reply is t;
- `succ`: the content of the counter is incremented by one and the reply is t;
- `pred`: if the content of the counter is greater than zero, then the content of the counter is decremented by one and the reply is t; otherwise, nothing changes and the reply is f;
- `iszero`: if the content of the counter equals zero, then nothing changes and the reply is t; otherwise, nothing changes and the reply is f.

In Appendix B, some results concerning functional units for natural numbers are given. The main results concern universal computable functional units for natural numbers.

3.3 Functional Unit Related Additional Instructions

In this section, we present instruction sequence notations with indirect jump instructions, returning jump instructions and an accompanying return instruction, and dynamically instantiated instructions. These notations are explained with the help of functional units defined in Sect. 3.2. Unlike the instruction sequence notations introduced in Sect. 2.3, the notations introduced here cannot be explained in terms of SPISA instruction sequences only.

3.3.1 *Indirect absolute jump instructions*

In this section, we introduce a variant of ISNA with indirect jump instructions. This variant is called $\mathrm{ISNA}_{\mathrm{ij}}$.

In $\mathrm{ISNA}_{\mathrm{ij}}$, it is assumed that a fixed but arbitrary number $i_{\max} \in \mathbb{N}^+$ has been given, which is considered the number of natural number registers available. It is also assumed that a fixed but arbitrary number $n_{\max} \in \mathbb{N}^+$ has been given, which is considered the greatest natural number that can be contained in a natural number register.

In ISNA, it is assumed that a fixed but arbitrary set $\mathfrak{A}$ of basic instructions has been given. In ISNA_{ij}, the following additional assumptions relating to $\mathfrak{A}$ are made:

- a fixed but arbitrary set $\mathcal{F}$ of foci with $\{\text{nnr}{:}i \mid i \in [1, i_{\text{max}}]\} \subseteq \mathcal{F}$ has been given;
- a fixed but arbitrary set $\mathcal{M}$ of methods with $\mathcal{I}(NNR) \subseteq \mathcal{M}$ has been given;
- $\mathfrak{A} = \{\boldsymbol{f}.\boldsymbol{m} \mid \boldsymbol{f} \in \mathcal{F} \setminus \{\text{nnr}{:}i \mid i \in [1, i_{\text{max}}]\} \wedge \boldsymbol{m} \in \mathcal{M}\}$.

ISNA_{ij} has the following primitive instructions in addition to the primitive instructions of ISNA:

- for each $i \in [1, i_{\text{max}}]$ and $n \in [0, n_{\text{max}}]$, a *register set instruction* $\text{set}{:}i{:}n$;
- for each $i \in [1, i_{\text{max}}]$, an *indirect absolute jump instruction* $\text{i}\#\#i$.

ISNA_{ij} instruction sequences have the form $\boldsymbol{u}_1 ; \ldots ; \boldsymbol{u}_k$, where $\boldsymbol{u}_1, \ldots, \boldsymbol{u}_k$ are primitive instructions of ISNA_{ij}.

On execution of an ISNA_{ij} instruction sequence, the effects of the plain basic instructions, the positive test instructions, the negative test instructions, the direct absolute jump instructions, and the termination instructions are as in ISNA. The effect of a register set instruction $\text{set}{:}i{:}n$ is that the contents of register i is set to n and execution proceeds with the next primitive instruction. If there is no primitive instruction to proceed with, inaction occurs. Initially, the contents of all registers is 0. The effect of an indirect absolute jump instruction $\text{i}\#\#i$ is the same as the effect of $\#\#l$, where l is the content of register i.

We define the meaning of ISNA_{ij} instruction sequences by means of a projection `isnaij2isna` from the set of all ISNA_{ij} instruction sequences to the set of all ISNA instruction sequences. This function is defined by

$$
\begin{array}{l}
\texttt{isnaij2isna}(\boldsymbol{u}_1 ; \ldots ; \boldsymbol{u}_k) = \\
\quad \psi(\boldsymbol{u}_1) ; \ldots ; \psi(\boldsymbol{u}_k) ; \#\#0 ; \#\#0 ; \\
\quad +\text{nnr}{:}1.\text{eq}{:}1 ; \#\#1 ; \ldots ; +\text{nnr}{:}1.\text{eq}{:}n ; \#\#n ; \#\#0 ; \\
\quad \ \vdots \\
\quad +\text{nnr}{:}i_{\text{max}}.\text{eq}{:}1 ; \#\#1 ; \ldots ; +\text{nnr}{:}i_{\text{max}}.\text{eq}{:}n ; \#\#n ; \#\#0 \, ,
\end{array}
$$

where $n = \min(k, n_{\text{max}})$ and the auxiliary function ψ from the set of all primitive instructions of ISNA_{ij} to the set of all primitive instructions of ISNA is defined as follows:

$$
\begin{aligned}
&\psi(\mathsf{set}{:}i{:}n) = \mathtt{nnr}{:}i.\mathtt{set}{:}n\ , && \\
&\psi(\#\#l) \quad = \#\#l && \text{if } l \leq k\ , \\
&\psi(\#\#l) \quad = \#\#0 && \text{if } l > k\ , \\
&\psi(\mathsf{i}\#\#i) \quad = \#\#l_i\ , && \\
&\psi(\boldsymbol{u}) \qquad = \boldsymbol{u} && \text{if } \boldsymbol{u} \text{ is not a register set instruction or} \\
& && \quad \text{jump instruction}\ ,
\end{aligned}
$$

and for each $i \in [1, i_{\max}]$:

$$l_i = k + 3 + (2 \cdot \min(k, n_{\max}) + 1) \cdot (i - 1)\ .$$

The idea is that each indirect absolute jump can be replaced by a direct absolute jump to the beginning of the instruction sequence

$$+\mathtt{nnr}{:}i.\mathsf{eq}{:}1\ ;\ \#\#1\ ;\ \ldots\ ;\ +\mathtt{nnr}{:}i.\mathsf{eq}{:}n\ ;\ \#\#n\ ;\ \#\#0\ ,$$

where i is the register concerned and $n = \min(k, n_{\max})$. The execution of this instruction sequence leads to the intended jump after the content of the register concerned has been found by a linear search. To enforce that inaction occurs after execution of the last instruction of the instruction sequence if the last instruction is a plain basic instruction, a positive test instruction or a negative test instruction, $\#\#0;\#\#0$ is appended to $\psi(\boldsymbol{u}_1);\ldots;\psi(\boldsymbol{u}_k)$. Because the length of the translated instruction sequence is greater than k, care is taken that there are no direct absolute jumps to instructions with a position greater than k. Obviously, the linear search for the content of a register can be replaced by a binary search in this projection and forthcoming ones.

Let $\boldsymbol{p}$ be an ISNA$_{\mathrm{ij}}$ instruction sequence. Then $\mathtt{isnaij2isna}(\boldsymbol{p})$ is the meaning of $\boldsymbol{p}$ as an ISNA instruction sequence. The intended behaviour of $\boldsymbol{p}$ under execution is the behaviour of $\mathtt{isnaij2isna}(\boldsymbol{p})$ under execution on interaction with a register file. That is, the *behaviour* of $\boldsymbol{p}$, written $|\boldsymbol{p}|_{\mathrm{ISNA_{ij}}}$, is $|\mathtt{isnaij2isna}(\boldsymbol{p})|_{\mathrm{ISNA}} \mathbin{/\!/} (\bigoplus_{i=1}^{i_{\max}} \mathtt{nnr}{:}i.\mathit{NNR}(0))$.

For example, the behaviour of the ISNA$_{\mathrm{ij}}$ instruction sequence

$$\mathsf{a}\ ;\ \mathsf{set}{:}1{:}8\ ;\ +\mathsf{b}\ ;\ \mathsf{set}{:}1{:}6\ ;\ \mathsf{i}\#\#1\ ;\ \mathsf{c}\ ;\ \#\#2\ ;\ +\mathsf{d}\ ;\ !\mathsf{t}\ ;\ !\mathsf{f}$$

is the x-component of the solution of the guarded recursive specification consisting of the following two equations:

$$x = \mathsf{a} \circ y\ , \qquad y = (\mathsf{c} \circ y) \trianglelefteq \mathsf{b} \trianglerighteq (\mathsf{S{+}} \trianglelefteq \mathsf{d} \trianglerighteq \mathsf{S{-}})\ .$$

Remark 3.3. More than one instruction is needed in ISNA to obtain the effect of a single indirect absolute jump instruction. The projection isnaij2isna deals with that in such a way that there is no need for the unit instruction operator introduced in [Ponse (2002)] or the distinction between first-level instructions and second-level instructions introduced in [Bergstra and Bethke (2007)].

3.3.2 *Indirect relative jump instructions*

In this section, we introduce a variant of ISNR with indirect jump instructions. This variant is called $\mathrm{ISNR_{ij}}$.

In $\mathrm{ISNR_{ij}}$, the same assumptions are made as in $\mathrm{ISNA_{ij}}$.

$\mathrm{ISNR_{ij}}$ has the following primitive instructions in addition to the primitive instructions of ISNR:

- for each $i \in [1, i_{\max}]$ and $n \in [0, n_{\max}]$, a *register set instruction* $\mathsf{set}{:}i{:}n$;
- for each $i \in [1, i_{\max}]$, an *indirect forward jump instruction* $\mathsf{i}\#i$;
- for each $i \in [1, i_{\max}]$, an *indirect backward jump instruction* $\mathsf{i}\backslash\#i$.

$\mathrm{ISNR_{ij}}$ instruction sequences have the form $\boldsymbol{u}_1 ; \ldots ; \boldsymbol{u}_k$, where $\boldsymbol{u}_1, \ldots, \boldsymbol{u}_k$ are primitive instructions of $\mathrm{ISNR_{ij}}$.

On execution of an $\mathrm{ISNR_{ij}}$ instruction sequence, the effects of the plain basic instructions, the positive test instructions, the negative test instructions, the direct forward jump instructions, the direct backward jump instructions, and the termination instructions are as in ISNR. The effects of the register set instructions are as in $\mathrm{ISNA_{ij}}$. The effect of an indirect forward jump instruction $\mathsf{i}\#i$ is the same as the effect of $\#l$, where l is the content of register i. The effect of an indirect backward jump instruction $\mathsf{i}\backslash\#i$ is the same as the effect of $\backslash\#l$, where l is the content of register i.

We define the meaning of $\mathrm{ISNR_{ij}}$ instruction sequences by means of a projection `isnrij2isnr` from the set of all $\mathrm{ISNR_{ij}}$ instruction sequences to the set of all ISNR instruction sequences. This function is defined by

$$
\begin{array}{l}
\mathtt{isnrij2isnr}(\boldsymbol{u}_1 ; \ldots ; \boldsymbol{u}_k) = \\
\quad \psi_1(\boldsymbol{u}_1) ; \ldots ; \psi_k(\boldsymbol{u}_k) ; \#0 ; \#0 ; \\
\quad +\mathtt{nnr}{:}1.\mathsf{eq}{:}0 ; \backslash\#l'_{1,1,0} ; \ldots ; +\mathtt{nnr}{:}1.\mathsf{eq}{:}n_{\max} ; \backslash\#l'_{1,1,n_{\max}} ; \\
\qquad \vdots \\
\quad +\mathtt{nnr}{:}1.\mathsf{eq}{:}0 ; \backslash\#l'_{1,k,0} ; \ldots ; +\mathtt{nnr}{:}1.\mathsf{eq}{:}n_{\max} ; \backslash\#l'_{1,k,n_{\max}} ; \\
\qquad\quad \vdots
\end{array}
$$

$$
\begin{array}{l}
+\mathtt{nnr}{:}i_{\max}.\mathtt{eq}{:}0\ ;\ \backslash\#l'_{i_{\max},1,0}\ ;\ \ldots\ ;\ +\mathtt{nnr}{:}i_{\max}.\mathtt{eq}{:}n_{\max}\ ;\ \backslash\#l'_{i_{\max},1,n_{\max}}\ ;\\
\quad\vdots\\
+\mathtt{nnr}{:}i_{\max}.\mathtt{eq}{:}0\ ;\ \backslash\#l'_{i_{\max},k,0}\ ;\ \ldots\ ;\ +\mathtt{nnr}{:}i_{\max}.\mathtt{eq}{:}n_{\max}\ ;\ \backslash\#l'_{i_{\max},k,n_{\max}}\ ;\\
+\mathtt{nnr}{:}1.\mathtt{eq}{:}0\ ;\ \backslash\#\underline{l}'_{1,1,0}\ ;\ \ldots\ ;\ +\mathtt{nnr}{:}1.\mathtt{eq}{:}n_{\max}\ ;\ \backslash\#\underline{l}'_{1,1,n_{\max}}\ ;\\
\quad\vdots\\
+\mathtt{nnr}{:}1.\mathtt{eq}{:}0\ ;\ \backslash\#\underline{l}'_{1,k,0}\ ;\ \ldots\ ;\ +\mathtt{nnr}{:}1.\mathtt{eq}{:}n_{\max}\ ;\ \backslash\#\underline{l}'_{1,k,n_{\max}}\ ;\\
\qquad\vdots\\
+\mathtt{nnr}{:}i_{\max}.\mathtt{eq}{:}0\ ;\ \backslash\#\underline{l}'_{i_{\max},1,0}\ ;\ \ldots\ ;\ +\mathtt{nnr}{:}i_{\max}.\mathtt{eq}{:}n_{\max}\ ;\ \backslash\#\underline{l}'_{i_{\max},1,n_{\max}}\ ;\\
\quad\vdots\\
+\mathtt{nnr}{:}i_{\max}.\mathtt{eq}{:}0\ ;\ \backslash\#\underline{l}'_{i_{\max},k,0}\ ;\ \ldots\ ;\ +\mathtt{nnr}{:}i_{\max}.\mathtt{eq}{:}n_{\max}\ ;\ \backslash\#\underline{l}'_{i_{\max},k,n_{\max}}\ ,
\end{array}
$$

where the auxiliary functions ψ_j from the set of all primitive instructions of $\mathrm{ISNR}_{\mathrm{ij}}$ to the set of all primitive instructions of ISNR is defined as follows ($1 \leq j \leq k$):

$$
\begin{array}{lll}
\psi_j(\mathsf{set}{:}i{:}n) = \mathtt{nnr}{:}i.\mathtt{set}{:}n\ , & & \\
\psi_j(\#l) & = \#l & \text{if } j + l \leq k\ ,\\
\psi_j(\#l) & = \backslash\#j & \text{if } j + l > k\ ,\\
\psi_j(\backslash\#l) & = \backslash\#l\ , & \\
\psi_j(\mathsf{i}\#i) & = \#l_{i,j}\ , & \\
\psi_j(\mathsf{i}\backslash\#i) & = \#\underline{l}_{i,j}\ , & \\
\psi_j(u) & = u & \text{if } u \text{ is not a register set instruction or}\\
 & & \quad\text{jump instruction}\ ,
\end{array}
$$

and for each $i \in [1, i_{\max}]$, $j \in [1, k]$, and $h \in [0, n_{\max}]$:

$$
\begin{array}{ll}
l_{i,j} = k + 3 + 2 \cdot (n_{\max} + 1) \cdot (k \cdot (i - 1) + (j - 1))\ , & \\
\underline{l}_{i,j} = k + 3 + 2 \cdot (n_{\max} + 1) \cdot (k \cdot (i_{\max} + i - 1) + (j - 1))\ , & \\
l'_{i,j,h} = l_{i,j} + 2 \cdot h + 1 - (j + h) & \text{if } j + h \leq k\ ,\\
l'_{i,j,h} = k + 3 + 2 \cdot (n_{\max} + 1) \cdot k \cdot i_{\max} & \text{if } j + h > k\ ,\\
\underline{l}'_{i,j,h} = \underline{l}_{i,j} + 2 \cdot h + 1 - (j - h) & \text{if } j - h \geq 0\ ,\\
\underline{l}'_{i,j,h} = k + 3 + 4 \cdot (n_{\max} + 1) \cdot k \cdot i_{\max} & \text{if } j - h < 0\ .
\end{array}
$$

Like in the case of indirect absolute jumps, the idea is that each indirect forward jump and each indirect backward jump can be replaced by a direct forward jump to the beginning of an instruction sequence whose execution leads to the intended jump after the content of the register concerned has been found by a linear search. However, the direct backward jump instructions occurring in that instruction sequence now depend upon the position of the indirect jump concerned in $u_1 ; \ldots ; u_k$. To enforce that inaction occurs after execution of the last instruction of the instruction sequence if the last instruction is a plain basic instruction, a positive test instruction or a negative test instruction, $\#0 ; \#0$ is appended to $\psi_1(u_1) ; \ldots ; \psi_k(u_k)$. Because the length of the translated instruction sequence is greater than k, care is taken that there are no direct forward jumps to instructions with a position greater than k.

Let p be an ISNR$_{\text{ij}}$ instruction sequence. Then $\mathtt{isnrij2isnr}(p)$ is the meaning of p as an ISNR instruction sequence. The intended behaviour of p under execution is the behaviour of $\mathtt{isnrij2isnr}(p)$ under execution on interaction with a register file. That is, the *behaviour* of p, written $|p|_{\text{ISNR}_{\text{ij}}}$, is $|\mathtt{isnrij2isnr}(p)|_{\text{ISNR}} /\!/ (\bigoplus_{i=1}^{i_{\max}} \mathtt{nnr}{:}i.NNR(0))$.

For example, the behaviour of the ISNR$_{\text{ij}}$ instruction sequence

$$\mathsf{a} ; \mathsf{set}{:}1{:}3 ; +\mathsf{b} ; \mathsf{set}{:}1{:}1 ; \mathsf{i}\#1 ; \mathsf{c} ; \backslash\#5 ; +\mathsf{d} ; !\mathsf{t} ; !\mathsf{f}$$

is the x-component of the solution of the guarded recursive specification consisting of the following two equations:

$$x = \mathsf{a} \circ y\,, \qquad y = (\mathsf{c} \circ y) \trianglelefteq \mathsf{b} \trianglerighteq (\mathsf{S+} \trianglelefteq \mathsf{d} \trianglerighteq \mathsf{S-})\,.$$

The projection $\mathtt{isnrij2isnr}$ yields needlessly long ISNR instruction sequences because it does not take into account the fact that there is at most one indirect jump instruction at each position in an ISNR$_{\text{ij}}$ instruction sequence being projected. Taking this fact into account would lead to a projection with a much more complicated definition. Whatever projection is taken, indirect jump instructions are eliminated. In Sect. 6.1, the effect of indirect jump instruction elimination on the interactive performance of instruction sequences is studied.

3.3.3 *Double indirect jump instructions*

In this section, we introduce a variant of ISNA$_{\text{ij}}$ with double indirect jump instructions. This variant is called ISNA$_{\text{dij}}$.

In ISNA$_{\text{dij}}$, the same assumptions are made as in ISNA$_{\text{ij}}$.

ISNA$_{\text{dij}}$ has the following primitive instructions in addition to the primitive instructions of ISNA$_{\text{ij}}$:

- for each $i \in [1, i_{\max}]$, a *double indirect absolute jump instruction* $\mathsf{ii}\#\#i$.

ISNA$_{\text{dij}}$ instruction sequences have the form $u_1 ; \ldots ; u_k$, where $u_1, \ldots, u_k$ are primitive instructions of $\mathrm{ISNA_{dij}}$.

On execution of an $\mathrm{ISNA_{dij}}$ instruction sequence, the effects of the plain basic instructions, the positive test instructions, the negative test instructions, the direct absolute jump instructions, the register set instructions, the indirect absolute jump instructions, and the termination instructions are as in $\mathrm{ISNA_{ij}}$. The effect of a double indirect absolute jump instruction $\mathsf{ii}\#\#i$ is the same as the effect of $\mathsf{i}\#\#i'$, where i' is the content of register i.

Like before, we define the meaning of $\mathrm{ISNA_{dij}}$ instruction sequences by means of a projection `isnadij2isnaij` from the set of all $\mathrm{ISNA_{dij}}$ instruction sequences to the set of all $\mathrm{ISNA_{ij}}$ instruction sequences. This function is defined by

$$\begin{aligned}
&\mathtt{isnadij2isnaij}(u_1\,;\ldots;u_k) = \\
&\quad \psi(u_1)\,;\ldots;\psi(u_k)\,;\#\#0\,;\#\#0\,;\overbrace{\#\#0\,;\ldots;\#\#0}^{\max(k+2,n_{\max})-(k+2)}\,; \\
&\quad +\mathtt{nnr}{:}1.\mathsf{eq}{:}1\,;\mathsf{i}\#\#1\,;\ldots;+\mathtt{nnr}{:}1.\mathsf{eq}{:}n\,;\mathsf{i}\#\#n\,;\#\#0\,; \\
&\quad \vdots \\
&\quad +\mathtt{nnr}{:}i_{\max}.\mathsf{eq}{:}1\,;\mathsf{i}\#\#1\,;\ldots;+\mathtt{nnr}{:}i_{\max}.\mathsf{eq}{:}n\,;\mathsf{i}\#\#n\,;\#\#0\,,
\end{aligned}$$

where $n = \min(i_{\max}, n_{\max})$ and the auxiliary function ψ from the set of all primitive instructions of $\mathrm{ISNA_{dij}}$ to the set of all primitive instructions of $\mathrm{ISNA_{ij}}$ is defined as follows:

$$\begin{aligned}
\psi(\#\#l) &= \#\#l && \text{if } l \leq k\,, \\
\psi(\#\#l) &= \#\#0 && \text{if } l > k\,, \\
\psi(\mathsf{i}\#\#i) &= \mathsf{i}\#\#i\,, \\
\psi(\mathsf{ii}\#\#i) &= \#\#l_i\,, \\
\psi(u) &= u && \text{if } u \text{ is not a jump instruction}\,,
\end{aligned}$$

and for each $i \in [1, i_{\max}]$:

$$l_i = \max(k+2, n_{\max}) + 1 + (2 \cdot \min(i_{\max}, n_{\max}) + 1) \cdot (i-1)\,.$$

The idea is that each double indirect absolute jump can be replaced by a direct absolute jump to the beginning of the instruction sequence

$$+\mathtt{nnr}{:}i.\mathsf{eq}{:}1\,;\mathsf{i}\#\#1\,;\ldots;+\mathtt{nnr}{:}i.\mathsf{eq}{:}n\,;\mathsf{i}\#\#n\,;\#\#0\,,$$

where i is the register concerned and $n = \min(i_{\max}, n_{\max})$. The execution of this instruction sequence leads to the intended jump after the content of the register concerned has been found by a linear search. To enforce that inaction occurs after execution of the last instruction of the instruction sequence if the last instruction is a plain basic instruction, a positive test instruction or a negative test instruction, $\#\#0\,;\#\#0$ is appended to $\psi(u_1)\,;\ldots;\psi(u_k)$. Because the length of the translated instruction sequence is greater than k, care is taken that there are no direct absolute jumps to instructions with a position greater than k. To deal properly with indirect absolute jumps to instructions with a position greater than k, the instruction $\#\#0$ is appended to $\psi(\boldsymbol{u}_1) ; \ldots ; \psi(\boldsymbol{u}_k) ; \#\#0 ; \#\#0$ a sufficient number of times.

Let $\boldsymbol{p}$ be an ISNA_{dij} instruction sequence. Then $\mathtt{isnadij2isnaij}(\boldsymbol{p})$ is the meaning of $\boldsymbol{p}$ as an ISNA_{ij} instruction sequence. The intended behaviour of $\boldsymbol{p}$ under execution is the behaviour of the ISNA_{ij} instruction sequence $\mathtt{isnadij2isnaij}(\boldsymbol{p})$ under execution. That is, the behaviour of $\boldsymbol{p}$ under execution, written $|\boldsymbol{p}|_{\text{ISNA}_{\text{dij}}}$, is $|\mathtt{isnadij2isnaij}(\boldsymbol{p})|_{\text{ISNA}_{\text{ij}}}$.

For example, the behaviour of the ISNA_{dij} instruction sequence

$$\mathsf{set{:}1{:}2} ; \mathsf{a} ; \mathsf{set{:}2{:}9} ; +\mathsf{b} ; \mathsf{set{:}2{:}7} ; \mathsf{ii}\#\#1 ; \mathsf{c} ; \#\#3 ; +\mathsf{d} ; !\mathsf{t} ; !\mathsf{f}$$

is the x-component of the solution of the guarded recursive specification consisting of the following two equations:

$$x = \mathtt{a} \circ y\,, \qquad y = (\mathtt{c} \circ y) \trianglelefteq \mathtt{b} \trianglerighteq (\mathsf{S+} \trianglelefteq \mathtt{d} \trianglerighteq \mathsf{S-})\,.$$

The projection $\mathtt{isnadij2isnaij}$ uses indirect absolute jumps to obtain the effect of a double indirect absolute jump in the same way as the projection $\mathtt{isnaij2isna}$ uses direct absolute jumps to obtain the effect of an indirect absolute jump. Likewise, indirect relative jumps can be used in that way to obtain the effect of a double indirect relative jump. Moreover, double indirect jumps can be used in that way to obtain the effect of a triple indirect jump, and so on.

3.3.4 *Returning jump and return instructions*

In this section, we introduce a variant of ISNA with returning jump instructions and an accompanying return instruction. This variant is called ISNA_{rj}.

In ISNA_{rj}, it is assumed that a fixed but arbitrary number $l_{\mathrm{max}} \in \mathbb{N}^+$ has been given, which is considered the maximal length of a natural number stack. It is also assumed that a fixed but arbitrary number $n_{\mathrm{max}} \in \mathbb{N}^+$ has been given, which is considered the greatest natural number that can be contained in the elements of the natural number stack.

In ISNA, it is assumed that a fixed but arbitrary set $\mathfrak{A}$ of basic instructions has been given. In ISNA_{rj}, the following additional assumptions relating to $\mathfrak{A}$ are made:

- a fixed but arbitrary set $\mathcal{F}$ of foci with $\mathtt{nns} \in \mathcal{F}$ has been given;
- a fixed but arbitrary set $\mathcal{M}$ of methods with $\mathcal{I}(\mathit{NNS}) \subseteq \mathcal{M}$ has been given;
- $\mathfrak{A} = \{\boldsymbol{f}.\boldsymbol{m} \mid \boldsymbol{f} \in \mathcal{F} \setminus \{\mathtt{nns}\} \wedge \boldsymbol{m} \in \mathcal{M}\}$.

ISNA_{rj} has the following primitive instructions in addition to the primitive instructions of ISNA:

- for each $l \in \mathbb{N}$, a *returning absolute jump instruction* $\mathsf{r}\#\#l$;
- an *absolute return instruction* $\#\#\mathsf{r}$.

ISNA_{rj} instruction sequences have the form $u_1 ; \ldots ; u_k$, where $u_1, \ldots, u_k$ are primitive instructions of ISNA_{rj}.

On execution of an ISNA_{rj} instruction sequence, the effects of the plain basic instructions, the positive test instructions, the negative test instructions, the non-returning absolute jump instructions, and the termination instructions are as in ISNA. The effect of a returning absolute jump instruction $\mathsf{r}\#\#l$ is that execution proceeds with the lth instruction of the instruction sequence concerned, but execution returns to the next primitive instruction on encountering a return instruction. If $\mathsf{r}\#\#l$ is itself the lth instruction or there is no primitive instruction to proceed with, inaction occurs. The effect of a return instruction $\#\#\mathsf{r}$ is that execution proceeds with the primitive instruction immediately following the last executed returning absolute jump instruction to which a return has not yet taken place. If there is no primitive instruction following that returning absolute jump instruction, inaction occurs.

Most assembly languages provide variants of the returning jump and return instructions of ISNA_{rj} as the means to make use of recursion in assembly language programming. An example of the use of the returning jump and return instructions of ISNA_{rj} for that purpose will be given below.

Like before, we define the meaning of ISNA_{rj} instruction sequences by means of a projection `isnarj2isna` from the set of all ISNA_{rj} instruction sequences to the set of all ISNA instruction sequences. This function is defined by

$$
\begin{aligned}
&\texttt{isnarj2isna}(u_1 ; \ldots ; u_k) = \\
&\quad \psi_1(u_1) ; \ldots ; \psi_k(u_k) ; \#\#0 ; \#\#0 ; \\
&\quad +\mathbf{nns.push}{:}1 ; \#\#1 ; \#\#0 ; \ldots ; +\mathbf{nns.push}{:}1 ; \#\#k ; \#\#0 ; \\
&\qquad \vdots \\
&\quad +\mathbf{nns.push}{:}n ; \#\#1 ; \#\#0 ; \ldots ; +\mathbf{nns.push}{:}n ; \#\#k ; \#\#0 ; \\
&\quad -\mathbf{nns.topeq}{:}1 ; \#\#l'_1 ; \mathbf{nns.pop} ; \#\#1{+}1 ; \\
&\qquad \vdots \\
&\quad -\mathbf{nns.topeq}{:}n ; \#\#l'_n ; \mathbf{nns.pop} ; \#\#n{+}1 ; \\
&\quad \#\#0 \,,
\end{aligned}
$$

where $n = \min(k, n_{\max})$ and the auxiliary functions ψ_j from the set of all primitive instructions of $\mathrm{ISNA}_{\mathrm{rj}}$ to the set of all primitive instructions of ISNA is defined as follows $(1 \leq j \leq k)$:

$$
\begin{aligned}
\psi_j(\#\#l) &= \#\#l && \text{if } l \leq k \,, \\
\psi_j(\#\#l) &= \#\#0 && \text{if } l > k \,, \\
\psi_j(\mathsf{r}\#\#l) &= \#\#l_{j,l} \,, \\
\psi_j(\#\#\mathsf{r}) &= \#\#l' \,, \\
\psi_j(\boldsymbol{u}) &= \boldsymbol{u} && \text{if } \boldsymbol{u} \text{ is not a jump instruction} \,,
\end{aligned}
$$

and for each $j \in [1,k]$, $l \in \mathbb{N}$, and $h \in [1, \min(k, n_{\max})]$:

$$
\begin{aligned}
l_{j,l} &= k + 3 + 3 \cdot k \cdot (j-1) + 3 \cdot (l-1) && \text{if } l \leq k \wedge j \leq n_{\max} \,, \\
l_{j,l} &= 0 && \text{if } l > k \vee j > n_{\max} \,, \\
l' &= k + 3 + 3 \cdot k \cdot \min(k, n_{\max}) \,, \\
l'_h &= l' + 4 \cdot h \,.
\end{aligned}
$$

The first idea is that each returning absolute jump can be replaced by an absolute jump to the beginning of the instruction sequence

$$
+\mathtt{nns.push}{:}j \,;\, \#\#l \,;\, \#\#0 \,,
$$

where j is the position of the returning absolute jump instruction concerned and l is the position of the instruction to jump to. The execution of this instruction sequence leads to the intended jump after the return position has been put on the stack. In the case of stack overflow, inaction occurs. The second idea is that each return can be replaced by an absolute jump to the beginning of the instruction sequence

$$
\begin{aligned}
&-\mathtt{nns.topeq}{:}1 \,;\, \#\#l'_1 \,;\, \mathtt{nns.pop} \,;\, \#\#1{+}1 \,; \\
&\quad\vdots \\
&-\mathtt{nns.topeq}{:}n \,;\, \#\#l'_n \,;\, \mathtt{nns.pop} \,;\, \#\#n{+}1 \,; \\
&\#\#0 \,,
\end{aligned}
$$

where $n = \min(k, n_{\max})$. The execution of this instruction sequence leads to the intended jump after the position on the top of the stack has been found by a linear search and has been removed from the stack. In the case of an empty stack, inaction occurs. To enforce that inaction occurs after execution of the last instruction of the instruction sequence if the last instruction is a plain basic instruction, a positive test instruction or a negative test instruction, $\#\#0 \,;\, \#\#0$ is appended to $\psi_1(\boldsymbol{u}_1) \,;\, \ldots \,;\, \psi_k(\boldsymbol{u}_k)$. Because the length of the translated instruction sequence is greater than k, care is taken that there are no non-returning or returning absolute jumps to instructions with a position greater than k.

Let $\boldsymbol{p}$ be an $\mathrm{ISNA}_{\mathrm{rj}}$ instruction sequence. Then $\mathtt{isnarj2isna}(\boldsymbol{p})$ is the meaning of $\boldsymbol{p}$ as an ISNA instruction sequence. The intended behaviour of $\boldsymbol{p}$ under execution is the behaviour of $\mathtt{isnarj2isna}(\boldsymbol{p})$ under execution on interaction with a stack. That is, the *behaviour* of $\boldsymbol{p}$, written $|\boldsymbol{p}|_{\mathrm{ISNA}_{\mathrm{rj}}}$, is $|\mathtt{isnarj2isna}(\boldsymbol{p})|_{\mathrm{ISNA}} \mathbin{/\!/} nns.NNS(\epsilon)$.

For example, the behaviour of the $\mathrm{ISNA}_{\mathrm{rj}}$ instruction sequence

$$\mathsf{r\#\#3} \mathbin{;} \mathsf{S} \mathbin{;} \mathsf{+a} \mathbin{;} \mathsf{r\#\#3} \mathbin{;} \mathsf{b} \mathbin{;} \mathsf{\#\#r}$$

is the x_0-component of the solution of the guarded recursive specification consisting of the following equations:

$$\begin{aligned}
x_n &= x_{n+1} \trianglelefteq \mathsf{a} \trianglerighteq y_n && \text{for all } n \leq l_{\max} \;, \\
x_{l_{\max}+1} &= \mathsf{D} \;, \\
y_0 &= \mathsf{S} \;, \\
y_{n+1} &= \mathsf{b} \circ y_n && \text{for all } n < l_{\max} \;.
\end{aligned}$$

This thread can, for each $n < l_{\max}$, first perform $n+1$ times a, next perform n times b, and then terminate; and it can first perform $l_{\max} + 1$ times a and then become inactive. Recall that $l_{\max}$ is the maximal length of the stack involved. The $\mathrm{ISNA}_{\mathrm{rj}}$ instruction sequence involved in this example can be viewed as follows: the first two primitive instructions make up the main program and the last four instructions make up a subroutine. From this viewpoint, the primitive instruction $\mathsf{r\#\#3}$ serves as a subroutine call, and the subroutine is recursively called from itself until the execution of $\mathsf{+a}$ yields a negative reply. Because the realization of recursion makes use of a bounded stack, the depth of the recursion is limited to $l_{\max}$.

According to the definition of the behaviour of $\mathrm{ISNA}_{\mathrm{rj}}$ instruction sequences given above, the execution of a returning jump instruction leads to inaction in the case where its position cannot be pushed on the stack (as in the example given above) and the execution of a return instruction leads to inaction in the case where there is no position to be popped from the stack. In the latter case, the return instruction is wrongly used. In the former case, however, the returning jump instruction is not wrongly used, but the finiteness of the stack comes into play. This shows that the definition of the behaviour of $\mathrm{ISNA}_{\mathrm{rj}}$ instruction sequences given here takes into account the finiteness of the execution environment of instruction sequences.

3.3.5 *Dynamically instantiated instructions*

In this section, we introduce a variant of ISNA with dynamically instantiated instructions. This variant is called ISNA_{dii}. In Appendix C, the usefulness of dynamic instruction instantiation is illustrated by means of an example.

In ISNA_{dii}, it is assumed that a fixed but arbitrary number $i_{\max} \in \mathbb{N}^+$ has been given, which is considered the number of natural number registers in a register file. It is also assumed that a fixed but arbitrary number $n_{\max} \in \mathbb{N}^+$ has been given, which is considered the greatest natural number that can be contained in the registers of the register file. The functions from $[1, i_{\max}]$ to $[0, n_{\max}]$ are taken for the states of the register file. For every function $g : [1, i_{\max}] \to [0, n_{\max}]$, g is the state in which, for each $i \in [1, i_{\max}]$, the content of register i is $g(i)$.

It is also assumed that a fixed but arbitrary set $\mathfrak{A}_{\mathsf{proto}}$ of *basic proto-instructions* and a fixed but arbitrary *dynamic instantiation* function $\theta : \mathfrak{A}_{\mathsf{proto}} \times ([1, i_{\max}] \to [0, n_{\max}]) \to \mathfrak{A}$ have been given. $\mathfrak{A}_{\mathsf{proto}}$ is a set whose members can be turned into basic instructions and θ gives, for each e from $\mathfrak{A}_{\mathsf{proto}}$ and function $g : [1, i_{\max}] \to [0, n_{\max}]$, the basic instruction into which e is turned when it is encountered during execution and the state of the register file is g at that moment.

In ISNA, it is assumed that a fixed but arbitrary set $\mathfrak{A}$ of basic instructions has been given. In ISNA_{dii}, the following additional assumptions relating to $\mathfrak{A}$ are made:

- a fixed but arbitrary set $\mathcal{F}$ of foci with $\{\mathtt{nnr}{:}i \mid i \in [1, i_{\max}]\} \subseteq \mathcal{F}$ has been given;
- a fixed but arbitrary set $\mathcal{M}$ of methods with $\mathcal{I}(NNR) \subseteq \mathcal{M}$ has been given;
- $\mathfrak{A} = \{f.m \mid f \in \mathcal{F} \setminus \{\mathtt{nnr}{:}i \mid i \in [1, i_{\max}]\} \wedge m \in \mathcal{M}\}$.

ISNA_{dii} has the following primitive instructions in addition to the primitive instructions of ISNA:

- for each $i \in [1, i_{\max}]$ and $n \in [0, n_{\max}]$, a *register set instruction* $\mathsf{set}{:}i{:}n$;
- for each $e \in \mathfrak{A}_{\mathsf{proto}}$, a *plain basic proto-instruction* e;
- for each $e \in \mathfrak{A}_{\mathsf{proto}}$, a *positive test proto-instruction* $+e$;
- for each $e \in \mathfrak{A}_{\mathsf{proto}}$, a *negative test proto-instruction* $-e$.

ISNA_{dii} instruction sequences have the form $u_1 ; \ldots ; u_k$, where $u_1, \ldots, u_k$ are primitive instructions of ISNA_{dii}.

On execution of an ISNA_{dii} instruction sequence, the effects of the plain basic instructions, the positive test instructions, the negative test instructions, the absolute jump instructions, and the the termination instructions are as in ISNA. The effects of the register set instructions are as in ISNA_{ij}. The effect of a plain basic proto-instruction e is the same as the effect of the plain basic instruction $\theta(e, g)$, where g is the state of the register file involved in the instantiation of proto-instructions. The effect of a positive or negative test proto-instruction is similar.

We define the meaning of ISNA_{dii} instruction sequences only for the case where $i_{\max} = 1$. The generalization of the definition to arbitrary $i_{\max}$ is obvious, but leads to a definition that is hard to read. The meaning of ISNA_{dii} instruction sequences is given by a projection `isnadii2isna` from the set of all ISNA_{dii} instruction sequences to the set of all ISNA instruction sequences. For the case where $i_{\max} = 1$, this function is defined by

$$\texttt{isnadii2isna}(\boldsymbol{u}_1 \,;\ldots;\, \boldsymbol{u}_k) = \psi_1(\boldsymbol{u}_1) \,;\ldots;\, \psi_k(\boldsymbol{u}_k)\ ,$$

where the auxiliary functions ψ_j from the set of all primitive instructions of ISNA_{dii} to the set of all ISNA instruction sequences are defined as follows ($1 \leq j \leq k$):

$$
\begin{aligned}
\psi_j(\mathsf{set}{:}1{:}n) &= \mathtt{nnr}{:}1.\mathtt{set}{:}n\ ,\\
\psi_j(\boldsymbol{e}) &= +\mathtt{nnr}{:}1.\mathsf{eq}{:}0 \,;\, \#\#l''_{j,0} \,;\\
&\quad \vdots\\
&\quad +\mathtt{nnr}{:}1.\mathsf{eq}{:}n_{\max}{-}1 \,;\, \#\#l''_{j,n_{\max}-1} \,;\\
&\quad \#\#l''_{j,n_{\max}} \,;\\
&\quad \theta(\boldsymbol{e}, 0) \,;\, \#\#l'_{j+1} \,;\, \#\#l'_{j+2} \,;\\
&\quad \vdots\\
&\quad \theta(\boldsymbol{e}, n_{\max}{-}1) \,;\, \#\#l'_{j+1} \,;\, \#\#l'_{j+2} \,;\\
&\quad \theta(\boldsymbol{e}, n_{\max})\ ,\\
\psi_j(+\boldsymbol{e}) &= +\mathtt{nnr}{:}1.\mathsf{eq}{:}0 \,;\, \#\#l''_{j,0} \,;\\
&\quad \vdots\\
&\quad +\mathtt{nnr}{:}1.\mathsf{eq}{:}n_{\max}{-}1 \,;\, \#\#l''_{j,n_{\max}-1} \,;\\
&\quad \#\#l''_{j,n_{\max}} \,;\\
&\quad +\theta(\boldsymbol{e}, 0) \,;\, \#\#l'_{j+1} \,;\, \#\#l'_{j+2} \,;\\
&\quad \vdots\\
&\quad +\theta(\boldsymbol{e}, n_{\max}{-}1) \,;\, \#\#l'_{j+1} \,;\, \#\#l'_{j+2} \,;\\
&\quad +\theta(\boldsymbol{e}, n_{\max})\ ,
\end{aligned}
$$

$$
\begin{aligned}
\psi_j(-e) &= +\mathtt{nnr}{:}1.\mathrm{eq}{:}0 \,;\, \#\#l''_{j,0} \,; \\
&\quad\vdots \\
&\quad +\mathtt{nnr}{:}1.\mathrm{eq}{:}n_{\max}{-}1 \,;\, \#\#l''_{j,n_{\max}-1} \,; \\
&\quad \#\#l''_{j,n_{\max}} \,; \\
&\quad -\theta(e,0) \,;\, \#\#l'_{j+1} \,;\, \#\#l'_{j+2} \,; \\
&\quad\vdots \\
&\quad -\theta(e,n_{\max}{-}1) \,;\, \#\#l'_{j+1} \,;\, \#\#l'_{j+2} \,; \\
&\quad -\theta(e,n_{\max}) \,, \\
\psi_j(\#\#l) &= \#\#l'_j \,, \\
\psi_j(u) &= u \qquad \text{if } u \text{ is not a register set instruction, proto-instruction or jump instruction} \,,
\end{aligned}
$$

and for each $j \in [1,k]$ and $h \in [0,n_{\max}]$:

$$
\begin{aligned}
l'_j &= j + (5 \cdot n_{\max} + 2) \cdot n_j \,, \\
l''_{j,h} &= l'_j + 2 \cdot n_{\max} + 3 \cdot h + 1 \,,
\end{aligned}
$$

and n_j is the number of proto-instructions preceding position j.

The idea is that each proto-instruction can be replaced by an instruction sequence of which the execution leads to the execution of the intended instruction after the content of the register has been found by a linear search. Because the length of the replacing instruction sequence is greater than 1, the direct absolute jump instructions are adjusted so as to compensate for the introduction of additional instructions.

We will proceed as if `isnadii2isna` has been defined for arbitrary $i_{\max}$. Let p be an ISNA$_{\mathrm{dii}}$ instruction sequence. Then $\mathtt{isnadii2isna}(p)$ is the meaning of p as an ISNA instruction sequence. The intended behaviour of p under execution is the behaviour of $\mathtt{isnadii2isna}(p)$ under execution on interaction with a register file. That is, the *behaviour* of p under execution, written $|p|_{\mathrm{ISNA_{dii}}}$, is $|\mathtt{isnadii2isna}(p)|_{\mathrm{ISNA}} \,/\!/\, (\bigoplus_{i=1}^{i_{\max}} \mathtt{nnr}{:}i.\mathit{NNR}(0))$.

Chapter 4

Expressiveness of Instruction Sequences

This chapter concerns the expressiveness of SPISA instruction sequences. In this case, expressiveness is basically about which behaviours can be produced by instruction sequences under execution, which primitive instructions can be removed without reducing the class of behaviours that can be produced by instruction sequences under execution, how to enlarge the class of behaviours that can be produced by instruction sequences under execution, et cetera.

We present answers to the basic expressiveness issues. Because the reach of jump instructions in SPISA is not bounded from above, the set of primitive instructions is infinite, even if the set $\mathfrak{A}$ of basic instructions is finite. One of the basic expressiveness results is that the expressiveness would be reduced by making the reach of jump instructions bounded from above. On the other hand, it is rather implausible that there exist execution mechanisms that can deal with sequences of instructions from an infinite set. We demonstrate that bounding the reach of jump instructions from above does not reduce the expressiveness if a special primitive instruction is added. By interaction between instruction sequences under execution and services, it is possible to enlarge the class of behaviours that can be produced. We also demonstrate that the reduction of the expressiveness resulting from the complete removal of jump instructions can be compensated for by means of interaction with Boolean registers.

This chapter is also concerned with some issues that arise from the investigation of expressiveness issues regarding SPISA. We show that, even in the case where the set of primitive instructions concerned is finite, a finite-state execution mechanism for a set of instruction sequences that by itself can produce each thread producible by a SPISA instruction sequence from an instruction sequence belonging to the set in question is unfeasible. We also show that in a variation on SPISA in which jump instructions are replaced by labels and goto instructions, but which is as expressive as SPISA, an upper bound on the number of labels reduces the expressiveness.

4.1 Basic Expressiveness Results

In this section, we provide the basic expressiveness results concerning SPISA. That is, we provide results about which threads can be produced by SPISA instruction sequences under execution, which primitive instructions of SPISA can be removed without reducing the class of threads that can be produced, and which primitive instructions of SPISA cannot be removed without reducing the class of threads that can be produced.

In this chapter, we assume that a model $\mathcal{M}$ of BTA+TSI+REC+AIP has been given.

Before we provide the basic expressiveness results concerning SPISA, we show that ISNR instruction sequences and ISNA instruction sequences can produce the same threads as SPISA instruction sequences.

Proposition 4.1.

(1) *For each thread t, there exists a closed* SPISA *term* $\mathbf{t}$ *such that the interpretation of* $|\mathbf{t}|$ *in* $\mathcal{M}$ *is t iff there exists an* ISNR *instruction sequence* $\mathbf{p}$ *such that the interpretation of* $|\mathbf{p}|_{\mathrm{ISNR}}$ *in* $\mathcal{M}$ *is t.*

(2) *For each thread t, there exists a closed* SPISA *term* $\mathbf{t}$ *such that the interpretation of* $|\mathbf{t}|$ *in* $\mathcal{M}$ *is t iff there exists an* ISNA *instruction sequence* $\mathbf{p}$ *such that the interpretation of* $|\mathbf{p}|_{\mathrm{ISNA}}$ *in* $\mathcal{M}$ *is t.*

Proof. For Property 1, by Lemma 2.2, it is sufficient to show that there exists a function `spisa2isnr` from the set of all closed SPISA terms in first canonical form to the set of all ISNR instruction sequences such that, for all closed SPISA terms t in first canonical form, $|\mathtt{isnr2spisa}(\mathtt{spisa2isnr}(t))| = |t|$. It is easy to see that a witnessing function is the one defined by

$$\begin{aligned}
&\mathtt{spisa2isnr}(u_1 \,;\ldots;\, u_n) &&= u_1 \,;\ldots;\, u_n\,,\\
&\mathtt{spisa2isnr}(u_1 \,;\ldots;\, u_k \,;\, (u_{k+1} \,;\ldots;\, u_{k+n})^{\omega}) &&= u_1 \,;\ldots;\, u_{k+n} \,;\, (\backslash\#n)^m\,,
\end{aligned}$$

where m is 2 if $u_1 \,;\ldots;\, u_{k+n}$ is jump-free and the maximum of 2 and the highest l such that $u_i \equiv \#l$ for some $i \in [1, k+n]$ otherwise.

Property 2 follows immediately from Property 1 and Proposition 2.3. □

The following proposition puts the expressiveness of SPISA in terms of producible threads.

Proposition 4.2. *For each thread t, there exists a closed* SPISA *term* $\boldsymbol{t}$ *such that the interpretation of* $|\boldsymbol{t}|$ *in* $\mathcal{M}$ *is* t *iff* t *is regular.*

Proof. The implication from left to right follows immediately from the axioms for the thread extraction operator (Table 2.6).

The implication from right to left is proved as follows. By Proposition 2.1, t is a component of the solution of some finite linear recursive specification $\boldsymbol{E}$ over BTA. There occur finitely many variables $\boldsymbol{x}_0, \ldots, \boldsymbol{x}_n$ in $\boldsymbol{E}$. Assume that t is the $\boldsymbol{x}_0$-component of the solution of $\boldsymbol{E}$. Let $\boldsymbol{p}$ be the ISNA instruction sequence $\boldsymbol{p}_0 \,;\ldots;\, \boldsymbol{p}_n$, where $\boldsymbol{p}_i$ is defined as follows ($0 \leq i \leq n$):

$$
\boldsymbol{p}_i = \begin{cases}
\mathsf{!t} \,;\, \mathsf{!t} \,;\, \mathsf{!t} & \text{if } \boldsymbol{x}_i = \mathsf{S+} \in \boldsymbol{E} \\
\mathsf{!f} \,;\, \mathsf{!f} \,;\, \mathsf{!f} & \text{if } \boldsymbol{x}_i = \mathsf{S-} \in \boldsymbol{E} \\
\mathsf{!} \,;\, \mathsf{!} \,;\, \mathsf{!} & \text{if } \boldsymbol{x}_i = \mathsf{S} \in \boldsymbol{E} \\
\#\#3{\cdot}i{+}1 \,;\, \#\#3{\cdot}i{+}1 \,;\, \#\#3{\cdot}i{+}1 & \text{if } \boldsymbol{x}_i = \mathsf{D} \in \boldsymbol{E} \\
+\boldsymbol{a} \,;\, \#\#3{\cdot}j{+}1 \,;\, \#\#3{\cdot}k{+}1 & \text{if } \boldsymbol{x}_i = \boldsymbol{x}_j \trianglelefteq \boldsymbol{a} \trianglerighteq \boldsymbol{x}_k \in \boldsymbol{E}\,.
\end{cases}
$$

Then $\mathtt{isna2spisa}(\boldsymbol{p})$ is a closed SPISA term such that the interpretation of $|\mathtt{isna2spisa}(\boldsymbol{p})|$ in $\mathcal{M}$ is t. □

The following proposition shows that the expressiveness of SPISA would not be reduced by removing plain basic instructions and negative test instructions.

Proposition 4.3. *For each closed* SPISA *term* $\boldsymbol{t}$*, there exists a closed* SPISA *term* $\boldsymbol{t}'$ *without occurrences of plain basic instructions and negative test instructions such that* $|\boldsymbol{t}| = |\boldsymbol{t}'|$.

Proof. This follows immediately from the proof of Proposition 4.2: the witnessing closed SPISA term is a term without occurrences of plain basic instructions and negative test instructions. □

The following proposition shows that the expressiveness of SPISA would not be reduced by increasing the lower bound of the reach of forward jump instructions.

Proposition 4.4. *For each $n > 0$, for each closed* SPISA *term* $\boldsymbol{t}$*, there exists a closed* SPISA *term* $\boldsymbol{t}'$ *without occurrences of jump instructions* $\#l$ *with* $l < n$ *such that* $|\boldsymbol{t}| = |\boldsymbol{t}'|$.

Proof. By Lemma 2.6, it is sufficient to consider only closed SPISA terms $\boldsymbol{t}$ that are of the form

$$
(\boldsymbol{u}_1 \,;\ldots;\, \boldsymbol{u}_k)^{\omega}\,.
$$

Let $i \in [1, k]$ be such that $\boldsymbol{u}_i$ is of the form $\#l$, and let $\boldsymbol{t}''$ be $\boldsymbol{t}$ with $\boldsymbol{u}_i$ replaced by $\#l{+}k$. Then it follows from SC3, together with SPISA1, SPISA4 and SC5, that $\boldsymbol{t} \cong_{\mathrm{s}} \boldsymbol{t}''$. By Proposition 2.2, $\boldsymbol{t} \cong_{\mathrm{s}} \boldsymbol{t}''$ implies $|\boldsymbol{t}| = |\boldsymbol{t}''|$. Hence, for each $j \in [1, k]$ for which $\boldsymbol{u}_j$ is of the form $\#l$ with $l < n$, $\boldsymbol{u}_j$ can be replaced by $\#l'$ with $l' \geq n$ where l' is obtained by adding k sufficiently many times to l. □

The following proposition shows that the expressiveness of SPISA would be reduced by making the reach of forward jump instructions bounded from above.

Proposition 4.5. *Assume that* $\mathrm{card}(\mathfrak{A}) > 0$. *Then, for each* $n > 0$, *there exists a closed* SPISA *term* $\boldsymbol{t}$ *for which there does not exist a closed* SPISA *term* $\boldsymbol{t}'$ *without occurrences of jump instructions* $\#l$ *with* $l > n$ *such that* $|\boldsymbol{t}| = |\boldsymbol{t}'|$.

Proof. Take an $n > 0$ and a basic instruction a. Let $\boldsymbol{t}$ be the closed SPISA term

$$\boldsymbol{t}_1 \,;\, \ldots \,;\, \boldsymbol{t}_{n+1} \,;\, ! \,;\, (\boldsymbol{t}'_1 \,;\, \ldots \,;\, \boldsymbol{t}'_{n+1})^\omega$$

with

$$\boldsymbol{t}_i = {+}\mathsf{a} \,;\, \#l_i \,, \qquad \boldsymbol{t}'_i = \mathsf{a}^i \,;\, {+}\mathsf{a} \,;\, ! \,;\, \#l'_i \,,$$

where l_i and l'_i are such that on execution of $\boldsymbol{t}$ the effect of $\#l_i$ and $\#l'_i$ is that execution proceeds with the first primitive instruction of $\boldsymbol{t}'_i$. Then $\boldsymbol{t}$ produces the x_1-component of the solution of the guarded recursive specification consisting of the following equations:

$$\begin{aligned} x_i &= y_i \trianglelefteq \mathsf{a} \trianglerighteq x_{i+1} && \text{for all } i \in [1, n+1] \,, \\ x_{n+2} &= \mathsf{S} \,, \\ y_i &= \mathsf{a}^i \circ (\mathsf{S} \trianglelefteq \mathsf{a} \trianglerighteq y_i) && \text{for all } i \in [1, n+1] \,. \end{aligned}$$

For every $i \in [1, n+1]$, let t_i be the y_i-component of the solution of this guarded recursive specification. Now suppose that there exists a closed SPISA term without occurrences of jump instructions $\#l$ with $l > n$ that produces the same thread as $\boldsymbol{t}$. Then, by Lemma 2.6, there exists such a term that is of the form

$$(\boldsymbol{u}_1 \,;\, \ldots \,;\, \boldsymbol{u}_k)^\omega \,.$$

Because $\mathit{Res}(t_i) \cap \mathit{Res}(t_j) = \{\mathsf{S}\}$ for each $i, j \in [1, n+1]$ with $i \neq j$, it is easy to see that each of the primitive instructions $\boldsymbol{u}_1, \ldots, \boldsymbol{u}_k$ can contribute to at most one of the threads $t_1, \ldots, t_{n+1}$. By the upper bound on the reach of jump instructions we know that, for each $i \in [1, n+1]$, there are at most $n-1$ other primitive instructions between two successive primitive instructions contributing to t_i. This means that, for each $i \in [1, n+1]$, $\boldsymbol{u}_1 ; \ldots ; \boldsymbol{u}_k$

contains at least $\lceil k/n \rceil$ primitive instructions contributing to t_i.[1] Hence, in total $u_1 ; \ldots ; u_k$ contains at least $(n+1) \cdot \lceil k/n \rceil$ primitive instructions. Because $(n+1) \cdot \lceil k/n \rceil > k$, this contradicts the fact that $u_1 ; \ldots ; u_k$ contains k primitive instructions. □

Proposition 4.5 does not go through under the implicit assumption that $\mathrm{card}(\mathfrak{A}) \geq 0$: in the case where $\mathrm{card}(\mathfrak{A}) = 0$, each closed SPISA term is behaviourally congruent to a closed SPISA term without occurrences of jump instructions.

4.2 Jump-Free Instruction Sequences

In this section, we show that each regular thread can be produced by some single-pass instruction sequence without jump instructions through interaction with Boolean registers.

In the proof of the theorem presented below, we associate a closed SPISA term $\boldsymbol{t}$ in which jump instructions do not occur with a finite linear recursive specification $\boldsymbol{E}$ of the form

$$\{\boldsymbol{x}_i = \boldsymbol{x}_{l(i)} \trianglelefteq \boldsymbol{a}_i \trianglerighteq \boldsymbol{x}_{r(i)} \mid i \in [1,n]\}$$
$$\cup \{\boldsymbol{x}_{n+1} = \mathsf{S+}, \boldsymbol{x}_{n+2} = \mathsf{S-}, \boldsymbol{x}_{n+3} = \mathsf{S}, \boldsymbol{x}_{n+4} = \mathsf{D}\} .$$

In $\boldsymbol{t}$, a number of Boolean registers is used for specific purposes. The purpose of each individual Boolean register is reflected in the focus that serves as its name:

- for each $i \in [1, n+4]$, $\mathtt{s}{:}i$ serves as the name of a Boolean register that is used to indicate whether the current state of $\langle \boldsymbol{x}_1 | \boldsymbol{E} \rangle$ is $\langle \boldsymbol{x}_i | \boldsymbol{E} \rangle$;
- `rt` serves as the name of a Boolean register that is used to indicate whether the reply upon the action performed by $\langle \boldsymbol{x}_1 | \boldsymbol{E} \rangle$ in its current state is t;
- `rf` serves as the name of a Boolean register that is used to indicate whether the reply upon the action performed by $\langle \boldsymbol{x}_1 | \boldsymbol{E} \rangle$ in its current state is f;
- `e` serves as the name of a Boolean register that is used to achieve that instructions not related to the current state of $\langle \boldsymbol{x}_1 | \boldsymbol{E} \rangle$ are passed correctly;
- `o` serves as the name of a Boolean register that is used to achieve with the instruction $+\mathtt{o.set}{:}\mathsf{f}$ that the following instruction is skipped.

Now we turn to the theorem announced above. It states rigorously that each component of the solution of each finite linear recursive specification can be produced by a single-pass instruction sequence without forward jump instructions through interaction with Boolean registers.

[1] As usual, we write $\lceil q \rceil$ for the smallest integer not less than q.

Theorem 4.1. *Let $\boldsymbol{E}$ be a finite linear recursive specification*

$$\{\boldsymbol{x}_i = \boldsymbol{x}_{l(i)} \trianglelefteq \boldsymbol{a}_i \trianglerighteq \boldsymbol{x}_{r(i)} \mid i \in [1, n]\} \\ \cup \{\boldsymbol{x}_{n+1} = \mathsf{S+}, \boldsymbol{x}_{n+2} = \mathsf{S-}, \boldsymbol{x}_{n+3} = \mathsf{S}, \boldsymbol{x}_{n+4} = \mathsf{D}\} .$$

Then there exists a closed SPISA *term* $\boldsymbol{t}$ *in which jump instructions do not occur such that*

$$|\boldsymbol{t}| /\!/ ((\bigoplus_{i=1}^{n+4} \mathtt{s}{:}i.BR(\mathsf{f})) \oplus \mathtt{rt}.BR(\mathsf{f}) \oplus \mathtt{rf}.BR(\mathsf{f}) \oplus \mathtt{e}.BR(\mathsf{f}) \oplus \mathtt{o}.BR(\mathsf{f})) \\ = \langle \boldsymbol{x}_1 | \boldsymbol{E} \rangle .$$[2]

Proof. We associate a closed SPISA term $\boldsymbol{t}$ in which jump instructions do not occur with $\boldsymbol{E}$ as follows:

$$\boldsymbol{t} = \mathtt{s{:}1.set{:}t} \,;\, (\boldsymbol{t}_1 \,;\, \ldots \,;\, \boldsymbol{t}_{n+3})^\omega ,$$

where, for each $i \in [1, n]$:

$$\begin{aligned} \boldsymbol{t}_i \quad = \ & +\mathtt{s}{:}i.\mathtt{get} \,;\, \mathtt{e.set{:}t} \,; \\ & +\mathtt{s}{:}i.\mathtt{get} \,;\, \mathtt{s}{:}i.\mathtt{set{:}f} \,; \\ & +\mathtt{e.get} \,;\, -\boldsymbol{a}_i \,;\, +\mathtt{o.set{:}f} \,;\, \mathtt{rt.set{:}t} \,; \\ & +\mathtt{e.get} \,;\, +\mathtt{rt.get} \,;\, +\mathtt{o.set{:}f} \,;\, \mathtt{rf.set{:}t} \,; \\ & +\mathtt{rt.get} \,;\, \mathtt{s}{:}l(i).\mathtt{set{:}t} \,; \\ & +\mathtt{rf.get} \,;\, \mathtt{s}{:}r(i).\mathtt{set{:}t} \,; \\ & \mathtt{rt.set{:}f} \,;\, \mathtt{rf.set{:}f} \,;\, \mathtt{e.set{:}f} , \end{aligned}$$

and

$$\begin{aligned} \boldsymbol{t}_{n+1} &= +\mathtt{s}{:}n{+}1.\mathtt{get} \,;\, !\mathsf{t} , \\ \boldsymbol{t}_{n+2} &= +\mathtt{s}{:}n{+}2.\mathtt{get} \,;\, !\mathsf{f} , \\ \boldsymbol{t}_{n+3} &= +\mathtt{s}{:}n{+}3.\mathtt{get} \,;\, ! . \end{aligned}$$

We use the following abbreviations (for $i \in [1, n+3]$ and $j \in [1, n+4]$):

$\boldsymbol{t}'_i$ for $\boldsymbol{t}_i \,;\, \ldots \,;\, \boldsymbol{t}_{n+3} \,;\, (\boldsymbol{t}_1 \,;\, \ldots \,;\, \boldsymbol{t}_{n+3})^\omega$;
$|\boldsymbol{t}'_i|^{\mathrm{br}}_j$ for $|\boldsymbol{t}'_i| /\!/ ((\bigoplus_{i=1}^{n+4} \mathtt{s}{:}i.BR(b_i)) \oplus \mathtt{rt}.BR(\mathsf{f}) \oplus \mathtt{rf}.BR(\mathsf{f}) \oplus \mathtt{e}.BR(\mathsf{f}) \oplus \mathtt{o}.BR(\mathsf{f}))$,
where $b_j = \mathsf{t}$ and, for each $j' \in [1, n+4]$ such that $j' \neq j$, $b_{j'} = \mathsf{f}$.

From axioms TE2 and AU7, and the definition of the Boolean register functional unit BR, it follows that

$$|\boldsymbol{t}| /\!/ ((\bigoplus_{i=1}^{n+4} \mathtt{s}{:}i.BR(\mathsf{f})) \oplus \mathtt{rt}.BR(\mathsf{f}) \oplus \mathtt{rf}.BR(\mathsf{f}) \oplus \mathtt{e}.BR(\mathsf{f}) \oplus \mathtt{o}.BR(\mathsf{f})) \\ = |\boldsymbol{t}'_1|^{\mathrm{br}}_1 .$$

[2]The Boolean register functional unit BR has been defined in Sect. 3.2.2.

This leaves us to show that $\langle \boldsymbol{x}_1 | \boldsymbol{E} \rangle = |\boldsymbol{t}'_1|_1^{\mathrm{br}}$.

Using axioms P1, P5, TE2, TE4, TE6, TE13, TE15, TE17, AU1–AU4, AU7, AU8 and AU10, and the definition of the Boolean register functional unit, we easily prove the following:

1. $|\boldsymbol{t}'_i|_j^{\mathrm{br}} = |\boldsymbol{t}'_{i+1}|_j^{\mathrm{br}}$ if $1 \leq i \leq n+2 \wedge 1 \leq j \leq n+3 \wedge i \neq j$
2. $|\boldsymbol{t}'_i|_j^{\mathrm{br}} = |\boldsymbol{t}'_1|_j^{\mathrm{br}}$ if $i = n+3 \wedge 1 \leq j \leq n+3 \wedge i \neq j$
3. $|\boldsymbol{t}'_i|_i^{\mathrm{br}} = |\boldsymbol{t}'_{i+1}|_{l(i)}^{\mathrm{br}} \trianglelefteq \boldsymbol{a}_i \trianglerighteq |\boldsymbol{t}'_{i+1}|_{r(i)}^{\mathrm{br}}$ if $1 \leq i \leq n$
4. $|\boldsymbol{t}'_i|_i^{\mathrm{br}} = \mathsf{S+}$ if $i = n+1$
5. $|\boldsymbol{t}'_i|_i^{\mathrm{br}} = \mathsf{S-}$ if $i = n+2$
6. $|\boldsymbol{t}'_i|_i^{\mathrm{br}} = \mathsf{S}$ if $i = n+3$
7. $|\boldsymbol{t}'_i|_j^{\mathrm{br}} = \mathsf{D}$ if $1 \leq i \leq n+3 \wedge j = n+4$

From Properties 1 and 2, it follows that

$$|\boldsymbol{t}'_i|_j^{\mathrm{br}} = |\boldsymbol{t}'_j|_j^{\mathrm{br}} \text{ if } 1 \leq i \leq n+3 \wedge 1 \leq j \leq n+3 \wedge i \neq j\,.$$

From this and Property 3, it follows that

$$|\boldsymbol{t}'_i|_i^{\mathrm{br}} = |\boldsymbol{t}'_{l(i)}|_{l(i)}^{\mathrm{br}} \trianglelefteq \boldsymbol{a}_i \trianglerighteq |\boldsymbol{t}'_{r(i)}|_{r(i)}^{\mathrm{br}} \text{ if } 1 \leq i \leq n\,.$$

From this and Properties 4–7, it follows that $|\boldsymbol{t}'_1|_1^{\mathrm{br}}$ is the $\boldsymbol{x}_1$-component of a solution of $\boldsymbol{E}$. Because linear recursive specifications have unique solutions, it follows that $\langle \boldsymbol{x}_1 | \boldsymbol{E} \rangle = |\boldsymbol{t}'_1|_1^{\mathrm{br}}$. □

Theorem 4.1 goes through in the cases where $\boldsymbol{E} = \{\boldsymbol{x}_1 = \mathsf{S+}\}$, $\boldsymbol{E} = \{\boldsymbol{x}_1 = \mathsf{S-}\}$, $\boldsymbol{E} = \{\boldsymbol{x}_1 = \mathsf{S}\}$ and $\boldsymbol{E} = \{\boldsymbol{x}_1 = \mathsf{D}\}$. The first three cases are trivial. In the last case, a witnessing SPISA term $\boldsymbol{t}$ is $\mathtt{o.get}^{\omega}$. It follows from the proof of Proposition 2.1 that, for each regular thread t, either there exists a finite linear recursive specification $\boldsymbol{E}$ of the form considered in Theorem 4.1 such that t is the $\boldsymbol{x}_1$-component of the solution of $\boldsymbol{E}$ or t is the $\boldsymbol{x}_1$-component of the solution of $\{\boldsymbol{x}_1 = \mathsf{S+}\}$, $\{\boldsymbol{x}_1 = \mathsf{S-}\}$, $\{\boldsymbol{x}_1 = \mathsf{S}\}$ or $\{\boldsymbol{x}_1 = \mathsf{D}\}$. Hence, we have the following corollary of Proposition 2.1 and Theorem 4.1:

Corollary 4.1. *For each regular thread t, there exists a closed* SPISA *term* $\boldsymbol{t}$ *in which jump instructions do not occur such that t is the thread denoted by*

$$|\boldsymbol{t}| \mathbin{/\!/} \left(\left(\textstyle\bigoplus_{i=1}^{n+4} \mathtt{s}{:}i.BR(\mathsf{f})\right) \oplus \mathtt{rt}.BR(\mathsf{f}) \oplus \mathtt{rf}.BR(\mathsf{f}) \oplus \mathtt{e}.BR(\mathsf{f}) \oplus \mathtt{o}.BR(\mathsf{f})\right)\,.$$

In other words, each regular thread can be produced by an instruction sequence without jump instructions through interaction with Boolean registers.

Remark 4.1. The construction of such instructions sequences given in the proof of Theorem 4.1 is weakly reminiscent of the construction of structured programs from flow charts found in [Cooper (1967)]. However, our construction is more extreme: it yields instruction sequences that contain neither unstructured jumps nor a rendering of the conditional and loop constructs used in structured programming.

4.3 Gotos and a Bounded Number of Labels

In this section, we introduce $\mathrm{SPISA_g}$, a variation on SPISA in which jump instructions are replaced by labels and goto instructions, which does not reduce the expressiveness, and show that an upper bound on the number of labels reduces the expressiveness.

4.3.1 *Labels and gotos*

In $\mathrm{SPISA_g}$, like in SPISA, it is assumed that a fixed but arbitrary set $\mathfrak{A}$ of basic instructions has been given. $\mathrm{SPISA_g}$ has the primitive instructions of SPISA except the forward jump instructions and in addition:

- for each $l \in \mathbb{N}$, a *label instruction* $[l]$;
- for each $l \in \mathbb{N}$, a *goto instruction* $\#[l]$.

We write $\mathfrak{I}_\mathrm{g}$ for the set of all primitive instructions of $\mathrm{SPISA_g}$.

On execution of a $\mathrm{SPISA_g}$ instruction sequence, the effects of the plain basic instructions, the positive test instructions, the negative test instructions, and the terminations instructions are as in SPISA. The effects of the label and goto instructions are as follows:

- the effect of a label instruction $[l]$ is simply that execution proceeds with the next primitive instruction — if there is no primitive instruction to proceed with, inaction occurs;
- the effect of a goto instruction $\#[l]$ is that execution proceeds with the occurrence of the label instruction $[l]$ next following — if there is no occurrence of the label instruction $[l]$ to proceed with, inaction occurs.

$\mathrm{SPISA_g}$ has a constant $\boldsymbol{u}$ for each $\boldsymbol{u} \in \mathfrak{I}_\mathrm{g}$. $\mathrm{SPISA_g}$ has the same operators as SPISA. Likewise, $\mathrm{SPISA_g}$ has the same axioms as SPISA.

Some simple examples of closed $\mathrm{SPISA_g}$ terms are

$$+\mathtt{a} \,;\, \#[0] \,;\, \#[1] \,;\, [0] \,;\, \mathtt{b} \,;\, ! \;, \qquad ([0] \,;\, -\mathtt{a} \,;\, \#[0] \,;\, !)^{\omega} \;.$$

On execution of the instruction sequence denoted by the first term, the basic instruction a is executed first, if the execution of a produces the reply t, the basic instruction b is executed next and after that execution terminates, and if the execution of a produces the reply f, inaction occurs. On execution of the instruction sequence denoted by the second term, the basic instruction a is executed repeatedly until its execution produces the reply t and after that execution terminates.

Just like in the case of SPISA, all closed SPISA_g terms have first canonical forms. We assume that a fixed but arbitrary function *rewr* has been given that assigns to each closed SPISA_g term one of its first canonical forms.

Just like in the case of SPISA, the behaviours produced by instruction sequences denoted by closed SPISA_g terms are represented by threads. The behaviours produced by instruction sequences denoted by closed SPISA_g terms are indirectly given by the behaviour preserving function spisag2spisa from the set of all closed SPISA_g terms to the set of all closed SPISA terms defined by

$$\mathtt{spisag2spisa}(t) = \mathtt{spisagfcf2spisa}(\mathit{rewr}(t)) ,$$

where the function spisagfcf2spisa from the set of all closed SPISA_g terms in first canonical form to the set of all closed SPISA terms is defined by

$$\mathtt{spisagfcf2spisa}(u_1 ; \ldots ; u_n) = \mathtt{spisagfcf2spisa}(u_1 ; \ldots ; u_n ; (\#[0])^\omega) ,$$

$$\begin{aligned}&\mathtt{spisagfcf2spisa}(u_1 ; \ldots ; u_n ; (u_{n+1} ; \ldots ; u_m)^\omega)\\ &\quad = \varphi_1(u_1) ; \ldots ; \varphi_n(u_n) ; (\varphi_{n+1}(u_{n+1}) ; \ldots ; \varphi_m(u_m))^\omega ,\end{aligned}$$

and the auxiliary functions φ_j from the set of all primitive instructions of SPISA_g to the set of all primitive instructions of SPISA are defined as follows ($1 \leq j \leq m$):

$$\begin{aligned}\varphi_j([l]) &= \#1 ,\\ \varphi_j(\#[l]) &= \#\mathit{tgt}_j(l) ,\\ \varphi_j(u) &= u \qquad \text{if } u \text{ is not a label or goto instruction} ,\end{aligned}$$

where

- $\mathit{tgt}_j(l) = i$ if the label instruction $[l]$ occurs in the instruction sequence denoted by $u_j ; \ldots ; u_m ; u_{n+1} ; \ldots ; u_m$ and i is the position of the leftmost occurrence of $[l]$;
- $\mathit{tgt}_j(l) = 0$ if the label instruction $[l]$ does not occur in the instruction sequence denoted by $u_j ; \ldots ; u_m ; u_{n+1} ; \ldots ; u_m$.

For example, the behaviour produced by the instruction sequence denoted by the closed $\mathrm{SPISA_g}$ term

$$(\mathtt{a} \,;\, [0] \,;\, +\mathtt{b} \,;\, \#[1] \,;\, \#[2] \,;\, [1] \,;\, \mathtt{c} \,;\, \#[0] \,;\, [2] \,;\, \mathtt{d} \,;\, \#[0])^{\omega}$$

is the same as the behaviour produced by the instruction sequence denoted by the closed SPISA term

$$(\mathtt{a} \,;\, \#1 \,;\, +\mathtt{b} \,;\, \#2 \,;\, \#4 \,;\, \#1 \,;\, \mathtt{c} \,;\, \#5 \,;\, \#1 \,;\, \mathtt{d} \,;\, \#2)^{\omega}$$

Let t be a closed $\mathrm{SPISA_g}$ term. Then the behaviour of t under execution is $|\mathtt{spisag2spisa}(t)|$.

For example, the instruction sequence denoted by the closed $\mathrm{SPISA_g}$ term displayed above produces the x-component of the solution of the guarded recursive specification consisting of the following two equations:

$$x = \mathtt{a} \circ y \,, \qquad y = (\mathtt{c} \circ y) \trianglelefteq \mathtt{b} \trianglerighteq (\mathtt{d} \circ y) \,.$$

4.3.2 *A bounded number of labels*

In this section, we show that an upper bound on the number of labels restricts the expressiveness of $\mathrm{SPISA_g}$. Let $k > 0$. Then we will refer to $\mathrm{SPISA_g}$ terms without occurrences of label instructions $[l]$ with $l \geq k$ as $\mathrm{SPISA_g^k}$ terms, and to the primitive instructions from which the $\mathrm{SPISA_g^k}$ terms are generated as the primitive instructions of $\mathrm{SPISA_g^k}$.

We define an alternative projection for closed $\mathrm{SPISA_g^k}$ terms, which takes into account that these terms contain only label instructions $[l]$ with $l < k$. The alternative projection $\mathtt{spisag2spisa}^k$ from the set of all closed $\mathrm{SPISA_g^k}$ terms to the set of all closed SPISA terms is defined by

$$\mathtt{spisag2spisa}^k(t) = \mathtt{spisagfcf2spisa}^k(\mathit{rewr}(t)) \,,$$

where the function $\mathtt{spisagfcf2spisa}^k$ from the set of all closed $\mathrm{SPISA_g}$ terms in first canonical form to the set of all closed SPISA terms is defined by

$$\begin{aligned}
&\mathtt{spisagfcf2spisa}^k(u_1 \,;\, \ldots \,;\, u_n) \\
&\quad = \mathtt{spisagfcf2spisa}^k(u_1 \,;\, \ldots \,;\, u_n \,;\, (\#[0])^{\omega}) \,, \\
&\mathtt{spisagfcf2spisa}^k(u_1 \,;\, \ldots \,;\, u_n \,;\, (u_{n+1} \,;\, \ldots \,;\, u_m)^{\omega}) \\
&\quad = \psi(u_1, u_2) \,;\, \ldots \,;\, \psi(u_n, u_{n+1}) \,; \\
&\qquad (\psi(u_{n+1}, u_{n+2}) \,;\, \ldots \,;\, \psi(u_{m-1}, u_m) \,;\, \psi(u_m, u_{n+1}))^{\omega} \,,
\end{aligned}$$

where the auxiliary function ψ from the set of all pairs of primitive instructions of SPISA_g^k to the set of all closed SPISA terms is defined as follows:

$$\psi(\boldsymbol{u}', \boldsymbol{u}'') = \psi'(\boldsymbol{u}') \,;\, \#k{+}2 \,;\, \#k{+}2 \,;\, \psi''(\boldsymbol{u}'') \;,$$

where the auxiliary function ψ' from the set of all primitive instructions of SPISA_g^k to the set of all primitive instructions of SPISA is defined as follows:

$$\begin{aligned}
\psi'([l]) &= \#1 \;, \\
\psi'(\#[l]) &= \#l{+}3 \quad \text{if } l < k \;, \\
\psi'(\#[l]) &= \#0 \qquad \text{if } l \geq k \;, \\
\psi'(\boldsymbol{u}) &= \boldsymbol{u} \qquad \text{if } \boldsymbol{u} \text{ is not a label or goto instruction}
\end{aligned}$$

and the auxiliary function ψ'' from the set of all primitive instructions of SPISA_g^k to the set of all closed SPISA terms is defined as follows:

$$\begin{aligned}
\psi''([l]) &= (\#k{+}3)^l \,;\, \#k{-}l \,;\, (\#k{+}3)^{k-l-1} \;, \\
\psi''(\boldsymbol{u}) &= (\#k{+}3)^k \quad \text{if } \boldsymbol{u} \text{ is not a label instruction} \;.
\end{aligned}$$

In order to clarify the alternative projection, we explain how the intended effect of a goto instruction is obtained. If $\boldsymbol{u}_j$ is $\#[l]$, then $\psi'(\boldsymbol{u}_j)$ is $\#l{+}3$. The effect of $\#l{+}3$ is a jump to the $(l{+}1)$st instruction in $\psi''(\boldsymbol{u}_{j+1})$ if $j < m$ and a jump to the $(l{+}1)$st instruction in $\psi''(\boldsymbol{u}_{n+1})$ if $j = m$. If this instruction is $\#k{-}l$, then its effect is a jump to the occurrence of $\#1$ that replaces $[l]$. However, if this instruction is $\#k{+}3$, then its effect is a jump to the $(l{+}1)$st instruction in $\psi''(\boldsymbol{u}_{j+2})$ if $j < m - 1$, a jump to the $(l{+}1)$st instruction in $\psi''(\boldsymbol{u}_{n+1})$ if $j = m - 1$, and a jump to the $(l{+}1)$st instruction in $\psi''(\boldsymbol{u}_{n+2})$ if $j = m$.

In the proof of Theorem 4.2 below, chained jumps are changed into single jumps. The following lemma justifies these removals.

Lemma 4.1. *For each* SPISA *term* $\boldsymbol{t}$ *and variable* $\boldsymbol{X}$*:*

$$\begin{aligned}
|\boldsymbol{t}\,[\#n{+}1 \,;\, \boldsymbol{u}_1 \,;\, \ldots \,;\, \boldsymbol{u}_n \,;\, \#0/\boldsymbol{X}]\,| &= |\boldsymbol{t}\,[\#0 \,;\, \boldsymbol{u}_1 \,;\, \ldots \,;\, \boldsymbol{u}_n \,;\, \#0/\boldsymbol{X}]\,| \;, \\
|\boldsymbol{t}\,[\#n{+}1 \,;\, \boldsymbol{u}_1 \,;\, \ldots \,;\, \boldsymbol{u}_n \,;\, \#l/\boldsymbol{X}]\,| &= |\boldsymbol{t}\,[\#l{+}n{+}1 \,;\, \boldsymbol{u}_1 \,;\, \ldots \,;\, \boldsymbol{u}_n \,;\, \#l/\boldsymbol{X}]\,| \;.
\end{aligned}$$

Proof. This follows immediately from axioms SC1, SC2 and SC9, and Proposition 2.2. □

The following theorem states that the projections spisag2spisa and $\texttt{spisag2spisa}^k$ give rise to instruction sequences with the same behaviour.

Theorem 4.2. *For each* $k > 0$, *for each closed* SPISA_g^k *term* $\boldsymbol{t}$, $|\texttt{spisag2spisa}(\boldsymbol{t})| = |\texttt{spisag2spisa}^k(\boldsymbol{t})|$.

Proof. By the definitions of spisag2spisa and spisag2spisa^k, it is sufficient to consider only the case where t is of the form $u_1 ; \ldots ; u_n ; (u_{n+1} ; \ldots ; u_m)^\omega$.

We make use of the following auxiliary notation: we write

$$\begin{array}{ll} |i, u_1 ; \ldots ; u_n ; (u_{n+1} ; \ldots ; u_m)^\omega| & \\ \quad \text{for } |u_i ; \ldots ; u_m ; (u_{n+1} ; \ldots ; u_m)^\omega| & \text{if } 1 \leq i \leq m , \\ \quad \text{for } \mathsf{D} & \text{if } i = 0 \vee i > m . \end{array}$$

Let $t = u_1 ; \ldots ; u_n ; (u_{n+1} ; \ldots ; u_m)^\omega$ be a closed SPISA$_\mathrm{g}^k$ term, let $t' =$ spisag2spisa(t), and let $t'' =$ spisag2spisa^k(t). Moreover, let $\rho{:}\mathbb{N} \to \mathbb{N}$ be such that $\rho(i) = (k+3) \cdot (i-1) + 1$. Then it follows easily from the definitions of spisag2spisa and spisag2spisa^k, the axioms of SPISA, the axioms for the thread extraction operator, and Lemma 4.1 that for $1 \leq i \leq m$:

$$\begin{array}{ll}
|i, t'| = a \circ |i+1, t'| & \text{if } u_i = a , \\
|i, t'| = |i+1, t'| \trianglelefteq a \trianglerighteq |i+2, t'| & \text{if } u_i = +a , \\
|i, t'| = |i+2, t'| \trianglelefteq a \trianglerighteq |i+1, t'| & \text{if } u_i = -a , \\
|i, t'| = |i+1, t'| & \text{if } u_i = [l] , \\
|i, t'| = |i+n, t'| & \text{if } u_i = \#[l] \wedge tgt_i(l) = n , \\
|i, t'| = \mathsf{S+} & \text{if } u_i = \mathsf{!t} , \\
|i, t'| = \mathsf{S-} & \text{if } u_i = \mathsf{!f} , \\
|i, t'| = \mathsf{S} & \text{if } u_i = \mathsf{!}
\end{array}$$

and

$$\begin{array}{ll}
|\rho(i), t''| = a \circ |\rho(i+1), t''| & \text{if } u_i = a , \\
|\rho(i), t''| = |\rho(i+1), t''| \trianglelefteq a \trianglerighteq |\rho(i+2), t''| & \text{if } u_i = +a , \\
|\rho(i), t''| = |\rho(i+2), t''| \trianglelefteq a \trianglerighteq |\rho(i+1), t''| & \text{if } u_i = -a , \\
|\rho(i), t''| = |\rho(i+1), t''| & \text{if } u_i = [l] , \\
|\rho(i), t''| = |\rho(i+n), t''| & \text{if } u_i = \#[l] \wedge tgt_i(l) = n , \\
|\rho(i), t''| = \mathsf{S+} & \text{if } u_i = \mathsf{!t} , \\
|\rho(i), t''| = \mathsf{S-} & \text{if } u_i = \mathsf{!f} , \\
|\rho(i), t''| = \mathsf{S} & \text{if } u_i = \mathsf{!} ,
\end{array}$$

where tgt_i is defined as before in the definition of spisag2spisa. Because we have that |spisag2spisa(t)| $= |1, t'|$ and |spisag2spisa^k(t)| $= |\rho(1), t''|$, this means that |spisag2spisa(t)| and |spisag2spisa^k(t)| denote solutions of the same guarded recursive specification over BTA. Because guarded recursive specifications over BTA have unique solutions, it follows that |spisag2spisa(t)| $=$ |spisag2spisa^k(t)|. □

The projection $\texttt{spisag2spisa}^k(t)$ yields only closed SPISA terms that do not contain jump instructions $\#l$ with $l > k + 3$. Hence, we have the following corollary of Theorem 4.2:

Corollary 4.2. *For each closed* SPISA_g^k *term* t*, there exists a closed* SPISA *term* t' *not containing jump instructions* $\#l$ *with* $l > k + 3$ *such that* $|\texttt{spisag2spisa}(t)| = |t'|$.

It follows from Corollary 4.2 that, if a regular thread cannot be denoted by a closed SPISA term without occurrences of jump instructions $\#l$ with $l > k + 3$, it cannot be denoted by a closed SPISA_g^k term. Moreover, by Proposition 4.5, for each $k \in \mathbb{N}$, there exists a closed SPISA term for which there does not exist a closed SPISA term without occurrences of jump instructions $\#l$ with $l > k + 3$ that denotes the same thread. Hence, we also have the following corollary:

Corollary 4.3. *For each* $k > 0$*, there exists a closed* SPISA *term* t *for which there does not exist a closed* SPISA_g^k *term* t' *such that* $|t| = |\texttt{spisag2spisa}(t')|$.

4.4 The Jump-Shift Instruction and Finiteness Issues

In this section, we introduce SPISA_js, the extension of SPISA with a jump-shift instruction, and show that the set of all closed SPISA_js terms that do not contain forward jump instructions $\#l$ with $l > 0$ are as expressive as the set of all closed SPISA terms. We also introduce an alternative thread extraction operator for this restricted set of closed SPISA_js terms, that fits in better with the idea of single-pass execution of instruction sequences, and show that the threads yielded by the alternative thread extraction become the threads yielded by the original thread extraction through interaction with an unbounded counter. To get perspective on this result, we introduce the notion of an execution mechanism and show that there does not exist a finite-state execution mechanism that by itself, therefore without interaction with an unbounded counter, can produce each regular thread from an instruction sequence that is a finite or eventually periodic infinite sequence of instructions from a finite set.

4.4.1 *The jump-shift instruction*

We extend SPISA with the jump-shift instruction, resulting in SPISA_js. The merit of the jump-shift instruction is that the expressiveness of SPISA_js is not reduced if the reach of jump instructions is bounded from above.

Table 4.1 Axioms for the jump-shift instruction

$\#' ; \#l = \#l{+}1$	JSI1
$\#' ; u = u$	JSI2
$\#'^{\omega} = (\#0)^{\omega}$	JSI3

In SPISA$_{\mathrm{js}}$, like in SPISA, it is assumed that a fixed but arbitrary set $\mathfrak{A}$ of basic instructions has been given. SPISA$_{\mathrm{js}}$ has the primitive instructions of SPISA and in addition:

- a *jump-shift instruction* $\#'$.

We write $\mathfrak{I}_{\mathrm{js}}$ for the set of all primitive instructions of SPISA$_{\mathrm{js}}$. Moreover, we write $\mathfrak{I}_{\mathrm{jmp}}$ for the set of all forward jump instructions.

On execution of an instruction sequence, the effect of one or more jump-shift instructions preceding a jump instruction is that each of those jump-shift instructions increases the position to jump to by one. One or more jump-shift instructions preceding an instruction different from a jump instruction, do not have an effect.

SPISA$_{\mathrm{js}}$ has a constant u for each $u \in \mathfrak{I}_{\mathrm{js}}$. SPISA$_{\mathrm{js}}$ has the same operators as SPISA. SPISA$_{\mathrm{js}}$ has the axioms of SPISA and in addition the axioms for the jump-shift instruction given in Table 4.1. In this table, u stands for an arbitrary primitive instruction from $\mathfrak{I} \setminus \mathfrak{I}_{\mathrm{jmp}}$.

Some simple examples of closed SPISA$_{\mathrm{js}}$ terms are

$$\#' ; \mathtt{a} ; \mathtt{b} ; \mathtt{c} \,, \qquad +\mathtt{a} ; \#' ; \#' ; \#0 ; \#0 ; \mathtt{b} ; ! \,, \qquad (-\mathtt{a} ; \#' ; \#' ; \#0 ; !)^{\omega} \,.$$

On execution of the instruction sequence denoted by the first term, the basic instructions a, b and c are executed in that order and after that inaction occurs. On execution of the instruction sequence denoted by the second term, the basic instruction a is executed first, if the execution of a produces the reply t, the basic instruction b is executed next and after that execution terminates, and if the execution of a produces the reply f, inaction occurs. On execution of the instruction sequence denoted by the third term, the basic instruction a is executed repeatedly until its execution produces the reply t and after that execution terminates. The last two examples show that the jump-shift instruction could lead to some confusion with regard to the effects of test instructions.

In the case of SPISA$_{\mathrm{js}}$, the axioms for the structural congruence predicate are the axioms SC1–SC9 (Table 2.2), on the understanding that $u_1, \ldots, u_n, v_1, \ldots, v_{n'+1}$ still

Table 4.2 Additional axiom for the thread extraction operator

$\lvert x\rvert = \lvert x \,;\, \#0\rvert$	TE19

stand for arbitrary primitive instructions from $\mathfrak{J}$. We write SPISA_{js}+SC for SPISA_{js} extended with the predicate $\cong_{\text{s}}$, and the axioms SC1–SC9.

In the case of SPISA_{js}, the axioms for the thread extraction operator are the axioms TE1–TE18 (Table 2.6), on the understanding that u still stands for an arbitrary primitive instruction from $\mathfrak{J}$, and in addition the axiom given in Table 4.2.

The additional axiom $\lvert x\rvert = \lvert x \,;\, \#0\rvert$ expresses that a missing termination instruction leads to inaction. For all closed SPISA terms t, the equation $\lvert t\rvert = \lvert t \,;\, \#0\rvert$ is derivable from the axioms of SPISA and axioms TE1–TE18. For all closed SPISA_{js} terms t, the equation $\lvert \#l{+}2 \,;\, \#' \,;\, t\rvert = \lvert \#l{+}2 \,;\, t\rvert$ is derivable from the axioms of SPISA_{js} and axioms TE1–TE19.

Below, we consider closed SPISA_{js} terms that contain no other jump instruction than $\#0$. We will refer to SPISA_{js} terms without occurrences of jump instructions $\#l$ with $l > 0$ as $\text{SPISA}^0_{\text{js}}$ terms.

An interesting point of the set of all closed $\text{SPISA}^0_{\text{js}}$ terms is that the set of primitive instructions from which it is generated is finite if the set $\mathfrak{A}$ of basic instructions is finite. The set of primitive instructions from which the set of all closed SPISA terms is generated is infinite, even if the set $\mathfrak{A}$ of basic instructions is finite. It happens that all threads that are expressible by SPISA terms are also expressible by $\text{SPISA}^0_{\text{js}}$ terms.

Proposition 4.6. *For each closed* SPISA *term* t*, there exists a closed* $\text{SPISA}^0_{\text{js}}$ *term* t' *such that* $\lvert t\rvert = \lvert t'\rvert$.

Proof. Let t be a closed SPISA term, and let t' be t with, for all $l > 0$, all occurrences of $\#l$ in t replaced by $\#'^{l} \,;\, \#0$. Clearly, t' is a closed $\text{SPISA}^0_{\text{js}}$ term. It is easily proved by induction on l that, for each $l > 0$, the equation $\#l = \#'^{l} \,;\, \#0$ is derivable from the axioms of SPISA_{js}. From this it follows immediately that the equation $t = t'$ is derivable from the axioms of SPISA_{js}. Consequently, $\lvert t\rvert = \lvert t'\rvert$. □

For example,

$$\lvert {+}\mathtt{a} \,;\, \#2 \,;\, \#3 \,;\, \mathtt{b} \,;\, !\mathtt{t}\rvert = \lvert {+}\mathtt{a} \,;\, \#' \,;\, \#' \,;\, \#0 \,;\, \#' \,;\, \#' \,;\, \#' \,;\, \#0 \,;\, \mathtt{b} \,;\, !\mathtt{t}\rvert$$

We have the following corollary of Propositions 4.2 and 4.6.

Corollary 4.4. *For each regular thread t, there exists a closed* $\mathrm{SPISA}^0_{\mathrm{js}}$ *term* t *such that the interpretation of* $|t|$ *in* $\mathcal{M}$ *is t.*

This means that each finite-state thread can be produced by a finite or eventually periodic infinite sequence of instructions from a finite set if the set $\mathcal{A}$ of basic actions is finite.

Notice that, by the way the jump-shift instruction is handled, the thread extraction operator for $\mathrm{SPISA}_{\mathrm{js}}$ is not in accordance with the idea of single pass execution of instruction sequences.

4.4.2 *An alternative thread extraction operator*

We introduce an alternative thread extraction operator for $\mathrm{SPISA}^0_{\mathrm{js}}$, which is in accordance with the idea of single pass execution of instruction sequences, and show that the threads extracted in the alternative way become the threads extracted in the original way through interaction with an unbounded counter.

In $\mathrm{SPISA}_{\mathrm{js}}$, it is assumed that a fixed but arbitrary set $\mathfrak{A}$ of basic instructions has been given. In the case of the alternative thread extraction operator, the following additional assumptions relating to $\mathfrak{A}$ are made:

- a fixed but arbitrary set $\mathcal{F}$ of foci with $\mathtt{nnc} \in \mathcal{F}$ has been given;
- a fixed but arbitrary set $\mathcal{M}$ of methods with $\mathcal{I}(NNC) \subseteq \mathcal{M}$ has been given;
- $\mathfrak{A} = \{f.m \mid f \in \mathcal{F} \setminus \{\mathtt{nnc}\} \wedge m \in \mathcal{M}\}$.

Thereby no real restriction is imposed on the set $\mathfrak{A}$: in the case where the cardinality of $\mathcal{F}$ equals 2, all basic instructions have the same focus and the set $\mathcal{M}$ of methods can be looked upon as the set $\mathfrak{A}$ of basic instructions.

The axioms for the alternative thread extraction operator $|\_|'$ are given in Table 4.3. In this table, a stands for an arbitrary basic instruction from $\mathfrak{A}$ and u stands for an arbitrary primitive instruction from $\mathfrak{I} \setminus \mathfrak{I}_{\mathrm{jmp}}$. The auxiliary operator $|\_|'_{\mathrm{skp}}$ is used to deal with the skipping induced by test and jump instructions.

In this case, the thread extracted from an instruction sequence is not the behaviour of the instruction sequence under execution. That behaviour arises from interaction of the extracted thread with an unbounded counter.

Table 4.3 Axioms for the alternative thread extraction operator

$\lvert X \rvert' = \lvert X \,;\, \#0 \rvert'$	ATE1
$\lvert a \,;\, X \rvert' = \mathtt{nnc.setzero} \circ (a \circ \lvert X \rvert')$	ATE2
$\lvert +a \,;\, X \rvert' = \mathtt{nnc.setzero} \circ (\lvert X \rvert' \unlhd a \unrhd (\mathtt{nnc.succ}^2 \circ \lvert X \rvert'_{\mathrm{skp}}))$	ATE3
$\lvert -a \,;\, X \rvert' = \mathtt{nnc.setzero} \circ ((\mathtt{nnc.succ}^2 \circ \lvert X \rvert'_{\mathrm{skp}}) \unlhd a \unrhd \lvert X \rvert')$	ATE4
$\lvert \#' \,;\, X \rvert' = \mathtt{nnc.succ} \circ \lvert X \rvert'$	ATE5
$\lvert \#0 \,;\, X \rvert' = \mathsf{D} \unlhd \mathtt{nnc.iszero} \unrhd \lvert X \rvert'_{\mathrm{skp}}$	ATE6
$\lvert !\mathsf{t} \,;\, X \rvert' = \mathsf{S}+$	ATE7
$\lvert !\mathsf{f} \,;\, X \rvert' = \mathsf{S}-$	ATE8
$\lvert ! \,;\, X \rvert' = \mathsf{S}$	ATE9
$\lvert \#' \,;\, X \rvert'_{\mathrm{skp}} = \lvert X \rvert'_{\mathrm{skp}}$	ATES1
$\lvert \#0 \,;\, X \rvert'_{\mathrm{skp}} = \mathtt{nnc.pred} \circ (\mathsf{D} \unlhd \mathtt{nnc.iszero} \unrhd \lvert X \rvert'_{\mathrm{skp}})$	ATES2
$\lvert u \,;\, X \rvert'_{\mathrm{skp}} = \mathtt{nnc.pred} \circ (\lvert u \,;\, X \rvert' \unlhd \mathtt{nnc.iszero} \unrhd \lvert X \rvert'_{\mathrm{skp}})$	ATES3

For example,

$$\begin{aligned}&\lvert +\mathsf{a} \,;\, \#' \,;\, \#' \,;\, \#0 \,;\, !\mathsf{f} \,;\, !\mathsf{t} \rvert' = \\ &\quad \mathtt{nnc.setzero} \circ \big((\mathtt{nnc.succ}^2 \circ t) \unlhd \mathsf{a} \unrhd (\mathtt{nnc.succ}^2 \circ (\mathtt{nnc.pred} \circ t))\big)\;,\end{aligned}$$

where t is the following closed BTA term:

$$\begin{aligned}&\mathsf{D} \unlhd \mathtt{nnc.iszero} \unrhd \\ &\quad (\mathtt{nnc.pred} \circ (\mathsf{S}- \unlhd \mathtt{nnc.iszero} \unrhd \\ &\qquad\qquad (\mathtt{nnc.pred} \circ (\mathsf{S}+ \unlhd \mathtt{nnc.iszero} \unrhd \langle x \vert E \rangle))))\;,\end{aligned}$$

where E is the guarded recursive specification consisting of the following equation:

$$x = \mathtt{nnc.pred} \circ (\mathsf{D} \unlhd \mathtt{nnc.iszero} \unrhd x)\;.$$

We have that

$$\lvert +\mathsf{a} \,;\, \#' \,;\, \#' \,;\, \#0 \,;\, !\mathsf{f} \,;\, !\mathsf{t} \rvert' \,/\!/\, \mathtt{nnc}.\mathit{NNC}(0) = \mathsf{S}+ \unlhd \mathsf{a} \unrhd \mathsf{S}-$$

and also

$$\lvert +\mathsf{a} \,;\, \#' \,;\, \#' \,;\, \#0 \,;\, !\mathsf{f} \,;\, !\mathsf{t} \rvert = \mathsf{S}+ \unlhd \mathsf{a} \unrhd \mathsf{S}-\;.$$ [3]

[3] The counter functional unit NNC has been defined in Sect. 3.2.5.

The following proposition states rigorously how the two ways of thread extraction are related.

Proposition 4.7. *For all closed* SPISA$^0_{\mathrm{js}}$ *terms* $\boldsymbol{t}$, $|\boldsymbol{t}| = |\boldsymbol{t}|' \mathbin{/\!/} \mathtt{nnc}.NNC(0)$.

Proof. Strictly speaking, we prove this theorem in the algebraic theory obtained by combining SPISA$_{\mathrm{js}}$+SC with BTA+TSI+REC+AIP+ABSTR, and extending the result with the operators $|\_|$, $|\_|'$ and $|\_|'_{\mathrm{skp}}$ and the axioms for these operators. We write $\mathcal{IS}$ for the set of all closed terms of sort **IS** from the language of the resulting theory and $\mathcal{T}$ for the set of all closed terms of sort **T** from the language of the resulting theory. Moreover, we write $\mathcal{IS}^0$ for the set of all closed terms from $\mathcal{IS}$ that contain no other jump instructions than $\#0$.

Let

$$
\begin{aligned}
T &= \{|\boldsymbol{t}| \mid \boldsymbol{t} \in \mathcal{IS}^0\}\,,\\
T' &= \{|\boldsymbol{t}|' \mathbin{/\!/} \mathtt{nnc}.NNC(i) \mid i \in \mathbb{N} \wedge \boldsymbol{t} \in \mathcal{IS}^0\}\\
&\quad \cup \{|\boldsymbol{t}|'_{\mathrm{skp}} \mathbin{/\!/} \mathtt{nnc}.NNC(i+1) \mid i \in \mathbb{N} \wedge \boldsymbol{t} \in \mathcal{IS}^0\}\,,
\end{aligned}
$$

and let $\beta : T' \to T$ be the function defined by

$$
\begin{aligned}
&\beta(|\boldsymbol{t}|' \mathbin{/\!/} \mathtt{nnc}.NNC(0)) = |\boldsymbol{t}|\,,\\
&\beta(|\boldsymbol{t}|' \mathbin{/\!/} \mathtt{nnc}.NNC(i+1)) = |\#'^{i+1} \,;\, \boldsymbol{t}|\,,\\
&\beta(|\boldsymbol{t}|'_{\mathrm{skp}} \mathbin{/\!/} \mathtt{nnc}.NNC(i+1)) = |\#'^{i+1} \,;\, \#0 \,;\, \boldsymbol{t}|\,.
\end{aligned}
$$

For each $\boldsymbol{t} \in \mathcal{T}$, write $\beta^*(\boldsymbol{t})$ for $\boldsymbol{t}$ with, for all $\boldsymbol{t}' \in T'$, all occurrences of $\boldsymbol{t}'$ in $\boldsymbol{t}$ replaced by $\beta(\boldsymbol{t}')$. Then, it is straightforward to prove that there exists a set $\boldsymbol{E}$ consisting of one derivable equation $\boldsymbol{t}' = \boldsymbol{t}''$ for each $\boldsymbol{t}' \in T'$ such that, for all equations $\boldsymbol{t}' = \boldsymbol{t}''$ in $\boldsymbol{E}$:

- the equation $\beta(\boldsymbol{t}') = \beta^*(\boldsymbol{t}'')$ is also derivable;
- if $\boldsymbol{t}'' \in T'$, then $\boldsymbol{t}''$ can always be rewritten to a $\boldsymbol{t}''' \notin T'$ using the equations in $\boldsymbol{E}$ from left to right.

Because $\beta(|\boldsymbol{t}|' \mathbin{/\!/} \mathtt{nnc}.NNC(0)) = |\boldsymbol{t}|$ for all $\boldsymbol{t} \in \mathcal{IS}^0$, this means that, for all $\boldsymbol{t} \in \mathcal{IS}^0$, $|\boldsymbol{t}|' \mathbin{/\!/} \mathtt{nnc}.NNC(0)$ and $|\boldsymbol{t}|$ are solutions of the same guarded recursive specification. Because guarded recursive specifications have unique solutions, it follows immediately that, for all $\boldsymbol{t} \in \mathcal{IS}^0$, $|\boldsymbol{t}|' \mathbin{/\!/} \mathtt{nnc}.NNC(0) = |\boldsymbol{t}|$. □

We have the following corollary of Corollary 4.4 and Proposition 4.7.

Corollary 4.5. *For each regular thread t, there exists a closed* SPISA$^0_{\mathrm{js}}$ *term* $\boldsymbol{t}$ *such that the interpretation of* $|\boldsymbol{t}|' \mathbin{/\!/} \mathtt{nnc}.NNC(0)$ *in* $\boldsymbol{\mathcal{M}}$ *is t.*

4.4.3 *On finite-state execution mechanisms*

We investigate whether a finite-state execution mechanism can produce by itself, therefore without interaction with an unbounded counter, each regular thread from an instruction sequence that is a finite or eventually periodic infinite sequence of instructions from a finite set.

Below, we will introduce a notion of an execution mechanism. The intuition is that, for a function that assigns a finite-state behaviour to each member of some set of instruction sequences, an execution mechanism is a deterministic behaviour that can produce the behaviour assigned to each of these instruction sequences from the instruction sequence concerned by going through the instructions in the sequence one by one. In Appendix D, the notion of an analytic execution architecture is discussed. An execution mechanism is basically a realization of the component of an analytic execution architecture that contains an instruction sequence.

We believe that there do not exist execution mechanisms that can deal with sequences of instructions from an infinite set. Therefore, we restrict ourselves to finite instruction sets.

It is assumed that a finite set I of *instructions*, a set IS of finite or eventually periodic infinite sequences over I, and a function $|\_|$ that assigns a regular thread to each member of IS have been given. Moreover, it is assumed that $\mathtt{isc} \in \mathcal{F}$, that $\mathtt{hdeq}{:}u \in \mathcal{M}$ for all $u \in I$, that $\mathtt{drop} \in \mathcal{M}$, and that basic actions of the form $\mathtt{isc}.m$ do not occur in $|U|$ for all $U \in \mathit{IS}$.

We define a functional unit in $\mathcal{FU}(\mathit{IS})$ that is a container whose possible contents are the sequences of instructions from IS. The functional unit in question is defined as follows:

$$\mathit{ISC} = \{(\mathtt{hdeq}{:}u, \mathit{Hdeq}{:}u) \mid u \in I\} \cup \{(\mathtt{drop}, \mathit{Drop})\} ,$$

where the method operations are defined as follows:

$$\begin{aligned}
\mathit{Hdeq}{:}u(v\sigma) &= \begin{cases} (\mathtt{t}, v\sigma) & \text{if } u = v \\ (\mathtt{f}, v\sigma) & \text{if } u \neq v \,. \end{cases} \\
\mathit{Hdeq}{:}u(\epsilon) &= (\mathtt{f}, \epsilon) \,, \\
\mathit{Drop}(v\sigma) &= (\mathtt{t}, \sigma) \,, \\
\mathit{Drop}(\epsilon) &= (\mathtt{f}, \epsilon) \,.
\end{aligned}$$

The interface $\mathcal{I}(\mathit{ISC})$ of ISC can be explained as follows:

- $\mathtt{hdeq}{:}u$: if there is an instruction sequence left and its first instruction is u, then nothing changes and the reply is $\mathtt{t}$; otherwise, nothing changes and the reply is $\mathtt{f}$;

- drop: if there is an instruction sequence left, then its first instruction is dropped and the reply is t; otherwise, nothing changes and the reply is f.

In order to execute an instruction sequence $U \in IS$, an execution mechanism can interact with a container, loaded with U, to go through the instructions in that sequence one by one. Notice that an instruction sequence container does not have to hold an infinite object: there exists an adequate finite representation for each finite or eventually periodic infinite sequence of instructions.

Definition 4.1. An *execution mechanism* for $|\_|$ is a thread t such that $t \mathbin{/\!/} \mathtt{isc}.ISC(U) = |U|$ for all $U \in IS$. An execution mechanism is called a *finite-state* execution mechanism if it is a regular thread.

It is easy to see that, in the case of $\text{SPISA}^0_{\text{js}}$, there exists a finite-state execution mechanism for the thread extraction operation $|\_|'$. From this and Corollary 4.5, it follows immediately that there exists a finite-state execution mechanism that through interaction with an unbounded counter can produce each regular thread from some instruction sequence that is a finite or eventually periodic infinite sequence of instructions from a finite set.

We also have that there does not exist a finite-state execution mechanism that by itself can produce each regular thread from an instruction sequence that is a finite or eventually periodic infinite sequence of instructions from a finite set.

Theorem 4.3. *Assume that* $\text{card}(\mathcal{A}) > 1$. *Assume further that, for each regular thread* t, *there exists a* $U \in IS$ *such that* $|U| = t$. *Then there does not exist a finite-state execution mechanism for* $|\_|$.

Proof. Suppose that there exists a finite-state execution mechanism, say t_{exec}. Let n be the number of states of t_{exec}. Consider the thread t that is the x_0-component of the solution of the guarded recursive specification consisting of the following equations:

$$
\begin{aligned}
x_i &= x_{i+1} \trianglelefteq \mathtt{a} \trianglerighteq x'_{i+1,0} && \text{for } i \in [0, n] \,, \\
x_{n+1} &= \mathsf{S} \,, \\
x'_{i+1,i'} &= \mathtt{b} \circ x'_{i+1,i'+1} && \text{for } i \in [0, n], i' \in [0, i] \,, \\
x'_{i+1,i+1} &= \mathtt{a} \circ x'_{i+1,0} \,.
\end{aligned}
$$

We write t_i, where $i \in [0, n]$, for the x_i-component of the solution of this guarded recursive specification, and $t'_{i,i'}$, where $i \in [1, n]$ and $i' \in [0, i]$, for the $x'_{i,i'}$-component of the solution of this guarded recursive specification. Let U be a member of IS from which t_{exec} can produce t. Notice that t performs $\mathtt{a}$ at least once and at most $n + 1$ times after each other. Suppose that t has performed a for the jth time when the reply f is returned, while at that stage t_{exec} has gone through the first k_j instructions of U. Moreover, write U_j for what is left of U after its first k_j instructions have been dropped. Then t_{exec} still has to produce $t'_{j,0}$ from U_j. For each $j \in [1, n+1]$, a k_j as above can be found. Let j_0 be the unique $j \in [1, n+1]$ such that $k_{j'} \leq k_j$ for all $j' \in [1, n+1]$. Regardless the number of times t has performed a when the reply f is returned, t_{exec} must eventually have dropped the first k_{j_0} instructions of U. For each of the $n+1$ possible values of j, t_{exec} must be in a different state when t_{j_0} is left, because the thread that t_{exec} still has to produce is different. However, this is impossible with n states. □

In the light of Theorem 4.3, Corollary 4.5 can be considered a positive result: a finite-state execution mechanism that interacts with an unbounded counter is sufficient. However, this result is reached at the expense of an extremely inefficient way of representing jumps. We do not see how to improve on the linear representation of jumps. With a logarithmic representation, for instance, we expect that an unbounded counter will not do.

It is an open problem whether Theorem 4.3 goes through under the assumption that $\mathrm{card}(\mathcal{A}) > 0$.

Chapter 5

Computation-Theoretic Issues

This chapter concerns two subjects from the theory of computation, namely the halting problem and non-uniform computational complexity. Some issues concerning these subjects are investigated thinking in terms of instruction sequences.

Positioning Turing's result regarding the undecidability of the halting problem as a result about programs rather than machines, and taking single-pass instruction sequences as considered in SPISA as programs, we analyse the autosolvability requirement that a program of a certain kind must solve the halting problem for all programs of that kind. We present positive and negative results concerning the autosolvability of the halting problem for programs.

Thinking in terms of a single-pass instruction sequence as considered in SPISA, we define counterparts of the classical non-uniform complexity classes P/poly and $\mathrm{NP}/\mathrm{poly}$, introduce a notion of completeness for the counterpart of $\mathrm{NP}/\mathrm{poly}$ using a non-uniform reducibility relation, formulate several complexity hypotheses, including a counterpart of the well-known complexity theoretic conjecture that $\mathrm{NP} \not\subseteq \mathrm{P}/\mathrm{poly}$, and show that a problem closely related to $3\mathrm{SAT}$ is NP-complete as well as complete for the counterpart of $\mathrm{NP}/\mathrm{poly}$.

5.1 Autosolvability of Halting Problem Instances

Turing's result regarding the undecidability of the halting problem is a result about Turing machines. It says that there does not exist a single Turing machine that, given the description of an arbitrary Turing machine and input, will determine whether the computation of that Turing machine applied to that input eventually halts (see e.g. [Turing (1937)]). Implicit in this result is the autosolvability requirement that a machine of a certain kind must solve the halting problem for all machines of that kind. The halting problem is frequently paraphrased as a result about programs as follows: the halting problem is the problem to determine, given a program and an input to the program, whether execution of the program on that input will eventually terminate. If we position Turing's result regarding the undecidability of the halting problem as a result about programs rather than machines, we get the autosolvability requirement that a program of a certain kind must solve the halting problem for all programs of that kind. In this section, we investigate this autosolvability requirement in a setting in which programs take the form of instruction sequences.

5.1.1 *Functional units relating to Turing machine tapes*

First, we define some notions that have a bearing on the halting problem in the setting of $\mathrm{ISNR}^{\mathrm{s}}$ and functional units. The notions in question are defined in terms of functional units for the following state space:

$$\mathbb{T} = \{v\hat{\ }w \mid v, w \in \{0, 1, :\}^*\} \ .$$

The elements of $\mathbb{T}$ can be understood as the possible contents of the tape of a Turing machine whose tape alphabet is $\{0, 1, :\}$, including the position of the tape head. Consider an element $v\hat{\ }w \in \mathbb{T}$. Then v corresponds to the content of the tape to the left of the position of the tape head and w corresponds to the content of the tape from the position of the tape head to the right — the indefinite numbers of padding blanks at both ends are left out. The colon serves as a separator of bit sequences. This is for instance useful if the input of a program consists of another program and an input to the latter program, both encoded as a bit sequence. We could have taken any other tape alphabet whose cardinality is greater than one, but $\{0, 1, :\}$ is extremely handy when dealing with issues relating to the halting problem.

Below, we will use a computable injective function $\alpha : \mathbb{T} \to \mathbb{N}$ to encode the members of $\mathbb{T}$ as natural numbers. Because $\mathbb{T}$ is a countably infinite set, we assume that it is understood what is a computable function from $\mathbb{T}$ to $\mathbb{N}$. An obvious instance of a computable injective function $\alpha : \mathbb{T} \to \mathbb{N}$ is the one where $\alpha(a_1 \ldots a_n)$ is the natural number represented in the quinary number-system by $a_1 \ldots a_n$ if the symbols 0, 1, : and $\hat{\ }$ are taken as digits representing the numbers 1, 2, 3 and 4, respectively.

Definition 5.1. A method operation $M \in \mathcal{MO}(\mathbb{T})$ is *computable* if there exist computable functions $F, G : \mathbb{N} \to \mathbb{N}$ such that $M(v) = (\beta(F(\alpha(v))), \alpha^{-1}(G(\alpha(v))))$ for all $v \in \mathbb{T}$, where $\alpha : \mathbb{T} \to \mathbb{N}$ is a computable injective function and $\beta : \mathbb{N} \to \mathbb{B}$ is inductively defined by $\beta(0) = \mathsf{t}$ and $\beta(n + 1) = \mathsf{f}$. A functional unit $U \in \mathcal{FU}(\mathbb{T})$ is *computable* if, for each

$(m, M) \in U$, M is computable.

Definition 5.2. A computable $U \in \mathcal{FU}(\mathbb{T})$ is *universal* if for each computable $U' \in \mathcal{FU}(\mathbb{T})$, we have $U' \leq U$.

An example of a computable functional unit in $\mathcal{FU}(\mathbb{T})$ is the functional unit whose method operations correspond to the basic steps that a Turing machine with tape alphabet $\{0, 1, :\}$ can perform on its tape. It turns out that this functional unit is universal, which can be proved using simple programming in ISNR^{s}.

The universal functional unit mentioned above corresponds to the common part of all Turing machines with tape alphabet $\{0, 1, :\}$. The part that differs for different Turing machines is what is usually called their "transition function" or "program". In the current setting, the role of that part is filled by an instruction sequence whose instructions correspond to the method operations of this universal functional unit. This means that different instruction sequences are needed for different Turing machines with the tape alphabet concerned, but the same universal functional unit suffices for all of them. In particular, the same universal functional unit suffices for universal Turing machines and non-universal Turing machines.

It is assumed that, for each $U \in \mathcal{FU}(\mathbb{T})$, a computable injective function from $\mathcal{L}(\mathtt{f}.\mathcal{I}(U))$ to $\{0, 1\}^*$ with a computable image has been given that yields, for each $\boldsymbol{p} \in \mathcal{L}(\mathtt{f}.\mathcal{I}(U))$, an encoding of $\boldsymbol{p}$ as a bit sequence. If we consider the case where the jump lengths in jump instructions are character strings representing the jump lengths in decimal notation and method names are character strings, such an encoding function can easily be obtained using the ASCII character-encoding scheme. We use the notation $\overline{\boldsymbol{p}}$ to denote the encoding of $\boldsymbol{p}$ as a bit sequence.

Definition 5.3. Let $U \in \mathcal{FU}(\mathbb{T})$, and let $I \subseteq \mathcal{I}(U)$. Then:

- $\boldsymbol{p} \in \mathcal{L}(\mathtt{f}.\mathcal{I}(U))$ produces a *solution of the halting problem* for $\mathcal{L}(\mathtt{f}.I)$ with respect to U if:

$$\boldsymbol{p} \downarrow \mathtt{f}.U(v) \text{ for all } v \in \mathbb{T}\,,$$
$$\boldsymbol{p} \,!\, \mathtt{f}.U({\char`^}\overline{\boldsymbol{q}}{:}v) = \mathsf{t} \Leftrightarrow \boldsymbol{q} \downarrow \mathtt{f}.U({\char`^}v) \text{ for all } \boldsymbol{q} \in \mathcal{L}(\mathtt{f}.I) \text{ and } v \in \{0, 1, :\}^*\,;$$

- $\boldsymbol{p} \in \mathcal{L}(\mathtt{f}.\mathcal{I}(U))$ produces a *reflexive solution of the halting problem* for $\mathcal{L}(\mathtt{f}.I)$ with respect to U if $\boldsymbol{p}$ produces a solution of the halting problem for $\mathcal{L}(\mathtt{f}.I)$ with respect to U and $\boldsymbol{p} \in \mathcal{L}(\mathtt{f}.I)$;
- the halting problem for $\mathcal{L}(\mathtt{f}.I)$ with respect to U is *autosolvable* if there exists a $\boldsymbol{p} \in$

$\mathcal{L}(\mathtt{f}.\mathcal{I}(U))$ such that p produces a reflexive solution of the halting problem for $\mathcal{L}(\mathtt{f}.I)$ with respect to U;
- the halting problem for $\mathcal{L}(\mathtt{f}.I)$ with respect to U is *potentially autosolvable* if there exists an extension U' of U such that the halting problem for $\mathcal{L}(\mathtt{f}.\mathcal{I}(U'))$ with respect to U' is autosolvable;
- the halting problem for $\mathcal{L}(\mathtt{f}.I)$ with respect to U is *potentially recursively autosolvable* if there exists an extension U' of U such that the halting problem for $\mathcal{L}(\mathtt{f}.\mathcal{I}(U'))$ with respect to U' is autosolvable and U' is computable.

These definitions make clear that each combination of a $U \in \mathcal{FU}(\mathbb{T})$ and an $I \subseteq \mathcal{I}(U)$ gives rise to a *halting problem instance*.

In Sect. 5.1.2 and 5.1.3, we will make use of a method operation $Dup \in \mathcal{MO}(\mathbb{T})$ for duplicating bit sequences. This method operation is defined as follows:

$$\begin{aligned} Dup(v\,\hat{}\,w) &= Dup(\hat{}\,vw)\;, \\ Dup(\hat{}\,v) &= (\mathsf{t}, \hat{}\,v{:}v) && \text{if } v \in \{0,1\}^*\;, \\ Dup(\hat{}\,v{:}w) &= (\mathsf{t}, \hat{}\,v{:}v{:}w) && \text{if } v \in \{0,1\}^*\;. \end{aligned}$$

Proposition 5.1. *Let* $U \in \mathcal{FU}(\mathbb{T})$ *be such that* $(\mathsf{dup}, Dup) \in U$, *let* $I \subseteq \mathcal{I}(U)$ *be such that* $\mathsf{dup} \in I$, *let* $p \in \mathcal{L}(\mathtt{f}.I)$, *and let* $v \in \{0,1\}^*$ *and* $w \in \{0,1,:\}^*$ *be such that* $w = v$ *or* $w = v{:}w'$ *for some* $w' \in \{0,1,:\}^*$. *Then* $(\mathtt{f}.\mathsf{dup}\,;p)\ !\ \mathtt{f}.U(\hat{}\,w) = p\ !\ \mathtt{f}.U(\hat{}\,v{:}w)$.

Proof. This follows immediately from the definition of Dup and the axioms for !. □

The method operation Dup is a derived method operation of the above-mentioned functional unit whose method operations correspond to the basic steps that a Turing machine with tape alphabet $\{0,1,:\}$ can perform on its tape. This follows immediately from the computability of Dup and the universality of this functional unit.

In Sects. 5.1.2 and 5.1.3, we will make use of two simple transformations of ISNR^{s} instruction sequences that affect only their termination behaviour on execution and the Boolean value yielded at termination in the case of termination. Here, we introduce notations for those transformations.

Let p be a ISNR^{s} instruction sequence. Then we write $swap(p)$ for p with each occurrence of !t replaced by !f and each occurrence of !f replaced by !t, and we write $f2d(p)$ for p with each occurrence of !f replaced by #0. In the following proposition, the most important properties relating to these transformations are stated.

Proposition 5.2. *Let* p *be a* ISNR^{s} *instruction sequence and* t' *be a closed* SFA *term of sort* $\mathbf{SF}$. *Then:*

(1) if $\boldsymbol{p} \mathbin{!} \boldsymbol{t'} = \mathsf{t}$ *then* $swap(\boldsymbol{p}) \mathbin{!} \boldsymbol{t'} = \mathsf{f}$ *and* $f2d(\boldsymbol{p}) \mathbin{!} \boldsymbol{t'} = \mathsf{t}$*;*
(2) if $\boldsymbol{p} \mathbin{!} \boldsymbol{t'} = \mathsf{f}$ *then* $swap(\boldsymbol{p}) \mathbin{!} \boldsymbol{t'} = \mathsf{t}$ *and* $f2d(\boldsymbol{p}) \mathbin{!} \boldsymbol{t'} = \mathsf{d}$*.*

Proof. Let $\boldsymbol{t}$ be a closed BTA term of sort $\mathbf{T}$. Then we write $swap'(\boldsymbol{t})$ for $\boldsymbol{t}$ with each occurrence of $\mathsf{S}+$ replaced by $\mathsf{S}-$ and each occurrence of $\mathsf{S}-$ replaced by $\mathsf{S}+$, and we write $f2d'(\boldsymbol{t})$ for $\boldsymbol{t}$ with each occurrence of $\mathsf{S}-$ replaced by D. It is easy to prove that $|i, swap(\boldsymbol{p})| = swap'(|i, \boldsymbol{p}|)$ and $|i, f2d(\boldsymbol{p})| = f2d'(|i, \boldsymbol{p}|)$ for all $i \in \mathbb{N}$. By this result, Lemma 2.4, axioms RSP and R10, and Theorem 3.1, it is sufficient to prove the following for each closed BTA term $\boldsymbol{t}$ of sort $\mathbf{T}$:

if $\boldsymbol{t} \mathbin{!} \boldsymbol{t'} = \mathsf{t}$ then $swap'(\boldsymbol{t}) \mathbin{!} \boldsymbol{t'} = \mathsf{f}$ and $f2d'(\boldsymbol{t}) \mathbin{!} \boldsymbol{t'} = \mathsf{t}$;
if $\boldsymbol{t} \mathbin{!} \boldsymbol{t'} = \mathsf{f}$ then $swap'(\boldsymbol{t}) \mathbin{!} \boldsymbol{t'} = \mathsf{t}$ and $f2d'(\boldsymbol{t}) \mathbin{!} \boldsymbol{t'} = \mathsf{d}$.

This is easy by induction on the structure of $\boldsymbol{t}$. □

By the use of more than one focus and non-singleton service families, we can deal with cases that remind of multi-tape Turing machines, Turing machines that has random access memory, etc. However, in the remainder of Sect. 5.1, we will only consider the case that reminds of single-tape Turing machines. This means that we will use only one focus (`f`) and only singleton service families.

In Proposition 5.2 above, we do not comply with the relevant use conventions proposed in Sect. 3.1.7 because convergence forms a part of the real matter that we are concerned with. For the same reason, we do not comply with the relevant use conventions in Definition 5.4 and the proof of Theorem 5.4 below.

5.1.2 *Interpreters*

It is often mentioned in textbooks on computability that an interpreter, which is a program for simulating the execution of programs that it is given as input, cannot solve the halting problem because the execution of the interpreter will not terminate if the execution of its input program does not terminate. In this section, we have a look upon the termination behaviour of interpreters in the setting of $\mathrm{ISNR^s}$ and functional units.

Definition 5.4. Let $U \in \mathcal{FU}(\mathbb{T})$, let $I \subseteq \mathcal{I}(U)$, and let $I' \subseteq I$. Then $\boldsymbol{p} \in \mathcal{L}(\mathtt{f}.I)$ is an *interpreter* for $\mathcal{L}(\mathtt{f}.I')$ with respect to U if for all $\boldsymbol{q} \in \mathcal{L}(\mathtt{f}.I')$ and $v \in \{0,1,:\}^*$:

$$\boldsymbol{q} \downarrow \mathtt{f}.U(\hat{\ }v) \Rightarrow$$
$$\boldsymbol{p} \downarrow \mathtt{f}.U(\hat{\ }\overline{\boldsymbol{q}}{:}v) \land \boldsymbol{p} \bullet \mathtt{f}.U(\hat{\ }\overline{\boldsymbol{q}}{:}v) = \boldsymbol{q} \bullet \mathtt{f}.U(\hat{\ }v) \land \boldsymbol{p} \mathbin{!} \mathtt{f}.U(\hat{\ }\overline{\boldsymbol{q}}{:}v) = \boldsymbol{q} \mathbin{!} \mathtt{f}.U(\hat{\ }v)\,.$$

Moreover, $\boldsymbol{p} \in \mathcal{L}(\mathtt{f}.I)$ is a *reflexive interpreter* for $\mathcal{L}(\mathtt{f}.I')$ with respect to U if $\boldsymbol{p}$ is an interpreter for $\mathcal{L}(\mathtt{f}.I')$ with respect to U and $\boldsymbol{p} \in \mathcal{L}(\mathtt{f}.I')$.

The following theorem states that a reflexive interpreter that always terminates is impossible in the presence of the method operation Dup.

Theorem 5.1. *Let $U \in \mathcal{FU}(\mathbb{T})$ be such that $(\mathrm{dup}, Dup) \in U$, let $I \subseteq \mathcal{I}(U)$ be such that $\mathrm{dup} \in I$, and let $\boldsymbol{p} \in \mathcal{L}(\mathtt{f}.\mathcal{I}(U))$ be a reflexive interpreter for $\mathcal{L}(\mathtt{f}.I)$ with respect to U. Then there exist a $\boldsymbol{q} \in \mathcal{L}(\mathtt{f}.I)$ and a $v \in \{0, 1, :\}^*$ such that $\boldsymbol{p} \uparrow \mathtt{f}.U(\hat{}\,\overline{\boldsymbol{q}}{:}v)$.*

Proof. Assume the contrary. Take $\boldsymbol{q} = \mathtt{f}.\mathrm{dup} \mathbin{;} \mathit{swap}(\boldsymbol{p})$. By the assumption, $\boldsymbol{p} \downarrow \mathtt{f}.U(\hat{}\,\overline{\boldsymbol{q}}{:}\overline{\boldsymbol{q}})$. By Propositions 3.3 and 5.2, it follows that $\mathit{swap}(\boldsymbol{p}) \downarrow \mathtt{f}.U(\hat{}\,\overline{\boldsymbol{q}}{:}\overline{\boldsymbol{q}})$ and $\mathit{swap}(\boldsymbol{p}) \,!\, \mathtt{f}.U(\hat{}\,\overline{\boldsymbol{q}}{:}\overline{\boldsymbol{q}}) \neq \boldsymbol{p} \,!\, \mathtt{f}.U(\hat{}\,\overline{\boldsymbol{q}}{:}\overline{\boldsymbol{q}})$. By Propositions 3.3 and 5.1, it follows that $(\mathtt{f}.\mathrm{dup} \mathbin{;} \mathit{swap}(\boldsymbol{p})) \downarrow \mathtt{f}.U(\hat{}\,\overline{\boldsymbol{q}})$ and $(\mathtt{f}.\mathrm{dup} \mathbin{;} \mathit{swap}(\boldsymbol{p})) \,!\, \mathtt{f}.U(\hat{}\,\overline{\boldsymbol{q}}) \neq \boldsymbol{p} \,!\, \mathtt{f}.U(\hat{}\,\overline{\boldsymbol{q}}{:}\overline{\boldsymbol{q}})$. Since $\boldsymbol{q} = \mathtt{f}.\mathrm{dup} \mathbin{;} \mathit{swap}(\boldsymbol{p})$, we have $\boldsymbol{q} \downarrow \mathtt{f}.U(\hat{}\,\overline{\boldsymbol{q}})$ and $\boldsymbol{q} \,!\, \mathtt{f}.U(\hat{}\,\overline{\boldsymbol{q}}) \neq \boldsymbol{p} \,!\, \mathtt{f}.U(\hat{}\,\overline{\boldsymbol{q}}{:}\overline{\boldsymbol{q}})$. Because $\boldsymbol{p}$ is a reflexive interpreter, this implies $\boldsymbol{p} \,!\, \mathtt{f}.U(\hat{}\,\overline{\boldsymbol{q}}{:}\overline{\boldsymbol{q}}) = \boldsymbol{q} \,!\, \mathtt{f}.U(\hat{}\,\overline{\boldsymbol{q}})$ and $\boldsymbol{q} \,!\, \mathtt{f}.U(\hat{}\,\overline{\boldsymbol{q}}) \neq \boldsymbol{p} \,!\, \mathtt{f}.U(\hat{}\,\overline{\boldsymbol{q}}{:}\overline{\boldsymbol{q}})$. This is a contradiction. □

It is easy to see that Theorem 5.1 goes through for all functional units for $\mathbb{T}$ of which Dup is a derived method operation. Recall that the functional units concerned include the aforementioned functional unit whose method operations correspond to the basic steps that a Turing machine with tape alphabet $\{0, 1, :\}$ can perform on its tape.

For each $U \in \mathcal{FU}(\mathbb{T})$, $\boldsymbol{m} \in \mathcal{I}(U)$, and $v \in \mathbb{T}$, we have $(+\mathtt{f}.\boldsymbol{m} \mathbin{;} !\mathrm{t} \mathbin{;} !\mathrm{f}) \downarrow \mathtt{f}.U(v)$. This leads us to the following corollary of Theorem 5.1.

Corollary 5.1. *For all $U \in \mathcal{FU}(\mathbb{T})$ with $(\mathrm{dup}, Dup) \in U$ and $I \subseteq \mathcal{I}(U)$ with $\mathrm{dup} \in I$, there does not exist an $\boldsymbol{m} \in I$ such that $+\mathtt{f}.\boldsymbol{m} \mathbin{;} !\mathrm{t} \mathbin{;} !\mathrm{f}$ is a reflexive interpreter for $\mathcal{L}(\mathtt{f}.I)$ with respect to U.*

To the best of our knowledge, there are no existing results in computability theory or elsewhere directly related to Theorem 5.1. It looks as if the closest to this result are results on termination of particular interpreters for particular logic and functional programming languages.

5.1.3 *Autosolvability of the halting problem*

Because a reflexive interpreter that always terminates is impossible in the presence of the method operation Dup, we must conclude that solving the halting problem by means of a reflexive interpreter is out of the question in the presence of the method operation Dup. The question arises whether the proviso "by means of a reflexive interpreter" can be dropped. In this section, we answer this question in the affirmative. Before we present this negative result concerning autosolvability of the halting problem, we present a positive result.

Let $M \in \mathcal{MO}(\mathbb{T})$. Then we say that M *increases the number of colons* if for some $v \in \mathbb{T}$ the number of colons in $M^{\mathrm{e}}(v)$ is greater than the number of colons in v.

Theorem 5.2. *Let $U \in \mathcal{FU}(\mathbb{T})$ be such that no method operation of U increases the number of colons. Then there exist an extension U' of U, an $I' \subseteq \mathcal{I}(U')$, and a $\boldsymbol{p} \in \mathcal{L}(\mathtt{f}.\mathcal{I}(U'))$ such that $\boldsymbol{p}$ produces a reflexive solution of the halting problem for $\mathcal{L}(\mathtt{f}.I')$ with respect to U'.*

Proof. Take $\mathtt{halting} \in \mathcal{M}$ such that $\mathtt{halting} \notin \mathcal{I}(U)$. Moreover, let $U' = U \cup \{(\mathtt{halting}, \mathit{Halting})\}$, where $\mathit{Halting} \in \mathcal{MO}(\mathbb{T})$ is defined as follows:

$$\begin{aligned}
&\mathit{Halting}(v\,\hat{}\,w) = \mathit{Halting}(\hat{}\,vw)\,, && \\
&\mathit{Halting}(\hat{}\,v) \quad = (\mathsf{f}, \hat{}\,) && \text{if } v \in \{0,1\}^*\,, \\
&\mathit{Halting}(\hat{}\,v{:}w) = (\mathsf{f}, \hat{}\,) && \text{if } v \in \{0,1\}^* \wedge \forall \boldsymbol{p} \in \mathcal{L}(\mathtt{f}.I') \bullet v \neq \overline{\boldsymbol{p}}\,, \\
&\mathit{Halting}(\hat{}\,\overline{\boldsymbol{p}}{:}w) = (\mathsf{f}, \hat{}\,) && \text{if } \boldsymbol{p} \in \mathcal{L}(\mathtt{f}.I') \wedge \boldsymbol{p} \uparrow \mathtt{f}.U'(w)\,, \\
&\mathit{Halting}(\hat{}\,\overline{\boldsymbol{p}}{:}w) = (\mathsf{t}, \hat{}\,) && \text{if } \boldsymbol{p} \in \mathcal{L}(\mathtt{f}.I') \wedge \boldsymbol{p} \downarrow \mathtt{f}.U'(w)\,,
\end{aligned}$$

and let $I' = \mathcal{I}(U')$. Then $+\mathtt{f.halting}\,;!\mathsf{t}\,;!\mathsf{f}$ produces a reflexive solution of the halting problem for $\mathcal{L}(\mathtt{f}.I')$ with respect to U'. □

Theorem 5.2 tells us that there exist functional units $U \in \mathcal{FU}(\mathbb{T})$ with the property that the halting problem is potentially autosolvable for $\mathcal{L}(\mathtt{f}.\mathcal{I}(U))$ with respect to U. Thus, we know that there exist functional units $U \in \mathcal{FU}(\mathbb{T})$ with the property that the halting problem is autosolvable for $\mathcal{L}(\mathtt{f}.\mathcal{I}(U))$ with respect to U.

There exists a $U \in \mathcal{FU}(\mathbb{T})$ for which $\mathit{Halting}$ as defined in the proof of Theorem 5.2 is computable.

Theorem 5.3. *Let $U = \emptyset$ and $U' = U \cup \{(\mathtt{halting}, \mathit{Halting})\}$, where $\mathit{Halting}$ is as defined in the proof of Theorem 5.2. Then, $\mathit{Halting}$ is computable.*

Proof. It is sufficient to prove for an arbitrary $\boldsymbol{p} \in \mathcal{L}(\mathtt{f}.\mathcal{I}(U'))$ that, for all $v \in \mathbb{T}$, $\boldsymbol{p} \downarrow \mathtt{f}.U'(v)$ is decidable. We will prove this by induction on the number of colons in v.

The basis step. Because the number of colons in v equals 0, $\mathit{Halting}(v) = (\mathsf{f}, \hat{}\,)$. It follows that $\boldsymbol{p} \downarrow \mathtt{f}.U'(v) \Leftrightarrow \boldsymbol{p}' \downarrow \emptyset$, where $\boldsymbol{p}'$ is $\boldsymbol{p}$ with each occurrence of $\mathtt{f.halting}$

and $-\mathtt{f.halting}$ replaced by $\#1$ and each occurrence of $+\mathtt{f.halting}$ replaced by $\#2$. Because $\boldsymbol{p}'$ is finite, $\boldsymbol{p}' \downarrow \emptyset$ is decidable. Hence, $\boldsymbol{p} \downarrow \mathtt{f}.U'(v)$ is decidable.

The inductive step. Because the number of colons in v is greater than 0, either $\mathit{Halting}(v) = (\mathsf{t}, \hat{\ })$ or $\mathit{Halting}(v) = (\mathsf{f}, \hat{\ })$. It follows that $\boldsymbol{p} \downarrow \mathtt{f}.U'(v) \Leftrightarrow \boldsymbol{p}' \downarrow \emptyset$, where $\boldsymbol{p}'$ is $\boldsymbol{p}$ with:

- each occurrence of $\mathtt{f.halting}$ and $+\mathtt{f.halting}$ replaced by $\#1$ if the occurrence leads to the first application of *Halting* and $\mathit{Halting}^{\mathrm{r}}(v) = \mathsf{t}$, and by $\#2$ otherwise;
- each occurrence of $-\mathtt{f.halting}$ replaced by $\#2$ if the occurrence leads to the first application of *Halting* and $\mathit{Halting}^{\mathrm{r}}(v) = \mathsf{t}$, and by $\#1$ otherwise.

An occurrence of $\mathtt{f.halting}$, $+\mathtt{f.halting}$ or $-\mathtt{f.halting}$ in $\boldsymbol{p}$ leads to the first application of *Halting* iff $|1, \boldsymbol{p}| = |i, \boldsymbol{p}|$, where i is the position of the occurrence in $\boldsymbol{p}$. Because $\boldsymbol{p}$ is finite, it is decidable whether an occurrence of $\mathtt{f.halting}$, $+\mathtt{f.halting}$ or $-\mathtt{f.halting}$ leads to the first processing of $\mathtt{halting}$. Moreover, by the induction hypothesis, it is decidable whether $\mathit{Halting}^{\mathrm{r}}(v) = \mathsf{t}$. Because $\boldsymbol{p}'$ is finite, it follows that $\boldsymbol{p}' \downarrow \emptyset$ is decidable. Hence, $\boldsymbol{p} \downarrow \mathtt{f}.U'(v)$ is decidable. □

Theorems 5.2 and 5.3 together tell us that there exists a functional unit $U \in \mathcal{FU}(\mathbb{T})$, viz. $\emptyset$, with the property that the halting problem is potentially recursively autosolvable for $\mathcal{L}(\mathtt{f}.\mathcal{I}(U))$ with respect to U.

Let $U \in \mathcal{FU}(\mathbb{T})$ be such that all derived method operations of U are computable and do not increase the number of colons. Then the halting problem is potentially autosolvable for $\mathcal{L}(\mathtt{f}.\mathcal{I}(U))$ with respect to U. However, the halting problem is not always potentially recursively autosolvable for $\mathcal{L}(\mathtt{f}.\mathcal{I}(U))$ with respect to U because otherwise the halting problem would always be decidable.

The following theorem tells us essentially that potential autosolvability of the halting problem is precluded in the presence of the method operation *Dup*.

Theorem 5.4. *Let $U \in \mathcal{FU}(\mathbb{T})$ be such that $(\mathtt{dup}, \mathit{Dup}) \in U$, and let $I \subseteq \mathcal{I}(U)$ be such that $\mathtt{dup} \in I$. Then there does not exist a $\boldsymbol{p} \in \mathcal{L}(\mathtt{f}.\mathcal{I}(U))$ such that $\boldsymbol{p}$ produces a reflexive solution of the halting problem for $\mathcal{L}(\mathtt{f}.I)$ with respect to U.*

Proof. Assume the contrary. Let $\boldsymbol{p} \in \mathcal{L}(\mathtt{f}.\mathcal{I}(U))$ be such that $\boldsymbol{p}$ produces a reflexive solution of the halting problem for $\mathcal{L}(\mathtt{f}.I)$ with respect to U, and let $\boldsymbol{q} = \mathtt{f.dup}\ ;\ \mathit{f2d}(\mathit{swap}(\boldsymbol{p}))$. Then $\boldsymbol{p} \downarrow \mathtt{f}.U(\hat{\ }\overline{\boldsymbol{q}}\mathord{:}\overline{\boldsymbol{q}})$. By Propositions 3.3 and 5.2, it follows that $\mathit{swap}(\boldsymbol{p}) \downarrow \mathtt{f}.U(\hat{\ }\overline{\boldsymbol{q}}\mathord{:}\overline{\boldsymbol{q}})$ and either $\mathit{swap}(\boldsymbol{p})\ !\ \mathtt{f}.U(\hat{\ }\overline{\boldsymbol{q}}\mathord{:}\overline{\boldsymbol{q}}) = \mathsf{t}$ or $\mathit{swap}(\boldsymbol{p})\ !\ \mathtt{f}.U(\hat{\ }\overline{\boldsymbol{q}}\mathord{:}\overline{\boldsymbol{q}}) = \mathsf{f}$.

In the case where $\mathit{swap}(\boldsymbol{p}) \mathbin{!} \mathtt{f}.U(\hat{}\,\overline{\boldsymbol{q}}{:}\overline{\boldsymbol{q}}) = \mathsf{t}$, we have by Proposition 5.2 that (i) $\mathit{f2d}(\mathit{swap}(\boldsymbol{p})) \mathbin{!} \mathtt{f}.U(\hat{}\,\overline{\boldsymbol{q}}{:}\overline{\boldsymbol{q}}) = \mathsf{t}$ and (ii) $\boldsymbol{p} \mathbin{!} \mathtt{f}.U(\hat{}\,\overline{\boldsymbol{q}}{:}\overline{\boldsymbol{q}}) = \mathsf{f}$. By Proposition 5.1, it follows from (i) that $(\mathtt{f.dup};\mathit{f2d}(\mathit{swap}(\boldsymbol{p}))) \mathbin{!} \mathtt{f}.U(\hat{}\,\overline{\boldsymbol{q}}) = \mathsf{t}$. Since $\boldsymbol{q} = \mathtt{f.dup};\mathit{f2d}(\mathit{swap}(\boldsymbol{p}))$, we have $\boldsymbol{q} \mathbin{!} \mathtt{f}.U(\hat{}\,\overline{\boldsymbol{q}}) = \mathsf{t}$. On the other hand, because $\boldsymbol{p}$ produces a reflexive solution, it follows from (ii) that $\boldsymbol{q} \uparrow \mathtt{f}.U(\hat{}\,\overline{\boldsymbol{q}})$. By Proposition 3.3, this contradicts with $\boldsymbol{q} \mathbin{!} \mathtt{f}.U(\hat{}\,\overline{\boldsymbol{q}}) = \mathsf{t}$.

In the case where $\mathit{swap}(\boldsymbol{p}) \mathbin{!} \mathtt{f}.U(\hat{}\,\overline{\boldsymbol{q}}{:}\overline{\boldsymbol{q}}) = \mathsf{f}$, we have by Proposition 5.2 that (i) $\mathit{f2d}(\mathit{swap}(\boldsymbol{p})) \mathbin{!} \mathtt{f}.U(\hat{}\,\overline{\boldsymbol{q}}{:}\overline{\boldsymbol{q}}) = \mathsf{d}$ and (ii) $\boldsymbol{p} \mathbin{!} \mathtt{f}.U(\hat{}\,\overline{\boldsymbol{q}}{:}\overline{\boldsymbol{q}}) = \mathsf{t}$. By Proposition 5.1, it follows from (i) that $(\mathtt{f.dup};\mathit{f2d}(\mathit{swap}(\boldsymbol{p}))) \mathbin{!} \mathtt{f}.U(\hat{}\,\overline{\boldsymbol{q}}) = \mathsf{d}$. Since $\boldsymbol{q} = \mathtt{f.dup};\mathit{f2d}(\mathit{swap}(\boldsymbol{p}))$, we have $\boldsymbol{q} \mathbin{!} \mathtt{f}.U(\hat{}\,\overline{\boldsymbol{q}}) = \mathsf{d}$. On the other hand, because $\boldsymbol{p}$ produces a reflexive solution, it follows from (ii) that $\boldsymbol{q} \downarrow \mathtt{f}.U(\hat{}\,\overline{\boldsymbol{q}})$. By Proposition 3.3, this contradicts with $\boldsymbol{q} \mathbin{!} \mathtt{f}.U(\hat{}\,\overline{\boldsymbol{q}}) = \mathsf{d}$. □

It is easy to see that Theorem 5.4 goes through for all functional units for $\mathbb{T}$ of which *Dup* is a derived method operation. Recall that the functional units concerned include the aforementioned functional unit whose method operations correspond to the basic steps that a Turing machine with tape alphabet $\{0, 1, :\}$ can perform on its tape. Because of this, the unsolvability of the halting problem for Turing machines can be understood as a corollary of Theorem 5.4.

Below, we will give an alternative proof of Theorem 5.4. A case distinction is needed in both proofs, but in the alternative proof it concerns a minor issue. The issue in question is covered by the following lemma.

Lemma 5.1. *Let* $U \in \mathcal{FU}(\mathbb{T})$, *let* $I \subseteq \mathcal{I}(U)$, *let* $\boldsymbol{p} \in \mathcal{L}(\mathtt{f}.\mathcal{I}(U))$ *be such that* $\boldsymbol{p}$ *produces a reflexive solution of the halting problem for* $\mathcal{L}(\mathtt{f}.I)$ *with respect to* U, *let* $\boldsymbol{q} \in \mathcal{L}(\mathtt{f}.I)$, *and let* $v \in \{0, 1, :\}^*$. *Then* $\boldsymbol{q} \downarrow \mathtt{f}.U(\hat{}\,v)$ *implies* $\boldsymbol{q} \mathbin{!} \mathtt{f}.U(\hat{}\,v) = \boldsymbol{p} \mathbin{!} \mathtt{f}.U(\hat{}\,\overline{\mathit{f2d}(\boldsymbol{q})}{:}v)$.

Proof. By Proposition 3.3, it follows from $\boldsymbol{q} \downarrow \mathtt{f}.U(\hat{}\,v)$ that either $\boldsymbol{q} \mathbin{!} \mathtt{f}.U(\hat{}\,v) = \mathsf{t}$ or $\boldsymbol{q} \mathbin{!} \mathtt{f}.U(\hat{}\,v) = \mathsf{f}$.

In the case where $\boldsymbol{q} \mathbin{!} \mathtt{f}.U(\hat{}\,v) = \mathsf{t}$, we have by Propositions 3.3 and 5.2 that $\mathit{f2d}(\boldsymbol{q}) \downarrow \mathtt{f}.U(\hat{}\,v)$ and so $\boldsymbol{p} \mathbin{!} \mathtt{f}.U(\hat{}\,\overline{\mathit{f2d}(\boldsymbol{q})}{:}v) = \mathsf{t}$.

In the case where $\boldsymbol{q} \mathbin{!} \mathtt{f}.U(\hat{}\,v) = \mathsf{f}$, we have by Propositions 3.3 and 5.2 that $\mathit{f2d}(\boldsymbol{q}) \uparrow \mathtt{f}.U(\hat{}\,v)$ and so $\boldsymbol{p} \mathbin{!} \mathtt{f}.U(\hat{}\,\overline{\mathit{f2d}(\boldsymbol{q})}{:}v) = \mathsf{f}$. □

Proof. [Another proof of Theorem 5.4.] Assume the contrary. Let $\boldsymbol{p} \in \mathcal{L}(\mathtt{f}.\mathcal{I}(U))$ be such that $\boldsymbol{p}$ produces a reflexive solution of the halting problem for $\mathcal{L}(\mathtt{f}.I)$ with respect to U, and let $\boldsymbol{q} = \mathit{f2d}(\mathit{swap}(\mathtt{f.dup}\ ;\ \boldsymbol{p}))$. Then $\boldsymbol{p} \downarrow \mathtt{f}.U(\hat{}\,\overline{\boldsymbol{q}}{:}\overline{\boldsymbol{q}})$. By Propositions 3.3, 5.1 and 5.2, it follows that $\mathit{swap}(\mathtt{f.dup}\ ;\ \boldsymbol{p}) \downarrow \mathtt{f}.U(\hat{}\,\overline{\boldsymbol{q}})$. By Lemma 5.1, it follows that

$swap(\mathtt{f.dup}\,;\,\boldsymbol{p})\ !\ \mathtt{f}.U({}^{\frown}\overline{\boldsymbol{q}}) = \boldsymbol{p}\ !\ \mathtt{f}.U({}^{\frown}\overline{\boldsymbol{q}}{:}\overline{\boldsymbol{q}})$. By Proposition 5.2, it follows that $(\mathtt{f.dup}\,;\,\boldsymbol{p})\ !\ \mathtt{f}.U({}^{\frown}\overline{\boldsymbol{q}}) \neq \boldsymbol{p}\ !\ \mathtt{f}.U({}^{\frown}\overline{\boldsymbol{q}}{:}\overline{\boldsymbol{q}})$. On the other hand, by Proposition 5.1, we have that $(\mathtt{f.dup}\,;\,\boldsymbol{p})\ !\ \mathtt{f}.U({}^{\frown}\overline{\boldsymbol{q}}) = \boldsymbol{p}\ !\ \mathtt{f}.U({}^{\frown}\overline{\boldsymbol{q}}{:}\overline{\boldsymbol{q}})$. This contradicts with $(\mathtt{f.dup}\,;\,\boldsymbol{p})\ !\ \mathtt{f}.U({}^{\frown}\overline{\boldsymbol{q}}) \neq \boldsymbol{p}\ !\ \mathtt{f}.U({}^{\frown}\overline{\boldsymbol{q}}{:}\overline{\boldsymbol{q}})$. □

Both proofs of Theorem 5.4 given above are diagonalization proofs in disguise.

Let $U = \{(\mathtt{dup}, \mathit{Dup})\}$. By Theorem 5.4, the halting problem for $\mathcal{L}(\mathtt{f}.\{\mathtt{dup}\})$ with respect to U is not (potentially) autosolvable. However, it is decidable.

Theorem 5.5. *Let* $U = \{(\mathtt{dup}, \mathit{Dup})\}$. *Then the halting problem for* $\mathcal{L}(\mathtt{f}.\{\mathtt{dup}\})$ *with respect to* U *is decidable.*

Proof. Let $\boldsymbol{p} \in \mathcal{L}(\mathtt{f}.\{\mathtt{dup}\})$, and let $\boldsymbol{p}'$ be $\boldsymbol{p}$ with each occurrence of $\mathtt{f.dup}$ and $+\mathtt{f.dup}$ replaced by $\#1$ and each occurrence of $-\mathtt{f.dup}$ replaced by $\#2$. For all $v \in \mathbb{T}$, $\mathit{Dup}^{\mathrm{r}}(v) = \mathsf{t}$. Therefore, $\boldsymbol{p} \downarrow \mathtt{f}.U(v) \Leftrightarrow \boldsymbol{p}' \downarrow \emptyset$ for all $v \in \mathbb{T}$. Because $\boldsymbol{p}'$ is finite, $\boldsymbol{p}' \downarrow \emptyset$ is decidable. □

It follows from Theorem 5.5 that there exists a computable method operation by means of which a solution for the halting problem for $\mathcal{L}(\mathtt{f}.\{\mathtt{dup}\})$ can be produced. This leads us to the following corollary of Theorem 5.5.

Corollary 5.2. *There exist a computable* $U \in \mathcal{FU}(\mathbb{T})$ *with* $(\mathtt{dup}, \mathit{Dup}) \in U$, *an* $I \subseteq \mathcal{I}(U)$ *with* $\mathtt{dup} \in I$, *and a* $\boldsymbol{p} \in \mathcal{L}(\mathtt{f}.\mathcal{I}(U))$ *such that* $\boldsymbol{p}$ *produces a solution of the halting problem for* $\mathcal{L}(\mathtt{f}.I)$ *with respect to* U.

To the best of our knowledge, there are no existing results in computability theory directly related to Theorems 5.2–5.5. The closest to these results are probably the positive results in the setting of Turing machines that have been obtained with restrictions on the number of states, the minimum of the number of transitions where the tape head moves to the left and the number of transitions where the tape head moves to the right, or the number of different combinations of input symbol, direction of head move, and output symbol occurring in the transitions (see e.g. [Pavlotskaya (1973); Margenstern (1997)]).

5.2 Non-uniform Computational Complexity

In this section, we develop theory concerning non-uniform computational complexity based on the single-pass instruction sequences considered in SPISA.

In the first place, we define a counterpart of the classical non-uniform complexity class P/poly and formulate a counterpart of the well-known complexity theoretic conjecture that $\mathrm{NP} \not\subseteq \mathrm{P}/\mathrm{poly}$. Some evidence for this conjecture is the Karp-Lipton theorem [Karp and Lipton (1980)], which says that the polynomial time hierarchy collapses to the second level if $\mathrm{NP} \subseteq \mathrm{P}/\mathrm{poly}$. If the conjecture is right, then the conjecture that $\mathrm{P} \neq \mathrm{NP}$ is right as well.

Over and above that, we define a counterpart of the non-uniform complexity class $\mathrm{NP}/\mathrm{poly}$, introduce a notion of completeness for this complexity class using a non-uniform reducibility relation, and formulate three complexity hypotheses which concern restrictions on the instruction sequences used for computation. These three hypotheses are called super-polynomial feature elimination complexity hypotheses. The first of them is equivalent to the hypothesis that $\mathrm{NP}/\mathrm{poly} \not\subseteq \mathrm{P}/\mathrm{poly}$ and the second of them is equivalent to the hypothesis that $\mathrm{P}/\mathrm{poly} \not\subseteq \mathrm{L}/\mathrm{poly}$. We do not know whether there is an equivalent hypothesis for the third of them in well-known settings such as Turing machines with advice and Boolean circuits.

We show among other things that P/poly and $\mathrm{NP}/\mathrm{poly}$ coincide with their counterparts defined in this section and that a problem closely related to $\mathrm{3SAT}$ is NP-complete as well as complete for the counterpart of $\mathrm{NP}/\mathrm{poly}$.

5.2.1 *Instruction sequences acting on Boolean registers*

Our study of computational complexity is concerned with instruction sequences that act on Boolean registers. Preceding the study, we introduce special foci that serve as names of Boolean registers and describe the set of all closed SPISA terms that denote instruction sequences that matter to the counterpart of the classical non-uniform complexity class P/poly defined in Sect. 5.2.2.

In the instruction sequences which concern us in the remainder of Sect. 5.2, a number of Boolean registers is used as input registers, a number of Boolean registers is used as auxiliary registers, and one Boolean register is used as output register.

It is assumed that $\mathtt{in}{:}1, \mathtt{in}{:}2, \ldots \in \mathcal{F}$, $\mathtt{aux}{:}1, \mathtt{aux}{:}2, \ldots \in \mathcal{F}$, and $\mathtt{out} \in \mathcal{F}$. These foci play special roles:

- for each $i \in \mathbb{N}^+$, $\mathtt{in}{:}i$ serves as the name of the Boolean register that is used as ith input register in instruction sequences;
- for each $i \in \mathbb{N}^+$, $\mathtt{aux}{:}i$ serves as the name of the Boolean register that is used as ith auxiliary register in instruction sequences;

- $\mathtt{out}$ serves as the name of the Boolean register that is used as output register in instruction sequences.

We will write $\mathcal{F}_{\mathsf{in}}$ for $\{\mathtt{in}{:}i \mid i \in \mathbb{N}^+\}$ and $\mathcal{F}_{\mathsf{aux}}$ for $\{\mathtt{aux}{:}i \mid i \in \mathbb{N}^+\}$.

Definition 5.5. $\mathcal{IS}_{\mathrm{P}^*}$ is the set of all closed SPISA terms in which:

- plain basic instructions, positive test instructions and negative test instructions contain only basic instructions from the set

$$\{f.\mathtt{get} \mid f \in \mathcal{F}_{\mathsf{in}} \cup \mathcal{F}_{\mathsf{aux}}\} \cup \{f.\mathtt{set}{:}b \mid f \in \mathcal{F}_{\mathsf{aux}} \cup \{\mathtt{out}\} \land b \in \mathbb{B}\} \;;$$

- positive termination instructions and negative termination instructions do not occur;
- the repetition operator does not occur.

$\mathcal{IS}^{\mathrm{na}}_{\mathrm{P}^*}$ is the set of all closed SPISA terms from $\mathcal{IS}_{\mathrm{P}^*}$ in which:

- plain basic instructions, positive test instructions and negative test instructions contain only basic instructions from the set

$$\{f.\mathtt{get} \mid f \in \mathcal{F}_{\mathsf{in}}\} \cup \{\mathtt{out.set}{:}b \mid b \in \mathbb{B}\}\;.$$

$\mathcal{IS}_{\mathrm{P}^*}$ is the set of all closed SPISA terms denoting instruction sequences that matter to the complexity class P* which will be introduced in Sect. 5.2.2. $\mathcal{IS}^{\mathrm{na}}_{\mathrm{P}^*}$ is the set of all closed SPISA terms denoting instruction sequences that matter to this complexity class and in which no auxiliary registers are used.

We write $\mathrm{len}(t)$, where $t \in \mathcal{IS}_{\mathrm{P}^*}$, for the length of the SPISA instruction sequence denoted by t.

5.2.2 *The complexity class* P*

In the field of computational complexity, it is quite common to study the complexity of computing functions on finite strings over a binary alphabet. Since strings over an alphabet of any fixed size can be efficiently encoded as strings over a binary alphabet, it is sufficient to consider only a binary alphabet. We adopt the set $\mathbb{B}$ as preferred binary alphabet.

An important special case of functions on finite strings over a binary alphabet is the case where the value of functions is restricted to strings of length 1. Such a function is often identified with the set of strings of which it is the characteristic function. The set in question is usually called a language or a decision problem. The identification mentioned above allows of looking at the problem of computing a function $f : \mathbb{B}^* \to \mathbb{B}$ as the problem of deciding membership of the set $\{w \in \mathbb{B}^* \mid f(w) = \mathsf{t}\}$.

With each function $f : \mathbb{B}^* \to \mathbb{B}$, we can associate an infinite sequence $\langle f_n \rangle_{n \in \mathbb{N}}$ of functions, with $f_n : \mathbb{B}^n \to \mathbb{B}$ for every $n \in \mathbb{N}$, such that f_n is the restriction of f to $\mathbb{B}^n$ for each $n \in \mathbb{N}$. The complexity of computing such sequences of functions, which we call Boolean function families, by instruction sequences is studied in the remainder of Sect. 5.2. First, we introduce the class P* of all Boolean function families that can be computed by polynomial-length instruction sequences from $\mathcal{IS}_{\mathrm{P}^*}$.

An *n-ary Boolean function* is a function $f : \mathbb{B}^n \to \mathbb{B}$. Let φ be a Boolean formula containing the variables $v_1, \ldots, v_n$. Then φ induces an n-ary Boolean function f such that $f(b_1, \ldots, b_n) = \mathsf{t}$ iff φ is satisfied by the assignment σ to the variables $v_1, \ldots, v_n$ defined by $\sigma(v_1) = b_1, \ldots, \sigma(v_n) = b_n$. The Boolean function in question is called the Boolean function *induced* by φ.

A *Boolean function family* is an infinite sequence $\langle f_n \rangle_{n \in \mathbb{N}}$ of functions, where f_n is an n-ary Boolean function for each $n \in \mathbb{N}$. A Boolean function family $\langle f_n \rangle_{n \in \mathbb{N}}$ can be identified with the unique function $f : \mathbb{B}^* \to \mathbb{B}$ such that for each $n \in \mathbb{N}$, for each $w \in \mathbb{B}^n$, $f(w) = f_n(w)$. We are concerned with non-uniform complexity. Considering sets of Boolean function families as complexity classes looks to be most natural when studying non-uniform complexity. We will make the identification mentioned above only where connections with well-known complexity classes are made.

Definition 5.6. Let $n \in \mathbb{N}$, let $f : \mathbb{B}^n \to \mathbb{B}$, and let $t \in \mathcal{IS}_{\mathrm{P}^*}$. Then t *computes* f if there exists an $n' \in \mathbb{N}$ such that for all $b_1, \ldots, b_n \in \mathbb{B}$:

$$(|t| \,/\, ((\textstyle\bigoplus_{i=1}^{n} \mathtt{in}{:}i.BR(b_i)) \oplus (\bigoplus_{j=1}^{n'} \mathtt{aux}{:}j.BR(\mathsf{f})))) \bullet \mathtt{out}.BR(\mathsf{f})$$
$$= \mathtt{out}.BR(f(b_1, \ldots, b_n)) \;.$$

Definition 5.7. P* is the class of all Boolean function families $\langle f_n \rangle_{n \in \mathbb{N}}$ that satisfy:

> there exists a polynomial function $h : \mathbb{N} \to \mathbb{N}$ such that for all $n \in \mathbb{N}$ there exists a $t \in \mathcal{IS}_{\mathrm{P}^*}$ such that t computes f_n and $\mathrm{len}(t) \le h(n)$.

The question arises whether all n-ary Boolean functions can be computed by an instruction sequence from $\mathcal{IS}_{\mathrm{P}^*}$. This question can answered in the affirmative. They can even be computed, without using auxiliary Boolean registers, by an instruction sequence that contains no other jump instructions than #2.

Theorem 5.6. *For each $n \in \mathbb{N}$, for each n-ary Boolean function $f : \mathbb{B}^n \to \mathbb{B}$, there exists a*

$t \in \mathcal{IS}^{\mathrm{na}}_{\mathrm{P*}}$ in which no other jump instruction than #2 occurs such that t computes f and $\mathrm{len}(t) = O(2^n)$.

Proof. Let $inseq_n$ be the function from the set of all n-ary Boolean function $f : \mathbb{B}^n \to \mathbb{B}$ to $\mathcal{IS}^{\mathrm{na}}_{\mathrm{P*}}$ defined by induction on n as follows:

$$inseq_0(f) \quad = \begin{cases} -\mathtt{out.set{:}t}\,;\#2\,;! & \text{if } f() = \mathsf{t} \\ +\mathtt{out.set{:}f}\,;\#2\,;! & \text{if } f() = \mathsf{f}\,, \end{cases}$$
$$inseq_{n+1}(f) = -\mathtt{in{:}}n{+}1\mathtt{.get}\,;\#2\,;inseq_n(f_{\mathsf{t}})\,;inseq_n(f_{\mathsf{f}})\,,$$

where for each $f : \mathbb{B}^{n+1} \to \mathbb{B}$ and $b \in \mathbb{B}$, $f_b : \mathbb{B}^n \to \mathbb{B}$ is defined as follows:

$$f_b(b_1, \ldots, b_n) = f(b_1, \ldots, b_n, b)\,.$$

It is easy to prove by induction on n that $|\#2\,;inseq_n(f_{\mathsf{t}})\,;t| = |t|$. Using this fact, it is easy to prove by induction on n that $inseq_n(f)$ computes f. Moreover, it is easy to see that $\mathrm{len}(inseq_n(f)) = O(2^n)$. □

In the proof of Theorem 5.6, the instruction sequences yielded by the function $inseq_n$ contain the jump instruction #2. Each occurrence of #2 belongs to a jump chain ending in the instruction sequence $-\mathtt{out.set{:}t}\,;\#2\,;!$ or the instruction sequence $+\mathtt{out.set{:}f}\,;\#2\,;!$. Therefore, each occurrence of #2 can safely be replaced by the instruction $+\mathtt{out.set{:}f}$, which like #2 skips the next instruction. This point gives rise to the following interesting corollary.

Corollary 5.3. *For each $n \in \mathbb{N}$, for each n-ary Boolean function $f : \mathbb{B}^n \to \mathbb{B}$, there exists a $t \in \mathcal{IS}^{\mathrm{na}}_{\mathrm{P*}}$ in which jump instructions do not occur such that t computes f and* $\mathrm{len}(t) = O(2^n)$.

We consider the proof of Theorem 5.6 once again. Because the content of the Boolean register concerned is initially f, the question arises whether `out.set:f` can be dispensed with in instruction sequences computing Boolean functions. This question can be answered in the affirmative if we permit the use of auxiliary Boolean registers.

Theorem 5.7. *Let $n \in \mathbb{N}$, let $f : \mathbb{B}^n \to \mathbb{B}$, and let $t \in \mathcal{IS}_{\mathrm{P*}}$ be such that t computes f. Then there exists a $t' \in \mathcal{IS}_{\mathrm{P*}}$ in which the basic instruction `out.set:f` does not occur such that t' computes f and $\mathrm{len}(t')$ is linear in $\mathrm{len}(t)$.*

Proof. Let $o \in \mathbb{N}^+$ be such that the basic instructions $\mathtt{aux{:}}o\mathtt{.set{:}t}$, $\mathtt{aux{:}}o\mathtt{.set{:}f}$, and $\mathtt{aux{:}}o\mathtt{.get}$ do not occur in t. Let t'' be obtained from t by replacing each occurrence of the focus out by aux:o. Suppose that $t'' = u_1 ; \ldots ; u_k$. Let t' be obtained from $u_1 ; \ldots ; u_k$ as follows:

(1) stop if $u_1 \equiv\, !$;
(2) stop if there exists no $j \in [2, k]$ such that $u_{j-1} \not\equiv \mathtt{out.set{:}t}$ and $u_j \equiv\, !$;
(3) find the least $j \in [2, k]$ such that $u_{j-1} \not\equiv \mathtt{out.set{:}t}$ and $u_j \equiv\, !$;
(4) replace u_j by $+\mathtt{aux}{:}o.\mathtt{get}\, ;\, \mathtt{out.set{:}t}\, ;\, !$,
(5) for each $i \in [1, k]$, replace u_i by $\#l{+}2$ if $u_i \equiv \#l$ and $i < j < i + l$;
(6) repeat the preceding steps for the resulting instruction sequence.

It is easy to prove by induction on k that the Boolean function computed by t and the Boolean function computed by t' are the same. Moreover, it is easy to see that $\mathrm{len}(t') < 3 \cdot \mathrm{len}(t)$. Hence, $\mathrm{len}(t')$ is linear in $\mathrm{len}(t)$. □

Below, we dwell on obtaining instruction sequences that compute the Boolean functions induced by Boolean formulas from the Boolean formulas concerned. We will write $\varphi(b_1, \ldots, b_n)$, where φ is a Boolean formula containing the variables $v_1, \ldots, v_n$ and $b_1, \ldots, b_n \in \mathbb{B}$, to indicate that φ is satisfied by the assignment σ to the variables $v_1, \ldots, v_n$ defined by $\sigma(v_1) = b_1, \ldots, \sigma(v_n) = b_n$.

The Boolean function induced by a CNF-formula can be computed, without using auxiliary Boolean registers, by an instruction sequence from $\mathcal{IS}^{\mathrm{na}}_{\mathrm{P}*}$ that contains no other jump instructions than $\#2$ and whose length is linear in the size of the CNF-formula.

Theorem 5.8. *For each* CNF*-formula φ, there exists a $t \in \mathcal{IS}^{\mathrm{na}}_{\mathrm{P}*}$ in which no other jump instruction than $\#2$ occurs such that t computes the Boolean function induced by φ and* $\mathrm{len}(t)$ *is linear in the size of φ.*

Proof. Let $\mathit{inseq}_{\mathrm{cnf}}$ be the function from the set of all CNF-formulas containing the variables $v_1, \ldots, v_n$ to $\mathcal{IS}^{\mathrm{na}}_{\mathrm{P}*}$ as follows:

$$\begin{aligned}
&\mathit{inseq}_{\mathrm{cnf}}\big(\textstyle\bigwedge_{i\in[1,m]} \bigvee_{j\in[1,n_i]} \xi_{ij}\big) = \\
&\quad \mathit{inseq}'_{\mathrm{cnf}}(\xi_{11}) \,;\, \ldots \,;\, \mathit{inseq}'_{\mathrm{cnf}}(\xi_{1n_1}) \,;\, +\mathtt{out.set{:}f} \,;\, \#2 \,;\, ! \,; \\
&\quad \vdots \\
&\quad \mathit{inseq}'_{\mathrm{cnf}}(\xi_{m1}) \,;\, \ldots \,;\, \mathit{inseq}'_{\mathrm{cnf}}(\xi_{mn_m}) \,;\, +\mathtt{out.set{:}f} \,;\, \#2 \,;\, ! \,;\, +\mathtt{out.set{:}t} \,;\, ! \,,
\end{aligned}$$

where

$$\begin{aligned}
\mathit{inseq}'_{\mathrm{cnf}}(v_k) &= +\mathtt{in}{:}k.\mathtt{get} \,;\, \#2 \,, \\
\mathit{inseq}'_{\mathrm{cnf}}(\neg v_k) &= -\mathtt{in}{:}k.\mathtt{get} \,;\, \#2 \,.
\end{aligned}$$

It is easy to see that no other jump instruction than $\#2$ occurs in $inseq_{\mathrm{cnf}}(\varphi)$. Recall that a disjunction is satisfied if one of its disjuncts is satisfied and a conjunction is satisfied if each of its conjuncts is satisfied. Using these facts, it is easy to prove by induction on the number of clauses in a CNF-formula, and in the basis step by induction on the number of literals in a clause, that $inseq_{\mathrm{cnf}}(\varphi)$ computes the Boolean function induced by φ. Moreover, it is easy to see that $\mathrm{len}(inseq_{\mathrm{cnf}}(\varphi))$ is linear in the size of φ. □

In the proof of Theorem 5.8, it is shown that the Boolean function induced by a CNF-formula can be computed, without using auxiliary Boolean registers, by an instruction sequence from $\mathcal{IS}^{\mathrm{na}}_{\mathrm{P*}}$ that contains no other jump instructions than $\#2$. However, the instruction sequence concerned contains multiple termination instructions and both out.set:t and out.set:f. This raises the question whether further restrictions are possible. We have a negative result.

Theorem 5.9. *Let φ be the Boolean formula $v_1 \wedge v_2 \wedge v_3$. Then there does not exist a $t \in \mathcal{IS}^{\mathrm{na}}_{\mathrm{P*}}$ in which jump instructions do not occur, multiple termination instructions do not occur and the basic instruction* out.set:f *does not occur such that t computes the Boolean function induced by φ.*

Proof. Suppose that $t = u_1 \,;\, \ldots \,;\, u_k$ is an instruction sequence from $\mathcal{IS}^{\mathrm{na}}_{\mathrm{P*}}$ satisfying the restrictions and computing the Boolean function induced by φ. Consider the smallest $l \in [1, k]$ such that u_l is either out.set:t, +out.set:t or −out.set:t (there must be such an l). Because φ is not satisfied by all assignments to the variables v_1, v_2, v_3, it cannot be the case that $l = 1$. In the case where $l > 1$, for each $i \in [1, l-1]$, u_i is either in:j.get, +in:j.get or −in:j.get for some $j \in \{1, 2, 3\}$. This implies that, for each $i \in [0, l-1]$, there exists a basic Boolean formula ψ_i over the variables v_1, v_2, v_3 that is unique up to logical equivalence such that, for each $b_1, b_2, b_3 \in \mathbb{B}$, if the initial states of the Boolean registers named in:1, in:2 and in:3 are b_1, b_2 and b_3, respectively, then u_{i+1} will be executed iff $\psi_i(b_1, b_2, b_3)$. We have that $\psi_0 \Leftrightarrow \mathsf{t}$ and, for each $i \in [1, l-1]$, $\psi_i \Leftrightarrow (\psi_{i-1} \Rightarrow \mathsf{t})$ if $u_i \equiv$ in:j.get, $\psi_i \Leftrightarrow (\psi_{i-1} \Rightarrow v_j)$ if $u_i \equiv$ +in:j.get, and $\psi_i \Leftrightarrow (\psi_{i-1} \Rightarrow \neg v_j)$ if $u_i \equiv$ −in:j.get. Hence, for each $i \in [0, l-1]$, $\psi_i \Rightarrow \varphi$ implies $\mathsf{t} \Rightarrow \varphi$ or $v_j \Rightarrow \varphi$ or $\neg v_j \Rightarrow \varphi$ for some $j \in \{1, 2, 3\}$. Because the latter three Boolean formulas are no tautologies, $\psi_i \Rightarrow \varphi$ is no tautology either. This means that, for each $i \in [1, l-1]$, $\psi_i \Rightarrow \varphi$ is not satisfied by all assignments to the variables v_1, v_2, v_3. Hence, t cannot exist. □

According to Theorem 5.8, the Boolean function induced by a CNF-formula can be computed, without using auxiliary Boolean registers, by an instruction sequence from $\mathcal{IS}^{\mathrm{na}}_{\mathrm{P*}}$ that contains no other jump instructions than $\#2$ and whose length is linear in the size of the formula. If we permit arbitrary jump instructions, this result generalizes from CNF-formulas to arbitrary basic Boolean formulas, i.e. Boolean formulas in which no other connectives than $\neg$, $\vee$ and $\wedge$ occur.

Theorem 5.10. *For each basic Boolean formula φ, there exists a $\boldsymbol{t} \in \mathcal{IS}^{\mathrm{na}}_{\mathrm{P*}}$ in which the basic instruction* out.set:f *does not occur such that $\boldsymbol{t}$ computes the Boolean function induced by φ and $\mathrm{len}(\boldsymbol{t})$ is linear in the size of φ.*

Proof. Let $inseq_{\mathrm{bf}}$ be the function from the set of all basic Boolean formulas containing the variables $v_1, \ldots, v_n$ to $\mathcal{IS}^{\mathrm{na}}_{\mathrm{P*}}$ as follows:

$$inseq_{\mathrm{bf}}(\varphi) = inseq'_{\mathrm{bf}}(\varphi) \mathbin{;} {+}\mathtt{out.set{:}t} \mathbin{;} ! \,,$$

where

$$\begin{aligned}
inseq'_{\mathrm{bf}}(v_k) &= {+}\mathtt{in}{:}k\mathtt{.get} \,, \\
inseq'_{\mathrm{bf}}(\neg\varphi) &= inseq'_{\mathrm{bf}}(\varphi) \mathbin{;} \#2 \,, \\
inseq'_{\mathrm{bf}}(\varphi \vee \psi) &= inseq'_{\mathrm{bf}}(\varphi) \mathbin{;} \#\mathrm{len}(inseq'_{\mathrm{bf}}(\psi)){+}1 \mathbin{;} inseq'_{\mathrm{bf}}(\psi) \,, \\
inseq'_{\mathrm{bf}}(\varphi \wedge \psi) &= inseq'_{\mathrm{bf}}(\varphi) \mathbin{;} \#2 \mathbin{;} \#\mathrm{len}(inseq'_{\mathrm{bf}}(\psi)){+}2 \mathbin{;} inseq'_{\mathrm{bf}}(\psi) \,.
\end{aligned}$$

Using the same facts about disjunctions and conjunctions as in the proof of Theorem 5.8, it is easy to prove by induction on the structure of φ that $inseq_{\mathrm{bf}}(\varphi)$ computes the Boolean function induced by φ. Moreover, it is easy to see that $\mathrm{len}(inseq_{\mathrm{bf}}(\varphi))$ is linear in the size of φ. □

Because Boolean formulas can be looked upon as Boolean circuits in which all gates have out-degree 1, the question arises whether Theorem 5.10 generalizes from Boolean formulas to Boolean circuits. This question can be answered in the affirmative if we permit the use of auxiliary Boolean registers.

Theorem 5.11. *For each Boolean circuit C containing no other gates than $\neg$-gates, $\vee$-gates and $\wedge$-gates, there exists a $\boldsymbol{t} \in \mathcal{IS}_{\mathrm{P*}}$ in which the basic instruction* out.set:f *does not occur such that $\boldsymbol{t}$ computes the Boolean function induced by C and $\mathrm{len}(\boldsymbol{t})$ is linear in the size of C.*

Proof. Let $inseq_{\mathrm{bc}}$ be the function from the set of all Boolean circuits with input nodes $in_1, \ldots, in_n$ and gates $g_1, \ldots, g_m$ to $\mathcal{IS}^{\mathrm{na}}_{\mathrm{P*}}$ as follows:

$$inseq_{\mathrm{bc}}(C) = inseq'_{\mathrm{bc}}(g_1) \mathbin{;} \ldots \mathbin{;} inseq'_{\mathrm{bc}}(g_m) \mathbin{;} {+}\mathtt{aux}{:}m\mathtt{.get} \mathbin{;} {+}\mathtt{out.set{:}t} \mathbin{;} ! \,,$$

where

$$\begin{aligned}
&\mathit{inseq}'_{\mathrm{bc}}(g_k) = \\
&\quad \mathit{inseq}''_{\mathrm{bc}}(p)\ ;\ \#2\ ;\ {+}\mathtt{aux}{:}k.\mathtt{set}{:}\mathtt{t} \\
&\quad \text{if } g_k \text{ is a } \neg\text{-gate with direct preceding node } p\ , \\
&\mathit{inseq}'_{\mathrm{bc}}(g_k) = \\
&\quad \mathit{inseq}''_{\mathrm{bc}}(p)\ ;\ \#2\ ;\ \mathit{inseq}''_{\mathrm{bc}}(p')\ ;\ {+}\mathtt{aux}{:}k.\mathtt{set}{:}\mathtt{t} \\
&\quad \text{if } g_k \text{ is a } \lor\text{-gate with direct preceding nodes } p \text{ and } p'\ , \\
&\mathit{inseq}'_{\mathrm{bc}}(g_k) = \\
&\quad \mathit{inseq}''_{\mathrm{bc}}(p)\ ;\ \#2\ ;\ \#3\ ;\ \mathit{inseq}''_{\mathrm{bc}}(p')\ ;\ {+}\mathtt{aux}{:}k.\mathtt{set}{:}\mathtt{t} \\
&\quad \text{if } g_k \text{ is a } \land\text{-gate with direct preceding nodes } p \text{ and } p'\ ,
\end{aligned}$$

and

$$\begin{aligned}
\mathit{inseq}''_{\mathrm{bc}}(in_k) &= {+}\mathtt{in}{:}k.\mathtt{get}\ , \\
\mathit{inseq}''_{\mathrm{bc}}(g_k) &= {+}\mathtt{aux}{:}k.\mathtt{get}\ .
\end{aligned}$$

Using the same facts about disjunctions and conjunctions as in the proofs of Theorems 5.8 and 5.10, it is easy to prove by induction on the depth of C that $\mathit{inseq}_{\mathrm{bc}}(C)$ computes the Boolean function induced by C if $g_1, \ldots, g_m$ is a topological sorting of the gates of C. Moreover, it is easy to see that $\mathrm{len}(\mathit{inseq}_{\mathrm{bc}}(C))$ is linear in the size of C. □

P^* includes Boolean function families that correspond to uncomputable functions from $\mathbb{B}^*$ to $\mathbb{B}$. Take an undecidable set $N \subseteq \mathbb{N}$ and consider the Boolean function family $\langle f_n \rangle_{n \in \mathbb{N}}$ with, for each $n \in \mathbb{N}$, $f_n : \mathbb{B}^n \to \mathbb{B}$ defined by

$$\begin{aligned}
f_n(b_1, \ldots, b_n) &= \mathtt{t} \ \text{ if } n \in N\ , \\
f_n(b_1, \ldots, b_n) &= \mathtt{f} \ \text{ if } n \notin N\ .
\end{aligned}$$

For each $n \in N$, f_n is computed by the instruction sequence out.set:t;!. For each $n \notin N$, f_n is computed by the instruction sequence out.set:f ; !. The length of these instruction sequences is constant in n. Hence, $\langle f_n \rangle_{n \in \mathbb{N}}$ is in P^*. However, the corresponding function $f : \mathbb{B}^* \to \mathbb{B}$ is clearly uncomputable. This reminds of the fact that P/poly includes uncomputable functions from $\mathbb{B}^*$ to $\mathbb{B}$.

It happens that P^* and P/poly coincide, provided that we identify each Boolean function family $\langle f_n \rangle_{n \in \mathbb{N}}$ with the unique function $f : \mathbb{B}^* \to \mathbb{B}$ such that for each $n \in \mathbb{N}$, for each $w \in \mathbb{B}^n$, $f(w) = f_n(w)$.

Theorem 5.12. $\mathrm{P}^* = \mathrm{P}/\mathrm{poly}$.

Proof. We will prove the inclusion $\mathrm{P/poly} \subseteq \mathrm{P}^*$ using the definition of $\mathrm{P/poly}$ in terms of Boolean circuits and we will prove the inclusion $\mathrm{P}^* \subseteq \mathrm{P/poly}$ using the definition of $\mathrm{P/poly}$ in terms of Turing machines that take advice.

$\mathrm{P/poly} \subseteq \mathrm{P}^*$: Suppose that $\langle f_n \rangle_{n \in \mathbb{N}}$ in $\mathrm{P/poly}$. Then, for all $n \in \mathbb{N}$, there exists a Boolean circuit C such that C computes f_n and the size of C is polynomial in n. For each $n \in \mathbb{N}$, let C_n be such a C. From Theorem 5.11 and the fact that linear in the size of C_n implies polynomial in n, it follows that each Boolean function family in $\mathrm{P/poly}$ is also in P^*.

$\mathrm{P}^* \subseteq \mathrm{P/poly}$: Suppose that $\langle f_n \rangle_{n \in \mathbb{N}}$ in P^*. Then, for all $n \in \mathbb{N}$, there exists a $\boldsymbol{t} \in \mathcal{IS}_{\mathrm{P}^*}$ such that $\boldsymbol{t}$ computes f_n and $\mathrm{len}(\boldsymbol{t})$ is polynomial in n. For each $n \in \mathbb{N}$, let $\boldsymbol{t}_n$ be such a $\boldsymbol{t}$. Then f can be computed by a Turing machine that, on an input of size n, takes a binary description of $\boldsymbol{t}_n$ as advice and then just simulates the execution of $\boldsymbol{t}_n$. It is easy to see that, under the assumption that instructions of the forms $\mathtt{aux}{:}i.\boldsymbol{m}$, $+\mathtt{aux}{:}i.\boldsymbol{m}$, $-\mathtt{aux}{:}i.\boldsymbol{m}$ and $\#i$ with $i > \mathrm{len}(\boldsymbol{t}_n)$ do not occur in $\boldsymbol{t}_n$, the size of the description of $\boldsymbol{t}_n$ and the number of steps that it takes to simulate the execution of $\boldsymbol{t}_n$ are both polynomial in n. It is obvious that we can make the assumption without loss of generality. Hence, each Boolean function family in P^* is also in $\mathrm{P/poly}$. □

We do not know whether there are restrictions on the number of auxiliary Boolean registers in the definition of P^* (Definition 5.7) that lead to a class different from P^*. In particular, it is unknown to us whether the restriction to zero auxiliary Boolean registers leads to a class different from P^*.

5.2.3 *The non-uniform super-polynomial complexity hypothesis*

In this section, we introduce a complexity hypothesis which is a counterpart of the classical complexity theoretic conjecture that $3\mathrm{SAT} \notin \mathrm{P/poly}$ in the current setting. By the NP-completeness of 3SAT, $3\mathrm{SAT} \notin \mathrm{P/poly}$ is equivalent to $\mathrm{NP} \not\subseteq \mathrm{P/poly}$. If the conjecture that $3\mathrm{SAT} \notin \mathrm{P/poly}$ is right, then the conjecture that $\mathrm{NP} \neq \mathrm{P}$ is right as well. We talk here about a hypothesis instead of a conjecture because we are primarily interested in its consequences.

To formulate the hypothesis, we need a Boolean function family $\langle 3\mathrm{SAT}'_n \rangle_{n \in \mathbb{N}}$ that corresponds to 3SAT. We obtain this Boolean function family by encoding 3CNF-formulas as sequences of Boolean values.

We write $H(k)$ for $\binom{2k}{1} + \binom{2k}{2} + \binom{2k}{3}$.[1] $H(k)$ is the number of combinations of at most

[1] As usual, we write $\binom{k}{l}$ for the number of l-element subsets of a k-element set.

3 elements from a set with $2k$ elements. Notice that $H(k) = (4k^3 + 5k)/3$.

It is assumed that a countably infinite set $\{v_1, v_2, \ldots\}$ of propositional variables has been given. Moreover, it is assumed that a family of bijections

$$\langle \alpha_k : [1, H(k)] \to \{L \subseteq \{v_1, \neg v_1, \ldots, v_k, \neg v_k\} \mid 1 \leq \mathrm{card}(L) \leq 3\} \rangle_{k \in \mathbb{N}}$$

has been given that satisfies the following two conditions:

$$\forall i \in \mathbb{N} \bullet \forall j \in [1, H(i)] \bullet {\alpha_i}^{-1}(\alpha_{i+1}(j)) = j \;,$$
$$\alpha \text{ is polynomial-time computable} \;,$$

where $\alpha : \mathbb{N}^+ \to \{L \subseteq \{v_1, \neg v_1, v_2, \neg v_2, \ldots\} \mid 1 \leq \mathrm{card}(L) \leq 3\}$ is defined by

$$\alpha(i) = \alpha_{\min\{j \mid i \in [1, H(j)]\}}(i) \;.$$

The function α is well-defined owing to the first condition on $\langle \alpha_k \rangle_{k \in \mathbb{N}}$. The second condition is satisfiable, but it is not satisfied by all $\langle \alpha_k \rangle_{k \in \mathbb{N}}$ satisfying the first condition.

The basic idea underlying the encoding of 3CNF-formulas as sequences of Boolean values is as follows:

- if $n = H(k)$ for some $k \in \mathbb{N}$, then the input of $3\mathrm{SAT}'_n$ consists of one Boolean value for each disjunction of at most three literals from the set $\{v_1, \neg v_1, \ldots, v_k, \neg v_k\}$;
- each Boolean value indicates whether the corresponding disjunction occurs in the encoded 3CNF-formula;
- if $H(k) < n < H(k+1)$ for some $k \in \mathbb{N}$, then only the first $H(k)$ Boolean values form part of the encoding.

For each $n \in \mathbb{N}$, $3\mathrm{SAT}'_n : \mathbb{B}^n \to \mathbb{B}$ is defined as follows:

- if $n = H(k)$ for some $k \in \mathbb{N}$:

  $$3\mathrm{SAT}'_n(b_1, \ldots, b_n) = \mathsf{t} \;\text{ iff }\; \bigwedge_{i \in [1,n] \text{ s.t. } b_i = \mathsf{t}} \bigvee \alpha_k(i) \;\text{ is satisfiable} \;,$$

  where k is such that $n = H(k)$;
- if $H(k) < n < H(k+1)$ for some $k \in \mathbb{N}$:

  $$3\mathrm{SAT}'_n(b_1, \ldots, b_n) = 3\mathrm{SAT}'_{H(k)}(b_1, \ldots, b_{H(k)}) \;,$$

  where k is such that $H(k) < n < H(k+1)$.

Because $\langle \alpha_k \rangle_{k \in \mathbb{N}}$ satisfies the condition that ${\alpha_i}^{-1}(\alpha_{i+1}(j)) = j$ for all $i \in \mathbb{N}$ and $j \in [1, H(i)]$, we have for each $n \in \mathbb{N}$, for all $b_1, \ldots, b_n \in \mathbb{B}$:

$$3\mathrm{SAT}'_n(b_1, \ldots, b_n) = 3\mathrm{SAT}'_{n+1}(b_1, \ldots, b_n, \mathsf{f}) \;.$$

In other words, for each $n \in \mathbb{N}$, $3\mathrm{SAT}'_{n+1}$ can in essence handle all inputs that $3\mathrm{SAT}'_n$ can handle. This means that $\langle 3\mathrm{SAT}'_n \rangle_{n\in\mathbb{N}}$ converges to the unique function $3\mathrm{SAT}' : \mathbb{B}^* \to \mathbb{B}$ such that for each $n \in \mathbb{N}$, for each $w \in \mathbb{B}^n$, $3\mathrm{SAT}'(w) = 3\mathrm{SAT}'_n(w)$.

$3\mathrm{SAT}'$ is meant to correspond to $3\mathrm{SAT}$. Therefore, the following theorem does not come as a surprise. Notice that we identify in this theorem the Boolean function family $3\mathrm{SAT}' = \langle 3\mathrm{SAT}'_n \rangle_{n\in\mathbb{N}}$ with the unique function $3\mathrm{SAT}' : \mathbb{B}^* \to \mathbb{B}$ such that for each $n \in \mathbb{N}$, for each $w \in \mathbb{B}^n$, $3\mathrm{SAT}'(w) = 3\mathrm{SAT}'_n(w)$.

Theorem 5.13. $3\mathrm{SAT}'$ *is* NP*-complete.*

Proof. $3\mathrm{SAT}'$ is NP-complete iff $3\mathrm{SAT}'$ is in NP and $3\mathrm{SAT}'$ is NP-hard. Because $3\mathrm{SAT}$ is NP-complete, it is sufficient to prove that $3\mathrm{SAT}'$ is polynomial-time Karp reducible to $3\mathrm{SAT}$ and $3\mathrm{SAT}$ is polynomial-time Karp reducible to $3\mathrm{SAT}'$, respectively. In the rest of the proof, α is defined as above.

$3\mathrm{SAT}' \leq_{\mathrm{P}} 3\mathrm{SAT}$: Take the function f from $\mathbb{B}^*$ to the set of all 3CNF-formulas containing the variables $v_1, \ldots, v_k$ for some $k \in \mathbb{N}$ that is defined by $f(b_1, \ldots, b_n) = \bigwedge_{i \in [1, \max\{H(k) \mid H(k) \leq n\}] \text{ s.t. } b_i = \mathrm{t}} \bigvee \alpha(i)$. Then we have that $3\mathrm{SAT}'(b_1, \ldots, b_n) = 3\mathrm{SAT}(f(b_1, \ldots, b_n))$. It remains to show that f is polynomial-time computable. To compute $f(b_1, \ldots, b_n)$, α has to be computed for a number of times that is not greater than n and α is computable in time polynomial in n. Hence, f is polynomial-time computable.

$3\mathrm{SAT} \leq_{\mathrm{P}} 3\mathrm{SAT}'$: Take the unique function g from the set of all 3CNF-formulas containing the variables $v_1, \ldots, v_k$ for some $k \in \mathbb{N}$ to $\mathbb{B}^*$ such that for all 3CNF-formulas φ containing the variables $v_1, \ldots, v_k$ for some $k \in \mathbb{N}$, $f(g(\varphi)) = \varphi$ and there exists no $w \in \mathbb{B}^*$ shorter than $g(\varphi)$ such that $f(w) = \varphi$. We have that $3\mathrm{SAT}(\varphi) = 3\mathrm{SAT}'(g(\varphi))$. It remains to show that g is polynomial-time computable. Let l be the size of φ. To compute $g(\varphi)$, α has to be computed for each clause a number of times that is not greater than $H(l)$ and α is computable in time polynomial in $H(l)$. Moreover, φ contains at most l clauses. Hence, g is polynomial-time computable. □

Before we turn to the non-uniform super-polynomial complexity hypothesis, we touch lightly on the choice of the family of bijections in the definition of $3\mathrm{SAT}'$. It is easy to see that the choice is not essential. Let $3\mathrm{SAT}''$ be the same as $3\mathrm{SAT}'$, but based on another family of bijections, say $\langle \alpha'_n \rangle_{n\in\mathbb{N}}$, and let, for each $i \in \mathbb{N}$, for each $j \in [1, H(i)]$, $b'_j = b_{\alpha_i{}^{-1}(\alpha'_i(j))}$. Then:

- if $n = H(k)$ for some $k \in \mathbb{N}$:

$$3\mathrm{SAT}'_n(b_1, \dots, b_n) = 3\mathrm{SAT}''_n(b'_1, \dots, b'_n) ;$$

- if $H(k) < n < H(k+1)$ for some $k \in \mathbb{N}$:

$$3\mathrm{SAT}'_n(b_1, \dots, b_n) = 3\mathrm{SAT}''_n(b'_1, \dots, b'_{H(k)}, b_{H(k)+1}, \dots, b_n) ,$$

  where k is such that $H(k) < n < H(k+1)$.

This means that the only effect of another family of bijections is another order of the relevant arguments.

The *non-uniform super-polynomial complexity hypothesis* is the following hypothesis:

Hypothesis 5.1. $3\mathrm{SAT}' \notin \mathrm{P}^*$.

$3\mathrm{SAT}' \notin \mathrm{P}^*$ expresses in short that there does not exist a polynomial function $h : \mathbb{N} \to \mathbb{N}$ such that for all $n \in \mathbb{N}$ there exists a $\boldsymbol{t} \in \mathcal{IS}_{\mathrm{P}^*}$ such that $\boldsymbol{t}$ computes $3\mathrm{SAT}'_n$ and $\mathrm{len}(\boldsymbol{t}) \leq h(n)$. This corresponds with the following informal formulation of the non-uniform super-polynomial complexity hypothesis:

> the lengths of the shortest instruction sequences that compute the Boolean functions $3\mathrm{SAT}'_n$ are not bounded by a polynomial in n.

The statement that Hypothesis 5.1 is a counterpart of the conjecture that $3\mathrm{SAT} \notin \mathrm{P}/\mathrm{poly}$ is made rigorous in the following theorem.

Theorem 5.14. $3\mathrm{SAT}' \notin \mathrm{P}^*$ *is equivalent to* $3\mathrm{SAT} \notin \mathrm{P}/\mathrm{poly}$.

Proof. This follows immediately from Theorems 5.12 and 5.13 and the fact that 3SAT is NP-complete. □

5.2.4 *Splitting instruction sequences*

The instruction sequences considered in SPISA are sufficient to define a counterpart of P/poly, but not to define a counterpart of $\mathrm{NP}/\mathrm{poly}$. For a counterpart of $\mathrm{NP}/\mathrm{poly}$, we introduce in this section an extension of SPISA that allows for single-pass instruction sequences to split. We also introduce an extension of BTA with a behavioural counterpart of instruction sequence splitting that is reminiscent of thread forking. First, we extend SPISA with instruction sequence splitting.

It is assumed that a fixed but arbitrary countably infinite set $\mathcal{BP}$ of *Boolean parameters* has been given. Boolean parameters are used to set up a simple form of parameterization for single-pass instruction sequences.

SPISA$_{\text{iss}}$ is SPISA with built-in basic instructions for instruction sequence splitting. In SPISA$_{\text{iss}}$, the following basic instructions belong to $\mathfrak{A}$:

- for each $\boldsymbol{bp} \in \mathcal{BP}$, a *splitting instruction* $\mathsf{split}(\boldsymbol{bp})$;
- for each $\boldsymbol{bp} \in \mathcal{BP}$, a *direct replying instruction* $\mathsf{reply}(\boldsymbol{bp})$.

On execution of the instruction sequence $+\mathsf{split}(\boldsymbol{bp})\ ;\ \boldsymbol{t}$, the primitive instruction $+\mathsf{split}(\boldsymbol{bp})$ brings about concurrent execution of the instruction sequence $\boldsymbol{t}$ with the Boolean parameter $\boldsymbol{bp}$ instantiated to t and the instruction sequence $\#2;\boldsymbol{t}$ with the Boolean parameter $\boldsymbol{bp}$ instantiated to f. The case where $+\mathsf{split}(\boldsymbol{bp})$ is replaced by $-\mathsf{split}(\boldsymbol{bp})$ and the case where $+\mathsf{split}(\boldsymbol{bp})$ is replaced by $\mathsf{split}(\boldsymbol{bp})$ differ in the obvious ways.

On execution of the instruction sequence $+\mathsf{reply}(\boldsymbol{bp})\ ;\ \boldsymbol{t}$, the primitive instruction $+\mathsf{reply}(\boldsymbol{bp})$ brings about execution of the instruction sequence $\boldsymbol{t}$ if the value taken by the Boolean parameter $\boldsymbol{bp}$ is t and execution of the instruction sequence $\#2;\boldsymbol{t}$ if the value taken by the Boolean parameter $\boldsymbol{bp}$ is f. The case where $+\mathsf{reply}(\boldsymbol{bp})$ is replaced by $-\mathsf{reply}(\boldsymbol{bp})$ and the case where $+\mathsf{reply}(\boldsymbol{bp})$ is replaced by $\mathsf{reply}(\boldsymbol{bp})$ differ in the obvious ways.

A simple example of a closed SPISA$_{\text{iss}}$ term is

$$\mathsf{split}(\mathsf{par{:}1})\ ;\ \mathsf{a}\ ;\ \mathsf{b}\ ;\ -\mathsf{reply}(\mathsf{par{:}1})\ ;\ \#3\ ;\ \mathsf{c}\ ;\ \#2\ ;\ \mathsf{d}\ ;\ \mathsf{e}\ ;\ !$$

We will come back to this example at the end of the current section.

The axioms of SPISA$_{\text{iss}}$ are the same as the axioms of SPISA. The thread extraction operator for SPISA$_{\text{iss}}$ instruction sequences is the same as for SPISA instruction sequences. However, in the presence of the built-in basic instructions of SPISA$_{\text{iss}}$, the intended behaviour of the instruction sequence denoted by a closed term $\boldsymbol{t}$ is not described by $|\boldsymbol{t}|$. In the notation of the extension of BTA introduced below, the intended behaviour is described by $\|(\langle|\boldsymbol{t}|\rangle)$.

Definition 5.8. $\mathcal{IS}_{\mathrm{P}**}$ is the set of all closed SPISA$_{\text{iss}}$ terms in which:

- plain basic instructions, positive test instructions and negative test instructions contain only basic instructions from the set
$$\{f.\mathtt{get} \mid f \in \mathcal{F}_{\mathsf{in}}\} \cup \{\mathtt{out.set{:}t}\}$$
$$\cup\, \{\mathsf{split}(\boldsymbol{bp}) \mid \boldsymbol{bp} \in \mathcal{BP}\} \cup \{\mathsf{reply}(\boldsymbol{bp}) \mid \boldsymbol{bp} \in \mathcal{BP}\}\ ;$$
- positive termination instructions and negative termination instructions do not occur;

- the repetition operator does not occur.

Notice that no auxiliary registers are used in instruction sequences from $\mathcal{IS}_{\mathrm{P}^{**}}$ and that the basic instruction `out.set:f` does not occur in instruction sequences from $\mathcal{IS}_{\mathrm{P}^{**}}$.

As for $t \in \mathcal{IS}_{\mathrm{P}^{*}}$, we write $\mathrm{len}(t)$, where $t \in \mathcal{IS}_{\mathrm{P}^{**}}$, for the length of the $\mathrm{SPISA_{iss}}$ instruction sequence denoted by t.

We continue with introducing an extension of BTA with a mechanism for multi-threading that supports thread splitting, the behavioural counterpart of instruction sequence splitting. This extension, called BTA+MTTS (BTA with Multi-Threading and Thread Splitting), is entirely tailored to the behaviours of the instruction sequences that can be denoted by closed $\mathrm{SPISA_{iss}}$ terms.

It is assumed that the collection of threads to be interleaved takes the form of a sequence of threads, called a *thread vector*.

The interleaving of threads is based on the simplest deterministic interleaving strategy treated in [Bergstra and Middelburg (2007c)], namely cyclic interleaving, but any other plausible deterministic interleaving strategy would be appropriate for our purpose.[2] Cyclic interleaving basically operates as follows: at each stage of the interleaving, the first thread in the thread vector gets a turn to perform a basic action and then the thread vector undergoes cyclic permutation. We mean by cyclic permutation of a thread vector that the first thread in the thread vector becomes the last one and all others move one position to the left. If one thread in the thread vector becomes inactive, the whole does not become inactive till all others have terminated or become inactive.

We introduce the additional sort $\mathbf{TV}$ of *thread vectors*. To build terms of sort $\mathbf{T}$, we introduce the following additional operators:

- the unary *cyclic interleaving* operator $\parallel\ : \mathbf{TV} \to \mathbf{T}$;
- the unary *inaction at termination* operator $\mathsf{S_D} : \mathbf{T} \to \mathbf{T}$;
- for each $\boldsymbol{bp} \in \mathcal{BP}$ and $b \in \mathbb{B}$, the unary *parameter instantiation* operator $\mathsf{I}_b^{\boldsymbol{bp}} : \mathbf{T} \to \mathbf{T}$;
- for each $\boldsymbol{bp} \in \mathcal{BP}$, the binary *postconditional composition* operators $\_ \trianglelefteq \mathsf{split}(\boldsymbol{bp}) \trianglerighteq \_ :$ $\mathbf{T} \times \mathbf{T} \to \mathbf{T}$ and $\_ \trianglelefteq \mathsf{reply}(\boldsymbol{bp}) \trianglerighteq \_ : \mathbf{T} \times \mathbf{T} \to \mathbf{T}$.

To build terms of sort $\mathbf{TV}$, we introduce the following constants and operators:

- the *empty thread vector* constant $\langle\rangle : \to \mathbf{TV}$;

[2]Fairness of the strategy is not an issue because the behaviours of the instruction sequences denoted by the closed $\mathrm{SPISA_{iss}}$ terms that belong to $\mathcal{IS}_{\mathrm{P}^{**}}$ are finite threads. However, inaction of one thread in the thread vector should not prevent others to proceed.

- the *singleton thread vector* operator $\langle \_ \rangle : \mathbf{T} \to \mathbf{TV}$;
- the *thread vector concatenation* operator $\_ \frown \_ : \mathbf{TV} \times \mathbf{TV} \to \mathbf{TV}$.

We assume that there are infinitely many variables of sort $\mathbf{TV}$, including α.

For an operational intuition, $\mathsf{split}(\boldsymbol{bp})$ can be considered a thread splitting action: when the thread denoted by a closed term of the form $\boldsymbol{t} \trianglelefteq \mathsf{split}(\boldsymbol{bp}) \trianglerighteq \boldsymbol{t'}$ gets a turn at some stage of interleaving, this thread is split into two threads, namely the thread denoted by $\boldsymbol{t}$ with the Boolean parameter $\boldsymbol{bp}$ instantiated to t and the thread denoted by $\boldsymbol{t'}$ with the Boolean parameter $\boldsymbol{bp}$ instantiated to f. For an operational intuition, $\mathsf{reply}(\boldsymbol{bp})$ can be considered a direct replying action: the thread denoted by a closed term of the form $\boldsymbol{t} \trianglelefteq \mathsf{reply}(\boldsymbol{bp}) \trianglerighteq \boldsymbol{t'}$ proceeds, without any further processing of the action, as the thread denoted by $\boldsymbol{t}$ if the value taken by the Boolean parameter $\boldsymbol{bp}$ is t and as the thread denoted by $\boldsymbol{t'}$ if the value taken by the Boolean parameter $\boldsymbol{bp}$ is f.

The thread denoted by a closed term of the form $\|(\boldsymbol{t})$ is the thread that results from cyclic interleaving of the threads in the thread vector denoted by $\boldsymbol{t}$, covering the above-mentioned splitting of a thread in the thread vector into two threads. This splitting involves instantiation of Boolean parameters in threads. The thread denoted by a closed term of the form $\mathsf{I}_b^{\boldsymbol{bp}}(\boldsymbol{t})$ is the thread that results from instantiating the Boolean parameter $\boldsymbol{bp}$ to b in the thread denoted by $\boldsymbol{t}$. In the event of inaction of one thread in the thread vector, the whole becomes inactive only after all others have terminated or become inactive. The auxiliary operator $\mathsf{S_D}$ is introduced to describe this fully precise. The thread denoted by a closed term of the form $\mathsf{S_D}(\boldsymbol{t})$ is the thread that results from turning termination into inaction in the thread denoted by $\boldsymbol{t}$.

The axioms for cyclic interleaving with thread splitting, inaction at termination, and parameter instantiation are given in Tables 5.1, 5.2 and 5.3. In these tables, $\boldsymbol{a}$ stands for an arbitrary action from $\mathcal{A}$. With the exception of CSI11 and BPI8, the axioms simply formalize the informal explanations given above. Axiom CSI11 expresses that inaction occurs when $\mathsf{reply}(\boldsymbol{bp})$ is encountered while threads are interleaved. Axiom BPI8 expresses that inaction occurs when $\mathsf{split}(\boldsymbol{bp})$ is encountered while Boolean parameter $\boldsymbol{bp}$ is instantiated.

To be fully precise, we should give axioms concerning the constants and operators to build terms of the sort $\mathbf{TV}$ as well. We refrain from doing so because the constants and operators concerned are the usual ones for sequences.

To simplify matters, we will henceforth take the set $\{\mathsf{par}{:}i \mid i \in \mathbb{N}^+\}$ for the set $\mathcal{BP}$ of Boolean parameters.

Recall that the intended behaviour of the instruction sequence denoted by a closed

Table 5.1 Axioms for the cyclic interleaving operator

$\Vert(\langle\rangle) = \mathsf{S}$	CSI1
$\Vert(\langle \mathsf{S+} \rangle) = \mathsf{S+}$	CSI2
$\Vert(\langle \mathsf{S+} \rangle \frown \langle x \rangle \frown \alpha) = \Vert(\langle x \rangle \frown \alpha)$	CSI3
$\Vert(\langle \mathsf{S-} \rangle) = \mathsf{S-}$	CSI4
$\Vert(\langle \mathsf{S-} \rangle \frown \langle x \rangle \frown \alpha) = \Vert(\langle x \rangle \frown \alpha)$	CSI5
$\Vert(\langle \mathsf{S} \rangle \frown \alpha) = \Vert(\alpha)$	CSI6
$\Vert(\langle \mathsf{D} \rangle \frown \alpha) = \mathsf{S}_{\mathsf{D}}(\Vert(\alpha))$	CSI7
$\Vert(\langle \mathsf{tau} \circ x \rangle \frown \alpha) = \mathsf{tau} \circ \Vert(\alpha \frown \langle x \rangle)$	CSI8
$\Vert(\langle x \unlhd \boldsymbol{a} \unrhd y \rangle \frown \alpha) = \Vert(\alpha \frown \langle x \rangle) \unlhd \boldsymbol{a} \unrhd \Vert(\alpha \frown \langle y \rangle)$	CSI9
$\Vert(\langle x \unlhd \mathsf{split}(\boldsymbol{bp}) \unrhd y \rangle \frown \alpha) = \mathsf{tau} \circ \Vert(\alpha \frown \langle \mathsf{I}_{\mathsf{t}}^{\boldsymbol{bp}}(x) \rangle \frown \langle \mathsf{I}_{\mathsf{f}}^{\boldsymbol{bp}}(y) \rangle)$	CSI10
$\Vert(\langle x \unlhd \mathsf{reply}(\boldsymbol{bp}) \unrhd y \rangle \frown \alpha) = \mathsf{S}_{\mathsf{D}}(\Vert(\alpha))$	CSI11

Table 5.2 Axioms for the inaction at termination operator

$\mathsf{S}_{\mathsf{D}}(\mathsf{S+}) = \mathsf{D}$	S2D1
$\mathsf{S}_{\mathsf{D}}(\mathsf{S-}) = \mathsf{D}$	S2D1
$\mathsf{S}_{\mathsf{D}}(\mathsf{S}) = \mathsf{D}$	S2D3
$\mathsf{S}_{\mathsf{D}}(\mathsf{D}) = \mathsf{D}$	S2D4
$\mathsf{S}_{\mathsf{D}}(\mathsf{tau} \circ x) = \mathsf{tau} \circ \mathsf{S}_{\mathsf{D}}(x)$	S2D5
$\mathsf{S}_{\mathsf{D}}(x \unlhd \boldsymbol{a} \unrhd y) = \mathsf{S}_{\mathsf{D}}(x) \unlhd \boldsymbol{a} \unrhd \mathsf{S}_{\mathsf{D}}(y)$	S2D6
$\mathsf{S}_{\mathsf{D}}(x \unlhd \mathsf{split}(\boldsymbol{bp}) \unrhd y) = \mathsf{S}_{\mathsf{D}}(x) \unlhd \mathsf{split}(\boldsymbol{bp}) \unrhd \mathsf{S}_{\mathsf{D}}(y)$	S2D7
$\mathsf{S}_{\mathsf{D}}(x \unlhd \mathsf{reply}(\boldsymbol{bp}) \unrhd y) = \mathsf{S}_{\mathsf{D}}(x) \unlhd \mathsf{reply}(\boldsymbol{bp}) \unrhd \mathsf{S}_{\mathsf{D}}(y)$	S2D8

SPISA$_{\mathrm{iss}}$ term $\boldsymbol{t}$ is described by $\Vert(\langle |\boldsymbol{t}| \rangle)$. Concerning the intended behaviour of the instruction sequence denoted by the closed SPISA$_{\mathrm{iss}}$ term

$$\mathsf{split}(\mathsf{par{:}1}) \,;\, \mathtt{a} \,;\, \mathtt{b} \,;\, -\mathsf{reply}(\mathsf{par{:}1}) \,;\, \#3 \,;\, \mathtt{c} \,;\, \#2 \,;\, \mathtt{d} \,;\, \mathtt{e} \,;\, ! \,,$$

we can derive the following:

Table 5.3 Axioms for the parameter instantiation operator

$\mathsf{I}_b^{bp}(\mathsf{S{+}}) = \mathsf{S{+}}$	BPI1
$\mathsf{I}_b^{bp}(\mathsf{S{-}}) = \mathsf{S{-}}$	BPI2
$\mathsf{I}_b^{bp}(\mathsf{S}) = \mathsf{S}$	BPI3
$\mathsf{I}_b^{bp}(\mathsf{D}) = \mathsf{D}$	BPI4
$\mathsf{I}_b^{bp}(\mathsf{tau} \circ x) = \mathsf{tau} \circ \mathsf{I}_b^{bp}(x)$	BPI5
$\mathsf{I}_b^{bp}(x \trianglelefteq \boldsymbol{a} \trianglerighteq y) = \mathsf{I}_b^{bp}(x) \trianglelefteq \boldsymbol{a} \trianglerighteq \mathsf{I}_b^{bp}(y)$	BPI6
$\mathsf{I}_b^{bp}(x \trianglelefteq \mathsf{split}(\boldsymbol{bp}') \trianglerighteq y) = \mathsf{I}_b^{bp}(x) \trianglelefteq \mathsf{split}(\boldsymbol{bp}') \trianglerighteq \mathsf{I}_b^{bp}(y)$ if $\boldsymbol{bp} \neq \boldsymbol{bp}'$	BPI7
$\mathsf{I}_b^{bp}(x \trianglelefteq \mathsf{split}(\boldsymbol{bp}) \trianglerighteq y) = \mathsf{D}$	BPI8
$\mathsf{I}_b^{bp}(x \trianglelefteq \mathsf{reply}(\boldsymbol{bp}') \trianglerighteq y) = \mathsf{I}_b^{bp}(x) \trianglelefteq \mathsf{reply}(\boldsymbol{bp}') \trianglerighteq \mathsf{I}_b^{bp}(y)$ if $\boldsymbol{bp} \neq \boldsymbol{bp}'$	BPI9
$\mathsf{I}_\mathsf{t}^{bp}(x \trianglelefteq \mathsf{reply}(\boldsymbol{bp}) \trianglerighteq y) = \mathsf{tau} \circ \mathsf{I}_\mathsf{t}^{bp}(x)$	BPI10
$\mathsf{I}_\mathsf{f}^{bp}(x \trianglelefteq \mathsf{reply}(\boldsymbol{bp}) \trianglerighteq y) = \mathsf{tau} \circ \mathsf{I}_\mathsf{f}^{bp}(y)$	BPI11

$$
\begin{aligned}
&\|(\langle|\mathsf{split}(\mathsf{par{:}1})\,;\mathsf{a}\,;\mathsf{b}\,;-\mathsf{reply}(\mathsf{par{:}1})\,;\#3\,;\mathsf{c}\,;\#2\,;\mathsf{d}\,;\mathsf{e}\,;!|\rangle)\\
&= \|(\langle\mathsf{split}(\mathsf{par{:}1}) \circ \mathsf{a} \circ \mathsf{b} \circ ((\mathsf{c} \circ \mathsf{e} \circ \mathsf{S}) \trianglelefteq \mathsf{reply}(\mathsf{par{:}1}) \trianglerighteq (\mathsf{d} \circ \mathsf{e} \circ \mathsf{S}))\rangle)\\
&= \mathsf{tau} \circ \|(\langle\mathsf{a} \circ \mathsf{b} \circ \mathsf{tau} \circ \mathsf{c} \circ \mathsf{e} \circ \mathsf{S}\rangle \curvearrowright \langle\mathsf{a} \circ \mathsf{b} \circ \mathsf{tau} \circ \mathsf{d} \circ \mathsf{e} \circ \mathsf{S}\rangle)\\
&= \mathsf{tau} \circ \mathsf{a} \circ \mathsf{a} \circ \mathsf{b} \circ \mathsf{b} \circ \mathsf{tau} \circ \mathsf{tau} \circ \mathsf{c} \circ \mathsf{d} \circ \mathsf{e} \circ \mathsf{e} \circ \mathsf{S}\,.
\end{aligned}
$$

5.2.5 *The complexity class* P**

In this section, we introduce the class P^{**} of all Boolean function families that can be computed by polynomial-length instruction sequences from $\mathcal{IS}_{\mathrm{P}^{**}}$.

Definition 5.9. Let $n \in \mathbb{N}$, let $f : \mathbb{B}^n \to \mathbb{B}$, and let $\boldsymbol{t} \in \mathcal{IS}_{\mathrm{P}^{**}}$. Then $\boldsymbol{t}$ *splitting computes* f if for all $b_1, \ldots, b_n \in \mathbb{B}$:

$$(\|(\langle|\boldsymbol{t}|\rangle) \,/\, (\bigoplus_{i=1}^{n} \mathtt{in}{:}i.BR(b_i))) \bullet \mathtt{out}.BR(\mathsf{f}) = \mathtt{out}.BR(f(b_1, \ldots, b_n))\,.$$

Definition 5.10. P^{**} is the class of all Boolean function families $\langle f_n \rangle_{n \in \mathbb{N}}$ that satisfy:

> there exists a polynomial function $h : \mathbb{N} \to \mathbb{N}$ such that for all $n \in \mathbb{N}$ there exists a $\boldsymbol{t} \in \mathcal{IS}_{\mathrm{P}^{**}}$ such that $\boldsymbol{t}$ splitting computes f_n and $\mathrm{len}(\boldsymbol{t}) \leq h(n)$.

A question that arises is how P^{*} and P^{**} are related. It happens that P^{*} is included in P^{**}.

Theorem 5.15. $\mathrm{P}^* \subseteq \mathrm{P}^{**}$.

Proof. Suppose that $\langle f_n \rangle_{n \in \mathbb{N}}$ in P^*. Let $n \in \mathbb{N}$, and let $t \in \mathcal{IS}_{\mathrm{P}^*}$ be such that t computes f_n and $\mathrm{len}(t)$ is polynomial in n. Assume that the basic instruction $\mathtt{out.set{:}f}$ does not occur in t. By Theorem 5.7, this assumption can be made without loss of generality. Then a $t'' \in \mathcal{IS}_{\mathrm{P}^{**}}$ such that t'' splitting computes f_n and $\mathrm{len}(t'')$ is polynomial in n can be obtained from t as described below.

Suppose that $t = u_1 ; \ldots ; u_k$. Let $t' \in \mathcal{IS}_{\mathrm{P}^*}$ be obtained from $u_1 ; \ldots ; u_k$ as follows:

(1) stop if there exists no $i \in [1,k]$ such that $u_i \equiv -\mathtt{aux}{:}j\mathtt{.set{:}t}$ or $u_i \equiv +\mathtt{aux}{:}j\mathtt{.set{:}f}$ for some $j \in \mathbb{N}^+$;
(2) find the least $i \in [1,k]$ such that $u_i \equiv -\mathtt{aux}{:}j\mathtt{.set{:}t}$ or $u_i \equiv +\mathtt{aux}{:}j\mathtt{.set{:}f}$ for some $j \in \mathbb{N}^+$;
(3) if $u_i \equiv -\mathtt{aux}{:}j\mathtt{.set{:}t}$ for some $j \in \mathbb{N}^+$, then replace u_i by $+\mathtt{aux}{:}j\mathtt{.set{:}t} ; \#2$;
(4) if $u_i \equiv +\mathtt{aux}{:}j\mathtt{.set{:}f}$ for some $j \in \mathbb{N}^+$, then replace u_i by $-\mathtt{aux}{:}j\mathtt{.set{:}f} ; \#2$;
(5) for each $i' \in [1,k]$, replace $u_{i'}$ by $\#l{+}1$ if $u_{i'} \equiv \#l$ and $i' < i < i' + l$;
(6) repeat the preceding steps for the resulting instruction sequence.

Now, suppose that $t' = u'_1 ; \ldots ; u'_{k'}$. Let $t'' \in \mathcal{IS}_{\mathrm{P}^{**}}$ be obtained from $u'_1 ; \ldots ; u'_{k'}$ as follows:

(1) stop if there exists no $i \in [1,k']$ such that $u'_i \equiv \mathtt{aux}{:}j\mathtt{.set}{:}b$ or $u'_i \equiv +\mathtt{aux}{:}j\mathtt{.set{:}t}$ or $u'_i \equiv -\mathtt{aux}{:}j\mathtt{.set{:}f}$ for some $j \in \mathbb{N}^+$ and $b \in \mathbb{B}$;
(2) find the greatest $i \in [1,k']$ such that $u'_i \equiv \mathtt{aux}{:}j\mathtt{.set}{:}b$ or $u'_i \equiv +\mathtt{aux}{:}j\mathtt{.set{:}t}$ or $u'_i \equiv -\mathtt{aux}{:}j\mathtt{.set{:}f}$ for some $j \in \mathbb{N}^+$ and $b \in \mathbb{B}$;
(3) find the unique $j \in \mathbb{N}^+$ such that focus $\mathsf{aux}{:}j$ occurs in u'_i;
(4) find the least $j' \in \mathbb{N}^+$ such that parameter $\mathsf{par}{:}j'$ does not occur in $u'_i ; \ldots ; u'_{k'}$;
(5) if $u'_i \equiv \mathtt{aux}{:}j\mathtt{.set{:}t}$ or $u'_i \equiv +\mathtt{aux}{:}j\mathtt{.set{:}t}$, then replace u'_i by $-\mathsf{split}(\mathsf{par}{:}j') ; !$;
(6) if $u'_i \equiv \mathtt{aux}{:}j\mathtt{.set{:}f}$ or $u'_i \equiv -\mathtt{aux}{:}j\mathtt{.set{:}f}$, then replace u'_i by $+\mathsf{split}(\mathsf{par}{:}j') ; !$;
(7) for each $i' \in [1,k']$, replace $u'_{i'}$ by $\#l{+}1$ if $u'_{i'} \equiv \#l$ and $i' < i < i' + l$;
(8) for each $i' \in [i+1,k']$:
    (a) if $u'_{i'} \equiv \mathtt{aux}{:}j\mathtt{.get}$, then replace $u'_{i'}$ by $\mathsf{reply}(\mathsf{par}{:}j')$,
    (b) if $u'_{i'} \equiv +\mathtt{aux}{:}j\mathtt{.get}$, then replace $u'_{i'}$ by $+\mathsf{reply}(\mathsf{par}{:}j')$,
    (c) if $u'_{i'} \equiv -\mathtt{aux}{:}j\mathtt{.get}$, then replace $u'_{i'}$ by $-\mathsf{reply}(\mathsf{par}{:}j')$;
(9) repeat the preceding steps for the resulting instruction sequence.

It is easy to prove by induction on k that the Boolean function computed by $\boldsymbol{t}$ and the Boolean function computed by $\boldsymbol{t}'$ are the same, and it is easy to prove by induction on k' that the Boolean function computed by $\boldsymbol{t}'$ and the Boolean function splitting computed by $\boldsymbol{t}''$ are the same. Moreover, it is easy to see that $\mathrm{len}(\boldsymbol{t}'') \leq 3 \cdot \mathrm{len}(\boldsymbol{t})$. Hence, $\mathrm{len}(\boldsymbol{t}'')$ is also polynomial in n. □

The chances are that $\mathrm{P}^{**} \not\subseteq \mathrm{P}^*$. In Sect. 5.2.6, we will hypothesize this.

In Sect. 5.2.3, we have hypothesized that $3\mathrm{SAT}' \notin \mathrm{P}^*$. The question arises whether $3\mathrm{SAT}' \in \mathrm{P}^{**}$. This question can be answered in the affirmative.

Theorem 5.16. $3\mathrm{SAT}' \in \mathrm{P}^{**}$.

Proof. Let $n \in \mathbb{N}$, let $k \in \mathbb{N}$ be the unique k such that $H(k) \leq n < H(k+1)$, and, for each $b_1, \ldots, b_n \in \mathbb{B}$, let $\varphi_{b_1,\ldots,b_n}$ be the formula $\bigwedge_{i \in [1,H(k)] \text{ s.t. } b_i = \mathrm{t}} \bigvee \alpha_k(i)$. We have that $3\mathrm{SAT}'_n(b_1, \ldots, b_n) = \mathrm{t}$ iff $\varphi_{b_1,\ldots,b_n}$ is satisfiable. Let ψ be the basic Boolean formula $\bigwedge_{i \in [1,n]} (\neg v_{k+i} \vee \bigvee \alpha_k(i))$. We have that $\varphi_{b_{k+1},\ldots,b_{k+n}}(b_1, \ldots, b_k)$ iff $\psi(b_1, \ldots, b_{k+n})$. Let $\boldsymbol{t} \in \mathcal{IS}^{\mathrm{na}}_{\mathrm{P}^*}$ be such that the basic instruction out.set:f does not occur in $\boldsymbol{t}$, $\boldsymbol{t}$ computes the Boolean function induced by ψ, and $\mathrm{len}(\boldsymbol{t})$ is polynomial in n. It follows from Theorem 5.10 that such a $\boldsymbol{t}$ exists. Assume that instructions in:i.get, +in:i.get, and −in:i.get with $i > k$ do not occur in $\boldsymbol{t}$. It is obvious that this assumption can be made without loss of generality. Let $\boldsymbol{t}' \in \mathcal{IS}_{\mathrm{P}^{**}}$ be the instruction sequence obtained from $\boldsymbol{t}$ by replacing, for each $i \in [1, k]$, all occurrences of the primitive instructions in:i.get, +in:i.get, and −in:i.get by the primitive instructions reply(par:i), +reply(par:i), and −reply(par:i), respectively, and let $\boldsymbol{t}'' = $ split(par:1) ; … ; split(par:k) ; $\boldsymbol{t}'$. We have that $\boldsymbol{t}'' \in \mathcal{IS}_{\mathrm{P}^{**}}$, $\boldsymbol{t}''$ splitting computes $3\mathrm{SAT}'_n$, and $\mathrm{len}(\boldsymbol{t}'')$ is polynomial in n. Hence, $3\mathrm{SAT}' \in \mathrm{P}^{**}$. □

Below we will define P^{**}-completeness. We would like to call P^{**}-completeness the counterpart of NP/poly-completeness in the current setting, but the notion of NP/poly-completeness looks to be absent in the literature on complexity theory. The closest to NP/poly-completeness that we could find is p-completeness for pD, a notion introduced in [Skyum and Valiant (1985)]. Like NP-completeness, P^{**}-completeness will be defined in terms of a reducibility relation. Because $3\mathrm{SAT}'$ is closely related to 3SAT and $3\mathrm{SAT}' \in \mathrm{P}^{**}$, we expect $3\mathrm{SAT}'$ to be P^{**}-complete.

Definition 5.11. Let $l, m, n \in \mathbb{N}$, and let $f : \mathbb{B}^n \to \mathbb{B}$ and $g : \mathbb{B}^m \to \mathbb{B}$. Then f is *length l reducible* to g, written $f \leq^l_{\mathrm{P}^*} g$, if there exist $h_1, \ldots, h_m : \mathbb{B}^n \to \mathbb{B}$ such that:

- there exist $\boldsymbol{t}_1, \ldots, \boldsymbol{t}_m \in \mathcal{IS}_{\mathrm{P}^*}$ such that $\boldsymbol{t}_1, \ldots, \boldsymbol{t}_m$ compute $h_1, \ldots, h_m$ and

$\mathrm{len}(\boldsymbol{t}_1), \ldots, \mathrm{len}(\boldsymbol{t}_m) \leq l$;
- for all $b_1, \ldots, b_n \in \mathbb{B}$, $f(b_1, \ldots, b_n) = g(h_1(b_1, \ldots, b_n), \ldots, h_m(b_1, \ldots, b_n))$.

Let $\langle f_n \rangle_{n \in \mathbb{N}}$ and $\langle g_n \rangle_{n \in \mathbb{N}}$ be Boolean function families. Then $\langle f_n \rangle_{n \in \mathbb{N}}$ is *non-uniform polynomial-length reducible* to $\langle g_n \rangle_{n \in \mathbb{N}}$, written $\langle f_n \rangle_{n \in \mathbb{N}} \leq_{\mathrm{P}^*} \langle g_n \rangle_{n \in \mathbb{N}}$, if there exists a polynomial function $q : \mathbb{N} \to \mathbb{N}$ such that:

- for all $n \in \mathbb{N}$, there exist $l, m \in \mathbb{N}$ with $l, m \leq q(n)$ such that $f_n \leq^l_{\mathrm{P}^*} g_m$.

Definition 5.12. Let $\langle f_n \rangle_{n \in \mathbb{N}}$ be a Boolean function family. Then $\langle f_n \rangle_{n \in \mathbb{N}}$ is P^{**}*-complete* if:

- $\langle f_n \rangle_{n \in \mathbb{N}} \in \mathrm{P}^{**}$;
- for all $\langle g_n \rangle_{n \in \mathbb{N}} \in \mathrm{P}^{**}$, $\langle g_n \rangle_{n \in \mathbb{N}} \leq_{\mathrm{P}^*} \langle f_n \rangle_{n \in \mathbb{N}}$.

The most important properties of non-uniform polynomial-length reducibility and P^{**}-completeness as defined above are stated in the following two propositions.

Proposition 5.3.

(1) if $\langle f_n \rangle_{n \in \mathbb{N}} \leq_{\mathrm{P}^*} \langle g_n \rangle_{n \in \mathbb{N}}$ and $\langle g_n \rangle_{n \in \mathbb{N}} \in \mathrm{P}^*$, then $\langle f_n \rangle_{n \in \mathbb{N}} \in \mathrm{P}^*$;
(2) $\leq_{\mathrm{P}^*}$ is reflexive and transitive.

Proof. Both properties follow immediately from the definition of $\leq_{\mathrm{P}^*}$. □

Proposition 5.4.

(1) if $\langle f_n \rangle_{n \in \mathbb{N}}$ is P^{**}-complete and $\langle f_n \rangle_{n \in \mathbb{N}} \in \mathrm{P}^*$, then $\mathrm{P}^{**} = \mathrm{P}^*$;
(2) if $\langle f_n \rangle_{n \in \mathbb{N}}$ is P^{**}-complete, $\langle g_n \rangle_{n \in \mathbb{N}} \in \mathrm{P}^{**}$ and $\langle f_n \rangle_{n \in \mathbb{N}} \leq_{\mathrm{P}^*} \langle g_n \rangle_{n \in \mathbb{N}}$, then $\langle g_n \rangle_{n \in \mathbb{N}}$ is P^{**}-complete.

Proof. The first property follows immediately from the definition of P^{**}-completeness, and the second property follows immediately from the definition of P^{**}-completeness and the transitivity of $\leq_{\mathrm{P}^*}$. □

The properties stated in Proposition 5.4 make P^{**}-completeness as defined above adequate for our purposes. In the following proposition, non-uniform polynomial-length reducibility is related to polynomial-time Karp reducibility ($\leq_{\mathrm{P}}$).

Proposition 5.5. *Let $\langle f_n \rangle_{n \in \mathbb{N}}$ and $\langle g_n \rangle_{n \in \mathbb{N}}$ be Boolean function families, and let f and g be the unique functions $f, g : \mathbb{B}^* \to \mathbb{B}$ such that for each $n \in \mathbb{N}$, for each $w \in \mathbb{B}^n$, $f(w) = f_n(w)$ and $g(w) = g_n(w)$. Then $f \leq_{\mathrm{P}} g$ only if $\langle f_n \rangle_{n \in \mathbb{N}} \leq_{\mathrm{P}^*} \langle g_n \rangle_{n \in \mathbb{N}}$.*

Proof. This property follows immediately from the definitions of $\leq_{\mathrm{P}}$ and $\leq_{\mathrm{P}^*}$, the well-known fact that $\mathrm{P} \subseteq \mathrm{P/poly}$ (see e.g. [Arora and Barak (2009)], Sect. 6.2) , and Theorem 5.12. □

The property stated in Proposition 5.5 allows for results concerning polynomial-time Karp reducibility to be reused in the current setting.

Now we turn to the anticipated P**-completeness of 3SAT′.

Theorem 5.17. 3SAT′ *is* P**-*complete.*

Proof. By Theorem 5.16, we have that $3\mathrm{SAT}' \in \mathrm{P}^{**}$. It remains to prove that for all $\langle f_n \rangle_{n \in \mathbb{N}} \in \mathrm{P}^{**}$, $\langle f_n \rangle_{n \in \mathbb{N}} \leq_{\mathrm{P}^*} 3\mathrm{SAT}'$.

Suppose that $\langle f_n \rangle_{n \in \mathbb{N}} \in \mathrm{P}^{**}$. Let $n \in \mathbb{N}$, and let $\boldsymbol{t} \in \mathcal{IS}_{\mathrm{P}^{**}}$ be such that $\boldsymbol{t}$ splitting computes f_n and $\mathrm{len}(\boldsymbol{t})$ is polynomial in n. Assume that out.set:t occurs only once in $\boldsymbol{t}$. This assumption can be made without loss of generality: multiple occurrences can always be eliminated by replacement by jump instructions (on execution, instructions possibly following those occurrences do not change the state of the Boolean register named out). Suppose that $\boldsymbol{t} = \boldsymbol{u}_1 ; \ldots ; \boldsymbol{u}_k$, and let $l \in [1, k]$ be such that $\boldsymbol{u}_l$ is either out.set:t, +out.set:t or −out.set:t.

We look for a transformation that gives, for each $b_1, \ldots, b_n \in \mathbb{B}$, a Boolean formula $\varphi_{b_1,\ldots,b_n}$ such that $f_n(b_1, \ldots, b_n) = \mathsf{t}$ iff $\varphi_{b_1,\ldots,b_n}$ is satisfiable. Notice that, for fixed initial states of the Boolean registers named in:1, …, in:n, it is possible that there exist several execution paths through $\boldsymbol{t}$ because of the split instructions that may occur in $\boldsymbol{t}$. We have that $f_n(b_1, \ldots, b_n) = \mathsf{t}$ iff there exists an execution path through $\boldsymbol{t}$ that reaches $\boldsymbol{u}_l$ if the initial states of the Boolean registers named in:1, …, in:n are $b_1, \ldots, b_n$, respectively. The existence of such an execution path corresponds to the satisfiability of the Boolean formula $v_1 \wedge v_l \wedge \bigwedge_{i \in [2,k]} (v_i \Leftrightarrow \bigvee_{j \in B(i)} v_j)$, where, for each $i \in [2, k]$, $B(i)$ is the set of all $j \in [1, i]$ for which execution may proceed with $\boldsymbol{u}_i$ after execution of $\boldsymbol{u}_j$ if the initial states of the Boolean registers named in:1, …, in:n are $b_1, \ldots, b_n$, respectively. Let $\varphi_{b_1,\ldots,b_n}$ be this Boolean formula. Then $f_n(b_1, \ldots, b_n) = \mathsf{t}$ iff $\varphi_{b_1,\ldots,b_n}$ is satisfiable.

For some $m \in \mathbb{N}$, $\varphi_{b_1,\ldots,b_n}$ still has to be transformed into a $w_{b_1,\ldots,b_n} \in \mathbb{B}^m$ such that $\varphi_{b_1,\ldots,b_n}$ is satisfiable iff $3\mathrm{SAT}'_m(w_{b_1,\ldots,b_n}) = \mathsf{t}$. We look upon this transformation as a composition of two transformations: first $\varphi_{b_1,\ldots,b_n}$ is transformed into a 3CNF-formula $\psi_{b_1,\ldots,b_n}$ such that $\varphi_{b_1,\ldots,b_n}$ is satisfiable iff $\psi_{b_1,\ldots,b_n}$ is satisfiable, and next, for some $m \in \mathbb{N}$, $\psi_{b_1,\ldots,b_n}$ is transformed into a $w_{b_1,\ldots,b_n} \in \mathbb{B}^m$ such that $\psi_{b_1,\ldots,b_n}$ is satisfiable iff $3\mathrm{SAT}'_m(w_{b_1,\ldots,b_n}) = \mathsf{t}$.

It is easy to see that the size of $\varphi_{b_1,\ldots,b_n}$ is polynomial in n and that $(b_1,\ldots,b_n)$ can be transformed into $\varphi_{b_1,\ldots,b_n}$ in time polynomial in n. It is well-known that each Boolean formula ψ can be transformed in time polynomial in the size of ψ into a 3CNF-formula ψ', with size and number of variables linear in the size of ψ, such that ψ is satisfiable iff ψ' is satisfiable (see e.g. [Balcázar *et al.* (1988)], Theorem 3.7). Moreover, it is known from the proof of Theorem 5.13 that each 3CNF-formula φ can be transformed in time polynomial in the size of φ into a $w \in \mathbb{B}^{H(k')}$, where k' is the number of variables in φ, such that $\mathrm{3SAT}(\varphi) = \mathrm{3SAT}'(w)$. From these facts, and Proposition 5.5, it follows easily that $\langle f_n \rangle_{n \in \mathbb{N}}$ is non-uniform polynomial-length reducible to 3SAT′. □

It happens that P^{**} and NP/poly coincide.

Theorem 5.18. $\mathrm{P}^{**} = \mathrm{NP/poly}$.

Proof. It follows easily from the definitions concerned that $f \in \mathrm{NP/poly}$ iff there exist a $k \in \mathbb{N}$ and a $g \in \mathrm{P/poly}$ such that, for all $w \in \mathbb{B}^*$:

$$f(w) = \mathsf{t} \Leftrightarrow \exists c \in \mathbb{B}^* \bullet (|c| \leq |w|^k \wedge g(w,c) = \mathsf{t}) .$$

Below, we will refer to such a g as a *checking function* for f. We will first prove the inclusion $\mathrm{NP/poly} \subseteq \mathrm{P}^{**}$ and then the inclusion $\mathrm{P}^{**} \subseteq \mathrm{NP/poly}$.

$\mathrm{NP/poly} \subseteq \mathrm{P}^{**}$: Suppose that $f \in \mathrm{NP/poly}$. Then there exists a checking function for f. Let g be a checking function for f, and let $\langle g_n \rangle_{n \in \mathbb{N}}$ be the Boolean function family corresponding to g. Because $g \in \mathrm{P/poly}$, we have by Theorem 5.12 that $\langle g_n \rangle_{n \in \mathbb{N}} \in \mathrm{P}^*$. This implies that, for all $n \in \mathbb{N}$, there exists a $\boldsymbol{t} \in \mathcal{IS}_{\mathrm{P}^*}$ such that $\boldsymbol{t}$ computes g_n and $\mathrm{len}(\boldsymbol{t})$ is polynomial in n. For each $n \in \mathbb{N}$, let $\boldsymbol{t}_n$ be such a $\boldsymbol{t}$. Moreover, let $\langle f_n \rangle_{n \in \mathbb{N}}$ be the Boolean function family corresponding to f. For each $n \in \mathbb{N}$, there exists an $m \in \mathbb{N}$ such that a $\boldsymbol{t}' \in \mathcal{IS}_{\mathrm{P}^{**}}$ can be obtained from $\boldsymbol{t}_m$ in the way followed in the proof of Theorem 5.15 such that $\boldsymbol{t}'$ splitting computes f_n and $\mathrm{len}(\boldsymbol{t}')$ is polynomial in n. Hence, each Boolean function family in NP/poly is also in P^{**}.

$\mathrm{P}^{**} \subseteq \mathrm{NP/poly}$: Suppose that $\langle f_n \rangle_{n \in \mathbb{N}} \in \mathrm{P}^{**}$. Then, for all $n \in \mathbb{N}$, there exists a $\boldsymbol{t} \in \mathcal{IS}_{\mathrm{P}^{**}}$ such that $\boldsymbol{t}$ splitting computes f_n and $\mathrm{len}(\boldsymbol{t})$ is polynomial in n. For each $n \in \mathbb{N}$, let $\boldsymbol{t}_n$ be such a $\boldsymbol{t}$. Moreover, let $f : \mathbb{B}^* \to \mathbb{B}$ be the function corresponding to $\langle f_n \rangle_{n \in \mathbb{N}}$. Then a checking function g for f can be computed by a Turing machine as follows: on a proper input of size n, it takes a binary description of $\boldsymbol{t}_n$ as advice and then simulates the execution of $\boldsymbol{t}_n$ treating the proper input as a description of the choices to make at each split. It is easy to see that, under the assumption that instructions $\mathsf{split}(\mathsf{par}{:}i)$, $+\mathsf{split}(\mathsf{par}{:}i)$,

$-$split(par:i), reply(par:i), $+$reply(par:i), $-$reply(par:i) and $\#i$ with $i > \mathrm{len}(\boldsymbol{t}_n)$ do not occur in $\boldsymbol{t}_n$, the size of the description of $\boldsymbol{t}_n$ and the number of steps that it takes to simulate the execution of $\boldsymbol{t}_n$ are both polynomial in n. It is obvious that we can make the assumption without loss of generality. Hence, each Boolean function family in P** is also in NP/poly.

□

A known result about classical complexity classes turns out to be a corollary of Theorems 5.12, 5.13, 5.17 and 5.18.

Corollary 5.4. $\mathrm{NP} \not\subseteq \mathrm{P/poly}$ *is equivalent to* $\mathrm{NP/poly} \not\subseteq \mathrm{P/poly}$.

Notice that it is justified by Theorem 5.18 to regard the definition of P**-completeness given in this section (Definition 5.12) as a definition of NP/poly-completeness in the setting of single-pass instruction sequences and consequently to read Theorem 5.17 as $3\mathrm{SAT}'$ is NP/poly-complete.

5.2.6 *Super-polynomial feature elimination complexity hypotheses*

In this section, we introduce three complexity hypotheses which concern restrictions on the instruction sequences with which Boolean functions are computed.

By Theorem 5.15, we have that $\mathrm{P}^* \subseteq \mathrm{P}^{**}$. We hypothesize that $\mathrm{P}^{**} \not\subseteq \mathrm{P}^*$. We can think of P^* as roughly obtained from P^{**} by restricting the computing instruction sequences to non-splitting instruction sequences. This motivates the formulation of the hypothesis that $\mathrm{P}^{**} \not\subseteq \mathrm{P}^*$ as a feature elimination complexity hypothesis.

The *first super-polynomial feature elimination complexity hypothesis* is the following hypothesis:

Hypothesis 5.2. *Let* $\rho : \mathcal{IS}_{\mathrm{P}^{**}} \to \mathcal{IS}_{\mathrm{P}^*}$ *be such that, for each* $\boldsymbol{t} \in \mathcal{IS}_{\mathrm{P}^{**}}$, $\rho(\boldsymbol{t})$ *computes the same Boolean function as* $\boldsymbol{t}$. *Then* $\mathrm{len}(\rho(\boldsymbol{t}))$ *is not polynomially bounded in* $\mathrm{len}(\boldsymbol{t})$.

We can also think of complexity classes obtained from P^* by restricting the computing instruction sequences further. They can, for instance, be restricted to instruction sequences in which:

- primitive instructions of the forms $f.m$, $+f.m$ and $-f.m$ with $f \in \mathcal{F}_{\mathsf{aux}}$ do not occur;
- for some fixed $k \in \mathbb{N}$, primitive instructions of the form $\#l$ with $l > k$ do not occur;
- primitive instructions out.set:f, $+$out.set:f and $-$out.set:f do not occur;

- multiple termination instructions do not occur.

Below we introduce two hypotheses that concern the first two of these restrictions.

The *second super-polynomial feature elimination complexity hypothesis* is the following hypothesis:

Hypothesis 5.3. *Let* $\rho : \mathcal{IS}_{\mathrm{P}*} \to \mathcal{IS}^{\mathrm{na}}_{\mathrm{P}*}$ *be such that, for each* $\boldsymbol{t} \in \mathcal{IS}_{\mathrm{P}*}$, $\rho(\boldsymbol{t})$ *computes the same Boolean function as* $\boldsymbol{t}$. *Then* $\mathrm{len}(\rho(\boldsymbol{t}))$ *is not polynomially bounded in* $\mathrm{len}(\boldsymbol{t})$.

The *third super-polynomial feature elimination complexity hypothesis* is the following hypothesis:

Hypothesis 5.4. *Let* $k \in \mathbb{N}$, *and let* $\rho : \mathcal{IS}^{\mathrm{na}}_{\mathrm{P}*} \to \mathcal{IS}^{\mathrm{na}}_{\mathrm{P}*}$ *be such that, for each* $\boldsymbol{t} \in \mathcal{IS}^{\mathrm{na}}_{\mathrm{P}*}$, $\rho(\boldsymbol{t})$ *computes the same Boolean function as* $\boldsymbol{t}$ *and, for each jump instruction* $\#l$ *occurring in* $\rho(\boldsymbol{t})$, $l \leq k$. *Then* $\mathrm{len}(\rho(\boldsymbol{t}))$ *is not polynomially bounded in* $\mathrm{len}(\boldsymbol{t})$.

These hypotheses motivate the introduction of subclasses of P^*. For each $k, l \in \mathbb{N}$, P^k_l is the class of all Boolean function families $\langle f_n \rangle_{n \in \mathbb{N}}$ that satisfy:

> there exists a polynomial function $h : \mathbb{N} \to \mathbb{N}$ such that for all $n \in \mathbb{N}$ there exists a $\boldsymbol{t} \in \mathcal{IS}_{\mathrm{P}*}$ such that:
>
> - $\boldsymbol{t}$ computes f_n and $\mathrm{len}(\boldsymbol{t}) \leq h(n)$;
> - primitive instructions of the forms $\boldsymbol{f}.m$, $+\boldsymbol{f}.m$ and $-\boldsymbol{f}.m$ with $\boldsymbol{f} = \mathtt{aux}{:}i$ for some $i > k$ do not occur in $\boldsymbol{t}$;
> - primitive instructions of the form $\#l'$ with $l' > l$ do not occur in $\boldsymbol{t}$.

Moreover, for each $k, l \in \mathbb{N}$, P^k_* is the class $\bigcup_{l \in \mathbb{N}} \mathrm{P}^k_l$, and P^*_l is the class $\bigcup_{k \in \mathbb{N}} \mathrm{P}^k_l$.

The hypotheses formulated above, can also be expresses in terms of these subclasses of P^*: Hypotheses 5.2, 5.3, and 5.4 are equivalent to $\mathrm{P}^{**} \not\subseteq \mathrm{P}^*$, $\mathrm{P}^* \not\subseteq \mathrm{P}^0_*$, and $\mathrm{P}^0_* \not\subseteq \mathrm{P}^0_k$ for all $k \in \mathbb{N}$, respectively.

Remark 5.1. It is well-known that, for all $f : \mathbb{B}^* \to \mathbb{B}$, $f \in \mathrm{L/poly}$ iff f has polynomial-size branching programs (see e.g. [Thierauf (2000)]). Moreover, the threads produced by the instruction sequences from $\mathcal{IS}^{\mathrm{na}}_{\mathrm{P}*}$ are in essence the polynomial-size branching programs. Hence, $\mathrm{P}^0_* = \mathrm{L/poly}$. This means that Hypothesis 5.3 is also equivalent to $\mathrm{P/poly} \not\subseteq \mathrm{L/poly}$.

Chapter 6

Computer-Architectural Issues

This chapter concerns two subjects from the area of computer architecture which have to do with instruction sequences and instruction processing, namely instruction sequence performance and instruction set architectures.

Although instruction sequences with direct and indirect jump instructions are as expressive as instruction sequences with direct jump instructions only, indirect jump instructions are widely used to implement features of contemporary high-level programming languages. Therefore, we consider a further analysis of indirect jump instructions relevant. We study the effect of eliminating indirect jump instructions from instruction sequences with direct and indirect jump instructions on the interactive performance of instruction sequences.

We propose a strict version of the concept of a load/store instruction set architecture for theoretical work relevant to the design of instruction set architectures. The idea underlying this concept is that there is a main memory whose elements contain data, an operating unit with a small internal memory by which data can be manipulated, and an interface between the main memory and the operating unit for data transfer between them. We study how the transformations on the states of the main memory of a strict load/store instruction set architecture that can be achieved by executing instruction sequences on it depend on parameters such as the size of its operating unit memory, the cardinality of its instruction set, and the maximal number of states of the behaviours produced by instruction sequences executed on it.

6.1 Instruction Sequence Performance

In this section, we introduce the maximal internal delay of an $\mathrm{ISNR}_{\mathrm{ij}}$ instruction sequence as a performance measure for such an instruction sequence and show that, in the case where the number of instructions is not bounded, there exist instruction sequences with direct and indirect jump instructions from which elimination of indirect jump instructions is possible without a super-linear increase of their maximal internal delay on execution only at the cost of a super-linear increase of their length.

It is assumed that a fixed but arbitrary set $\mathfrak{X} \subset \mathfrak{A}$ of *auxiliary basic instructions* has been given. The view is that, in common with the effect of jump instructions, the effect of auxiliary basic instructions is wholly unobservable externally, but contributes to the realization of externally observable behaviour. Typical examples of auxiliary basic instructions are basic instructions for storing and fetching data of a temporary nature. Typical examples of non-auxiliary basic instructions are basic instructions for reading input data from a keyboard, showing output data on a screen and writing data of a permanent nature on a disk.

The maximal internal delay of an ISNR_{ij} instruction sequence concerns the delays that takes place between successive non-auxiliary basic instructions on execution of the instruction sequence. That is why it is considered a measure of interactive performance. Another conceivable performance measure is the largest possible sum of the delays that takes place between successive non-auxiliary basic instructions on execution of the instruction sequence. However, this measure looks to be less adequate to the interactive performance of instruction sequences.

Before we define the maximal internal delay of an ISNR_{ij} instruction sequence, we define the execution traces of an ISNR_{ij} instruction sequence. Recall that, in ISNR_{ij}, it is assumed that fixed but arbitrary positive natural numbers i_{max} and n_{max} have been given, which are considered the number of natural number registers available and the greatest natural number that can be contained in a natural number register, respectively.

Let $\rho : [1, i_{\text{max}}] \to [0, n_{\text{max}}]$, $j \in \mathbb{N}$, and let $\boldsymbol{u}_1 \,;\ldots;\, \boldsymbol{u}_k$ be an ISNR_{ij} instruction sequence. Then $tr(\rho, j, \boldsymbol{u}_1 \,;\ldots;\, \boldsymbol{u}_k)$ is the set of all finite sequences of primitive instructions of ISNR_{ij} that may be encountered successively on execution of $\boldsymbol{u}_1 \,;\ldots;\, \boldsymbol{u}_k$ if execution starts with $\boldsymbol{u}_j$, with the registers used for indirect jumps set according to ρ. The set $tr(\rho, j, \boldsymbol{u}_1 \,;\ldots;\, \boldsymbol{u}_k)$ is inductively defined by the following clauses:

(1) $\epsilon \in tr(\rho, j, \boldsymbol{u}_1 \,;\ldots;\, \boldsymbol{u}_k)$;

(2) if $\boldsymbol{u}_j \equiv \boldsymbol{a}$ or $\boldsymbol{u}_j \equiv +\boldsymbol{a}$ or $\boldsymbol{u}_j \equiv -\boldsymbol{a}$, and $\sigma \in tr(\rho, j+1, \boldsymbol{u}_1 \,;\ldots;\, \boldsymbol{u}_k)$, then $\boldsymbol{u}_j\sigma \in tr(\rho, j, \boldsymbol{u}_1 \,;\ldots;\, \boldsymbol{u}_k)$;

(3) if $\boldsymbol{u}_j \equiv +\boldsymbol{a}$ or $\boldsymbol{u}_j \equiv -\boldsymbol{a}$, and $\sigma \in tr(\rho, j+2, \boldsymbol{u}_1 \,;\ldots;\, \boldsymbol{u}_k)$, then $\boldsymbol{u}_j\sigma \in tr(\rho, j, \boldsymbol{u}_1 \,;\ldots;\, \boldsymbol{u}_k)$;

(4) if $\boldsymbol{u}_j \equiv \#l$ and $\sigma \in tr(\rho, j+l, \boldsymbol{u}_1 \,;\ldots;\, \boldsymbol{u}_k)$, then $\boldsymbol{u}_j\sigma \in tr(\rho, j, \boldsymbol{u}_1 \,;\ldots;\, \boldsymbol{u}_k)$;

(5) if $\boldsymbol{u}_j \equiv \backslash\#l$ and $\sigma \in tr(\rho, j \dot{-} l, \boldsymbol{u}_1 ; \ldots ; \boldsymbol{u}_k)$, then $\boldsymbol{u}_j\sigma \in tr(\rho, j, \boldsymbol{u}_1 ; \ldots ; \boldsymbol{u}_k)$;

(6) if $\boldsymbol{u}_j \equiv \mathsf{set}{:}i{:}n$ and $\sigma \in tr(\rho \oplus [i \mapsto n], j+1, \boldsymbol{u}_1 ; \ldots ; \boldsymbol{u}_k)$, then $\boldsymbol{u}_j\sigma \in tr(\rho, j, \boldsymbol{u}_1 ; \ldots ; \boldsymbol{u}_k)$;

(7) if $\boldsymbol{u}_j \equiv \mathsf{i}\#i$ and $\sigma \in tr(\rho, j + \rho(i), \boldsymbol{u}_1 ; \ldots ; \boldsymbol{u}_k)$, then $\boldsymbol{u}_j\sigma \in tr(\rho, j, \boldsymbol{u}_1 ; \ldots ; \boldsymbol{u}_k)$;

(8) if $\boldsymbol{u}_j \equiv \mathsf{i}\backslash\#i$ and $\sigma \in tr(\rho, j \dot{-} \rho(i), \boldsymbol{u}_1 ; \ldots ; \boldsymbol{u}_k)$, then $\boldsymbol{u}_j\sigma \in tr(\rho, j, \boldsymbol{u}_1 ; \ldots ; \boldsymbol{u}_k)$;

(9) if $\boldsymbol{u}_j \equiv \mathsf{!t}$ or $\boldsymbol{u}_j \equiv \mathsf{!f}$ or $\boldsymbol{u}_j \equiv \mathsf{!}$, then $\boldsymbol{u}_j \in tr(\rho, j, \boldsymbol{u}_1 ; \ldots ; \boldsymbol{u}_k)$.

For example,

$$tr(\rho_0, 1, +\mathsf{a} ; \#3 ; \mathsf{set}{:}1{:}3 ; \#2 ; \mathsf{set}{:}1{:}1 ; \mathsf{i}\#1 ; \mathsf{b} ; \#2 ; \mathsf{c} ; \mathsf{!})\ ,$$

where ρ_0 is defined by $\rho_0(i) = 0$ for all $i \in [1, i_{\max}]$, contains

$$+\mathsf{a}\ \ \#3\ \ \mathsf{set}{:}1{:}1\ \ \mathsf{i}\#1\ \ \mathsf{b}\ \ \#2\ \ \mathsf{!}\ ,$$
$$+\mathsf{a}\ \ \mathsf{set}{:}1{:}3\ \ \#2\ \ \mathsf{i}\#1\ \ \mathsf{c}\ \ \mathsf{!}\ ,$$

and all prefixes of these two sequences, including the empty sequence.

Definition 6.1. The set of *execution traces* of an $\mathrm{ISNR_{ij}}$ instruction sequence $\boldsymbol{p}$, written $tr(\boldsymbol{p})$, is $tr(\rho_0, 1, \boldsymbol{p})$, where ρ_0 is defined by $\rho_0(i) = 0$ for all $i \in [1, i_{\max}]$.

Definition 6.2. The *maximal internal delay* of an $\mathrm{ISNR_{ij}}$ instruction sequence $\boldsymbol{p}$, written $MID(\boldsymbol{p})$, is the largest $n \in \mathbb{N}$ for which there exists an execution trace $\boldsymbol{u}_1 \ldots \boldsymbol{u}_k \in tr(\boldsymbol{p})$ and $i_1, i_2 \in [1, k]$ with $i_1 \leq i_2$ such that $ID(\boldsymbol{u}_j) \neq 0$ for all $j \in [i_1, i_2]$ and $ID(\boldsymbol{u}_{i_1}) + \ldots + ID(\boldsymbol{u}_{i_2}) = n$, where $ID(\boldsymbol{u})$ is defined as follows:

$$\begin{array}{lll}
ID(\boldsymbol{a}) = 0 \quad \text{if } \boldsymbol{a} \notin \mathfrak{X}\ , & ID(\#l) = 1\ , & ID(\mathsf{!t}) = 0\ , \\
ID(\boldsymbol{a}) = 1 \quad \text{if } \boldsymbol{a} \in \mathfrak{X}\ , & ID(\backslash\#l) = 1\ , & ID(\mathsf{!f}) = 0\ , \\
ID(+\boldsymbol{a}) = 0 \ \text{if } \boldsymbol{a} \notin \mathfrak{X}\ , & ID(\mathsf{set}{:}i{:}n) = 1\ , & ID(\mathsf{!}) = 0\ . \\
ID(+\boldsymbol{a}) = 1 \ \text{if } \boldsymbol{a} \in \mathfrak{X}\ , & ID(\mathsf{i}\#i) = 2\ , & \\
ID(-\boldsymbol{a}) = 0 \ \text{if } \boldsymbol{a} \notin \mathfrak{X}\ , & ID(\mathsf{i}\backslash\#i) = 2\ , & \\
ID(-\boldsymbol{a}) = 1 \ \text{if } \boldsymbol{a} \in \mathfrak{X}\ , & &
\end{array}$$

Suppose that in the example given above a, b and c are non-auxiliary basic instructions. Then

$$MID(+\mathsf{a} ; \#3 ; \mathsf{set}{:}1{:}3 ; \#2 ; \mathsf{set}{:}1{:}1 ; \mathsf{i}\#1 ; \mathsf{b} ; \#2 ; \mathsf{c} ; \mathsf{!}) = 4\ .$$

This delay takes place between the execution of a and the execution of b or c.

Remark 6.1. In [Bergstra and van der Zwaag (2008)], an extension of BTA is proposed which allows for internal delays to be described and analysed. We could formally describe the behaviours produced by ISNR$_{\text{ij}}$ instruction sequences under execution, internal delays included, using this extension of BTA. The notion of maximal internal delay of an ISNR$_{\text{ij}}$ instruction sequence has been defined above so as to be justifiable by such a formal description of the behaviours produced by ISNR$_{\text{ij}}$ instruction sequences under execution.

The time that it takes to execute one basic instruction is taken for the time unit in the definition of the maximal internal delay of an ISNR$_{\text{ij}}$ instruction sequence given above. By that $MID(\boldsymbol{p})$ can be looked upon as the number of basic instruction that can be executed during the maximal internal delay of $\boldsymbol{p}$. It is customary to refer to the time that it takes to execute one basic instruction as a *step*.

Below, we will show that indirect jump instructions are needed for instruction sequence performance. It is assumed that $\mathtt{br{:}1} \in \mathcal{F}$ and $\mathcal{I}(BR) \subseteq \mathcal{M}$.

For each $k \in \mathbb{N}$, let $\boldsymbol{p}_k$ be the following ISNR$_{\text{ij}}$ program:

$$\begin{array}{l}
;_{i=1}^{2^k}(-\mathtt{br{:}1.get}\ ;\ \#3\ ;\ \mathsf{set{:}1{:}}2{\cdot}i{-}1\ ;\ \#(2^k{-}i){\cdot}4{+}2)\ ;\ !\ ;\\
;_{i=1}^{2^k}(-\mathtt{br{:}1.get}\ ;\ \#3\ ;\ \mathsf{set{:}2{:}}2{\cdot}i{-}1\ ;\ \#(2^k{-}i){\cdot}4{+}2)\ ;\ !\ ;\\
\mathsf{i\#1}\ ;\ ;_{i=1}^{2^k}(\mathsf{a}_i\ ;\ \#(2^k{-}i){\cdot}2{+}1)\ ;\ \mathsf{i\#2}\ ;\ ;_{i=1}^{2^k}(\mathsf{a}'_i\ ;\ !)\ .
\end{array}$$

First, $\boldsymbol{p}_k$ repeatedly tests the Boolean register $\mathtt{br{:}1}$. If $\mathtt{t}$ is not returned for 2^k tests, $\boldsymbol{p}_k$ terminates. Otherwise, in case it takes i tests until $\mathtt{t}$ is returned, the content of register 1 is set to $2{\cdot}i{-}1$. If $\boldsymbol{p}_k$ has not yet terminated, it once again repeatedly tests the Boolean register $\mathtt{br{:}1}$. If $\mathtt{t}$ is not returned for 2^k tests, $\boldsymbol{p}_k$ terminates. Otherwise, in case it takes j tests until $\mathtt{t}$ is returned, the content of register 2 is set to $2 \cdot j - 1$. If $\boldsymbol{p}_k$ has not yet terminated, it performs $\boldsymbol{a}_i$ after an indirect jump and following this $\boldsymbol{a}'_j$ after another indirect jump. After that, $\boldsymbol{p}_k$ terminates. The length of $\boldsymbol{p}_k$ is $12 \cdot 2^k + 4$ instructions and the maximal internal delay of $\boldsymbol{p}_k$ is 4 steps.

The ISNR$_{\text{ij}}$ programs $\boldsymbol{p}_1, \boldsymbol{p}_2, \ldots$ defined above will be used in the proof of the result concerning the elimination of indirect jump instructions stated below.

Like before, we will write $\mathrm{len}(\boldsymbol{p})$, where $\boldsymbol{p}$ is a ISNR$_{\text{ij}}$ program, for the length of $\boldsymbol{p}$.

Definition 6.3. A mapping $\mathtt{proj}$ from the set of all ISNR$_{\text{ij}}$ programs to the set of all ISNR programs has a *linear upper bound on the increase in maximal internal delay* if for some $c', c'' \in \mathbb{N}$, for all ISNR$_{\text{ij}}$ programs $\boldsymbol{p}$, $MID(\mathtt{proj}(\boldsymbol{p})) \leq c' \cdot MID(\boldsymbol{p}) + c''$. A mapping $\mathtt{proj}$ from a subset $\mathcal{P}$ of the set of all ISNR$_{\text{ij}}$ programs to the set of all ISNR programs has a *quadratic lower bound on the increase in length* if for some $c', c'' \in \mathbb{N}$ with $c' \neq 0$, for all $\boldsymbol{p} \in \mathcal{P}$, $\mathrm{len}(\mathtt{proj}(\boldsymbol{p})) \geq c' \cdot \mathrm{len}(\boldsymbol{p})^2 + c''$.

Theorem 6.1. *Suppose* `proj` *is a behaviour-preserving mapping from the set of all* ISNR$_{\mathrm{ij}}$ *programs to the set of all* ISNR *programs with a linear upper bound on the increase in maximal internal delay. Moreover, suppose that the number of basic instructions is not bounded. Then there exists a set* $\mathcal{P}$ *of* ISNR$_{\mathrm{ij}}$ *programs such that the restriction of* `proj` *to* $\mathcal{P}$ *has a quadratic lower bound on the increase in length.*

Proof. For each $k \in \mathbb{N}$, let $\boldsymbol{p}_k$ be defined as above. We show that the restriction of `proj` to $\{\boldsymbol{p}_1, \boldsymbol{p}_2, \ldots\}$ has a quadratic lower bound on its increase in length. Take an arbitrary $k \in \mathbb{N}$. Because `proj` has a linear upper bound on the increase in maximal internal delay, we have $\mathit{MID}(\mathtt{proj}(\boldsymbol{p}_k)) \leq c' \cdot \mathit{MID}(\boldsymbol{p}_k) + c'' = c' \cdot 4 + c''$ for some $c', c'' \in \mathbb{N}$. Let $c = c' \cdot 4 + c''$. Suppose that k is much greater than c. This supposition requires that the number of basic instructions is not bounded. If the use of auxiliary basic instructions (such as basic instructions working on auxiliary Boolean registers) is allowed, then there are at most 2^c different basic instructions reachable in c steps. Let $i \in [1, 2^k]$. Then, in $\mathtt{proj}(\boldsymbol{p}_k)$, for each $j \in [1, 2^k]$, some occurrence of $\boldsymbol{a}'_j$ is reachable from each occurrence of $\boldsymbol{a}_i$ without intermediate occurrences of $\boldsymbol{a}_i$ and $\boldsymbol{a}'_1, \ldots, \boldsymbol{a}'_{2^k}$. From one occurrence of $\boldsymbol{a}_i$, at most 2^c basic instructions are reachable, but there are 2^k different instructions to reach. Therefore, there must be at least $2^k/2^c = 2^{k-c}$ different occurrences of $\boldsymbol{a}_i$ in $\mathtt{proj}(\boldsymbol{p}_k)$. Consequently, $\mathrm{len}(\mathtt{proj}(\boldsymbol{p}_k)) \geq 2^k \cdot 2^{k-c} = 2^{2 \cdot k - c}$. Moreover, $\mathrm{len}(\boldsymbol{p}_k) = 12 \cdot 2^k + 4$. Hence, the restriction of `proj` to $\{\boldsymbol{p}_1, \boldsymbol{p}_2, \ldots\}$ has a quadratic lower bound on its increase in length. □

We conclude from Theorem 6.1 that we are faced with super-linear increases of maximal internal delays if we strive for acceptable increases of instruction sequence lengths on elimination of indirect jump instructions. In other words, indirect jump instructions are needed for instruction sequence performance. Semantically, we can eliminate indirect jump instructions by means of a projection, but we meet here two challenges for the viewpoint which has led to the approach of projection semantics: explosion of size and degradation of performance. In Appendix A, these challenges and three other challenges for this viewpoint are discussed.

6.2 Load/Store Instruction Set Architectures

In this section, we introduce a strict version of the concept of a load/store ISA (Instruction Set Architecture) and study how the transformations on the states of the main memory of a strict load/store ISA that can be achieved by executing instruction sequences on it depend on various parameters.

We describe the concept of a load/store ISA in the setting of Maurer machines. Maurer machines are based on the view that a computer has a memory, the contents of all memory elements make up the state of the computer, the computer processes instructions, and the processing of an instruction amounts to performing an operation on the state of the computer which results in changes of the contents of certain memory elements. The design of ISAs must deal with these aspects of real computers. Turing machines and the other kinds of machines known from theoretical computer science (see e.g. [Hopcroft *et al.* (2001)]) abstract from these aspects of real computers.

The idea underlying the concept of a load/store ISA is that there is a main memory whose elements contain data, an operating unit with a small internal memory by which data can be manipulated, and an interface between the main memory and the operating unit for data transfer between them. This means that, in a load/store ISA, all data manipulation takes place in the operating unit. This raises among other things the question whether, if the operating unit size is reduced by one, it is possible with new instructions for data manipulation to yield the same state changes on the data memory. We answer this question in the affirmative.

For strict load/store ISAs with address width aw and word length wl, the number of possible transformations on the states of the data memory is $2^{(2^{(2^{aw} \cdot wl + aw)} \cdot wl)}$. We also show how the possibility to achieve all these state transformation by executing an instruction sequence on a strict load/store ISA with this address width and word length depends on the size of the memory of its operating unit, the cardinality of its instruction set, and the maximal number of states of the behaviours produced by instruction sequences executed on it.

6.2.1 *Maurer machines*

We introduce the concept of a Maurer machine. This concept originates from a model for computers proposed in [Maurer (1966)]. A Maurer machine induces a functional unit. It represents a rather concrete view on a functional unit, which is intended for studying higher-level issues from the area of computer architecture.

Because the apply operator from BTA+TSI will be used, the assumptions relating to $\mathcal{A}$ made in BTA+TSI are made here as well.

Definition 6.4. A *Maurer machine* H consists of the following components:

- a set M with $\mathrm{card}(M) > 0$;
- a set B with $\mathrm{card}(B) > 1$;
- a set $\mathcal{S}$ of functions $S : M \to B$;
- a set $\mathcal{O}$ of functions $O : \mathcal{S} \to \mathcal{S}$;
- a set $I \subseteq \mathcal{M}$;
- a function $[\![\_]\!] : I \to (\mathcal{O} \times M)$;

and satisfies the following conditions:

- if $S_1, S_2 \in \mathcal{S}$, $M' \subseteq M$, and $S_3 : M \to B$ is such that $S_3(x) = S_1(x)$ if $x \in M'$ and $S_3(x) = S_2(x)$ if $x \notin M'$, then $S_3 \in \mathcal{S}$;
- if $S_1, S_2 \in \mathcal{S}$, then the set $\{x \in M \mid S_1(x) \neq S_2(x)\}$ is finite;
- if $S \in \mathcal{S}$, $m \in I$, and $[\![m]\!] = (O, r)$, then $S(r) \in \mathbb{B}$.

Let $H = (M, B, \mathcal{S}, \mathcal{O}, I, [\![\_]\!])$ be a Maurer machine. Then M is called the *memory* of H, B is called the *base set* of H, the members of $\mathcal{S}$ are called the *states* of H, the members of $\mathcal{O}$ are called the *operations* of H, the members of I are called the *instructions* of H, and $[\![\_]\!]$ is called the *instruction interpretation function* of H.

We write M_H, B_H, $\mathcal{S}_H$, $\mathcal{O}_H$, I_H and $[\![\_]\!]_H$, where $H = (M, B, \mathcal{S}, \mathcal{O}, I, [\![\_]\!])$ is a Maurer machine, for M, B, $\mathcal{S}$, $\mathcal{O}$, I and $[\![\_]\!]$, respectively.

A Maurer machine has much in common with a real computer. The memory of a Maurer machine consists of memory elements whose contents are elements from its base set. The term memory must not be taken too strict. For example, register files and caches must be regarded as parts of the memory. The contents of all memory elements together make up a state of the Maurer machine. State changes are accomplished by performing its operations. Every state change amounts to changes of the contents of certain memory elements. The instructions of a Maurer machine are the instructions that it is able to process. The processing of an instruction amounts to performing the operation associated with the instruction by the instruction interpretation function. At completion of the processing, the content of the memory element associated with the instruction by the instruction interpretation function is the reply produced by the Maurer machine.

The first condition on the states of a Maurer machine is a structural condition and the second one is a finite variability condition. We return to these conditions, which are met by any real computer, after the introduction of the input region and output region of an operation. The third condition on the states of a Maurer machine restricts the possible replies at completion of the processing of an instruction to t and f.

Remark 6.2. In [Maurer (1966)], Maurer proposed a model for computers. In [Bergstra and Middelburg (2007b)], the term Maurer computer was introduced for what is a computer according to Maurer's definition. Leaving out the set of instructions and the instruction interpretation function from a Maurer machine yields a Maurer computer. The set of instructions and the instruction interpretation function constitute the interface of a Maurer machine with its environment, which effectuates state changes by issuing instructions.

The notions of input region of an operation and output region of an operation, which originate from [Maurer (1966)], are used in the rest of Sect. 6.2.

Definition 6.5. Let $H = (M, B, \mathcal{S}, \mathcal{O}, I, [\![\_]\!])$ be a Maurer machine, and let $O : \mathcal{S} \to \mathcal{S}$. Then the *input region* of O, written $IR(O)$, and the *output region* of O, written $OR(O)$, are the subsets of M defined as follows:

$$\begin{aligned} IR(O) = \{x \in M \mid \exists S_1, S_2 \in \mathcal{S} \bullet (\forall z \in M \setminus \{x\} \bullet S_1(z) = S_2(z) \wedge \\ \exists y \in OR(O) \bullet O(S_1)(y) \neq O(S_2)(y))\}\ , \end{aligned}$$

$$OR(O) = \{x \in M \mid \exists S \in \mathcal{S} \bullet S(x) \neq O(S)(x)\}\ .$$

$OR(O)$ is the set of all memory elements that are possibly affected by O; and $IR(O)$ is the set of all memory elements that possibly affect elements of $OR(O)$ under O. For example, the input region and output region of an operation that adds the content of a given main memory cell, say x, to the content of a given register, say y, are $\{x, y\}$ and $\{y\}$, respectively.

Let $H = (M, B, \mathcal{S}, \mathcal{O}, I, [\![\_]\!])$ be a Maurer machine, let $S_1, S_2 \in \mathcal{S}$, and let $O \in \mathcal{O}$. Then $S_1 \restriction IR(O) = S_2 \restriction IR(O)$ implies $O(S_1) \restriction OR(O) = O(S_2) \restriction OR(O)$. In other words, every operation transforms states that coincide on the input region of the operation to states that coincide on the output region of the operation. The second condition on the states of a Maurer machine is necessary for this fundamental property to hold. The first condition on the states of a Maurer machine could be relaxed somewhat.

Remark 6.3. In [Maurer (1966)], more results relating to input regions and output regions are given. Recently, a revised and expanded version of [Maurer (1966)], which includes all the proofs, has appeared in [Maurer (2006)].

Definition 6.6. Let $H = (M, B, \mathcal{S}, \mathcal{O}, I, [\![\_]\!])$ be a Maurer machine, and let $(O_m, r_m) = [\![m]\!]$ for all $m \in I$. Then the functional unit $U_H \in \mathcal{FU}(\mathcal{S})$ *induced by* H is defined by

$$U_H = \{(m, M_m) \mid m \in I\}\ ,$$

where the method operations M_m are defined as follows ($m \in I$):

$$M_m(S) = (O_m(S)(r_m), O_m(S))\ .^1$$

The apply operator introduced in Sect. 3.1.2 allows for instruction sequences to effectuate state changes of a Maurer machine by means of its operations. Let $H = (M, B, \mathcal{S}, \mathcal{O}, I, [\![\_]\!])$ be a Maurer machine, let $S \in \mathcal{S}$, and let $p \in \mathcal{L}(\mathtt{f}.\mathcal{I}(U_H))$. If $p \bullet \mathtt{f}.U_H(S) = \mathtt{f}.U_H(S')$, then S' is the state of the Maurer machine H that results from processing the instruction m of each basic action $\mathtt{f}.m$ that the thread produced by p performs by the Maurer machine H, starting from state S. The processing of an instruction m by H amounts to a state change according to the operation associated with m by $[\![\_]\!]$. In the resulting state, the reply produced by H is contained in the memory element associated with m by $[\![\_]\!]$.

6.2.2 *Strict load/store Maurer ISAs*

In this section, we introduce the concept of a strict load/store Maurer instruction set architecture. This concept takes its name from the following: it is described in the setting of Maurer machines, it concerns only load/store architectures, and the load/store architectures concerned are strict in some respects that will be explained after its formalization.

The concept of a strict load/store Maurer instruction set architecture, or shortly a strict load/store Maurer ISA, is an approximation of the concept of a load/store instruction set architecture (see e.g. [Hennessy and Patterson (2003)]). It is focussed on instructions for data manipulation and data transfer. Transfer of program control is treated in a uniform way over different strict load/store Maurer ISAs by working at the abstraction level of threads. All that is left of transfer of program control at this level is postconditional composition.

The idea underlying the concept of a strict load/store Maurer ISA is that there is a main memory whose elements contain data, an operating unit with a small internal memory by which data can be manipulated, and an interface between the main memory and the operating unit for data transfer between them. For the sake of simplicity, data is restricted to the natural numbers between 0 and some upper bound. Other types of data that could be supported can always be represented by the natural numbers provided. Moreover, the data manipulation instructions offered by a strict load/store Maurer ISA are not restricted and may include ones that are tailored to manipulation of representations of other types of data. Therefore, we believe that nothing essential is lost by the restriction to natural numbers.

[1]Notice the double use of M here: M is the memory of the Maurer machine H, and M_m is the method operation with name m.

The concept of a strict load/store Maurer ISA is parametrized by:

- an address width aw;
- a word length wl;
- an operating unit size ous;
- a number $nrpl$ of pairs of data and address registers for load instructions;
- a number $nrps$ of pairs of data and address registers for store instructions;
- a set I_{dm} of basic instructions for data manipulation;

where $aw, ous \geq 0$, $wl, nrpl, nrps > 0$ and $I_{dm} \subseteq \mathcal{M}$.

The address width aw can be regarded as the number of bits used for the binary representation of addresses of data memory elements. The word length wl can be regarded as the number of bits used to represent data in data memory elements. The operating unit size ous can be regarded as the number of bits that the internal memory of the operating unit contains. The operating unit size is measured in bits because this allows for establishing results in which no assumption about the internal structure of the operating unit are involved.

It is assumed that, for each $n \in \mathbb{N}$, a fixed but arbitrary countably infinite set $\mathsf{M}^n_{\mathsf{data}}$ and a fixed but arbitrary bijection $\mathsf{m}^n_{\mathsf{data}} : \mathbb{N} \to \mathsf{M}^n_{\mathsf{data}}$ have been given. The members of $\mathsf{M}^n_{\mathsf{data}}$ are called *data memory elements*. The contents of data memory elements are taken as data. The data memory elements from $\mathsf{M}^n_{\mathsf{data}}$ can contain natural numbers in the interval $[0, 2^n - 1]$.

It is assumed that a fixed but arbitrary countably infinite set M_{ou} and a fixed but arbitrary bijection $\mathsf{m}_{\mathsf{ou}} : \mathbb{N} \to \mathsf{M}_{\mathsf{ou}}$ have been given. The members of M_{ou} are called *operating unit memory elements*. They can contain natural numbers in the set $\{0, 1\}$, i.e. bits. Usually, a part of the operating unit memory is partitioned into groups to which data manipulation instructions can refer.

It is assumed that, for each $n \in \mathbb{N}$, fixed but arbitrary countably infinite sets $\mathsf{M}^n_{\mathsf{ld}}$, $\mathsf{M}^n_{\mathsf{la}}$, $\mathsf{M}^n_{\mathsf{sd}}$ and $\mathsf{M}^n_{\mathsf{sa}}$ and fixed but arbitrary bijections $\mathsf{m}^n_{\mathsf{ld}} : \mathbb{N} \to \mathsf{M}^n_{\mathsf{ld}}$, $\mathsf{m}^n_{\mathsf{la}} : \mathbb{N} \to \mathsf{M}^n_{\mathsf{la}}$, $\mathsf{m}^n_{\mathsf{sd}} : \mathbb{N} \to \mathsf{M}^n_{\mathsf{sd}}$ and $\mathsf{m}^n_{\mathsf{sa}} : \mathbb{N} \to \mathsf{M}^n_{\mathsf{sa}}$ have been given. The members of $\mathsf{M}^n_{\mathsf{ld}}$, $\mathsf{M}^n_{\mathsf{la}}$, $\mathsf{M}^n_{\mathsf{sd}}$ and $\mathsf{M}^n_{\mathsf{sa}}$ are called *load data registers*, *load address registers*, *store data registers* and *store address registers*, respectively. The contents of load data registers and store data registers are taken as data, whereas the contents of load address registers and store address registers are taken as addresses. The load data registers from $\mathsf{M}^n_{\mathsf{ld}}$, the load address registers from $\mathsf{M}^n_{\mathsf{la}}$, the store data registers from $\mathsf{M}^n_{\mathsf{sd}}$ and the store address registers from $\mathsf{M}^n_{\mathsf{sa}}$ can contain natural numbers in the interval $[0, 2^n - 1]$. The load and store registers are special memory elements designated for transferring data between the data memory and the operating unit memory.

A single special memory element rr is taken for passing on the replies resulting from the processing of basic instructions. This special memory element is called the *reply register*.

It is assumed that, for each $n, n' \in \mathbb{N}$, $\mathsf{M}^n_{\mathsf{data}}$, M_{ou}, $\mathsf{M}^n_{\mathsf{ld}}$, $\mathsf{M}^{n'}_{\mathsf{la}}$, $\mathsf{M}^n_{\mathsf{sd}}$, $\mathsf{M}^{n'}_{\mathsf{sa}}$ and $\{\mathsf{rr}\}$ are pairwise disjoint sets.

If $M \subseteq \mathsf{M}^n_{\mathsf{data}}$ and $\mathsf{m}^n_{\mathsf{data}}(i) \in M$, then we write $M[i]$ for $\mathsf{m}^n_{\mathsf{data}}(i)$. If $M \subseteq \mathsf{M}^n_{\mathsf{ld}}$ and $\mathsf{m}^n_{\mathsf{ld}}(i) \in M$, then we write $M[i]$ for $\mathsf{m}^n_{\mathsf{ld}}(i)$. If $M \subseteq \mathsf{M}^n_{\mathsf{la}}$ and $\mathsf{m}^n_{\mathsf{la}}(i) \in M$, then we write $M[i]$ for $\mathsf{m}^n_{\mathsf{la}}(i)$. If $M \subseteq \mathsf{M}^n_{\mathsf{sd}}$ and $\mathsf{m}^n_{\mathsf{sd}}(i) \in M$, then we write $M[i]$ for $\mathsf{m}^n_{\mathsf{sd}}(i)$. If $M \subseteq \mathsf{M}^n_{\mathsf{sa}}$ and $\mathsf{m}^n_{\mathsf{sa}}(i) \in M$, then we write $M[i]$ for $\mathsf{m}^n_{\mathsf{sa}}(i)$.

Definition 6.7. Let $aw, ous \geq 0$, $wl, nrpl, nrps > 0$ and $I_{dm} \subseteq \mathcal{M}$. Then a *strict load/store Maurer instruction set architecture* with parameters aw, wl, ous, $nrpl$, $nrps$ and I_{dm} is a Maurer machine $H = (M, B, \mathcal{S}, \mathcal{O}, I, [\![\_]\!])$ with

$$
\begin{aligned}
M &= M_{data} \cup M_{ou} \cup M_{ld} \cup M_{la} \cup M_{sd} \cup M_{sa} \cup \{\mathsf{rr}\}\ , \\
B &= [0, 2^{wl} - 1] \cup [0, 2^{aw} - 1] \cup \mathbb{B}\ , \\
\mathcal{S} &= \{S : M \to B \mid \\
&\qquad \forall m \in M_{data} \cup M_{ld} \cup M_{sd} \bullet S(m) \in [0, 2^{wl} - 1] \land \\
&\qquad \forall m \in M_{la} \cup M_{sa} \bullet S(m) \in [0, 2^{aw} - 1] \land \\
&\qquad \forall m \in M_{ou} \bullet S(m) \in \{0, 1\} \land S(\mathsf{rr}) \in \mathbb{B}\}\ , \\
\mathcal{O} &= \{O_{\boldsymbol{m}} \mid \boldsymbol{m} \in I\}\ , \\
I &= \{\mathtt{load}{:}n \mid n \in [0, nrpl - 1]\} \cup \{\mathtt{store}{:}n \mid n \in [0, nrps - 1]\} \cup I_{dm}\ , \\
[\![\boldsymbol{m}]\!] &= (O_{\boldsymbol{m}}, \mathsf{rr}) \quad \text{for all } \boldsymbol{m} \in I\ ,
\end{aligned}
$$

where

$$
\begin{aligned}
M_{data} &= \{\mathsf{m}^{wl}_{\mathsf{data}}(i) \mid i \in [0, 2^{aw} - 1]\}\ , \\
M_{ou} &= \{\mathsf{m}_{\mathsf{ou}}(i) \mid i \in [0, ous - 1]\}\ , \\
M_{ld} &= \{\mathsf{m}^{wl}_{\mathsf{ld}}(i) \mid i \in [0, nrpl - 1]\}\ , \\
M_{la} &= \{\mathsf{m}^{aw}_{\mathsf{la}}(i) \mid i \in [0, nrpl - 1]\}\ , \\
M_{sd} &= \{\mathsf{m}^{wl}_{\mathsf{sd}}(i) \mid i \in [0, nrps - 1]\}\ , \\
M_{sa} &= \{\mathsf{m}^{aw}_{\mathsf{sa}}(i) \mid i \in [0, nrps - 1]\}\ ,
\end{aligned}
$$

and, for all $n \in [0, nrpl - 1]$, $O_{\mathtt{load}:n}$ is the unique function from $\mathcal{S}$ to $\mathcal{S}$ such that for all

$S \in \mathcal{S}$:

$$
\begin{aligned}
O_{\mathtt{load}:n}(S) \restriction (M \setminus \{M_{ld}[n], \mathsf{rr}\}) &= S \restriction (M \setminus \{M_{ld}[n], \mathsf{rr}\}) \,, \\
O_{\mathtt{load}:n}(S)(M_{ld}[n]) &= S(M_{data}[S(M_{la}[n])]) \,, \\
O_{\mathtt{load}:n}(S)(\mathsf{rr}) &= \mathsf{t} \,,
\end{aligned}
$$

and, for all $n \in [0, nrps - 1]$, $O_{\mathtt{store}:n}$ is the unique function from $\mathcal{S}$ to $\mathcal{S}$ such that for all $S \in \mathcal{S}$:

$$
\begin{aligned}
O_{\mathtt{store}:n}(S) \restriction (M \setminus \{M_{data}[S(M_{sa}[n])], \mathsf{rr}\}) &= \\
S \restriction (M \setminus \{M_{data}[S(M_{sa}[n])], \mathsf{rr}\}) \,, \\
O_{\mathtt{store}:n}(S)(M_{data}[S(M_{sa}[n])]) &= S(M_{sd}[n]) \,, \\
O_{\mathtt{store}:n}(S)(\mathsf{rr}) &= \mathsf{t} \,,
\end{aligned}
$$

and, for all $m \in I_{dm}$, O_m is a function from $\mathcal{S}$ to $\mathcal{S}$ such that:

$$
\begin{aligned}
IR(O_m) &\subseteq M_{ou} \cup M_{ld} \,, \\
OR(O_m) &\subseteq M_{ou} \cup M_{la} \cup M_{sd} \cup M_{sa} \cup \{\mathsf{rr}\} \,.
\end{aligned}
$$

We will write $\mathcal{MISA}_{\mathrm{sls}}(aw, wl, ous, nrpl, nrps, I_{dm})$ for the set of all strict load/store Maurer ISAs with parameters aw, wl, ous, $nrpl$, $nrps$ and I_{dm}.

In our opinion, load/store architectures give rise to a relatively simple interface between the data memory and the operating unit.

A strict load/store Maurer ISA is strict in the following respects:

- with data transfer between the data memory and the operating unit, a strict separation is made between data registers for loading, address registers for loading, data registers for storing, and address registers for storing;
- from these registers, only the registers of the first kind are allowed in the input regions of data manipulation operations, and only the registers of the other three kinds are allowed in the output regions of data manipulation operations;
- a data memory whose size is less than the number of addresses determined by the address width is not allowed.

The first two ways in which a strict load/store Maurer ISA is strict concern the interface between the data memory and the operating unit. We believe that they yield the most conveniently arranged interface for theoretical work relevant to the design of instruction set architectures. The third way in which a strict load/store Maurer ISA is strict saves the need to deal with addresses that do not address a memory element. Such addresses can be dealt with in many different ways, each of which complicates the architecture considerably.

We consider their exclusion desirable in much theoretical work relevant to the design of instruction set architectures.

Remark 6.4. A strict separation between data registers for loading, address registers for loading, data registers for storing, and address registers for storing is also made in Cray and Thornton's design of the CDC 6600 computer, see [Thornton (1970)], which is arguably the first implemented load/store architecture. However, in their design, data registers for storing are also allowed in the input regions of data manipulation operations.

6.2.3 *Reducing the operating unit size*

In a strict load/store Maurer ISA, data manipulation takes place in the operating unit. This raises questions concerning the consequences of changing the operating unit size. One of the questions is whether, if the operating unit size is reduced by one, it is possible with new instructions for data manipulation to yield the same state changes on the data memory. This question can be answered in the affirmative.

Theorem 6.2. *Let* $aw \geq 0$, $wl, ous, nrpl, nrps > 0$ *and* $I_{dm} \subseteq \mathcal{M}$, *let* $H = (M, B, \mathcal{S}, \mathcal{O}, I, [\![\_]\!]) \in \mathcal{MISA}_{\mathrm{sls}}(aw, wl, ous, nrpl, nrps, I_{dm})$, *and let* $M_{data} = \{\mathsf{m}^{wl}_{\mathsf{data}}(i) \mid i \in [0, 2^{aw} - 1]\}$ *and* $\mathsf{bc} = \mathsf{m}_{\mathsf{ou}}(ous - 1)$. *Then there exist an* $I'_{dm} \subseteq \mathcal{M}$ *and an* $H' = (M', B, \mathcal{S}', \mathcal{O}', I', [\![\_]\!]') \in \mathcal{MISA}_{\mathrm{sls}}(aw, wl, ous - 1, nrpl, nrps, I'_{dm})$ *such that for all closed* BTA+REC *terms* $\boldsymbol{t}$ *denoting a regular thread over* $\{\mathtt{f}.\boldsymbol{m} \mid \boldsymbol{m} \in I\}$ *there exist closed* BTA+REC *terms* $\boldsymbol{t}'_0, \boldsymbol{t}'_1$ *denoting regular threads over* $\{\mathtt{f}.\boldsymbol{m} \mid \boldsymbol{m} \in I'\}$ *such that*

$$\begin{aligned}&\{(S_0 \restriction M_{data}, S \restriction M_{data}) \mid S_0 \in \mathcal{S} \wedge \boldsymbol{t} \bullet \mathtt{f}.U_H(S_0) = \mathtt{f}.U_H(S) \wedge S_0(\mathsf{bc}) = 0\}\\ &\quad = \{(S'_0 \restriction M_{data}, S' \restriction M_{data}) \mid S'_0 \in \mathcal{S}' \wedge \boldsymbol{t}'_0 \bullet \mathtt{f}.U_H(S'_0) = \mathtt{f}.U_H(S')\}\end{aligned}$$

and

$$\begin{aligned}&\{(S_0 \restriction M_{data}, S \restriction M_{data}) \mid S_0 \in \mathcal{S} \wedge \boldsymbol{t} \bullet \mathtt{f}.U_H(S_0) = \mathtt{f}.U_H(S) \wedge S_0(\mathsf{bc}) = 1\}\\ &\quad = \{(S'_0 \restriction M_{data}, S' \restriction M_{data}) \mid S'_0 \in \mathcal{S}' \wedge \boldsymbol{t}'_1 \bullet \mathtt{f}.U_H(S'_0) = \mathtt{f}.U_H(S')\}\ .\end{aligned}$$

Notice that bc is the operating unit memory element of H that is missing in H'. In the proof of Theorem 6.2 given below, we take I'_{dm} such that, for each instruction $\boldsymbol{m}$ in I_{dm}, there are four instructions $\boldsymbol{m}(0)$, $\boldsymbol{m}(1)$, $\overline{\boldsymbol{m}}(0)$ and $\overline{\boldsymbol{m}}(1)$ in I'_{dm}. $O_{\boldsymbol{m}(0)}$ and $O_{\boldsymbol{m}(1)}$ affect the memory elements of H' like $O_{\boldsymbol{m}}$ would affect them if the content of the missing operating unit memory element would be 0 and 1, respectively. The effect that $O_{\boldsymbol{m}}$ would have on the missing operating unit memory element is made available by $O_{\overline{\boldsymbol{m}}(0)}$ and $O_{\overline{\boldsymbol{m}}(1)}$, respectively. They do nothing but replying f if the content of the missing operating unit memory element would become 0 and t if the content of the missing operating unit memory element would become 1.

Proof. [Proof of Theorem 6.2] Instead of the result to be proved, we prove that there exist an $I'_{dm} \subseteq \mathcal{M}$ and an $H' = (M', B, \mathcal{S}', \mathcal{O}', I', [\![\_]\!]') \in \mathcal{MISA}_{\mathrm{sls}}(aw, wl, ous - 1, nrpl, nrps, I'_{dm})$ such that for all closed BTA+REC terms t denoting a regular thread over $\{\mathtt{f}.m \mid m \in I\}$ there exist closed BTA+REC terms t'_0, t'_1 denoting regular threads over $\{\mathtt{f}.m \mid m \in I'\}$ such that

$$\begin{aligned}&\{(S_0 \restriction M'', S \restriction M'') \mid S_0 \in \mathcal{S} \wedge t \bullet \mathtt{f}.U_H(S_0) = \mathtt{f}.U_H(S) \wedge S_0(\mathsf{bc}) = 0\}\\ &\quad = \{(S'_0 \restriction M'', S' \restriction M'') \mid S'_0 \in \mathcal{S}' \wedge t'_0 \bullet \mathtt{f}.U_H(S'_0) = \mathtt{f}.U_H(S')\}\end{aligned}$$

and

$$\begin{aligned}&\{(S_0 \restriction M'', S \restriction M'') \mid S_0 \in \mathcal{S} \wedge t \bullet \mathtt{f}.U_H(S_0) = \mathtt{f}.U_H(S) \wedge S_0(\mathsf{bc}) = 1\}\\ &\quad = \{(S'_0 \restriction M'', S' \restriction M'') \mid S'_0 \in \mathcal{S}' \wedge t'_1 \bullet \mathtt{f}.U_H(S'_0) = \mathtt{f}.U_H(S')\}\ ,\end{aligned}$$

where $M'' = M' \setminus \{\mathsf{rr}\}$. This is sufficient because $M_{data} \subseteq M' \setminus \{\mathsf{rr}\}$.

We take

$$I'_{dm} = \{m(k) \mid m \in I_{dm} \wedge k \in \{0,1\}\} \cup \{\overline{m}(k) \mid m \in I_{dm} \wedge k \in \{0,1\}\}\ ,$$

and we take $H' = (M', B, \mathcal{S}', \mathcal{O}', I', [\![\_]\!]')$ such that, for each $m \in I_{dm}$ and $k \in \{0,1\}$, $O_{m(k)}$ and $O_{\overline{m}(k)}$ are the unique functions from $\mathcal{S}'$ to $\mathcal{S}'$ such that for all $S' \in \mathcal{S}'$:

$$\begin{aligned}O_{m(k)}(S') &= O_m(\rho_k(S')) \restriction M'\ ,\\ O_{\overline{m}(k)}(S') \restriction (M' \setminus \{\mathsf{rr}\}) &= S' \restriction (M' \setminus \{\mathsf{rr}\})\ ,\\ O_{\overline{m}(k)}(S')(\mathsf{rr}) &= \gamma(O_m(\rho_k(S'))(\mathsf{bc}))\ ,\end{aligned}$$

where, for each $k \in \{0,1\}$, ρ_k is the unique function from $\mathcal{S}'$ to $\mathcal{S}$ such that

$$\begin{aligned}\rho_k(S') \restriction M' &= S'\ ,\\ \rho_k(S')(\mathsf{bc}) &= k\end{aligned}$$

and $\gamma : \{0,1\} \to \mathbb{B}$ is defined by

$$\begin{aligned}\gamma(0) &= \mathsf{f}\ ,\\ \gamma(1) &= \mathsf{t}\ .\end{aligned}$$

By Proposition 2.1, we can restrict ourselves to closed BTA+REC terms t that are constants $\langle x | E \rangle$ where E is a finite linear recursive specification in which only basic actions from $\{\mathtt{f}.m \mid m \in I\}$ occur.

We define transformation functions φ_k on such finite linear recursive specifications, for $k \in \{0, 1\}$, as follows:

$$\varphi_k(\langle \boldsymbol{x} | \boldsymbol{E} \rangle) = \langle \boldsymbol{x}_k | \varphi'_k(\boldsymbol{E}) \rangle \;,$$

where φ'_k, for $k \in \{0, 1\}$ is defined as follows:

$$\begin{aligned}
\varphi'_k(\{\boldsymbol{x} = \boldsymbol{y} \trianglelefteq \mathtt{f}.\boldsymbol{m} \trianglerighteq \boldsymbol{z}\}) &= \{\boldsymbol{x}_k = \boldsymbol{x}'_k \trianglelefteq \mathtt{f}.\overline{\boldsymbol{m}}(k) \trianglerighteq \boldsymbol{x}''_k, \\
&\qquad \boldsymbol{x}'_k = \boldsymbol{y}_1 \trianglelefteq \mathtt{f}.\boldsymbol{m}(k) \trianglerighteq \boldsymbol{z}_1, \\
&\qquad \boldsymbol{x}''_k = \boldsymbol{y}_0 \trianglelefteq \mathtt{f}.\boldsymbol{m}(k) \trianglerighteq \boldsymbol{z}_0\} \quad \text{if } \boldsymbol{m} \in I_{\mathit{dm}} \;, \\
\varphi'_k(\{\boldsymbol{x} = \boldsymbol{y} \trianglelefteq \mathtt{f}.\boldsymbol{m} \trianglerighteq \boldsymbol{z}\}) &= \{\boldsymbol{x}_k = \boldsymbol{y}_k \trianglelefteq \mathtt{f}.\boldsymbol{m} \trianglerighteq \boldsymbol{z}_k\} \qquad \text{if } \boldsymbol{m} \notin I_{\mathit{dm}} \;, \\
\varphi'_k(\{\boldsymbol{x} = \mathsf{S+}\}) &= \{\boldsymbol{x}_k = \mathsf{S+}\} \;, \\
\varphi'_k(\{\boldsymbol{x} = \mathsf{S-}\}) &= \{\boldsymbol{x}_k = \mathsf{S-}\} \;, \\
\varphi'_k(\{\boldsymbol{x} = \mathsf{S}\}) &= \{\boldsymbol{x}_k = \mathsf{S}\} \;, \\
\varphi'_k(\{\boldsymbol{x} = \mathsf{D}\}) &= \{\boldsymbol{x}_k = \mathsf{D}\} \;, \\
\varphi'_k(\boldsymbol{E}' \cup \boldsymbol{E}'') &= \varphi'_k(\boldsymbol{E}') \cup \varphi'_k(\boldsymbol{E}'') \;.
\end{aligned}$$

Here, for each variable $\boldsymbol{x}$, the new variables $\boldsymbol{x}_0$, $\boldsymbol{x}'_0$, $\boldsymbol{x}''_0$, $\boldsymbol{x}_1$, $\boldsymbol{x}'_1$ and $\boldsymbol{x}''_1$ are taken such that: (i) they are mutually different variables; (ii) for each variable $\boldsymbol{y}$ different from $\boldsymbol{x}$, $\{\boldsymbol{x}_0, \boldsymbol{x}'_0, \boldsymbol{x}''_0, \boldsymbol{x}_1, \boldsymbol{x}'_1, \boldsymbol{x}''_1\}$ and $\{\boldsymbol{y}_0, \boldsymbol{y}'_0, \boldsymbol{y}''_0, \boldsymbol{y}_1, \boldsymbol{y}'_1, \boldsymbol{y}''_1\}$ are disjoint sets.

Let $\boldsymbol{t}_0$ be a constant $\langle \boldsymbol{x} | \boldsymbol{E} \rangle$ where $\boldsymbol{E}$ is a finite linear recursive specification in which only basic actions from $\{\mathtt{f}.\boldsymbol{m} \mid \boldsymbol{m} \in I\}$ occur, let $S_0 \in \mathcal{S}$ and $S'_0 \in \mathcal{S}'$ be such that $S_0 \restriction M' = S'_0$, and let $\boldsymbol{t}'_0 = \varphi_{S_0(\mathsf{bc})}(\boldsymbol{t}_0)$. Assume that an equation of the form $\boldsymbol{t}_0 \bullet \mathtt{f}.U_H(S_0) = \mathtt{f}.U_H(S)$ is derivable, and let $n \in \mathbb{N}^+$ be the number of times that axiom A7 or axiom A8 has to be applied from left to right to derive an equation of the form $\boldsymbol{t}_0 \bullet \mathtt{f}.U_H(S_0) = \boldsymbol{t} \bullet \mathtt{f}.U_H(S)$ where $\boldsymbol{t}$ is either $\mathsf{S+}$, $\mathsf{S-}$ or S. For each $i \in [1, n]$, let $\boldsymbol{t}_0 \bullet \mathtt{f}.U_H(S_0) = \boldsymbol{t}_i \bullet \mathtt{f}.U_H(S_i)$ be the equation that has been derived after i applications of axiom A7 or axiom A8 from left to right, and let $\boldsymbol{m}_i$ be the method involved in the ith application. For each $i \in [1, n]$, let $\boldsymbol{t}'_0 \bullet \mathtt{f}.U_H(S'_0) = \boldsymbol{t}'_i \bullet \mathtt{f}.U_H(S'_i)$ be the equation that has been derived after i applications of axiom A7 or axiom A8 from left to right where the method involved is not of the form $\boldsymbol{m}(k)$. Then, it is easy to prove by induction on i that if $i \in [0, n-1]$ and $\boldsymbol{m}_{i+1} \in I_{\mathit{dm}}$:

$$\begin{aligned}
O_{\boldsymbol{m}_{i+1}}(S_i)(\mathsf{bc}) &= \gamma^{-1}(O_{\overline{\boldsymbol{m}_{i+1}}(S_i(\mathsf{bc}))}(S'_i)(\mathsf{rr})) \;, \\
O_{\boldsymbol{m}_{i+1}}(S_i)(\mathsf{rr}) &= O_{\boldsymbol{m}_{i+1}(S_i(\mathsf{bc}))}(O_{\overline{\boldsymbol{m}}_{i+1}(S_i(\mathsf{bc}))}(S'_i))(\mathsf{rr}) \;.
\end{aligned}$$

Now, using these two properties, it is easy to prove by induction on i that:

$$\begin{aligned}
&\varphi_{S_i(\mathsf{bc})}(\boldsymbol{t}_i) = \boldsymbol{t}'_i \;, \\
&S_i \restriction (M \setminus \{\mathsf{rr}\}) = \rho_{S_i(\mathsf{bc})}(S'_i) \restriction (M \setminus \{\mathsf{rr}\}) \;.
\end{aligned}$$

From this, the result follows immediately. □

Theorem 6.2 and its proof give us some upper bounds:

- for each thread that can be applied to the original ISA, the number of threads that can together produce the same state changes on the data memory of the ISA with the reduced operating unit does not have to be more than 2;
- the number of states of the new threads does not have to be more than 6 times the number of states of the original thread;
- the number of steps that the new threads take to produce some state change does not have to be more than 2 times the number of steps that the original thread takes to produce that state change;
- the number of instructions of the ISA with the reduced operating unit does not have to be more than 4 times the number of instructions of the original ISA.

Notice further that more efficient new threads are sometimes possible: equations of the form $\boldsymbol{x} = \boldsymbol{y} \trianglelefteq \texttt{f}.\boldsymbol{m} \trianglerighteq \boldsymbol{z}$ with $\boldsymbol{m} \in I_{dm}$ can be treated as if $\boldsymbol{m} \notin I_{dm}$ in the case where the operating unit memory element bc is not in $IR(O_{\boldsymbol{m}})$.

It follows from the proof of Theorem 6.2 that only one transformed thread is needed if the input region of the operation associated with the first instruction performed by the original thread does not include the operating unit memory element bc. It also follows from the proof of Theorem 6.2 that the operating unit size can even be reduced to zero. However, we have that, if the operating unit size is reduced from ous to zero, up to 2^{ous} transformed threads may be needed for an original thread.

Theorem 6.2 is phrased at the level of threads, i.e. the behaviours of instruction sequences under execution. By Propositions 4.1 and 4.2, it can also be phrased at the level of instruction sequences.

Corollary 6.1. *Let* $aw \geq 0$, $wl, ous, nrpl, nrps > 0$ *and* $I_{dm} \subseteq \mathcal{M}$, *let* $H = (M, B, \mathcal{S}, \mathcal{O}, I, [\![\_]\!]) \in \mathcal{MISA}_{\mathsf{sls}}(aw, wl, ous, nrpl, nrps, I_{dm})$, *and let* $M_{data} = \{\mathsf{m}^{wl}_{\mathsf{data}}(i) \mid i \in [0, 2^{aw} - 1]\}$ *and* $\mathsf{bc} = \mathsf{m}_{\mathsf{ou}}(ous - 1)$. *Then there exist an* $I'_{dm} \subseteq \mathcal{M}$ *and an* $H' = (M', B, \mathcal{S}', \mathcal{O}', I', [\![\_]\!]') \in \mathcal{MISA}_{\mathsf{sls}}(aw, wl, ous - 1, nrpl, nrps, I'_{dm})$ *such that for all* $\boldsymbol{p} \in \mathcal{L}(\texttt{f}.\mathcal{I}(U_H))$ *there exist* $\boldsymbol{p}'_0, \boldsymbol{p}'_1 \in \mathcal{L}(\texttt{f}.\mathcal{I}(U_{H'}))$ *such that*

$$\{(S_0 \upharpoonright M_{data}, S \upharpoonright M_{data}) \mid S_0 \in \mathcal{S} \wedge \boldsymbol{p} \bullet \texttt{f}.U_H(S_0) = \texttt{f}.U_H(S) \wedge S_0(\mathsf{bc}) = 0\}$$
$$= \{(S'_0 \upharpoonright M_{data}, S' \upharpoonright M_{data}) \mid S'_0 \in \mathcal{S}' \wedge \boldsymbol{p}'_0 \bullet \texttt{f}.U_H(S'_0) = \texttt{f}.U_H(S')\}$$

and

$$\{(S_0 \upharpoonright M_{data}, S \upharpoonright M_{data}) \mid S_0 \in \mathcal{S} \wedge \boldsymbol{p} \bullet \mathtt{f}.U_H(S_0) = \mathtt{f}.U_H(S) \wedge S_0(\mathsf{bc}) = 1\}$$
$$= \{(S'_0 \upharpoonright M_{data}, S' \upharpoonright M_{data}) \mid S'_0 \in \mathcal{S}' \wedge \boldsymbol{p}'_1 \bullet \mathtt{f}.U_H(S'_0) = \mathtt{f}.U_H(S')\} .$$

6.2.4 *Thread powered function classes*

A simple calculation shows that, for a strict load/store Maurer ISA with address width aw and word length wl, the number of possible transformations on the states of the data memory is $2^{(2^{(2^{aw} \cdot wl + aw)} \cdot wl)}$. This raises questions concerning the possibility to achieve all these state transformation by executing an instruction sequence on a strict load/store Maurer ISA with this address width and word length. One of the questions is how this possibility depends on the operating unit size of the ISAs, the size of the instruction set of the ISAs, and the maximal number of states of the threads produced by the instruction sequences. This brings us to introduce the concept of a thread powered function class.

The concept of a thread powered function class is parametrized by:

- an address width aw;
- a word length wl;
- an operating unit size ous;
- an instruction set size iss;
- a state space bound ssb;
- a working area flag waf;

where $aw, ous \geq 0$, $wl, iss, ssb > 0$ and $waf \in \mathbb{B}$.

The instruction set size iss is the number of basic instructions, excluding load and store instructions. To simplify the setting, we consider only the case where there is one load instruction and one store instruction. The state space bound ssb is a bound on the number of states of the thread that is applied. The working area flag waf indicates whether a part of the data memory is taken as a working area. A part of the data memory is taken as a working area if we are not interested in the state transformations with respect to that part. To simplify the setting, we always set aside half of the data memory for working area if a working area is in order.

Intuitively, the thread powered function class with parameters aw, wl, ous, iss, ssb and waf are the transformations on the states of the data memory or the first half of the data memory, depending on waf, that can be achieved by applying threads with not more than ssb states to a strict load/store Maurer ISA of which the address width is aw, the word length is wl, the operating unit size is ous, the number of register pairs for load instructions is 1, the number of register pairs for store instructions is 1, and the cardinality of the set of instructions for data manipulation is iss. Henceforth, we will use the term *external memory* for the data memory if $waf = \mathsf{f}$ and for the first half of the data memory if $waf = \mathsf{t}$. Moreover, if $waf = \mathsf{t}$, we will use the term *internal memory* for the second half of the data memory.

For $aw \geq 0$ and $wl > 0$, we define $\mathsf{M}_{\mathsf{data}}^{aw,wl}$, $\mathsf{S}_{\mathsf{data}}^{aw,wl}$ and $\mathsf{T}_{\mathsf{data}}^{aw,wl}$ as follows:

$$\begin{aligned}
\mathsf{M}_{\mathsf{data}}^{aw,wl} &= \{\mathsf{m}_{\mathsf{data}}^{wl}(i) \mid i \in [0, 2^{aw} - 1]\} , \\
\mathsf{S}_{\mathsf{data}}^{aw,wl} &= \{S \mid S : \mathsf{M}_{\mathsf{data}}^{aw,wl} \to [0, 2^{wl} - 1]\} , \\
\mathsf{T}_{\mathsf{data}}^{aw,wl} &= \{T \mid T : \mathsf{S}_{\mathsf{data}}^{aw,wl} \to \mathsf{S}_{\mathsf{data}}^{aw,wl}\} .
\end{aligned}$$

$\mathsf{M}_{\mathsf{data}}^{aw,wl}$ is the data memory of a strict load/store Maurer ISA with address width aw and word length wl, $\mathsf{S}_{\mathsf{data}}^{aw,wl}$ is the set of possible states of that data memory, and $\mathsf{T}_{\mathsf{data}}^{aw,wl}$ is the set of possible transformations on those states.

Definition 6.8. Let $aw, ous \geq 0$ and $wl, iss, ssb > 0$, and let $waf \in \mathbb{B}$ be such that $waf = \mathsf{f}$ if $aw = 0$. Then the *thread powered function class* with parameters aw, wl, ous, iss, ssb and waf, written $\mathcal{TPFC}(aw, wl, ous, iss, ssb, waf)$, is the subset of $\mathsf{T}_{\mathsf{data}}^{aw,wl}$ that is defined as follows:

$$\begin{aligned}
& T \in \mathcal{TPFC}(aw, wl, ous, iss, ssb, waf) \\
& \Leftrightarrow \exists I_{dm} \subseteq \mathcal{M} \bullet \\
& \quad \exists H \in \mathcal{MISA}_{\mathsf{sls}}(aw, wl, ous, 1, 1, I_{dm}) \bullet \\
& \quad\quad \exists \boldsymbol{t} \in \mathcal{T}_{\mathsf{reg}}(\{\mathtt{f}.\boldsymbol{m} \mid \boldsymbol{m} \in I_H\}) \bullet \\
& \quad\quad\quad (\mathrm{card}(I_{dm}) = iss \land \mathrm{card}(Res(\boldsymbol{t})) \leq ssb \land \\
& \quad\quad\quad \forall S \in \mathcal{S}_H \bullet \\
& \quad\quad\quad\quad \exists S' \in \mathcal{S}_H \bullet \\
& \quad\quad\quad\quad\quad (\boldsymbol{t} \bullet \mathtt{f}.U_H(S) = \mathtt{f}.U_H(S') \land \\
& \quad\quad\quad\quad\quad (waf = \mathsf{f} \Rightarrow T(S \restriction \mathsf{M}_{\mathsf{data}}^{aw,wl}) = S' \restriction \mathsf{M}_{\mathsf{data}}^{aw,wl}) \land \\
& \quad\quad\quad\quad\quad (waf = \mathsf{t} \Rightarrow T(S \restriction \mathsf{M}_{\mathsf{data}}^{aw,wl}) \restriction \mathsf{M}_{\mathsf{data}}^{aw-1,wl} = S' \restriction \mathsf{M}_{\mathsf{data}}^{aw-1,wl}))) ,
\end{aligned}$$

where $\mathcal{T}_{\mathsf{reg}}(A)$ is the set of all closed BTA+REC terms $\boldsymbol{t}$ denoting regular threads over A.

Definition 6.9. A thread powered function class $\mathcal{TPFC}(aw, wl, ous, iss, ssb, waf)$ is *complete* if $\mathcal{TPFC}(aw, wl, ous, iss, ssb, waf) = \mathsf{T}_{\mathsf{data}}^{aw,wl}$.

The following theorem states that $\mathcal{TPFC}(aw, wl, ous, iss, ssb, waf)$ is complete if $ous = 2^{aw} \cdot wl + aw + 1$, $iss = 5$ and $ssb = 8$. Because $2^{aw} \cdot wl$ is the data memory size, i.e. the number of bits that the data memory contains, this means that completeness can be obtained with 5 data manipulation instructions and threads whose number of states is less than or equal to 8 by taking the operating unit size slightly greater than the data memory size.

Theorem 6.3. *Let* $aw \geq 0$, $wl > 0$ *and* $waf \in \mathbb{B}$, *and let* $dms = 2^{aw} \cdot wl$. *Then* $\mathcal{TPFC}(aw, wl, dms + aw + 1, 5, 8, waf)$ *is complete.*

Proof. The full proof, which can be found in [Bergstra and Middelburg (2010b)], is straightforward but tedious. Therefore, we give here a very brief overview of that proof and the idea behind the construction of a strict load/store Maurer ISA which plays an important role in the proof.

The proof amounts to constructing, for an arbitrary $T \in \mathsf{T}_{\mathsf{data}}^{aw,wl}$, a strict load/store Maurer ISA H and a closed BTA+REC term $\boldsymbol{t}$ witnessing $T \in \mathcal{TPFC}(aw, wl, dms + aw + 1, 5, 8, waf)$. We can prove in the same inductive style as used in the proof of Theorem 6.2 a number of properties regarding the constructed H and $\boldsymbol{t}$ from which it follows immediately that they really witness $T \in \mathcal{TPFC}(aw, wl, dms + aw + 1, 5, 8, waf)$.

The idea behind the construction of a suitable strict load/store Maurer ISA is that first the content of the whole data memory is copied data memory element by data memory element via the load data register to the operating unit, after that the intended state transformation is applied to the copy in the operating unit, and finally the result is copied back data memory element by data memory element via the store data register to the data memory. The data manipulation instructions used to accomplish this are an initialization instruction, a pre-load instruction, a post-load instruction, a pre-store instruction, and a transformation instruction. The pre-load instruction is used to update the load address register before a data memory element is loaded, the post-load instruction is used to store the content of the load data register in the operating unit after a data memory element has been loaded, and the pre-store instruction is used to update the store address register and to load the content of the store data register from the operating unit before a data memory element is stored. The transformation instruction is used to apply the intended state transformation to the copy in the operating unit. □

As a corollary of the proofs of Theorems 6.2 and 6.3, we have that completeness can even be obtained if we take zero as the operating unit size.

Corollary 6.2. *Let* $aw \geq 0$ *and* $wl > 0$, *let* $waf \in \mathbb{B}$ *be such that* $waf = \mathsf{f}$ *if* $aw = 0$, *and let* $dms = 2^{aw} \cdot wl$. *Then* $\mathcal{TPFC}(aw, wl, 0, 5 \cdot 4^{dms+aw+1}, 8 \cdot 6^{dms+aw+1}, waf)$ *is* *complete.*

From Corollary 6.2, we know that it is possible to achieve all transformations on the states of the external memory of a strict load/store Maurer ISA with given address width and word length even if the operating unit size is zero. However, this may require a very large number of data manipulation instructions and threads with a very large number of states. This raises the question whether the operating unit size of the ISAs, the size of the instructions set of the ISAs and the maximal number of states of the threads can be taken such that it is impossible to achieve all transformations on the states of the external memory.

The following theorem states that $\mathcal{TPFC}(aw, wl, ous, iss, ssb, \mathrm{t})$ is not complete if the operating unit size is not greater than half the external memory size, the instruction set size is not greater than $2^{wl} - 4$, and the maximal number of states of the threads is not greater than 2^{aw-2}. Notice that 2^{wl} is the number of instructions that can be represented in memory elements with word length wl and that 2^{aw-2} is half the number of memory elements in the internal memory.

Theorem 6.4. *Let* $aw, wl > 1$ *and* $ous, iss, ssb > 0$*, and let* $ems = 2^{aw-1} \cdot wl$*. Then* $\mathcal{TPFC}(aw, wl, ous, iss, ssb, \mathrm{t})$ *is not complete if* $ous \leq ems/2$ *and* $iss \leq 2^{wl} - 4$ *and* $ssb \leq 2^{aw-2}$.

Proof. The proof is a simple counting argument, and can be found in [Bergstra and Middelburg (2010b)]. □

Chapter 7

Instruction Sequences and Process Algebra

This chapter concerns two subjects related to process algebra, namely protocols to deal with remote instruction processing and instruction sequence producible processes.

On execution of an instruction sequence, the processing of instructions increasingly takes place remotely. This involves the generation of a stream of instructions to be processed and a remote execution unit that handles the processing of this stream of instructions. We use process algebra to describe two protocols to deal with this phenomenon.

Process algebra is considered relevant to computer science, as is witnesses by the extent of the work on algebraic theories of processes such as ACP, CCS and CSP in theoretical computer science. This means that there must be programmed systems whose behaviours are taken for processes as considered in process algebra. We show that, by apposite choice of basic instructions, all finite-state processes can be produced by single-pass instruction sequences as considered in SPISA, provided that the cluster fair abstraction rule known from ACP is valid.

7.1 Process Algebra

In this section, we review the particular algebraic theory of processes that will be used in this chapter, namely ACP$^{\tau}$ (Algebra of Communicating Processes with abstraction). For a comprehensive overview of ACP$^{\tau}$, the reader is referred to [Baeten and Weijland (1990); Fokkink (2000)].

Threads as considered in BTA represent in a direct way behaviours produced by instruction sequences under execution. It is rather awkward to describe and analyse behaviours of this kind using algebraic theories of processes such as ACP [Bergstra and Klop (1984); Baeten and Weijland (1990)], CCS [Hennessy and Milner (1985); Milner (1989)] and CSP [Brookes *et al.* (1984); Hoare (1985)]. However, threads as considered in BTA can be viewed as representations of processes as considered in process algebra. We use ACP^τ, an extension of ACP which supports abstraction from internal actions, to make precise which processes are represented by threads. This allows among other things for the protocols for remote processing of instructions to be described using ACP^τ.

7.1.1 *Algebra of communicating processes*

In ACP^τ, it is assumed that a fixed but arbitrary set A of *atomic actions*, with $\tau, \delta \notin \mathsf{A}$, has been given. We write A_τ for $\mathsf{A} \cup \{\tau\}$ and A_δ for $\mathsf{A} \cup \{\delta\}$. In ACP^τ, it is also assumed that a fixed but arbitrary commutative and associative function $| : \mathsf{A}_\tau \times \mathsf{A}_\tau \to \mathsf{A}_\delta$, with $\tau \,|\, a = \delta$ for all $a \in \mathsf{A}_\tau$, has been given. The function $|$ is regarded to give the result of synchronously performing any two atomic actions for which this is possible, and to give δ otherwise. In ACP^τ, τ is a special atomic action, called the silent step. The act of performing the silent step is considered unobservable. Because it would otherwise be observable, the silent step is considered an atomic action that cannot be performed synchronously with other atomic actions.

ACP^τ has one sort: the sort $\mathbf{P}$ of *processes*. To build terms of sort $\mathbf{P}$, ACP^τ has the following constants and operators:

- for each $a \in \mathsf{A}$, the *atomic action* constant $a : \to \mathbf{P}$;
- the *silent step* constant $\tau : \to \mathbf{P}$;
- the *inaction* constant $\delta : \to \mathbf{P}$;
- the binary *alternative composition* operator $\_ + \_ : \mathbf{P} \times \mathbf{P} \to \mathbf{P}$;
- the binary *sequential composition* operator $\_ \cdot \_ : \mathbf{P} \times \mathbf{P} \to \mathbf{P}$;
- the binary *parallel composition* operator $\_ \parallel \_ : \mathbf{P} \times \mathbf{P} \to \mathbf{P}$;
- the binary *left merge* operator $\_ \mathbin{\|\!\!\_} \_ : \mathbf{P} \times \mathbf{P} \to \mathbf{P}$;
- the binary *communication merge* operator $\_ \mid \_ : \mathbf{P} \times \mathbf{P} \to \mathbf{P}$;
- for each $A \subseteq \mathsf{A}$, the unary *encapsulation* operator $\partial_A : \mathbf{P} \to \mathbf{P}$;
- for each $A \subseteq \mathsf{A}$, the unary *abstraction* operator $\tau_A : \mathbf{P} \to \mathbf{P}$.

We assume that there are infinitely many variables, including x, y, z. ACP^τ terms are built as usual. We use infix notation for the binary operators. The precedence conventions used with respect to the operators of ACP^τ are as follows: $+$ binds weaker than all others, $\cdot$ binds stronger than all others, and the remaining operators bind equally strong.

Let t and t' be closed ACP^τ terms, $a \in \mathsf{A}$, and $A \subseteq \mathsf{A}$. Intuitively, the constants and operators to build ACP^τ terms can be explained as follows:

- the process denoted by a first performs atomic action a and next terminates successfully;
- the process denoted by τ performs an unobservable atomic action and next terminates successfully;
- the process denoted by δ can neither perform an atomic action nor terminate successfully;
- the process denoted by $t + t'$ behaves either as the process denoted by t or as the process denoted by t', but not both;
- the process denoted by $t \cdot t'$ first behaves as the process denoted by t and on successful termination of that process it next behaves as the process denoted by t';
- the process denoted by $t \parallel t'$ behaves as the process that proceeds with the processes denoted by t and t' in parallel;
- the process denoted by $t \mathbin{⌊\!⌊} t'$ behaves the same as the process denoted by $t \parallel t'$, except that it starts with performing an atomic action of the process denoted by t;
- the process denoted by $t \mid t'$ behaves the same as the process denoted by $t \parallel t'$, except that it starts with performing an atomic action of the process denoted by t and an atomic action of the process denoted by t' synchronously;
- the process denoted by $\partial_A(t)$ behaves the same as the process denoted by t, except that atomic actions from A are blocked;
- the process denoted by $\tau_A(t)$ behaves the same as the process denoted by t, except that atomic actions from A are turned into unobservable atomic actions.

The operators $⌊\!⌊$ and $\mid$ are of an auxiliary nature. They are needed to axiomatize ACP$^\tau$.

The axioms of ACP$^\tau$ are given in Table 7.1. In this table, a, b and c stand for arbitrary constants of ACP$^\tau$, and A stands for an arbitrary subset of A. ACP$^\tau$ is extended with guarded recursion like BTA.

Definition 7.1. A *recursive specification* over ACP$^\tau$ is a set of recursion equations $\{x = t_x \mid x \in \mathcal{V}\}$, where $\mathcal{V}$ is a set of variables and each t_x is an ACP$^\tau$ term containing only variables from $\mathcal{V}$. Let t be an ACP$^\tau$ term without occurrences of abstraction operators containing a variable x. Then an occurrence of x in t is *guarded* if t has a subterm of the form $a \cdot t'$ where $a \in \mathsf{A}$ and t' is a term containing this occurrence of x. Let E be a recursive specification over ACP$^\tau$. Then E is a *guarded recursive specification* if, in each equation $x = t_x \in E$: (i) abstraction operators do not occur in t_x and (ii) all occurrences of variables in t_x are guarded or t_x can be rewritten to such a term using the axioms of ACP$^\tau$ in either direction and/or the equations in E except the equation $x = t_x$ from left to

Table 7.1 Axioms of ACP^{τ}

$x + y = y + x$	A1	$x \cdot \tau = x$	B1
$(x + y) + z = x + (y + z)$	A2	$x \cdot (\tau \cdot (y + z) + y) = x \cdot (y + z)$	B2
$x + x = x$	A3		
$(x + y) \cdot z = x \cdot z + y \cdot z$	A4	$\partial_{\boldsymbol{A}}(\boldsymbol{a}) = \boldsymbol{a}$ if $\boldsymbol{a} \notin \boldsymbol{A}$	D1
$(x \cdot y) \cdot z = x \cdot (y \cdot z)$	A5	$\partial_{\boldsymbol{A}}(\boldsymbol{a}) = \delta$ if $\boldsymbol{a} \in \boldsymbol{A}$	D2
$x + \delta = x$	A6	$\partial_{\boldsymbol{A}}(x + y) = \partial_{\boldsymbol{A}}(x) + \partial_{\boldsymbol{A}}(y)$	D3
$\delta \cdot x = \delta$	A7	$\partial_{\boldsymbol{A}}(x \cdot y) = \partial_{\boldsymbol{A}}(x) \cdot \partial_{\boldsymbol{A}}(y)$	D4
$x \parallel y = x \mathbin{⌊\!⌊} y + y \mathbin{⌊\!⌊} x + x \mid y$	CM1	$\tau_{\boldsymbol{A}}(\boldsymbol{a}) = \boldsymbol{a}$ if $\boldsymbol{a} \notin \boldsymbol{A}$	TI1
$\boldsymbol{a} \mathbin{⌊\!⌊} x = \boldsymbol{a} \cdot x$	CM2	$\tau_{\boldsymbol{A}}(\boldsymbol{a}) = \tau$ if $\boldsymbol{a} \in \boldsymbol{A}$	TI2
$\boldsymbol{a} \cdot x \mathbin{⌊\!⌊} y = \boldsymbol{a} \cdot (x \parallel y)$	CM3	$\tau_{\boldsymbol{A}}(x + y) = \tau_{\boldsymbol{A}}(x) + \tau_{\boldsymbol{A}}(y)$	TI3
$(x + y) \mathbin{⌊\!⌊} z = x \mathbin{⌊\!⌊} z + y \mathbin{⌊\!⌊} z$	CM4	$\tau_{\boldsymbol{A}}(x \cdot y) = \tau_{\boldsymbol{A}}(x) \cdot \tau_{\boldsymbol{A}}(y)$	TI4
$\boldsymbol{a} \cdot x \mid \boldsymbol{b} = (\boldsymbol{a} \mid \boldsymbol{b}) \cdot x$	CM5		
$\boldsymbol{a} \mid \boldsymbol{b} \cdot x = (\boldsymbol{a} \mid \boldsymbol{b}) \cdot x$	CM6	$\boldsymbol{a} \mid \boldsymbol{b} = \boldsymbol{b} \mid \boldsymbol{a}$	C1
$\boldsymbol{a} \cdot x \mid \boldsymbol{b} \cdot y = (\boldsymbol{a} \mid \boldsymbol{b}) \cdot (x \parallel y)$	CM7	$(\boldsymbol{a} \mid \boldsymbol{b}) \mid \boldsymbol{c} = \boldsymbol{a} \mid (\boldsymbol{b} \mid \boldsymbol{c})$	C2
$(x + y) \mid z = x \mid z + y \mid z$	CM8	$\delta \mid \boldsymbol{a} = \delta$	C3
$x \mid (y + z) = x \mid y + x \mid z$	CM9	$\tau \mid \boldsymbol{a} = \delta$	C4

right.

We are only interested models of ACP^{τ} in which guarded recursive specifications have unique solutions, such as the models of ACP^{τ} presented in [Baeten and Weijland (1990)].

We write $\text{V}(\boldsymbol{E})$, where $\boldsymbol{E}$ is a recursive specification over ACP^{τ}, for the set of all variables that occur in $\boldsymbol{E}$.

For each guarded recursive specification $\boldsymbol{E}$ and each $\boldsymbol{x} \in \text{V}(\boldsymbol{E})$, we introduce a constant $\langle \boldsymbol{x} | \boldsymbol{E} \rangle$ standing for the $\boldsymbol{x}$-component of the unique solution of $\boldsymbol{E}$. We write $\langle \boldsymbol{t} | \boldsymbol{E} \rangle$ for $\boldsymbol{t}$ with, for all $\boldsymbol{y} \in \text{V}(\boldsymbol{E})$, all occurrences of $\boldsymbol{y}$ in $\boldsymbol{t}$ replaced by $\langle \boldsymbol{y} | \boldsymbol{E} \rangle$. The axioms for the constants standing for the components of the unique solutions of guarded recursive specifications are RDP and RSP, which are given in Table 7.2. In this table, $\boldsymbol{x}$ stands for an arbitrary variable, $\boldsymbol{t}_{\boldsymbol{x}}$ stands for an arbitrary ACP^{τ} term, and $\boldsymbol{E}$ stands for an arbitrary guarded recursive specification over ACP^{τ}. Side conditions are added to restrict what $\boldsymbol{x}$,

Table 7.2 Axioms for guarded recursion

$\langle \boldsymbol{x} \vert \boldsymbol{E} \rangle = \langle \boldsymbol{t_x} \vert \boldsymbol{E} \rangle$	if $\boldsymbol{x} = \boldsymbol{t_x} \in \boldsymbol{E}$	RDP
$\boldsymbol{E} \Rightarrow \boldsymbol{x} = \langle \boldsymbol{x} \vert \boldsymbol{E} \rangle$	if $\boldsymbol{x} \in \mathrm{V}(\boldsymbol{E})$	RSP

Table 7.3 AIP and axioms for the projection operators

$\bigwedge_{n \geq 0} \pi_n(x) = \pi_n(y) \Rightarrow x = y$	AIP
$\pi_0(\boldsymbol{a}) = \delta$	PR1
$\pi_{n+1}(\boldsymbol{a}) = \boldsymbol{a}$	PR2
$\pi_0(\boldsymbol{a} \cdot x) = \delta$	PR3
$\pi_{n+1}(\boldsymbol{a} \cdot x) = \boldsymbol{a} \cdot \pi_n(x)$	PR4
$\pi_n(x + y) = \pi_n(x) + \pi_n(y)$	PR5
$\pi_n(\tau) = \tau$	PR6
$\pi_n(\tau \cdot x) = \tau \cdot \pi_n(x)$	PR7

$\boldsymbol{t_x}$ and $\boldsymbol{E}$ stand for.

Closed terms of ACP$^\tau$ extended with constants for the components of the unique solutions of guarded recursive specifications that denote the same process cannot always be proved equal by means of the axioms of ACP$^\tau$ together with RDP and RSP. We introduce AIP to remedy this. AIP is based on the view that two processes are identical if their approximations up to any finite depth are identical. The approximation up to depth n of a process behaves the same as that process, except that it cannot perform any further atomic action after n atomic actions have been performed. In AIP, approximation up to depth n is phrased in terms of a unary *projection* operator $\pi_n : \mathbf{P} \to \mathbf{P}$. AIP and the axioms for the projection operators are given in Table 7.3. In this table, $\boldsymbol{a}$ stands for arbitrary constants of ACP$^\tau$ different from τ and n stands for an arbitrary natural number.

We write ACP$^\tau$+REC for ACP$^\tau$ extended with the constants $\langle \boldsymbol{x} \vert \boldsymbol{E} \rangle$ and the axioms RDP and RSP, and we write ACP$^\tau$+REC+AIP for ACP$^\tau$+REC extended with the operators π_n and the axioms AIP and PR1–PR7.

In the remainder of this chapter, we assume that a fixed but arbitrary model $\mathcal{M}^{\tau}_{\mathrm{ACP}}$ of ACP$^{\tau}$+REC+AIP has been given. As in the case of models of BTA or some extension thereof, we denote the interpretations of sorts, constants and operators in $\mathcal{M}^{\tau}_{\mathrm{ACP}}$ by the sorts, constants and operators themselves.

From Sect. 7.3.2, we will sometimes assume that CFAR (Cluster Fair Abstraction Rule) is valid in $\mathcal{M}^{\tau}_{\mathrm{ACP}}$. CFAR says that a cluster of silent steps that has exits can be eliminated if all exits are reachable from everywhere in the cluster. A precise formulation of CFAR can be found in [Fokkink (2000)].

We use the term *process* for the elements of the interpretation of the sort $\mathbf{P}$ in $\mathcal{M}^{\tau}_{\mathrm{ACP}}$.

Definition 7.2. Let p be a process. Then the set of *states* or *subprocesses* of p, written $Sub(p)$, is inductively defined as follows:

- $p \in Sub(p)$;
- if $\boldsymbol{a} \cdot p' \in Sub(p)$, then $p' \in Sub(p)$;
- if $\boldsymbol{a} \cdot p' + p'' \in Sub(p)$, then $p' \in Sub(p)$.

Definition 7.3. Let p be a process and let $\boldsymbol{A} \subseteq \mathsf{A}_{\tau}$. Then p is *regular over* $\boldsymbol{A}$ if the following conditions are satisfied:

- $Sub(p)$ is finite;
- for all $p' \in Sub(p)$ and $\boldsymbol{a} \in \mathsf{A}_{\tau}$, $\boldsymbol{a} \cdot p' \in Sub(p)$ implies $\boldsymbol{a} \in \boldsymbol{A}$;
- for all $p', p'' \in Sub(p)$ and $\boldsymbol{a} \in \mathsf{A}_{\tau}$, $\boldsymbol{a} \cdot p' + p'' \in Sub(p)$ implies $\boldsymbol{a} \in \boldsymbol{A}$.

We say that p is *regular* if p is regular over A_{τ}.

We will make use of the fact that being a regular process over A coincides with being the solution of a finite guarded recursive specification in which the right-hand sides of the recursion equations are linear terms.

Definition 7.4. *Linearity* of ACP$^{\tau}$ terms is inductively defined as follows:

- δ is linear;
- if $\boldsymbol{a} \in \mathsf{A}_{\tau}$, then $\boldsymbol{a}$ is linear;
- if $\boldsymbol{a} \in \mathsf{A}_{\tau}$ and $\boldsymbol{x}$ is a variable, then $\boldsymbol{a} \cdot \boldsymbol{x}$ is linear;
- if $\boldsymbol{t}$ and $\boldsymbol{t}'$ are linear, then $\boldsymbol{t} + \boldsymbol{t}'$ is linear.

A *linear recursive specification* over ACP$^{\tau}$ is a guarded recursive specification $\{\boldsymbol{x} = \boldsymbol{t}_{\boldsymbol{x}} \mid \boldsymbol{x} \in \mathcal{V}\}$ over ACP$^{\tau}$ where each $\boldsymbol{t}_{\boldsymbol{x}}$ is linear.

Proposition 7.1. *Let p be a process and let $\boldsymbol{A} \subseteq \mathsf{A}$. Then p is regular over $\boldsymbol{A}$ iff there exists a finite linear recursive specification $\boldsymbol{E}$ over* ACP$^\tau$ *in which only atomic actions from $\boldsymbol{A}$ occur such that p is a component of the solution of $\boldsymbol{E}$.*

Proof. The proof follows the same line as the proof of Proposition 2.1. □

Proposition 7.1 is concerned with processes that are regular over A. We can also prove that being a regular process over A_τ coincides with being the solution of a finite linear recursive specification over ACP$^\tau$ if we assume that the cluster fair abstraction rule [Fokkink (2000)] holds in the model $\mathcal{M}^\tau_{\text{ACP}}$. However, we do not need this more general result.

We will write $\sum_{i \in S} t_i$, where $S = \{i_1, \ldots, i_n\}$ and $t_{i_1}, \ldots, t_{i_n}$ are terms of sort $\mathbf{P}$, for $t_{i_1} + \ldots + t_{i_n}$. The convention is that $\sum_{i \in S} t_i$ stands for δ if $S = \emptyset$. We will sometimes write x for $\langle x | \boldsymbol{E} \rangle$ if $\boldsymbol{E}$ is clear from the context. It should be borne in mind that, in such cases, we use x as a constant.

7.1.2 *Process extraction for threads*

In this section, we make precise in the setting of ACP$^\tau$ which processes are represented by threads whose basic actions are composed of a focus and a method. For that purpose, we combine BTA+REC+AIP with ACP$^\tau$+REC+AIP and extend the combination with an operator meant for the extraction of the processes that are represented by threads from the threads, assuming that:

- a fixed but arbitrary set $\mathcal{F}$ of foci has been given;
- a fixed but arbitrary set $\mathcal{M}$ of methods has been given;
- $\mathcal{A} = \{f.m \mid f \in \mathcal{F} \wedge m \in \mathcal{M}\}$.

A and | are taken such that the following conditions are satisfied:

$$\begin{aligned} \mathsf{A} \supseteq\; & \{\mathtt{s}_f(d) \mid f \in \mathcal{F} \wedge d \in \mathcal{M} \cup \mathbb{B}\} \cup \{\mathtt{r}_f(d) \mid f \in \mathcal{F} \wedge d \in \mathcal{M} \cup \mathbb{B}\} \\ & \cup \{\mathtt{stop}(r) \mid r \in \mathbb{B} \cup \{\mathsf{m}\}\} \cup \{\mathtt{i}\} \end{aligned}$$

and for all $f \in \mathcal{F}$, $d \in \mathcal{M} \cup \mathbb{B}$, $r \in \mathbb{B} \cup \{\mathsf{m}\}$, and $e \in \mathsf{A}$:

$$\begin{array}{lll} \mathtt{s}_f(d) \mid \mathtt{r}_f(d) = \mathtt{i}\;, & & \\ \mathtt{s}_f(d) \mid e = \delta & \text{if } e \neq \mathtt{r}_f(d)\;, & \mathtt{stop}(r) \mid e = \delta\;, \\ e \mid \mathtt{r}_f(d) = \delta & \text{if } e \neq \mathtt{s}_f(d)\;, & \mathtt{i} \mid e = \delta\;. \end{array}$$

Actions of the forms $\mathtt{s}_f(d)$ and $\mathtt{r}_f(d)$ are send and receive actions, respectively, actions of the form $\mathtt{stop}(r)$ are explicit termination actions, and $\mathtt{i}$ is a concrete internal action.

Table 7.4 Axioms for the process extraction operator

$\lvert \mathsf{S+} \rvert = \mathtt{stop(t)}$	PE1
$\lvert \mathsf{S-} \rvert = \mathtt{stop(f)}$	PE2
$\lvert \mathsf{S} \rvert = \mathtt{stop(m)}$	PE3
$\lvert \mathsf{D} \rvert = \mathtt{i} \cdot \delta$	PE4
$\lvert x \trianglelefteq \mathsf{tau} \trianglerighteq y \rvert = \mathtt{i} \cdot \mathtt{i} \cdot \lvert x \rvert$	PE5
$\lvert x \trianglelefteq f.m \trianglerighteq y \rvert = \mathtt{s}_f(m) \cdot (\mathtt{r}_f(\mathtt{t}) \cdot \lvert x \rvert + \mathtt{r}_f(\mathtt{f}) \cdot \lvert y \rvert)$	PE6

The resulting theory has the sorts, constants and operators of both BTA+REC+AIP and ACP$^\tau$+REC+AIP, and in addition the following operator:

- the *process extraction* operator $\lvert \_ \rvert : \mathbf{T} \to \mathbf{P}$.

The axioms of the resulting theory are the axioms of both BTA+REC+AIP and ACP$^\tau$+ REC+AIP, and in addition the axioms for the process extraction operator given in Table 7.4. In this table, f stands for an arbitrary focus from $\mathcal{F}$ and m stands for an arbitrary method from $\mathcal{M}$.

Let t, t' and t'' be closed terms of sort **IS**, sort $\mathbf{T}$ and sort $\mathbf{P}$, respectively. Then we loosely say that *thread t' produces process t''* if $\tau \cdot \tau_A(\lvert t' \rvert) = \tau \cdot t''$ for some $A \subseteq \mathsf{A}$, and we loosely say that *instruction sequence t produces process t''* if thread $\lvert t \rvert$ produces process t''.

Notice that two atomic actions are involved in performing a basic action of the form $f.m$: one for sending a request to process command m to the service named f and another for receiving a reply from that service upon completion of the processing. Notice also that, for each closed term t of sort $\mathbf{T}$, $\lvert t \rvert$ is a process that in the event of termination performs a special termination action just before termination.

The process extraction operator preserves the axioms of BTA+REC. Before we make this fully precise, we have a closer look at the axioms of BTA+REC.

A proper axiom is an equation or a conditional equation. In Table 2.4, we do not find proper axioms. Instead of proper axioms, we find axiom schemas (with side conditions to restrict their instances). The axioms of BTA+REC are obtained by replacing each axiom schema by all its instances.

In the following proposition, we identify $t_1 = t_2$ and $\emptyset \Rightarrow t_1 = t_2$.

Proposition 7.2. *Let* $E \Rightarrow t_1 = t_2$ *be a proper axiom of* BTA+REC. *Then* $\{|t'_1| = |t'_2| \mid t'_1 = t'_2 \in E\} \Rightarrow |t_1| = |t_2|$ *is derivable.*

Proof. The proof is trivial. □

7.2 Protocols for Remote Instruction Processing

The behaviour produced by an instruction sequence under execution is a behaviour to be controlled by some execution environment. It proceeds by performing steps in a sequential fashion. Each step performed actuates the processing of an instruction by the execution environment. A reply returned by the execution environment at completion of the processing of the instruction determines how the behaviour proceeds. Increasingly, the processing of instructions takes place remotely. This means that, on execution of an instruction sequence, a stream of instructions to be processed arises at one place and the processing of that stream of instructions is handled at another place. The main objective of the current section is to bring this phenomenon better into the picture. To achieve this objective, we describe two protocols to deal with this phenomenon. We use the phrase *protocols for instruction stream processing* to refer to such protocols.

The phenomenon sketched above is found if it is impracticable to load the instruction sequence to be executed as a whole. For instance, the storage capacity of the execution unit is too small or the execution unit is too far away. The phenomenon requires special attention because the transmission time of the messages involved in remote processing makes it hard to keep the execution unit busy without intermission. The more complex protocol for instruction stream processing described below is directed towards keeping the execution unit busy.

There is no reason to use the word "remote" in a narrow sense. It is convenient to consider processing remote if it involves message passing with transmission times that are not negligible. In that case, the more complex protocol provides a starting-point for studies of basic techniques aimed at increasing processor performance, such as pre-fetching and branch-prediction, at a more abstract level than usual. In particular, we think that the protocol can serve as a starting-point for the development of a model with which trade-offs encountered in the design of processor architectures can be clarified. Therefore, we consider protocols for instruction stream processing a subject relevant to the area of computer architecture.

7.2.1 *A simple protocol*

In this section and the next one, we consider protocols for instruction stream processing.

In BTA, it is assumed that a fixed but arbitrary set $\mathcal{A}$ of basic actions has been given. Here, the following additional assumptions relating to $\mathcal{A}$ are made:

- a fixed but arbitrary finite set $\mathcal{F}$ of foci has been given;
- a fixed but arbitrary finite set $\mathcal{M}$ of methods has been given;
- $\mathcal{A} = \{\boldsymbol{f}.\boldsymbol{m} \mid \boldsymbol{f} \in \mathcal{F} \wedge \boldsymbol{m} \in \mathcal{M}\}$.

The sets $\mathcal{F}$ and $\mathcal{M}$ are assumed to be finite because otherwise an extension of ACP with a relatively involved variable-binding operator generalizing alternative composition to countably infinite alternatives, like in μCRL [Groote and Ponse (1995, 1994)], would be needed.

In the remainder of Sect. 7.2, we assume that, in addition to the fixed but arbitrary model $\boldsymbol{\mathcal{M}}^{\tau}_{\mathrm{ACP}}$ of ACP$^{\tau}$+REC+AIP, a fixed but arbitrary model $\boldsymbol{\mathcal{M}}_{\mathrm{BTA}}$ of BTA+REC+AIP has been given.

Before the first protocol is described, a minor extension of ACP$^{\tau}$ is introduced to simplify the description of the protocols: the non-branching conditional operator $:\!\rightarrow$ over $\mathbb{B}$ from [Baeten and Bergstra (1992)]. The expression $\boldsymbol{t} :\!\rightarrow \boldsymbol{t}'$ is to be read as `if` $\boldsymbol{t}$ `then` $\boldsymbol{t}'$ `else` δ. The axioms for the non-branching conditional operator are

$$\mathsf{t} :\!\rightarrow x = x \quad \text{and} \quad \mathsf{f} :\!\rightarrow x = \delta\ .$$

The protocols concern systems whose main components are an *instruction stream generator* and an *instruction stream execution unit*. The instruction stream generator generates different instruction streams for different threads. This is considered to be accomplished by starting it in different states. The general idea of the protocols is that:

- the instruction stream generator generating an instruction stream for a thread $t \trianglelefteq \boldsymbol{a} \trianglerighteq t'$ sends $\boldsymbol{a}$ to the instruction stream execution unit;
- on receipt of $\boldsymbol{a}$, the instruction stream execution unit gets the execution of $\boldsymbol{a}$ done and sends the reply produced to the instruction stream generator;
- on receipt of the reply, the instruction stream generator proceeds with generating an instruction stream for t if the reply is t and for t' otherwise.

In the case where the thread is $\mathsf{S}{+}$, $\mathsf{S}{-}$, S or D, the instruction stream generator sends a special instruction ($\mathsf{stop_t}$, $\mathsf{stop_f}$, $\mathsf{stop_m}$ or dead) and the instruction stream execution unit does not send back a reply.

The first protocol for instruction stream processing that we consider is a very simple protocol that makes no effort to keep the execution unit busy without intermission.

We write $\mathcal{I}$ for the set $\mathcal{A} \cup \{\mathsf{stop_t}, \mathsf{stop_f}, \mathsf{stop_m}, \mathsf{dead}\}$ and $\mathcal{R}$ for the set $\{\mathsf{t}, \mathsf{f}, \mathsf{m}\}$. Elements from $\mathcal{I}$ will loosely be called instructions. The restriction of the domain of $\mathcal{M}_{\mathrm{BTA}}$ to the regular threads will be denoted by $\mathcal{RT}$.

The functions *act*, *thrt*, and *thrf* defined below give, for each thread t different from $\mathsf{S+}$, $\mathsf{S-}$, S and D, the basic action that t will perform first, the thread with which it will proceed if the reply from the execution environment is t, and the thread with which it will proceed if the reply from the execution environment is f, respectively. The functions $act : \mathcal{RT} \to \mathcal{I}$, $thrt : \mathcal{RT} \to \mathcal{RT}$, and $thrf : \mathcal{RT} \to \mathcal{RT}$ are defined as follows:

$$\begin{aligned}
&act(\mathsf{S+}) = \mathsf{stop_t}\,, && thrt(\mathsf{S+}) = \mathsf{D}\,, && thrf(\mathsf{S+}) = \mathsf{D}\,,\\
&act(\mathsf{S-}) = \mathsf{stop_f}\,, && thrt(\mathsf{S-}) = \mathsf{D}\,, && thrf(\mathsf{S-}) = \mathsf{D}\,,\\
&act(\mathsf{S}) = \mathsf{stop_m}\,, && thrt(\mathsf{S}) = \mathsf{D}\,, && thrf(\mathsf{S}) = \mathsf{D}\,,\\
&act(\mathsf{D}) = \mathsf{dead}\,, && thrt(\mathsf{D}) = \mathsf{D}\,, && thrf(\mathsf{D}) = \mathsf{D}\,,\\
&act(t \trianglelefteq \boldsymbol{a} \trianglerighteq t') = \boldsymbol{a}\,, && thrt(t \trianglelefteq \boldsymbol{a} \trianglerighteq t') = t\,, && thrf(t \trianglelefteq \boldsymbol{a} \trianglerighteq t') = t'\,.
\end{aligned}$$

The function nxt^0 defined below is used by the instruction stream generator to distinguish when it starts with handling the instruction to be executed next between the different instructions that it may be. The function $nxt^0 : \mathcal{I} \times \mathcal{RT} \to \mathbb{B}$ is defined as follows:

$$nxt^0(\boldsymbol{a}, t) = \begin{cases} \mathsf{t} & \text{if } act(t) = \boldsymbol{a} \\ \mathsf{f} & \text{if } act(t) \neq \boldsymbol{a}\,. \end{cases}$$

For the purpose of describing the simple protocol outlined above in ACP$^\tau$, A and $\mid$ are taken such that, in addition to the conditions mentioned at the beginning of Sect. 7.1.2, the following conditions are satisfied:

$$\begin{aligned}
\mathsf{A} \supseteq\; &\{\mathtt{s}_i(\boldsymbol{a}) \mid i \in \{1,2\} \wedge \boldsymbol{a} \in \mathcal{I}\} \cup \{\mathtt{r}_i(\boldsymbol{a}) \mid i \in \{1,2\} \wedge \boldsymbol{a} \in \mathcal{I}\}\\
\cup\; &\{\mathtt{s}_i(r) \mid i \in \{3,4\} \wedge r \in \mathbb{B}\} \cup \{\mathtt{r}_i(r) \mid i \in \{3,4\} \wedge r \in \mathbb{B}\} \cup \{\mathtt{j}\}
\end{aligned}$$

and for all $i \in \{1,2\}$, $j \in \{3,4\}$, $\boldsymbol{a} \in \mathcal{I}$, $r \in \mathbb{B}$, and $\boldsymbol{e} \in \mathsf{A}$:

$$\begin{aligned}
&\mathtt{s}_i(\boldsymbol{a}) \mid \mathtt{r}_i(\boldsymbol{a}) = \mathtt{j}\,, && && \mathtt{s}_j(r) \mid \mathtt{r}_j(r) = \mathtt{j}\,,\\
&\mathtt{s}_i(\boldsymbol{a}) \mid \boldsymbol{e} = \delta && \text{if } \boldsymbol{e} \neq \mathtt{r}_i(\boldsymbol{a})\,, && \mathtt{s}_j(r) \mid \boldsymbol{e} = \delta && \text{if } \boldsymbol{e} \neq \mathtt{r}_j(r)\,,\\
&\boldsymbol{e} \mid \mathtt{r}_i(\boldsymbol{a}) = \delta && \text{if } \boldsymbol{e} \neq \mathtt{s}_i(\boldsymbol{a})\,, && \boldsymbol{e} \mid \mathtt{r}_j(r) = \delta && \text{if } \boldsymbol{e} \neq \mathtt{s}_j(r)\,,\\
&\mathtt{j} \mid \boldsymbol{e} = \delta\,.
\end{aligned}$$

Let $t \in \mathcal{RT}$. Then the process representing the simple protocol for instruction stream processing with regard to thread t is described by

$$\partial_H(\mathit{ISG}^0_t \parallel \mathit{IMTC}^0 \parallel \mathit{RTC}^0 \parallel \mathit{ISEU}^0)\,,$$

where the process ISG^0_t is recursively specified by the following equations:

$$\begin{aligned}\mathit{ISG}^0_{t'} = {} & \sum_{f.m \in \mathcal{A}} \mathit{nxt}^0(\boldsymbol{f}.\boldsymbol{m}, t') :\to \\ & \quad \mathrm{s}_1(\boldsymbol{f}.\boldsymbol{m}) \cdot (\mathrm{r}_4(\mathsf{t}) \cdot \mathit{ISG}^0_{\mathit{thrt}(t')} + \mathrm{r}_4(\mathsf{f}) \cdot \mathit{ISG}^0_{\mathit{thrf}(t')}) \\ & + \sum_{r \in \mathcal{R}} \mathit{nxt}^0(\mathsf{stop}_r, t') :\to \mathrm{s}_1(\mathsf{stop}_r) \\ & + \mathit{nxt}^0(\mathsf{dead}, t') :\to \mathrm{s}_1(\mathsf{dead})\,, \\ & (\text{for every } t' \in \mathit{Res}(t))\,,\end{aligned}$$

the process IMTC^0 is recursively specified by the following equation:

$$\mathit{IMTC}^0 = \sum_{a \in \mathcal{I}} \mathrm{r}_1(\boldsymbol{a}) \cdot \mathrm{s}_2(\boldsymbol{a}) \cdot \mathit{IMTC}^0\,,$$

the process RTC^0 is recursively specified by the following equation:

$$\mathit{RTC}^0 = \sum_{r \in \mathbb{B}} \mathrm{r}_3(r) \cdot \mathrm{s}_4(r) \cdot \mathit{RTC}^0\,,$$

the process ISEU^0 is recursively specified by the following equation:

$$\begin{aligned}\mathit{ISEU}^0 = {} & \sum_{f.m \in \mathcal{A}} \mathrm{r}_2(\boldsymbol{f}.\boldsymbol{m}) \cdot \mathrm{s}_f(\boldsymbol{m}) \cdot (\mathrm{r}_f(\mathsf{t}) \cdot \mathrm{s}_3(\mathsf{t}) + \mathrm{r}_f(\mathsf{f}) \cdot \mathrm{s}_3(\mathsf{f})) \cdot \mathit{ISEU}^0 \\ & + \sum_{r \in \mathcal{R}} \mathrm{r}_2(\mathsf{stop}_r) \cdot \mathtt{stop}(r) + \mathrm{r}_2(\mathsf{dead}) \cdot \mathtt{i} \cdot \delta\end{aligned}$$

and

$$\begin{aligned}H = {} & \{\mathrm{s}_i(\boldsymbol{a}) \mid i \in \{1,2\} \wedge \boldsymbol{a} \in \mathcal{I}\} \cup \{\mathrm{r}_i(\boldsymbol{a}) \mid i \in \{1,2\} \wedge \boldsymbol{a} \in \mathcal{I}\} \\ \cup {} & \{\mathrm{s}_i(r) \mid i \in \{3,4\} \wedge r \in \mathbb{B}\} \cup \{\mathrm{r}_i(r) \mid i \in \{3,4\} \wedge r \in \mathbb{B}\}\,.\end{aligned}$$

ISG^0_t is the instruction stream generator for thread t, IMTC^0 is the transmission channel for messages containing instructions, RTC^0 is the transmission channel for replies, and ISEU^0 is the instruction stream execution unit.

Let $\boldsymbol{t}$ be a closed BTA term denoting a regular thread, and let t be that thread. If we abstract from all communications via the transmission channels, then the processes denoted by $\partial_H(\mathit{ISG}^0_t \parallel \mathit{IMTC}^0 \parallel \mathit{RTC}^0 \parallel \mathit{ISEU}^0)$ and $|\boldsymbol{t}|$ are equal modulo an initial silent step.

Theorem 7.1. *Let* $\mathbf{t}$ *be a closed* BTA+REC *term denoting a regular thread, and let* $t \in \mathcal{RT}$ *be the thread denoted by* $\mathbf{t}$*. Then we have that* $\tau \cdot \tau_{\{\mathrm{j}\}}(\partial_H(\mathit{ISG}^0_t \parallel \mathit{IMTC}^0 \parallel \mathit{RTC}^0 \parallel \mathit{ISEU}^0)) = \tau \cdot |\mathbf{t}|$.

Proof. By AIP, it is sufficient to prove that for all $n \geq 0$:

$$\pi_n(\tau \cdot \tau_{\{j\}}(\partial_H(ISG_t^o \parallel IMTC^o \parallel RTC^o \parallel ISEU^o))) = \pi_n(\tau \cdot |\boldsymbol{t}|) .$$

This is straightforwardly proved by induction on n, in the inductive step by case distinction on the structure of $\boldsymbol{t}$, and in the case $\boldsymbol{t} \equiv \boldsymbol{t}_1 \trianglelefteq \boldsymbol{f}.\boldsymbol{m} \trianglerighteq \boldsymbol{t}_2$ by case distinction between $n = 1$ and $n > 1$, using the axioms of BTA+REC, the axioms of ACP$^\tau$+REC+AIP and the axioms for the process extraction operator. □

7.2.2 *A more complex protocol*

In this section, we consider a more complex protocol for instruction stream processing that makes an effort to keep the execution unit busy without intermission.

The specifics of the more complex protocol considered here are that:

- the instruction stream generator may run ahead of the instruction stream execution unit by not waiting for the receipt of the replies resulting from the execution of instructions that it has sent earlier;
- to ensure that the instruction stream execution unit can handle the run-ahead, each instruction sent by the instruction stream generator is accompanied with the sequence of replies after which the instruction must be executed;
- to correct for replies that have not yet reached the instruction stream generator, each instruction sent is also accompanied with the number of replies received since the last sending of an instruction.

We write $\mathbb{B}^{\leq n}$, where $n \in \mathbb{N}$, for the set $\{u \in \mathbb{B}^* \mid \mathrm{len}(u) \leq n\}$.

It is assumed that a natural number ℓ has been given. The number ℓ is taken for the maximal number of steps that the instruction stream generator may run ahead of the instruction stream execution unit.

The set $\mathcal{IM}$ of *instruction messages* is defined as follows:

$$\mathcal{IM} = [0, \ell] \times \mathbb{B}^{\leq \ell} \times \mathcal{I} .$$

In an instruction message $(n, u, \boldsymbol{a}) \in \mathcal{IM}$:

- n is the number of replies that are acknowledged by the message;
- u is the sequence of replies after which the instruction that is part of the message must be executed;
- $\boldsymbol{a}$ is the instruction that is part of the message.

The instruction stream generator sends instruction messages via an instruction message transmission channel to the instruction stream execution unit. We refer to a succession of transmitted instruction messages as an *instruction stream*. An instruction stream is dynamic by nature, in contradistinction with an instruction sequence.

The set $\mathcal{S}_{\mathrm{ISG}}$ of *instruction stream generator states* is defined as follows:

$$\mathcal{S}_{\mathrm{ISG}} = [0, \ell] \times \mathcal{P}(\mathbb{B}^{\leq \ell+1} \times \mathcal{RT}) .$$

In an instruction stream generator state $(n, R) \in \mathcal{S}_{\mathrm{ISG}}$:

- n is the number of replies that has been received by the instruction stream generator since the last acknowledgement of received replies;
- in each $(u, t) \in R$, u is the sequence of replies after which the thread t must be performed.

The functions *updpm* and *updcr* defined below are used to model the updates of the instruction stream generator state on producing a message and consuming a reply, respectively. The function $\mathit{updpm} : (\mathbb{B}^{\leq \ell} \times \mathcal{RT}) \times \mathcal{S}_{\mathrm{ISG}} \to \mathcal{S}_{\mathrm{ISG}}$ is defined as follows:

$$\begin{aligned}
&\mathit{updpm}((u, t), (n, R)) = \\
&\quad \begin{cases} (0, (R \setminus \{(u, t)\}) \cup \{(u\mathrm{t}, \mathit{thrt}(t)), (u\mathrm{f}, \mathit{thrf}(t))\}) & \text{if } \mathit{act}(t) \in \mathcal{A} \\ (0, (R \setminus \{(u, t)\})) & \text{if } \mathit{act}(t) \notin \mathcal{A} . \end{cases}
\end{aligned}$$

The function $\mathit{updcr} : \mathbb{B} \times \mathcal{S}_{\mathrm{ISG}} \to \mathcal{S}_{\mathrm{ISG}}$ is defined as follows:

$$\mathit{updcr}(r, (n, R)) = (n + 1, \{(u, t) \mid (ru, t) \in R\}) .$$

The function *sel* defined below is used to model the selection of the sequence of replies and the instruction that will be part of the next message produced by the instruction stream generator. The function $\mathit{sel} : \mathcal{P}(\mathbb{B}^{\leq \ell} \times \mathcal{RT}) \to \mathcal{P}(\mathbb{B}^{\leq \ell} \times \mathcal{RT})$ is defined as follows:

$$\mathit{sel}(R) = \{(u, t) \in R \mid \forall (v, t') \in R \bullet \mathrm{len}(u) \leq \mathrm{len}(v) \wedge \mathrm{len}(u) \leq \ell\} .$$

Notice that $(u, t) \in \mathit{sel}(R)$ and $(v, t') \in R$ only if $\mathrm{len}(u) \leq \mathrm{len}(v)$. By that depth-first run-ahead is excluded. It happens that the performance of the protocol may change considerably if the function *sel* is replaced by another function.

The set $\mathcal{S}_{\mathrm{ISEU}}$ of *instruction stream execution unit states* is defined as follows:

$$\mathcal{S}_{\mathrm{ISEU}} = [0, \ell] \times \mathcal{P}(\mathbb{B}^{\leq \ell} \times \mathcal{I}) .$$

In an instruction stream execution unit state $(n, S) \in \mathcal{S}_{\mathrm{ISEU}}$:

- n is the number of replies for which the instruction stream execution unit still has to receive an acknowledgement;
- in each $(u, \boldsymbol{a}) \in S$, u is the sequence of replies after which the instruction $\boldsymbol{a}$ must be executed.

The functions *updcm* and *updpr* defined below are used to model the updates of the instruction stream execution unit state on consuming a message and producing a reply, respectively. The function $\mathit{updcm} : \mathcal{IM} \times \mathcal{S}_{\mathrm{ISEU}} \to \mathcal{S}_{\mathrm{ISEU}}$ is defined as follows:

$$\mathit{updcm}((k, u, \boldsymbol{a}), (n, S)) = (n \dot{-} k, S \cup \{(\mathrm{tl}^{n \dot{-} k}(u), \boldsymbol{a})\}) \,.$$[1]

The function $\mathit{updpr} : \mathbb{B} \times \mathcal{S}_{\mathrm{ISEU}} \to \mathcal{S}_{\mathrm{ISEU}}$ is defined as follows:

$$\mathit{updpr}(r, (n, S)) = (n + 1, \{(u, \boldsymbol{a}) \mid (ru, \boldsymbol{a}) \in S\}) \,.$$

The function *nxt* defined below is used by the instruction stream execution unit to distinguish when it starts with handling the instruction to be executed next between the different instructions that it may be. The function $\mathit{nxt} : \mathcal{I} \times \mathcal{P}(\mathbb{B}^{\leq \ell} \times \mathcal{I}) \to \mathbb{B}$ is defined as follows:

$$\mathit{nxt}(\boldsymbol{a}, S) = \begin{cases} \mathsf{t} & \text{if } (\epsilon, \boldsymbol{a}) \in S \\ \mathsf{f} & \text{if } (\epsilon, \boldsymbol{a}) \notin S \,. \end{cases}$$

The instruction stream execution unit sends replies via a reply transmission channel to the instruction stream generator. We refer to a succession of transmitted replies as a *reply stream*.

For the purpose of describing the transmission protocol in ACP^τ, A and $\mid$ are taken such that, in addition to the conditions mentioned at the beginning of Sect. 7.1.2, the following conditions are satisfied:

$$\begin{aligned} \mathsf{A} \supseteq\ & \{\mathtt{s}_i(d) \mid i \in \{1,2\} \land d \in \mathcal{IM}\} \cup \{\mathtt{r}_i(d) \mid i \in \{1,2\} \land d \in \mathcal{IM}\} \\ \cup\ & \{\mathtt{s}_i(r) \mid i \in \{3,4\} \land r \in \mathbb{B}\} \cup \{\mathtt{r}_i(r) \mid i \in \{3,4\} \land r \in \mathbb{B}\} \cup \{\mathtt{j}\} \end{aligned}$$

and for all $i \in \{1,2\}$, $j \in \{3,4\}$, $d \in \mathcal{IM}$, $r \in \mathbb{B}$, and $e \in \mathsf{A}$:

$$\begin{aligned} &\mathtt{s}_i(d) \mid \mathtt{r}_i(d) = \mathtt{j} \,, && && \mathtt{s}_j(r) \mid \mathtt{r}_j(r) = \mathtt{j} \,, \\ &\mathtt{s}_i(d) \mid e = \delta && \text{if } e \neq \mathtt{r}_i(d) \,, && \mathtt{s}_j(r) \mid e = \delta && \text{if } e \neq \mathtt{r}_j(r) \,, \\ &e \mid \mathtt{r}_i(d) = \delta && \text{if } e \neq \mathtt{s}_i(d) \,, && e \mid \mathtt{r}_j(r) = \delta && \text{if } e \neq \mathtt{s}_j(r) \,, \\ &\mathtt{j} \mid e = \delta \,. \end{aligned}$$

[1] $\mathrm{tl}^n(u)$ is defined by induction on n as usual: $\mathrm{tl}^0(u) = u$ and $\mathrm{tl}^{n+1}(u) = \mathrm{tl}(\mathrm{tl}^n(u))$.

Let $t \in \mathcal{RT}$. Then the process representing the more complex protocol for instruction stream processing with regard to thread t is described by

$$\partial_H(ISG_t \parallel IMTC \parallel RTC \parallel ISEU)\;,$$

where the process ISG_t is recursively specified by the following equations:

$$\begin{aligned}
ISG_t &= ISG'_{(0,\{(\epsilon,t)\})}\;,\\
ISG'_{(n,R)} &= \sum_{(u,t)\in sel(R)} \mathtt{s}_1((n,u,act(t))) \cdot ISG'_{updpm((u,t),(n,R))}\\
&+ \sum_{r\in\mathbb{B}} \mathtt{r}_4(r) \cdot ISG'_{updcr(r,(n,R))}\\
&\text{(for every } (n,R) \in \mathcal{S}_{\mathrm{ISG}} \text{ with } R \neq \emptyset)\;,\\
ISG'_{(n,\emptyset)} &= \mathtt{j}\\
&\text{(for every } (n,\emptyset) \in \mathcal{S}_{\mathrm{ISG}})\;,
\end{aligned}$$

the process $IMTC$ is recursively specified by the following equation:

$$IMTC = \sum_{d\in\mathcal{IM}} \mathtt{r}_1(d) \cdot \mathtt{s}_2(d) \cdot IMTC\;,$$

the process RTC is recursively specified by the following equation:

$$RTC = \sum_{r\in\mathbb{B}} \mathtt{r}_3(r) \cdot \mathtt{s}_4(r) \cdot RTC\;,$$

the process $ISEU$ is recursively specified by the following equations:

$$\begin{aligned}
ISEU &= ISEU'_{(0,\emptyset)}\;,\\
ISEU'_{(n,S)} &= \sum_{d\in\mathcal{IM}} \mathtt{r}_2(d) \cdot ISEU'_{updcm(d,(n,S))}\\
&+ \sum_{f.m\in\mathcal{A}} nxt(f.m,S) :\rightarrow \mathtt{s}_f(m) \cdot ISEU''_{(f,(n,S))}\\
&+ \sum_{r\in\mathcal{R}} nxt(\mathsf{stop}_r,S) :\rightarrow \mathtt{stop}(r) + nxt(\mathsf{dead},S) :\rightarrow \mathtt{i} \cdot \delta\\
&\text{(for every } (n,S) \in \mathcal{S}_{\mathrm{ISEU}})\;,\\
ISEU''_{(f,(n,S))} &= \sum_{r\in\mathbb{B}} \mathtt{r}_f(r) \cdot \mathtt{s}_3(r) \cdot ISEU'_{updpr(r,(n,S))}\\
&+ \sum_{d\in\mathcal{IM}} \mathtt{r}_2(d) \cdot ISEU''_{(f,updcm(d,(n,S)))}\\
&\text{(for every } (f,(n,S)) \in \mathcal{F} \times \mathcal{S}_{\mathrm{ISEU}})\;,
\end{aligned}$$

and

$$\begin{aligned} H = {} & \{\mathtt{s}_i(d) \mid i \in \{1,2\} \wedge d \in \mathcal{IM}\} \cup \{\mathtt{r}_i(d) \mid i \in \{1,2\} \wedge d \in \mathcal{IM}\} \\ \cup {} & \{\mathtt{s}_i(r) \mid i \in \{3,4\} \wedge r \in \mathbb{B}\} \cup \{\mathtt{r}_i(r) \mid i \in \{3,4\} \wedge r \in \mathbb{B}\} . \end{aligned}$$

ISG_t is the instruction stream generator for thread t, $IMTC$ is the transmission channel for instruction messages, RTC is the transmission channel for replies, and $ISEU$ is the instruction stream execution unit.

Like the simple protocol described in Sect. 7.2.1, the more complex protocol described above has been designed such that, for each closed BTA+REC term $\boldsymbol{t}$ denoting a regular thread, $\tau \cdot \tau_{\{\mathtt{j}\}}(\partial_H(ISG_t \parallel IMTC \parallel RTC \parallel ISEU)) = \tau \cdot |\boldsymbol{t}|$, where $t \in \mathcal{RT}$ is the thread denoted by $\boldsymbol{t}$. We refrain from presenting a proof of the claim that the protocol satisfies this because the proof is straightforward but tedious.

The transmission channels $IMTC$ and RTC can keep one instruction message and one reply, respectively. The protocol has been designed in such a way that the protocol will also work properly if these channels are replaced by channels with larger capacity and even by channels with unbounded capacity.

7.2.3 *Adaptations of the protocol*

In this section, we discuss some conceivable adaptations of the protocol for instruction stream processing described in Sect. 7.2.2.

Consider the case where, for each instruction, it is known what the probability is with which its execution leads to the reply $\mathtt{t}$. This might give reason to adapt the protocol described in Sect. 7.2.2. Suppose that the instruction stream generator states do not only keep the sequences of replies after which threads must be performed, but also the sequences of instructions involved in producing those sequences of replies. Then the probability with which the sequences of replies will happen can be calculated and several conceivable adaptations of the protocol to this probabilistic knowledge are possible by mere changes in the selection of the sequence of replies and the instruction that will be part of the next instruction message produced by the instruction stream generator. Among those adaptations are:

- restricting the instruction messages that are produced ahead to the ones where the sequence of replies after which the instruction must be executed will happen with a probability ≥ 0.50, but sticking to breadth-first run-ahead;
- restricting the instruction messages that are produced ahead to the ones where the se-

quence of replies after which the instruction must be executed will happen with a probability ≥ 0.95, but not sticking to breadth-first run-ahead.

Regular threads can be represented in such a way that it is effectively decidable whether the two threads with which a thread may proceed after performing its first action are identical. Consider the case where threads are represented in the instruction stream generator states in such a way. Then the protocol can be adapted such that no duplication of instruction messages takes place in the cases where the two threads with which a thread possibly proceeds after performing its first action are identical. This can be accomplished by using sequences of elements from $\mathbb{B} \cup \{*\}$, instead of sequences of elements from $\mathbb{B}$, in instruction messages, instruction stream generator states, and instruction stream execution unit states. The occurrence of $*$ at position i in a sequence indicates that the ith reply may be either $\mathtt{t}$ or $\mathtt{f}$. The impact of this change on the updates of instruction stream generator states and instruction stream execution unit states is minor.

7.3 Instruction Sequence Producible Processes

Process algebra is considered relevant to computer science, as is witnessed by the extent of the work on algebraic theories of processes in theoretical computer science. This means that there must be programmed systems whose behaviours are taken for processes as considered in process algebra. In this section, we establish a result concerning the processes as considered in ACP that can be produced by instruction sequences under execution: by apposite choice of basic instructions, all finite-state processes can be produced by instruction sequences provided that the cluster fair abstraction rule (see e.g. [Fokkink (2000)], Section 5.6) is valid.

7.3.1 SPISA *with alternative choice instructions*

For the purpose of producing processes as considered in ACP, we need a version of SPISA with special basic instructions. Recall that, in SPISA, it is assumed that a fixed but arbitrary set $\mathfrak{A}$ of basic instructions has been given. Here, we will make use a version of SPISA in which the following additional assumptions relating to $\mathfrak{A}$ are made:

- a fixed but arbitrary set $\mathcal{F}$ of foci has been given;
- a fixed but arbitrary set $\mathcal{M}$ of methods has been given;
- a fixed but arbitrary set $\mathcal{AA}$ of atomic actions, with $\mathtt{t} \notin \mathcal{AA}$, has been given;

Table 7.5 Additional axiom for the process extraction operator

$\lvert x \trianglelefteq \mathsf{ac}(e, e') \trianglerighteq y \rvert = e \cdot \lvert x \rvert + e' \cdot \lvert y \rvert$

- $\mathfrak{A} = \{f.m \mid f \in \mathcal{F} \land m \in \mathcal{M}\} \cup \{\mathsf{ac}(e_1, e_2) \mid e_1, e_2 \in \mathcal{AA} \cup \{\mathtt{t}\}\}$.

On execution of a basic instruction $\mathsf{ac}(e_1, e_2)$, first a non-deterministic choice between the atomic actions e_1 and e_2 is made and then the chosen atomic action is performed. The reply t is produced if e_1 is performed and the reply f is produced if e_2 is performed. Basic instructions of this kind are material to produce all regular processes by means of instruction sequences. A basic instruction of the form $\mathsf{ac}(e_1, e_2)$ is called an *alternative choice instruction*. Henceforth, we will write SPISA_{ac} for the version of SPISA with alternative choice instructions.

The intuition concerning alternative choice instructions given above will be made fully precise below using ACP^{τ}, i.e. by giving an additional axiom for the process extraction operator. It will not be made fully precise using an extension of BTA because it is considered a basic property of threads that they represent deterministic behaviours.

Because process extraction concerns extraction from threads, we are compelled to consider a version of BTA with basic actions of the form $\mathsf{ac}(e_1, e_2)$. A basic action of the form $\mathsf{ac}(e_1, e_2)$ is called an *alternative choice action*. We will write BTA_{ac} for the version of BTA with alternative choice actions.

For the purpose of making precise what processes are produced by the threads denoted by closed terms of BTA_{ac}+REC, A and $\mid$ are taken such that, in addition to the conditions mentioned at the beginning of Sect. 7.1.2, the following conditions are satisfied:

$$\mathsf{A} \supseteq \mathcal{AA} \cup \{\mathtt{t}\}$$

and for all $e, e' \in \mathsf{A}$:

$$e' \mid e = \delta \ \text{ if } e' \in \mathcal{AA} \cup \{\mathtt{t}\}\,.$$

The process extraction operator for BTA_{ac} has as axioms the axioms given in Table 7.4 and in addition the axiom given in Table 7.5. In this table, e and e' stand for arbitrary atomic actions from $\mathcal{AA} \cup \{\mathtt{t}\}$.

Proposition 7.2 goes through for BTA_{ac}.

7.3.2 *Producible processes*

It follows immediately from the axioms of the thread extraction and process extraction operators that the instruction sequences considered in SPISA$_{\mathrm{ac}}$ produce regular processes. The question is whether all regular processes are producible by these instruction sequences. This question can be answered in the affirmative.

All regular processes over $\mathcal{AA}$ can be produced by the instruction sequences considered in SPISA$_{\mathrm{ac}}$.

Theorem 7.2. *Assume that CFAR is valid in $\mathcal{M}^{\tau}_{\mathrm{ACP}}$. Then, for each process p that is regular over $\mathcal{AA}$, there exists a closed* SPISA$_{\mathrm{ac}}$ *term $\boldsymbol{t}$ in which only basic instructions of the form* $\mathsf{ac}(e,\mathtt{t})$ *occur such that the interpretation of $\tau \cdot \tau_{\{\mathtt{t}\}}(|\,|\boldsymbol{t}|\,|)$ in $\mathcal{M}^{\tau}_{\mathrm{ACP}}$ is $\tau \cdot p$.*

Proof. By Propositions 2.1, 4.2 and 7.1, it is sufficient to show that, for each finite linear recursive specification $\boldsymbol{E}$ over ACP$^{\tau}$ in which only atomic actions from $\mathcal{AA}$ occur, there exists a finite linear recursive specification $\boldsymbol{E}'$ over BTA$_{\mathrm{ac}}$ in which only basic actions of the form $\mathsf{ac}(e,\mathtt{t})$ occur such that $\tau \cdot \langle \boldsymbol{x}|\boldsymbol{E}\rangle = \tau \cdot \tau_{\{\mathtt{t}\}}(|\langle \boldsymbol{x}|\boldsymbol{E}'\rangle|)$ for all $\boldsymbol{x} \in \mathrm{V}(\boldsymbol{E})$.

Take the finite linear recursive specification $\boldsymbol{E}$ over ACP$^{\tau}$ that consists of the recursion equations

$$\boldsymbol{x}_i = \boldsymbol{e}_{i1} \cdot \boldsymbol{x}_{i1} + \ldots + \boldsymbol{e}_{ik_i} \cdot \boldsymbol{x}_{ik_i} + \boldsymbol{e}'_{i1} + \ldots + \boldsymbol{e}'_{il_i} \,,$$

where $\boldsymbol{e}_{i1}, \ldots, \boldsymbol{e}_{ik_i}, \boldsymbol{e}'_{i1}, \ldots, \boldsymbol{e}'_{il_i} \in \mathcal{AA}$, for $i \in \{1, \ldots n\}$. Then construct the finite linear recursive specification $\boldsymbol{E}'$ over BTA$_{\mathrm{ac}}$ that consists of the recursion equations

$$\begin{aligned}\boldsymbol{x}_i = \boldsymbol{x}_{i1} \trianglelefteq \mathsf{ac}(\boldsymbol{e}_{i1},\mathtt{t}) \trianglerighteq (\ldots (\boldsymbol{x}_{ik_i} \trianglelefteq \mathsf{ac}(\boldsymbol{e}_{ik_i},\mathtt{t}) \trianglerighteq \\ (\mathsf{S} \trianglelefteq \mathsf{ac}(\boldsymbol{e}'_{i1},\mathtt{t}) \trianglerighteq (\ldots (\mathsf{S} \trianglelefteq \mathsf{ac}(\boldsymbol{e}'_{il_i},\mathtt{t}) \trianglerighteq \boldsymbol{x}_i) \ldots))) \ldots)\end{aligned}$$

for $i \in \{1, \ldots n\}$; and the finite linear recursive specification $\boldsymbol{E}''$ over ACP$^{\tau}$ that consists of the recursion equations

$$\begin{aligned}
\boldsymbol{x}_i &= \boldsymbol{e}_{i1} \cdot \boldsymbol{x}_{i1} + \mathtt{t} \cdot \boldsymbol{y}_{i2} \,, & \boldsymbol{z}_{i1} &= \boldsymbol{e}'_{i1} + \mathtt{t} \cdot \boldsymbol{z}_{i2} \,, \\
\boldsymbol{y}_{i2} &= \boldsymbol{e}_{i2} \cdot \boldsymbol{x}_{i2} + \mathtt{t} \cdot \boldsymbol{y}_{i3} \,, & \boldsymbol{z}_{i2} &= \boldsymbol{e}'_{i2} + \mathtt{t} \cdot \boldsymbol{z}_{i3} \,, \\
&\ \vdots & &\ \vdots \\
\boldsymbol{y}_{ik_i} &= \boldsymbol{e}_{ik_i} \cdot \boldsymbol{x}_{ik_i} + \mathtt{t} \cdot \boldsymbol{z}_{i1} \,, & \boldsymbol{z}_{il_i} &= \boldsymbol{e}'_{il_i} + \mathtt{t} \cdot \boldsymbol{x}_i \,,
\end{aligned}$$

where $\boldsymbol{y}_{i2}, \ldots, \boldsymbol{y}_{ik_i}, \boldsymbol{z}_{i1}, \ldots, \boldsymbol{z}_{il_i}$ are fresh variables, for $i \in \{1, \ldots n\}$. It follows immediately from the axioms for the process extraction operator that $|\langle \boldsymbol{x}|\boldsymbol{E}'\rangle| = \langle \boldsymbol{x}|\boldsymbol{E}''\rangle$ for all $\boldsymbol{x} \in \mathrm{V}(\boldsymbol{E})$. Moreover, it follows from CFAR that $\tau \cdot \langle \boldsymbol{x}|\boldsymbol{E}\rangle = \tau \cdot \tau_{\{\mathtt{t}\}}(\langle \boldsymbol{x}|\boldsymbol{E}''\rangle)$ for all $\boldsymbol{x} \in \mathrm{V}(\boldsymbol{E})$. Hence, $\tau \cdot \langle \boldsymbol{x}|\boldsymbol{E}\rangle = \tau \cdot \tau_{\{\mathtt{t}\}}(|\langle \boldsymbol{x}|\boldsymbol{E}'\rangle|)$ for all $\boldsymbol{x} \in \mathrm{V}(\boldsymbol{E})$. □

Theorem 7.2 with "the interpretation of $\tau \cdot \tau_{\{\mathtt{t}\}}(||\boldsymbol{t}||)$ in $\mathcal{M}^{\tau}_{\mathrm{ACP}}$ is $\tau \cdot p$" replaced by "the interpretation of $||\boldsymbol{t}||$ in $\mathcal{M}^{\tau}_{\mathrm{ACP}}$ is p" can be established if SPISA is extended with multiple-reply test instructions, see [Bergstra and Middelburg (2008a)]. In that case, the assumption that CFAR is valid is superfluous.

Chapter 8

Variations on a Theme

This chapter concerns three variations of instruction sequences as considered in SPISA, namely polyadic instruction sequences, instruction sequences without a directional bias, and probabilistic instruction sequences.

We study the phenomenon that instruction sequences are split into fragments which somehow produce a joint behaviour. In order to bring this phenomenon better into the picture, we formalize a simple mechanism by which several instruction sequence fragments can produce a joint behaviour. The instruction sequences taken for fragments are parameterized instruction sequences of which the parameters are filled in each time they are made the one being executed. The instruction sequences in question are called polyadic instruction sequences. We show that, even in the case of the simple mechanism that we formalize, it is a non-trivial matter to explain by means of a translation into a single instruction sequence what takes place on execution of a collection of such instruction sequence fragments.

We introduce an algebraic theory of instruction sequences in which, for each instruction whose effect involves that execution proceeds in the forward direction, there is a counterpart whose effect involves that execution proceeds in the backward direction. The directional bias found in existing instruction sequence notations and program notations — there is always a left to right orientation — might admit an explanation in terms of complexity of design, expression or execution. The algebraic theory introduced provides a context in which this may be investigated.

We use the term probabilistic instruction sequence for an instruction sequence that contains probabilistic instructions, i.e. instructions that are themselves probabilistic by nature. We propose several kinds of probabilistic instructions, provide an informal operational meaning for each of them, and discuss related work. On purpose, we refrain from providing an ad hoc formal meaning for the proposed kinds of instructions.

8.1 Polyadic Instruction Sequences

This section concerns the phenomenon that instruction sequences are split into fragments which somehow produce a joint behaviour. We formalize a simple mechanism by which several instruction sequence fragments can produce a joint behaviour and show that, even in the case of this simple mechanism, it is a non-trivial matter to explain by means of a translation into a single instruction sequence what takes place on execution of a collection of instruction sequence fragments.

The question is how a joint behaviour of the fragments in a collection of fragments is achieved. The view of this matter is that there can only be a single fragment being executed at any stage, but the fragment in question may make any fragment in the collection the one being executed by means of a special instruction for switching over execution to another fragment. This does not fit in very well with the conception that the collection of fragments constitutes a sequential program. To our knowledge, a theoretical understanding of this matter has not yet been developed. This has motivated us to take up this topic.

The principal reason for splitting instruction sequences into fragments is that the execution environment at hand sets bounds to the size of instruction sequences. In the past, the phenomenon occurred explicitly in many software systems. At present, it often occurs rather implicitly, e.g. on execution of programs written in contemporary object-oriented programming languages, such as Java [Arnold and Gosling (1996)] and C# [Bishop and Horspool (2004)], classes are loaded as they are needed. The mechanisms in question are improvements upon the simple mechanism considered in this section, but they are also much more complicated. We believe that it is useful to consider the simple mechanism prior to the more complicated ones.

The instruction sequences taken for fragments are called polyadic instruction sequences. We introduce polyadic instruction sequences in the setting of SPISA. The behaviours produced by instruction sequences under execution are represented by threads as considered in BTA. We take the view that the possible joint behaviours produced by polyadic instruction sequences under execution can be represented by threads as considered in BTA as well. In a system that provides an execution environment for polyadic instruction sequences, a polyadic instruction sequence must be loaded in order to become the one being executed. Hence, making a polyadic instruction sequence the one being executed can be looked upon as loading it for execution.

8.1.1 *Executing polyadic instruction sequences*

In this section, we formalize a simple mechanism by which several instruction sequence fragments can produce a joint behaviour.

It is assumed that fixed but arbitrary instruction sequence notations $ISN_1, \ldots, ISN_n$ and, for each $i \in [1, n]$, a projection prj_i from the set of all ISN_i instruction sequences to the set of all closed SPISA terms have been given.

$ISN_1, \ldots, ISN_n$ may include some of the instruction sequence notations introduced in Sect. 2.3. In [Bergstra and Loots (2002)], a version of SPISA without the positive and negative termination instructions, called PGA, and a collection of instruction sequence notations with projections to closed PGA terms are presented. $ISN_1, \ldots, ISN_n$ may also include some of these instruction sequence notations. The important point is that a collection of well-defined instruction sequence notations rooted in an elementary instruction sequence notation, viz. the set of closed SPISA terms, has been given.

Instruction sequence fragments that can somehow produce a joint behaviour are viewed as instruction sequences that contain special instructions for switching over execution from one fragment to another. The instruction sequences in question are called polyadic instruction sequences. It is assumed that a special version of one of the instruction sequence notations $ISN_1, \ldots, ISN_n$, in which the special instructions for switching over execution from one fragment to another are available, is used for each polyadic instruction sequence. Moreover, it is assumed that a collection of polyadic instruction sequences between which execution can be switched takes the form of a sequence, called a polyadic instruction sequence vector, in which each polyadic instruction sequence is coupled with the instruction sequence notation used for it.

Our general view on the way of achieving a joint behaviour of the polyadic instruction sequences in a polyadic instruction sequence vector is as follows:

- there can only be a single polyadic instruction sequence being executed at any stage;
- the polyadic instruction sequence in question may make any polyadic instruction sequence in the vector the one being executed;
- making another polyadic instruction sequence the one being executed is effected by executing a special instruction for switching over execution;
- any polyadic instruction sequence can be taken for the one being executed initially.

In addition to special instructions for switching over execution, polyadic instruction sequences may contain two other kinds of special instructions:

- special instructions for putting instructions into instruction registers;
- special instructions of which the occurrences in a polyadic instruction sequence are replaced by instructions contained in instruction registers on making the polyadic instruction sequence the one being executed.

The special instructions of the latter kind serve as instruction place-holders. Their presence turns a polyadic instruction sequence into a parameterized instruction sequence of which the parameters are filled in each time it is made the one being executed. This feature accounts for the use of the prefix polyadic. Its merit is primarily that it allows for execution to proceed in effect from different positions each time a polyadic instruction sequence is loaded for execution. An example of this is given in Sect. 8.1.2.

We take the line that different instruction sequence notations can be used for different polyadic instruction sequences in a polyadic instruction sequence vector. On making a polyadic instruction sequence in the vector the one being executed, it is considered to be translated into a closed $\mathrm{SPISA_p}$ term.

$\mathrm{SPISA_p}$ is a variant of SPISA in which the above-mentioned special instructions are incorporated. In $\mathrm{SPISA_p}$, it is assumed that there is a fixed but arbitrary set $\mathfrak{A}_\mathrm{c}$ of *core basic instructions*. In $\mathrm{SPISA_p}$, a basic instruction is either a core basic instruction or a supplementary basic instruction.

$\mathrm{SPISA_p}$ has the following *core primitive instructions*:

- for each $\boldsymbol{a} \in \mathfrak{A}_\mathrm{c}$, a *plain basic instruction* $\boldsymbol{a}$;
- for each $\boldsymbol{a} \in \mathfrak{A}_\mathrm{c}$, a *positive test instruction* $+\boldsymbol{a}$;
- for each $\boldsymbol{a} \in \mathfrak{A}_\mathrm{c}$, a *negative test instruction* $-\boldsymbol{a}$;
- for each $l \in \mathbb{N}$, a *forward jump instruction* $\#l$;
- a *plain termination instruction* $!$;
- a *positive termination instruction* $!\mathsf{t}$;
- a *negative termination instruction* $!\mathsf{f}$.

We write $\mathfrak{I}_\mathrm{c}$ for the set of all core primitive instructions. The core primitive instructions of $\mathrm{SPISA_p}$ are the counterparts of the primitive instructions of SPISA.

$\mathrm{SPISA_p}$ has the following *supplementary basic instructions*:

- for each $i \in \mathbb{N}$, a *switch-over instruction* $\#\#\#i$;
- for each $i \in \mathbb{N}$ and $\boldsymbol{u} \in \mathfrak{I}_\mathrm{c}$, a *put instruction* $\$\mathsf{put}{:}i{:}\boldsymbol{u}$;
- for each $i \in \mathbb{N}$, a *get instruction* $\$\mathsf{get}{:}i$.

We write $\mathfrak{A}_s$ for the set of all supplementary basic instructions. In the presence of a polyadic instruction sequence vector, a switch-over instruction $\#\#\#i$ is the instruction for switching over execution to the ith polyadic instruction sequence in the vector. A put instruction $\$\mathsf{put}{:}i{:}\boldsymbol{u}$ is the instruction for putting instruction $\boldsymbol{u}$ in the instruction register with number i. A get instruction $\$\mathsf{get}{:}i$ is the instruction of which each occurrence in a polyadic instruction sequence is replaced by the content of the instruction register with number i on switching over execution to that polyadic instruction sequence. If a get instruction is encountered in the polyadic instruction sequence being executed, inaction occurs.

The supplementary basic instructions of SPISA_p can be viewed as built-in basic instructions. However, as laid down above, supplementary basic instructions do not occur in positive or negative test instructions. Thus, the core primitive instructions and supplementary basic instructions make up the primitive instructions of SPISA_p.

SPISA_p has one sort, namely the sort **IS** of instruction sequences, and the following constants and operators:

- for each $\boldsymbol{u} \in \mathfrak{I}_\text{c} \cup \mathfrak{A}_\text{s}$, an *instruction* constant $\boldsymbol{u} : \to \mathbf{IS}$;
- the binary *concatenation* operator $\_ \mathbin{;} \_ : \mathbf{IS} \times \mathbf{IS} \to \mathbf{IS}$;
- the unary *repetition* operator $\_^\omega : \mathbf{IS} \to \mathbf{IS}$.

The axioms of SPISA_p are the same as the axioms of SPISA.

SPISA_p can be viewed as the specialization of SPISA obtained by taking the set $\mathfrak{A}_\text{c} \cup \mathfrak{A}_\text{s}$ for $\mathfrak{A}$ and excluding terms in which basic instructions from $\mathfrak{A}_\text{s}$ occur in positive or negative test instructions. We will make use of this view to simplify the definitions of the different instruction sequence notations that can be used for polyadic instruction sequences and also to enable the use of the functions $prj_1, \ldots, prj_n$ for translating instruction sequences in those instruction sequence notations into closed SPISA_p terms.

The different instruction sequence notations that can be used for polyadic instruction sequences are $ISN_{\text{p}1}, \ldots, ISN_{\text{p}n}$. The set of all $ISN_{\text{p}i}$ instruction sequences is the subset of the set of all ISN_i instruction sequences, taking the set $\mathfrak{A}_\text{c} \cup \mathfrak{A}_\text{s}$ for $\mathfrak{A}$, in which the basic instructions from $\mathfrak{A}_\text{s}$ do not occur in positive or negative test instructions. If the set $\mathfrak{A}_\text{c} \cup \mathfrak{A}_\text{s}$ is taken for $\mathfrak{A}$, the function prj_i translates each $ISN_{\text{p}i}$ instruction sequence into a closed SPISA_p term that produces the same behaviour on execution.

A *polyadic instruction sequence* is a $ISN_{\text{p}1}$ instruction sequence or ... or a $ISN_{\text{p}n}$ instruction sequence.

Suppose that $ISN_1, \ldots, ISN_n$ include ISNR and ISNA. Consider the ISNA_p instruction sequence

$$+\mathsf{a}\,;\#\#5\,;\$\mathsf{put{:}1{:}\#3}\,;\#\#\#2\,;\$\mathsf{put{:}1{:}\#1}\,;\#\#\#2$$

and the ISNR_p instruction sequence

$$\$\mathsf{get{:}1}\,;\mathsf{b}\,;\#2\,;\mathsf{c}\,;\#\#\#1\,.$$

The idea is that, after abstraction from tau, the joint behaviour produced by these polyadic instruction sequences on execution is the solution of the guarded recursive specification consisting of the equation

$$x = (\mathsf{b} \circ x) \trianglelefteq \mathsf{a} \trianglerighteq (\mathsf{c} \circ x)$$

if execution begins with the ISNA_p instruction sequence.

A *polyadic instruction sequence vector* is a sequence of pairs consisting of a polyadic instruction sequence and a member of the set $[1, n]$ of *instruction sequence notation indices*. Let $\boldsymbol{\pi}$ be the polyadic instruction sequence vector $\langle(\boldsymbol{p}_1, c_1)\rangle \curvearrowright \ldots \curvearrowright \langle(\boldsymbol{p}_k, c_k)\rangle$,[1] where $\boldsymbol{p}_1, \ldots, \boldsymbol{p}_k$ and $c_1, \ldots, c_k$ are polyadic instruction sequences and instruction sequence notation indices, respectively, and let $i \in [1, k]$. Then we write $is(\boldsymbol{\pi}, i)$ and $isn(\boldsymbol{\pi}, i)$ for $\boldsymbol{p}_i$ and c_i, respectively. Moreover, we write $ind(\boldsymbol{\pi})$ for the set $[1, k]$.

Let $\boldsymbol{\pi}$ be a polyadic instruction sequence vector, and let $i \in ind(\boldsymbol{\pi})$. Then instruction sequence notation index $isn(\boldsymbol{\pi}, i)$ indicates which instruction sequence notation is used for polyadic instruction sequence $is(\boldsymbol{\pi}, i)$: if $isn(\boldsymbol{\pi}, i) = j$ then $\mathit{ISN}_{\mathrm{p}j}$ is used. The instruction sequence notation used is made explicit because it cannot always be determined uniquely from the polyadic instruction sequence concerned, whereas the behaviour that this polyadic instruction sequence produces on execution may be different for each of the instruction sequence notations in question. For example, every ISNRI_p instruction sequence is an ISNR_p instruction sequence in which no termination instructions occur. If such an instruction sequence leads to termination on execution as an ISNRI_p instruction sequence, it leads to inaction on execution as an ISNR_p instruction sequence.

The set of instruction registers that contain an instruction and the contents of each of those registers matter when a polyadic instruction sequence is made the one being executed. This makes us introduce the notion of an instruction register file state and special notation relating to this notion.

An *instruction register file state* is a function $\sigma : I \to \mathfrak{I}_\mathrm{c}$, where I is a finite subset of $\mathbb{N}$.

[1] For polyadic instruction sequence vectors, we use the sequence notation that is used for thread vectors in Sect. 5.2.4 instead of the common sequence notation that is also used elsewhere in this book.

Let t be a closed SPISA$_p$ term and σ be an instruction register file state. Then we write $t[\sigma]$ for t with, for all $i \in \mathrm{dom}(\sigma)$, all occurrences of \$get:i in t replaced by $\sigma(i)$.

Let $\boldsymbol{\pi}$ be a polyadic instruction sequence vector, let $j \in \mathit{ind}(\boldsymbol{\pi})$, and let σ be an instruction register file state. Then we write $\mathit{valid}(\boldsymbol{\pi}, j, \sigma)$ to indicate that instructions of the form \$get:i do not occur in $\mathit{prj}_{\mathit{isn}(\boldsymbol{\pi},j)}(\mathit{is}(\boldsymbol{\pi}, j))[\sigma]$.

An obvious choice of the thread extraction operator of SPISA$_p$ is the thread extraction operator of SPISA, taking the set $\mathfrak{A}_c \cup \mathfrak{A}_s$ for $\mathfrak{A}$, restricted to the set of closed terms of SPISA$_p$. This thread extraction operator is considered not to be the proper one, because it treats the supplementary basic instructions as arbitrary basic instructions and thus disregards the fixed effects that they should produce on execution. For example, a switch-over instruction $\#\#\#i$ would not have the effect that execution is switched over.

As regards the proper thread extraction for SPISA$_p$, the idea is that it yields, for each closed SPISA$_p$ term t, a function that assigns to each polyadic instruction sequence vector $\boldsymbol{\pi}$ the thread that represents the joint behaviour of t and the polyadic instruction sequences in $\boldsymbol{\pi}$ in the case where t is the polyadic instruction sequence being executed initially. Because this behaviour depends upon the set of instruction registers that contain an instruction and the contents of each of those registers, we need a thread extraction operator for each instruction register file state.

For each instruction register file state σ, we introduce a thread extraction operator $|\_|_\sigma$. The axioms for these thread extraction operators are the equations given in Table 8.1 and the rule that $|\#l \; ; \; x|_\sigma(\boldsymbol{\pi}) = \mathsf{D}$ if $\#l$ is the beginning of an infinite jump chain. In this table, $\boldsymbol{a}$ stands for an arbitrary core basic instruction from $\mathfrak{A}_c$, $\boldsymbol{u}$ stands for an arbitrary core primitive instruction or supplementary basic instruction from $\mathfrak{I}_c \cup \mathfrak{A}_s$, $\boldsymbol{v}$ stands for an arbitrary core primitive instruction from $\mathfrak{I}_c$, and l and i stand for arbitrary natural numbers.

We can couple nominal indices as labels with some of the polyadic instruction sequences in a polyadic instruction sequence vector. This would permit the use of alternative switch-over instructions with nominal indices instead of ordinal indices, like with the goto instructions from SPISA$_g$. In the notational style of Sect. 4.3, the form of those alternative switch-over instructions would be $\#\#\#[i]$.

8.1.2 *Example*

To illustrate the mechanism formalized in Sect. 8.1.1, we consider in this section the splitting of an ISNA instruction sequence $\boldsymbol{p}$ of 10000 instructions into two fragments.

We write $\nu_1(l)$ for the number of absolute jump instructions $\#\#l'$ with $l' > 5000$ from

Table 8.1 Axioms for the thread extraction operators of $\mathrm{SPISA_p}$

$\lvert \boldsymbol{a} \rvert_\sigma(\boldsymbol{\pi}) = \boldsymbol{a} \circ \mathsf{D}$	
$\lvert \boldsymbol{a} \,;\, x \rvert_\sigma(\boldsymbol{\pi}) = \boldsymbol{a} \circ \lvert x \rvert_\sigma(\boldsymbol{\pi})$	
$\lvert +\boldsymbol{a} \rvert_\sigma(\boldsymbol{\pi}) = \boldsymbol{a} \circ \mathsf{D}$	
$\lvert +\boldsymbol{a} \,;\, x \rvert_\sigma(\boldsymbol{\pi}) = \lvert x \rvert_\sigma(\boldsymbol{\pi}) \trianglelefteq \boldsymbol{a} \trianglerighteq \lvert \#2 \,;\, x \rvert_\sigma(\boldsymbol{\pi})$	
$\lvert -\boldsymbol{a} \rvert_\sigma(\boldsymbol{\pi}) = \boldsymbol{a} \circ \mathsf{D}$	
$\lvert -\boldsymbol{a} \,;\, x \rvert_\sigma(\boldsymbol{\pi}) = \lvert \#2 \,;\, x \rvert_\sigma(\boldsymbol{\pi}) \trianglelefteq \boldsymbol{a} \trianglerighteq \lvert x \rvert_\sigma(\boldsymbol{\pi})$	
$\lvert \#l \rvert_\sigma(\boldsymbol{\pi}) = \mathsf{D}$	
$\lvert \#0 \,;\, x \rvert_\sigma(\boldsymbol{\pi}) = \mathsf{D}$	
$\lvert \#1 \,;\, x \rvert_\sigma(\boldsymbol{\pi}) = \lvert x \rvert_\sigma(\boldsymbol{\pi})$	
$\lvert \#l{+}2 \,;\, \boldsymbol{u} \rvert_\sigma(\boldsymbol{\pi}) = \mathsf{D}$	
$\lvert \#l{+}2 \,;\, \boldsymbol{u} \,;\, x \rvert_\sigma(\boldsymbol{\pi}) = \lvert \#l{+}1 \,;\, x \rvert_\sigma(\boldsymbol{\pi})$	
$\lvert ! \rvert_\sigma(\boldsymbol{\pi}) = \mathsf{S}$	
$\lvert ! \,;\, x \rvert_\sigma(\boldsymbol{\pi}) = \mathsf{S}$	
$\lvert !\mathsf{t} \rvert_\sigma(\boldsymbol{\pi}) = \mathsf{S{+}}$	
$\lvert !\mathsf{t} \,;\, x \rvert_\sigma(\boldsymbol{\pi}) = \mathsf{S{+}}$	
$\lvert !\mathsf{f} \rvert_\sigma(\boldsymbol{\pi}) = \mathsf{S{-}}$	
$\lvert !\mathsf{f} \,;\, x \rvert_\sigma(\boldsymbol{\pi}) = \mathsf{S{-}}$	
$\lvert \#\#\#i \rvert_\sigma(\boldsymbol{\pi}) = \mathsf{tau} \circ \lvert prj_{isn(\boldsymbol{\pi},i)}(is(\boldsymbol{\pi},i))[\sigma] \rvert_\sigma(\boldsymbol{\pi})$	if $i \in ind(\boldsymbol{\pi}) \land valid(\boldsymbol{\pi},i,\sigma)$
$\lvert \#\#\#i \rvert_\sigma(\boldsymbol{\pi}) = \mathsf{D}$	if $i \in ind(\boldsymbol{\pi}) \land \neg valid(\boldsymbol{\pi},i,\sigma)$
$\lvert \#\#\#i \rvert_\sigma(\boldsymbol{\pi}) = \mathsf{S}$	if $i \notin ind(\boldsymbol{\pi})$
$\lvert \#\#\#i \,;\, x \rvert_\sigma(\boldsymbol{\pi}) = \mathsf{tau} \circ \lvert prj_{isn(\boldsymbol{\pi},i)}(is(\boldsymbol{\pi},i))[\sigma] \rvert_\sigma(\boldsymbol{\pi})$	if $i \in ind(\boldsymbol{\pi}) \land valid(\boldsymbol{\pi},i,\sigma)$
$\lvert \#\#\#i \,;\, x \rvert_\sigma(\boldsymbol{\pi}) = \mathsf{D}$	if $i \in ind(\boldsymbol{\pi}) \land \neg valid(\boldsymbol{\pi},i,\sigma)$
$\lvert \#\#\#i \,;\, x \rvert_\sigma(\boldsymbol{\pi}) = \mathsf{S}$	if $i \notin ind(\boldsymbol{\pi})$
$\lvert \$\mathsf{put}{:}i{:}\boldsymbol{v} \rvert_\sigma(\boldsymbol{\pi}) = \mathsf{tau} \circ \mathsf{D}$	
$\lvert \$\mathsf{put}{:}i{:}\boldsymbol{v} \,;\, x \rvert_\sigma(\boldsymbol{\pi}) = \mathsf{tau} \circ \lvert x \rvert_{\sigma \oplus [i \mapsto v]}(\boldsymbol{\pi})$	
$\lvert \$\mathsf{get}{:}i \rvert_\sigma(\boldsymbol{\pi}) = \mathsf{D}$	
$\lvert \$\mathsf{get}{:}i \,;\, x \rvert_\sigma(\boldsymbol{\pi}) = \mathsf{D}$	

position 1 up to position l and $\nu_2(l)$ for the number of absolute jump instructions $\#\#l'$ with $l' \leq 5000$ from position 5001 up to position l.

The polyadic instruction sequence p' corresponding to the first half of p is obtained from the first half of p as follows:

- the instruction $\texttt{\$get}{:}1$ is prefixed to it;
- each absolute jump instruction $\#\#l$ with $l \leq 5000$ is replaced by the absolute jump instructions $\#\#l'$, where $l' = l + \nu_1(l) + 1$;
- each absolute jump instruction $\#\#l$ with $l > 5000$ is replaced by the instruction sequence $\texttt{\$put}{:}2{:}\#l' \; ; \#\#\#2$, where $l' = (l - 5000) + \nu_2(l - 5000)$;

and the polyadic instruction sequence p'' corresponding to the second half of p is obtained from the second half of p as follows:

- the instruction $\texttt{\$get}{:}2$ is prefixed to it;
- each absolute jump instruction $\#\#l$ with $l > 5000$ is replaced by the absolute jump instructions $\#\#l'$, where $l' = (l - 5000) + \nu_2(l - 5000) + 1$;
- each absolute jump instruction $\#\#l$ with $l \leq 5000$ is replaced by the instruction sequence $\texttt{\$put}{:}1{:}\#l' \; ; \#\#\#1$, where $l' = l + \nu_1(l)$.

Notice that the positions occurring in jump instructions are adapted to the prefixing of a get instruction to each half of p and the replacement of each jump instructions that gives rise to a jump into the other half of p by two instructions.

Suppose that 2 is the instruction sequence notation index of $\mathrm{ISNA_p}$. Then, for any instruction register file state σ, we have that $|\texttt{\$put}{:}1{:}\#1 \; ; \#\#\#1|_\sigma(\langle(p', 2)\rangle \frown \langle(p'', 2)\rangle)$ coincides with $|p|$ after abstraction from the occurrences of the internal action tau in the former behaviour.

In this section, we have illustrated by means of an example that splitting an instruction sequence into fragments is relatively simple. In Sect. 8.1.4, we will show that synthesizing an instruction sequence from a collection of fragments is fairly complicated.

8.1.3 *Instruction register file functional unit*

In this section, we define a functional unit that is a register file consisting of a finite number of registers whose possible contents are the members of a finite set of core primitive instructions. This functional unit will be used in Sect. 8.1.4 to synthesize a single instruction sequence from a collection of instruction sequence fragments.

It is assumed that a fixed but arbitrary finite set $I \subseteq \mathbb{N}$ such that $I = [1, h]$ for some $h \in \mathbb{N}$ and a fixed but arbitrary finite set $U \subseteq \mathfrak{I}_c$ have been given. The set I is considered to consist of the positions of the registers in the instruction register file and the set U is considered to consist of the instructions that can be put in those registers.

The instruction register file functional unit is a functional unit for the following state space:

$$\mathcal{S}_{\mathrm{IRF}} = \bigcup_{I' \subseteq I} (I' \to U) \; .$$

It is assumed that a fixed but arbitrary bijection $\theta : \mathcal{S}_{\mathrm{IRF}} \to [1, \mathrm{card}(\mathcal{S}_{\mathrm{IRF}})]$ has been given.

The instruction register file functional unit is defined as follows:

$$\begin{aligned} \mathit{IRF} \;&=\; \{(\mathtt{put}{:}i{:}\boldsymbol{u}, \mathit{Put}{:}i{:}\boldsymbol{u}) \mid i \in I \wedge \boldsymbol{u} \in U\} \\ &\cup\; \{(\mathtt{eq}{:}n, \mathit{Eq}{:}n) \mid n \in \mathrm{rng}(\theta)\} \; , \end{aligned}$$

where the method operations are defined as follows:

$$\begin{aligned} \mathit{Put}{:}i{:}\boldsymbol{u}(\sigma) &= (\mathsf{t}, \sigma \oplus [i \mapsto \boldsymbol{u}]) \; , \\ \mathit{Eq}{:}n(\sigma) &= \begin{cases} (\mathsf{t}, \sigma) & \text{if } n = \theta(\sigma) \\ (\mathsf{f}, \sigma) & \text{if } n \neq \theta(\sigma) \; . \end{cases} \end{aligned}$$

The interface $\mathcal{I}(\mathit{IRF})$ of IRF can be explained as follows:

- $\mathtt{put}{:}i{:}\boldsymbol{u}$: the contents of register i becomes instruction $\boldsymbol{u}$ and the reply is t;
- $\mathtt{eq}{:}n$: if the state of the instruction register file equals $\theta^{-1}(n)$, then nothing changes and the reply is t; otherwise nothing changes and the reply is f.

8.1.4 *Instruction sequence synthesis*

In order to establish a connection between collections of instruction sequence fragments and instruction sequences, we show in this section that, for each possible joint behaviour of a collection of instruction sequence fragments, a single instruction sequence can be synthesized from the collection that produces on execution essentially the behaviour in question through interaction with an instruction register file. More precisely, we show that, for each closed $\mathrm{SPISA_p}$ term t and polyadic instruction sequence vector $\boldsymbol{\pi}$, a closed SPISA term t' can be synthesized from t and $\boldsymbol{\pi}$ such that, for all relevant instruction register file states σ, $|t'| \mathbin{/\!/} \mathtt{irf}.\mathit{IRF}(\sigma) = \tau_{\mathsf{tau}}(|t|_\sigma(\boldsymbol{\pi}))$.

Recall that, in $\mathrm{SPISA_p}$, it is assumed that a fixed but arbitrary set $\mathfrak{A}_\mathrm{c}$ of core basic instructions has been given. Here, the following additional assumptions relating to $\mathfrak{A}_\mathrm{c}$ are made:

- a fixed but arbitrary set $\mathcal{F}$ of foci with $\mathtt{irf} \in \mathcal{F}$ has been given;

- a fixed but arbitrary set $\mathcal{M}$ of methods with $\mathcal{I}(\mathit{IRF}) \subseteq \mathcal{M}$ has been given;
- $\mathfrak{A}_\mathrm{c} = \{f.m \mid f \in \mathcal{F} \setminus \{\mathtt{irf}\} \land m \in \mathcal{M}\}$.

Thereby no real restriction is imposed on the set $\mathfrak{A}_\mathrm{c}$: in the case where the cardinality of $\mathcal{F}$ equals 2, all core basic instructions have the same focus and the set $\mathcal{M}$ of methods can be looked upon as the set $\mathfrak{A}_\mathrm{c}$ of core basic instructions.

Let t be a closed $\mathrm{SPISA_p}$ term and π be a polyadic instruction sequence vector. The general idea is that:

- each polyadic instruction sequence in π is translated into a closed $\mathrm{SPISA_p}$ term and an appropriate finite collection of instances of this closed $\mathrm{SPISA_p}$ term in which occurrences of get instructions are replaced by core primitive instructions is generated;
- t and all the generated closed $\mathrm{SPISA_p}$ terms are translated into $\mathrm{ISNR_p}$ instruction sequences and these $\mathrm{ISNR_p}$ instruction sequences are concatenated;
- the resulting $\mathrm{ISNR_p}$ instruction sequence is translated into an $\mathrm{ISNA_p}$ instruction sequence and this instruction sequence is translated into an ISNA instruction sequence by replacing all occurrences of the supplementary instructions by core primitive instructions as follows:
  - a switch-over instruction $\#\#\#i$ is replaced by an absolute jump instruction whose effect is a jump to the beginning of an appended instruction sequence whose execution leads, after the state of the instruction register file has been found by a linear search, to a jump to the beginning of the right instance of the $\mathrm{ISNA_p}$ instruction sequence that corresponds to the ith polyadic instruction sequence in π;
  - a put instruction $\$\mathsf{put}{:}i{:}u$ is replaced by the plain basic instruction $\mathtt{irf}.\mathsf{put}{:}i{:}u$;
  - a get instruction $\$\mathsf{get}{:}i$ is replaced by the absolute jump instruction whose effect is a jump to the position of the instruction itself.

A collection of instances of the closed $\mathrm{SPISA_p}$ term corresponding to a polyadic instruction sequence in π is considered appropriate if it includes all instances that may become the one being executed. The closed $\mathrm{SPISA_p}$ term t and all the generated closed $\mathrm{SPISA_p}$ terms are translated into $\mathrm{ISNR_p}$ instruction sequences because $\mathrm{ISNR_p}$ instruction sequences are relocatable: they can be concatenated without disturbing the meaning of jump instructions. The $\mathrm{ISNR_p}$ instruction sequence resulting from the concatenation is translated into an $\mathrm{ISNA_p}$ instruction sequence before the supplementary instructions are replaced because the replacement of a switch-over instruction by an absolute jump instruction is simpler than its replacement by a relative jump instruction.

Following the general idea outlined above, we will define a function spisap2isna that yields, for each closed SPISA$_\mathrm{p}$ term $\boldsymbol{t}$, a function that yields, for each polyadic instruction sequence vector $\boldsymbol{\pi}$, an ISNA instruction sequence $\boldsymbol{p}$ such that, for each relevant instruction register file service state σ, $|\mathtt{isna2spisa}(\boldsymbol{p})| \mathbin{/\!/} \mathtt{irf}.\mathit{IRF}(\sigma) = \tau_{\mathsf{tau}}(|\boldsymbol{t}|_\sigma(\boldsymbol{\pi}))$.

Below, we will make use of the translation spisa2isnr from closed SPISA terms to ISNR instruction sequences that is the one defined in the proof of Proposition 4.1, but extended in the obvious way from closed SPISA terms in first canonical form to arbitrary closed SPISA terms, and the translation isnr2isna from ISNR instruction sequences to ISNA instruction sequences defined in Sect. 2.3.3. Taking $\mathfrak{A}_\mathrm{c} \cup \mathfrak{A}_\mathrm{s}$ for $\mathfrak{A}$, these translations can be used for translating closed SPISA$_\mathrm{p}$ terms to ISNR$_\mathrm{p}$ instruction sequences and translating ISNR$_\mathrm{p}$ instruction sequences to ISNA$_\mathrm{p}$ instruction sequences, respectively.

The function spisap2isna from the set of all closed SPISA$_\mathrm{p}$ terms to the set of all functions from the set of all polyadic instruction sequence vectors to the set of all ISNA instruction sequences is defined as follows:

$$
\begin{aligned}
&\mathtt{spisap2isna}(\boldsymbol{t})(\boldsymbol{\pi}) = \\
&\quad \mathit{translate}(\mathtt{isnr2isna}(\mathit{expand}(\boldsymbol{t})(\boldsymbol{\pi})))\ ; \\
&\quad {+}\mathtt{irf.eq}{:}1\ ;\ \#\#l_{1,1}\ ;\ \ldots\ ;\ {+}\mathtt{irf.eq}{:}n'\ ;\ \#\#l_{1,n'}\ ; \\
&\quad \vdots \\
&\quad {+}\mathtt{irf.eq}{:}1\ ;\ \#\#l_{n,1}\ ;\ \ldots\ ;\ {+}\mathtt{irf.eq}{:}n'\ ;\ \#\#l_{n,n'}\ ,
\end{aligned}
$$

where $n = \mathrm{len}(\boldsymbol{\pi})$, $n' = \max(\mathrm{rng}(\theta))$, the function *expand* from the set of all closed SPISA$_\mathrm{p}$ terms to the set of all functions from the set of all polyadic instruction sequence vectors to the set of all ISNR$_\mathrm{p}$ instruction sequences is defined as follows:

$$
\begin{aligned}
&\mathit{expand}(\boldsymbol{t})(\boldsymbol{\pi}) = \\
&\quad \mathtt{spisa2isnr}(\boldsymbol{t})\ ; \\
&\quad \mathtt{spisa2isnr}(\mathit{gen}(\boldsymbol{\pi}, 1, \theta^{-1}(1)))\ ;\ \ldots\ ;\ \mathtt{spisa2isnr}(\mathit{gen}(\boldsymbol{\pi}, 1, \theta^{-1}(n')))\ ; \\
&\quad \vdots \\
&\quad \mathtt{spisa2isnr}(\mathit{gen}(\boldsymbol{\pi}, n, \theta^{-1}(1)))\ ;\ \ldots\ ;\ \mathtt{spisa2isnr}(\mathit{gen}(\boldsymbol{\pi}, n, \theta^{-1}(n')))\ ,
\end{aligned}
$$

where $n = \mathrm{len}(\boldsymbol{\pi})$, $n' = \max(\mathrm{rng}(\theta))$, and the function *gen* from the set of all polyadic instruction sequence vectors, the set of all natural numbers and the set of all instruction register file states to the set of all closed SPISA$_\mathrm{p}$ terms is defined as follows:

$$
\begin{aligned}
&\mathit{gen}(\boldsymbol{\pi}, i, \sigma) = \mathit{prj}_{\mathit{isn}(\boldsymbol{\pi},i)}(\mathit{is}(\boldsymbol{\pi}, i))[\sigma] && \text{if } i \in \mathit{ind}(\boldsymbol{\pi}) \land \mathit{valid}(\boldsymbol{\pi}, i, \sigma)\ , \\
&\mathit{gen}(\boldsymbol{\pi}, i, \sigma) = \#0 && \text{if } i \in \mathit{ind}(\boldsymbol{\pi}) \land \neg \mathit{valid}(\boldsymbol{\pi}, i, \sigma)\ , \\
&\mathit{gen}(\boldsymbol{\pi}, i, \sigma) = \,! && \text{if } i \notin \mathit{ind}(\boldsymbol{\pi})\ ,
\end{aligned}
$$

the function *translate* from the set of all $\mathrm{ISNA_p}$ instruction sequences to the set of all ISNA instruction sequences is defined as follows:

$$translate(\boldsymbol{u}_1 \,;\ldots;\, \boldsymbol{u}_k) = \psi_1(\boldsymbol{u}_1) \,;\ldots;\, \psi_1(\boldsymbol{u}_k) \;,$$

where the functions ψ_j from the set of all primitive instructions of $\mathrm{ISNA_p}$ to the set of all primitive instructions of ISNA are defined as follows ($1 \leq j \leq k$):

$$\begin{aligned}
&\psi_j(\#\#\#i) &&= \#\#l_i && \text{if } i \in ind(\boldsymbol{\pi}) \;,\\
&\psi_j(\#\#\#i) &&= \,! && \text{if } i \notin ind(\boldsymbol{\pi}) \;,\\
&\psi_j(\$\mathsf{put}{:}i{:}\boldsymbol{u}) &&= \mathtt{irf.put}{:}i{:}\boldsymbol{u} \;, &&\\
&\psi_j(\$\mathsf{get}{:}i) &&= \#\#j \;, &&\\
&\psi_j(\boldsymbol{u}) &&= \boldsymbol{u} && \text{if } \boldsymbol{u} \text{ is a core primitive instruction} \;,
\end{aligned}$$

where for each $i \in [1, \mathrm{len}(\boldsymbol{\pi})]$:

$$\begin{aligned}
l_i = {} & \mathrm{len}(\mathtt{spisa2isnr}(\boldsymbol{t}))\\
& + \sum_{h \in [1,\mathrm{len}(\boldsymbol{\pi})], h' \in \mathrm{rng}(\theta)} \mathrm{len}(\mathtt{spisa2isnr}(prj_{\,isn(\boldsymbol{\pi},h)}(is(\boldsymbol{\pi}, h))[\theta^{-1}(h')]))\\
& + 2 \cdot \max(\mathrm{rng}(\theta)) \cdot (i-1) \;,
\end{aligned}$$

and for each $i \in [1, \mathrm{len}(\boldsymbol{\pi})]$ and $j \in \mathrm{rng}(\theta)$:

$$\begin{aligned}
l_{i,j} = {} & \mathrm{len}(\mathtt{spisa2isnr}(\boldsymbol{t}))\\
& + \sum_{h \in [1,i-1], h' \in \mathrm{rng}(\theta)} \mathrm{len}(\mathtt{spisa2isnr}(prj_{\,isn(\boldsymbol{\pi},h)}(is(\boldsymbol{\pi}, h))[\theta^{-1}(h')]))\\
& + \sum_{h' \in [1,j-1]} \mathrm{len}(\mathtt{spisa2isnr}(prj_{\,isn(\boldsymbol{\pi},i)}(is(\boldsymbol{\pi}, i))[\theta^{-1}(h')])) \;.
\end{aligned}$$

The following proposition states rigorously that, for any closed $\mathrm{SPISA_p}$ term $\boldsymbol{t}$ and polyadic instruction sequence vector $\boldsymbol{\pi}$, for all relevant instruction register file states σ, $|\mathtt{isna2spisa}(\mathtt{spisap2isna}(\boldsymbol{t})(\boldsymbol{\pi}))| \mathbin{/\!/} \mathtt{irf}.IRF(\sigma) = \tau_{\mathsf{tau}}(|\boldsymbol{t}|_\sigma(\boldsymbol{\pi}))$.

Proposition 8.1. *Let* $\boldsymbol{t}$ *be a closed* $\mathrm{SPISA_p}$ *term and* $\boldsymbol{\pi}$ *be a polyadic instruction sequence vector, and let* h *be the highest number occurring in instructions of the form* $\$\mathsf{put}{:}i{:}\boldsymbol{u}$ *or* $\$\mathsf{get}{:}i$ *in* $\boldsymbol{t}$ *or* $\boldsymbol{\pi}$*. Take the interval* $[1, h]$ *for* I *and the set of all core primitive instructions occurring in instructions of the form* $\$\mathsf{put}{:}i{:}\boldsymbol{u}$ *in* $\boldsymbol{t}$ *or* $\boldsymbol{\pi}$ *for* U*, and let* $\sigma \in \mathcal{S}_{\mathrm{IRF}}$*. Then* $\tau_{\mathsf{tau}}(|\boldsymbol{t}|_\sigma(\boldsymbol{\pi})) = |\mathtt{isna2spisa}(\mathtt{spisap2isna}(\boldsymbol{t})(\boldsymbol{\pi}))| \mathbin{/\!/} \mathtt{irf}.IRF(\sigma)$.

Proof. We refrain from presenting the proof of this proposition because it follows the same line as the proof of Proposition 4.7 but is extremely tedious. The definition of the function β needed here is much more complicated than the definition of the function β needed in the proof of Proposition 4.7. □

The synthesis of single instruction sequences from collections of instruction sequence fragments is reminiscent of the service-based variant of projection semantics followed in Sect. 3.3. The definition of `spisap2isna` shows that this synthesis is fairly complicated.

8.2 Backward Instructions

In this section, we introduce an algebraic theory of instruction sequences without a directional bias: for each instruction whose effect involves that execution proceeds in the forward direction, there is a counterpart whose effect involves that execution proceeds in the backward direction. An instruction whose effect involves that execution proceeds in the forward direction is called a forward instruction and an instruction whose effect involves that execution proceeds in the backward direction is called a backward instruction.

Instruction sequence notations, and more general program notations, invariably show a directional bias: there is always a left to right orientation. This fact might admit an explanation in terms of complexity of design, expression or execution, and the algebraic theory introduced in this section provides a context in which this may be investigated.

8.2.1 *C, a semigroup for code*

C is a variant of SPISA that has both forward instructions and backward instructions. In C, like in SPISA, it is assumed that there is a fixed but arbitrary set $\mathfrak{A}$ of basic instructions.

C has the following C *instructions*:

- for each $\boldsymbol{a} \in \mathfrak{A}$, a *forward plain basic instruction* $/\boldsymbol{a}$;
- for each $\boldsymbol{a} \in \mathfrak{A}$, a *forward positive test instruction* $+/\boldsymbol{a}$;
- for each $\boldsymbol{a} \in \mathfrak{A}$, a *forward negative test instruction* $-/\boldsymbol{a}$;
- for each $l \in \mathbb{N}^+$, a *forward jump instruction* $/\#l$;
- for each $\boldsymbol{a} \in \mathfrak{A}$, a *backward plain basic instruction* $\backslash\boldsymbol{a}$;
- for each $\boldsymbol{a} \in \mathfrak{A}$, a *backward positive test instruction* $+\backslash\boldsymbol{a}$;
- for each $\boldsymbol{a} \in \mathfrak{A}$, a *backward negative test instruction* $-\backslash\boldsymbol{a}$;
- for each $l \in \mathbb{N}^+$, a *backward jump instruction* $\backslash\#l$;
- an *abort instruction* $\#$;
- a *plain termination instruction* !;
- a *positive termination instruction* !t;
- a *negative termination instruction* !f.

We write $\mathfrak{I}_{\mathrm{C}}$ for the set of all C instructions.

On execution of a C instruction sequence, the C instructions have the following effects:

- the effects of forward instructions $/a$, $+/a$, $-/a$ and $/\#l$ are the same as the effects of a, $+a$, $-a$ and $\#l$, respectively, in SPISA;
- the effects of backward instructions $\backslash a$, $+\backslash a$, $-\backslash a$ and $\backslash\#l$ are the same as the effects of a, $+a$, $-a$ and $\#l$, respectively, in SPISA, but with the direction in which execution proceeds reversed;
- the effect of the abort instruction $\#$ is the same as the effect of $\#0$ in SPISA;
- the effects of the termination instructions $!$, $!\mathtt{t}$ and $!\mathtt{f}$ are the same as their effects in SPISA.

C has one sort, namely the sort **IS** of instruction sequences, and the following constants and operators:

- for each $u \in \mathfrak{I}_{\mathrm{C}}$, an *instruction* constant $u : \to \mathbf{IS}$;
- the binary *concatenation* operator $\_ \,;\, \_ : \mathbf{IS} \times \mathbf{IS} \to \mathbf{IS}$.

C has only one axiom, namely the associativity axiom $(X \,;\, Y) \,;\, Z = X \,;\, (Y \,;\, Z)$ for concatenation.

Some simple examples of closed C terms are

$$+/\mathtt{a} \,;\, /\#2 \,;\, \# \,;\, /\mathtt{b} \,;\, !\mathtt{t}\,, \qquad /\mathtt{a} \,;\, /\mathtt{b} \,;\, /\mathtt{c} \,;\, \backslash\#2\,, \qquad /\mathtt{a} \,;\, +/\mathtt{b} \,;\, \backslash\mathtt{c} \,;\, !\,.$$

8.2.2 *Thread extraction and code transformation*

We combine C with BTA+REC+AIP and extend the combination with:

- for each $i \in \mathbb{Z}$, the *thread extraction* operator $|\_|_i : \mathbf{IS} \to \mathbf{T}$

and the axioms given in Table 8.2. In this table, a stands for an arbitrary basic instruction from $\mathfrak{A}$, u stands for an arbitrary primitive instruction from $\mathfrak{I}_{\mathrm{C}}$, l and k stand for arbitrary positive natural numbers, and i stands for an arbitrary integer.

The thread extraction operators are meant for the extraction of the threads that represent the behaviours produced by C instruction sequences under execution from the C instruction sequences. For C instruction sequences whose length is greater than or equal to i, $|\_|_i$ yields the threads that represent the behaviours produced if execution starts at the ith instruction. For example,

$$|/\mathtt{a} \,;\, +/\mathtt{b} \,;\, \backslash\mathtt{c} \,;\, !|_1$$

Table 8.2 Axioms for the thread extraction operators of C

$\lvert u_1 ; \ldots ; u_k \rvert_i = \mathsf{D}$	if $i = 0 \lor i > k$
$\lvert u_1 ; \ldots ; u_k \rvert_i = a \circ \lvert u_1 ; \ldots ; u_k \rvert_{i+1}$	if $u_i = /a$
$\lvert u_1 ; \ldots ; u_k \rvert_i = \lvert u_1 ; \ldots ; u_k \rvert_{i+1} \trianglelefteq a \trianglerighteq \lvert u_1 ; \ldots ; u_k \rvert_{i+2}$	if $u_i = +/a$
$\lvert u_1 ; \ldots ; u_k \rvert_i = \lvert u_1 ; \ldots ; u_k \rvert_{i+2} \trianglelefteq a \trianglerighteq \lvert u_1 ; \ldots ; u_k \rvert_{i+1}$	if $u_i = -/a$
$\lvert u_1 ; \ldots ; u_k \rvert_i = \lvert u_1 ; \ldots ; u_k \rvert_{i+l}$	if $u_i = /\#l$
$\lvert u_1 ; \ldots ; u_k \rvert_i = a \circ \lvert u_1 ; \ldots ; u_k \rvert_{i-1}$	if $u_i = \backslash a$
$\lvert u_1 ; \ldots ; u_k \rvert_i = \lvert u_1 ; \ldots ; u_k \rvert_{i-1} \trianglelefteq a \trianglerighteq \lvert u_1 ; \ldots ; u_k \rvert_{i-2}$	if $u_i = +\backslash a$
$\lvert u_1 ; \ldots ; u_k \rvert_i = \lvert u_1 ; \ldots ; u_k \rvert_{i-2} \trianglelefteq a \trianglerighteq \lvert u_1 ; \ldots ; u_k \rvert_{i-1}$	if $u_i = -\backslash a$
$\lvert u_1 ; \ldots ; u_k \rvert_i = \lvert u_1 ; \ldots ; u_k \rvert_{i-l}$	if $u_i = \backslash\#l$
$\lvert u_1 ; \ldots ; u_k \rvert_i = \mathsf{D}$	if $u_i = \#$
$\lvert u_1 ; \ldots ; u_k \rvert_i = \mathsf{S}$	if $u_i = !$
$\lvert u_1 ; \ldots ; u_k \rvert_i = \mathsf{S+}$	if $u_i = !\mathsf{t}$
$\lvert u_1 ; \ldots ; u_k \rvert_i = \mathsf{S-}$	if $u_i = !\mathsf{f}$

is the x-component of the solution of the guarded recursive specification consisting of the following two equations:

$$x = \mathsf{a} \circ y \;, \qquad y = (\mathsf{c} \circ y) \trianglelefteq \mathsf{b} \trianglerighteq \mathsf{S} \;.$$

Henceforth, we will write $\lvert t \rvert^{\rightarrow}$, where t is a C term, for $\lvert t \rvert_1$.

We define a function c2c from the set of all closed C terms to the set of all closed C terms in which backward instructions other than backward jump instructions do not occur:

$$\mathsf{c2c}(u_1 ; \ldots ; u_k) = \varphi(u_1) ; \ldots ; \varphi(u_k) \;,$$

where the auxiliary function φ from the set of all primitive instructions of C to the set of all closed C terms is defined as follows:

$$\begin{aligned} \varphi(/a) &= /a \,; /\#2 \,; \# \;, \\ \varphi(+/a) &= +/a \,; /\#2 \,; /\#4 \;, \\ \varphi(-/a) &= -/a \,; /\#2 \,; /\#4 \;, \\ \varphi(/\#l) &= /\#3{\cdot}l \,; \# \,; \# \;, \end{aligned}$$

$$\begin{aligned}
\varphi(\backslash a) &= /a\,;\backslash\#4\,;\#\,,\\
\varphi(+\backslash a) &= +/a\,;\backslash\#4\,;\backslash\#8\,,\\
\varphi(-\backslash a) &= -/a\,;\backslash\#4\,;\backslash\#8\,,\\
\varphi(\backslash\#l) &= \backslash\#3{\cdot}l\,;\#\,;\#\,,\\
\varphi(\#) &= \#\,;\#\,;\#\,,\\
\varphi(!) &= !\,;\#\,;\#\,,\\
\varphi(!\mathsf{t}) &= !\mathsf{t}\,;\#\,;\#\,,\\
\varphi(!\mathsf{f}) &= !\mathsf{f}\,;\#\,;\#\,.
\end{aligned}$$

The function `c2c` preserves thread extraction, i.e. for all closed C terms t:

$$|t|^{\rightarrow} = |\mathtt{c2c}(t)|^{\rightarrow}\,.$$

This means that the expressiveness of C would not be reduced by excluding the backward instructions other than backward jump instructions. The function `c2c` is a very simple example of a program transformation. An example of this program transformation is

$$\mathtt{c2c}(+/\mathtt{a}\,;\backslash\mathtt{b}\,;!) = +/\mathtt{a}\,;/\#2\,;/\#4\,;/\mathtt{b}\,;\backslash\#4\,;\#\,;!\,;\#\,;\#\,.$$

8.2.3 *C programs and single-pass instruction sequences*

A C *program* is a closed C term $u_1\,;\ldots;\,u_k$ for which, for each $i \in [1,k]$, all derivable equations of the form $|u_1\,;\ldots;\,u_k|_i = t$ can be derived without using the first equation in Table 8.2.

The intuition is that execution of C programs can only end by executing one of the termination instructions or the abort instruction. For example,

$$+/\mathtt{a}\,;/\#2\,;/\#2\,;+\backslash\mathtt{b}\,;!\mathsf{t}$$

is a C program, but

$$+/\mathtt{a}\,;/\#2\,;/\#2\,;+/\mathtt{b}\,;!\mathsf{t} \quad \text{and} \quad +/\mathtt{a}\,;/\#2\,;/\#3\,;+\backslash\mathtt{b}\,;!\mathsf{t}$$

are not C programs.

We define a function `cp2spisa` from the set of all C programs to the set of all closed SPISA terms:

$$\mathtt{cp2spisa}(t) = \mathtt{cp2spisa}'(\mathtt{c2c}(t))\,,$$

where the function `cp2spisa`′ from the set of all C programs in which backward instructions other than backward jump instructions do not occur to the set of all closed SPISA terms is defined as follows:

$$\texttt{cp2spisa}'(u_1 \,;\ldots;\, u_k) = (\psi(u_1) \,;\ldots;\, \psi(u_k))^\omega \;,$$

where the auxiliary function ψ from the set of all primitive instructions of C to the set of all primitive instructions of SPISA is defined as follows:

$$\begin{aligned}
\psi(/a) &= a \;, \\
\psi(+/a) &= +a \;, \\
\psi(-/a) &= -a \;, \\
\psi(/\#l) &= \#l \;, \\
\psi(\backslash\#l) &= \#k{-}l \;, \\
\psi(\#) &= \#0 \;, \\
\psi(!) &= ! \;, \\
\psi(!\mathsf{t}) &= !\mathsf{t} \;, \\
\psi(!\mathsf{f}) &= !\mathsf{f} \;.
\end{aligned}$$

An example of this translation from C programs to closed SPISA terms is

$$\texttt{cp2spisa}(+/\texttt{a} \,;\, \backslash\texttt{b} \,;\, !) = (+\texttt{a} \,;\, \#2 \,;\, \#4 \,;\, \texttt{b} \,;\, \#5 \,;\, \#0 \,;\, ! \,;\, \#0 \,;\, \#0)^\omega \;.$$

The function `cp2spisa` is defined such that, for all C programs t:

$$|t|^{\rightarrow} = |\texttt{cp2spisa}(t)| \;.$$

The translation `spisa2isnr` defined in the proof of Proposition 4.1, extended in the obvious way from closed SPISA terms in first canonical form to arbitrary closed SPISA terms, maps each closed SPISA term to an ISNR instruction sequence producing the same thread. The translation from ISNR instruction sequences to C programs that maps each ISNR instruction sequence to a C program producing the same thread is trivial. This means that there also exists a function `spisa2cp` from the set of all closed SPISA terms to the set of all C program such that all closed SPISA terms t:

$$|t| = |\texttt{spisa2cp}(t)|^{\rightarrow} \;.$$

Hence, C programs and SPISA instruction sequences are equally expressive.

8.3 Probabilistic Instructions

In this section, we take the first step on a new direction of our work relating to instruction sequences: the study of probabilistic instruction sequences.

We use the term probabilistic instruction sequence for an instruction sequence that contains probabilistic instructions, i.e. instructions that are themselves probabilistic by nature. We will propose several kinds of probabilistic instructions, provide an informal operational meaning for each of them, and discuss related work. We will refrain from a formal semantic analysis of the proposed kinds of probabilistic instructions. Moreover, we will not claim any form of completeness for the proposed kinds of probabilistic instructions. Other convincing kinds might be found in the future.

Viewed from the perspective of machine-execution, execution of a probabilistic instruction sequence using an execution architecture without probabilistic features can only be a metaphor. Execution of a deterministic instruction sequence using an execution architecture with probabilistic features, i.e. an execution architecture that allows for probabilistic services, is far more plausible. Thus, it looks to be that probabilistic instruction sequences find their true meaning by translation into deterministic instruction sequences for execution architectures with probabilistic features. Indeed projection semantics, the approach to define the meaning of instruction sequences which was introduced in Sect. 2.3, need not be compromised when probabilistic instructions are taken into account.

8.3.1 *On the scope of Sect. 8.3*

We go into the scope of Sect. 8.3 to clarify and motivate its restrictions.

We will propose several kinds of probabilistic instructions, chosen because of their superficial similarity with kinds of deterministic instructions known from SPISA and the related instruction sequence notations presented in this book, and not because any computational intuition about them is known or assumed. For each of these kinds, we will provide an informal operational meaning. Moreover, we will show that the proposed unbounded probabilistic jump instructions can be simulated by means of bounded probabilistic test instructions and bounded deterministic jump instructions. We will also refer to related work that introduces something similar to what we call a probabilistic instruction and connect the proposed kinds of probabilistic instructions with similar features found in related work.

We will refrain from a formal semantic analysis of the proposed kinds of probabilistic instructions. The reasons for doing so are as follows:

- In the non-probabilistic case, the subject reduces to the semantics of instruction sequences as considered in SPISA. Although it seems obvious at first sight, different models, reflecting different levels of abstraction, can and have been distinguished. Probabilities introduce a further ramification.

- What we consider sensible is to analyse this double ramification fully. What we consider less useful is to provide one specific collection of design decisions and working out its details as a proof of concept.
- We notice that for process algebra the ramification of semantic options after the incorporation of probabilistic features is remarkable, and even frustrating (see e.g. [van Glabbeek *et al.* (1995); Jonsson *et al.* (2001)]). There is no reason to expect that the situation is much simpler here.
- Once that a semantic strategy is mainly judged on its preparedness for a setting with multi-threading, the subject becomes intrinsically complex (like the preparedness for a setting with arbitrary interleaving complicates the semantic modelling of deterministic processes in process algebra).
- We believe that a choice for a catalogue of kinds of probabilistic instructions can be made beforehand. Even if that choice will turn out to be wrong, because prolonged forthcoming semantic analysis may give rise to new, more natural, kinds of probabilistic instructions, it can at this stage best be driven by direct intuitions.

We will leave unanalysed the topic of probabilistic instruction sequence processing, which includes all phenomena concerning services and execution environments for probabilistic instruction sequences for which probabilistic analysis is necessary. At the same time, we admit that probabilistic instruction sequence processing is a much more substantial topic than probabilistic instruction sequences, because of its machine-oriented scope. We take the line that a probabilistic instruction sequence finds its operational meaning by translation into a deterministic instruction sequence and execution using an execution environment with probabilistic features.

In the remainder of Sect. 8.3, we will use the notation and terminology regarding instructions and instruction sequences from SPISA. The mathematical structure that we will use for quantities is a signed cancellation meadow.

8.3.2 *Signed cancellation meadows*

The signature of signed cancellation meadows consists of the following constants and operators:

- the constants 0 and 1;
- the binary *addition* operator $\_ + \_$;
- the binary *multiplication* operator $\_ \cdot \_$;

- the unary *additive inverse* operator $-\_$;
- the unary *multiplicative inverse* operator $\_^{-1}$;
- the unary *signum* operator s.

Terms are build as usual. We use infix notation for the binary operators $+$ and $\cdot$, prefix notation for the unary operator $-$, and postfix notation for the unary operator $^{-1}$. We use the usual precedence convention to reduce the need for parentheses. We introduce subtraction and division as abbreviations: $t_1 - t_2$ abbreviates $t_1 + (-t_2)$ and t_1/t_2 abbreviates $t_1 \cdot (t_2^{-1})$. We use the notation $\underline{n}$ for numerals and the notation t^n for exponentiation with a natural number as exponent. The term $\underline{n}$ is inductively defined as follows: $\underline{0} = 0$ and $\underline{n+1} = \underline{n} + 1$. The term t^n is inductively defined as follows: $t^0 = 1$ and $t^{n+1} = t^n \cdot t$.

The constants and operators from the signature of signed cancellation meadows are adopted from rational arithmetic, which gives an appropriate intuition about these constants and operators. The equational theory of signed cancellation meadows is given in [Bergstra and Ponse (2008)]. In signed cancellation meadows, the functions $\min$ and $\max$ have simple definitions (see also [Bergstra and Ponse (2008)]).

A signed cancellation meadow is a cancellation meadow expanded with a signum operation. The prime example of cancellation meadows is the field of rational numbers with the multiplicative inverse operation made total by imposing that the multiplicative inverse of zero is zero, see e.g. [Bergstra and Tucker (2007)].

In the remainder of Sect. 8.3, we assume that a fixed but arbitrary signed cancellation meadow $\mathfrak{M}$ has been given. As in the case of models of BTA or some extension thereof, we denote the interpretations of constants and operators in $\mathfrak{M}$ by the constants and operators themselves.

8.3.3 *Probabilistic basic and test instructions*

In this section, we propose several kinds of probabilistic basic and test instructions.

We propose the following *probabilistic basic instructions*:

- $\%()$, which produces t with probability $1/2$ and f with probability $1/2$;
- $\%(q)$, which produces t with probability $\max(0, \min(1, q))$ and f with probability $1 - \max(0, \min(1, q))$, for $q \in \mathfrak{M}$.

The probabilistic basic instructions have no side-effect on a state.

The basic instruction $\%()$ can be looked upon as a shorthand for $\%(1/2)$. We distinguish between $\%()$ and $\%(1/2)$ for reason of putting the emphasis on the fact that it is not necessary to bring in a notation for quantities ranging from 0 to 1 in order to design probabilistic instructions.

Once that probabilistic basic instructions of the form $\%(q)$ are chosen, an unbounded ramification of options for the notation of quantities is opened up. We will assume that closed terms over the signature of signed cancellation meadows are used to denote quantities. Instructions such as $\%(\sqrt{1+1})$ are implicit in the form $\%(q)$, assuming that it is known how to view $\sqrt{\ }$ as a notational extension of signed cancellation meadows (see e.g. [Bergstra and Bethke (2009)]).

Like all basic instructions, each probabilistic basic instruction gives rise to three probabilistic primitive instructions. Each probabilistic basic instruction of the form $\%(q)$ gives rise to

- the *probabilistic plain basic instruction* $\%(q)$;
- the *probabilistic test instructions* $+\%(q)$ and $-\%(q)$;

and likewise the probabilistic basic instruction $\%()$.

Probabilistic test instructions of the form $+\%(q)$ and $-\%(q)$ can be considered probabilistic branch instructions where q is the probability that the branch is not taken and taken, respectively.

We find that, different from $+\%(q)$ and $-\%(q)$, the plain basic instruction $\%(q)$ can be replaced by $\#1$ without loss of (intuitive) meaning. Of course, in a resource-aware model, $\#1$ may be much cheaper than $\%(q)$, especially if q is hard to compute. Suppose that $\%(q)$ is realized at a lower level by means of $\%()$, which is possible, and suppose that q is a computable real number. The question arises whether the expectation of the time to execute $\%(q)$ is finite.

To exemplify the possibility that $\%(q)$ is realized by means of $\%()$ in the case where q is a rational number, we look at the following probabilistic instruction sequences:

$$-\%(2/3) \,;\, \#3 \,;\, \mathtt{a} \,;\, ! \,;\, \mathtt{b} \,;\, ! \,,$$
$$(+\%() \,;\, \#3 \,;\, \mathtt{a} \,;\, ! \,;\, +\%() \,;\, \#3 \,;\, \mathtt{b} \,;\, !)^{\omega} \,.$$

It is easy to see that these instruction sequences produce on execution the same behaviour: with probability $2/3$, first $\mathtt{a}$ is performed and then termination follows; and with probability $1/3$, first $\mathtt{b}$ is performed and then termination follows. In the case of computable real numbers other than rational numbers, use must be made of a service that does duty for a Turing machine (see also Sect. 5.1.1).

Let $q \in \mathfrak{M}$, and let $\mathtt{random}(q)$ be a service with a method $\mathtt{get}$ whose reply is t with probability $\max(0, \min(1, q))$ and f with probability $1 - \max(0, \min(1, q))$. Then a reasonable view on the meaning of the probabilistic primitive instructions $\%(q)$, $+\%(q)$ and $-\%(q)$ is that they are translated into the deterministic primitive instructions $\texttt{random}(q)\texttt{.get}$, $+\texttt{random}(q)\texttt{.get}$ and $-\texttt{random}(q)\texttt{.get}$, respectively, and executed using an execution environment that provides the probabilistic service $\texttt{random}(q)$. Another option is possible here: instead of a different service $\texttt{random}(q)$ for each $q \in \mathfrak{M}$ and a single method get, we could have a single service random with a different method $\texttt{get}(q)$ for each $q \in \mathfrak{M}$. In the latter case, $\%(q)$, $+\%(q)$ and $-\%(q)$ would be translated into the deterministic primitive instructions $\texttt{random.get}(q)$, $+\texttt{random.get}(q)$ and $-\texttt{random.get}(q)$.

8.3.4 *Probabilistic jump instructions*

In this section, we propose several kinds of probabilistic jump instructions. It is assumed that the signed cancellation meadow $\mathfrak{M}$ has been expanded with an operation $\mathbb{N}$ such that, for all $q \in \mathfrak{M}$, $\mathbb{N}(q) = 0$ iff $q = \underline{n}$ for some $n \in \mathbb{N}$. We write $\bar{l}$, where $l \in \mathfrak{M}$ is such that $\mathbb{N}(l) = 0$, for the unique $n \in \mathbb{N}$ such that $l = \underline{n}$. Moreover, we write $\hat{q}$, where $q \in \mathfrak{M}$, for $\max(0, \min(1, q))$.

We propose the following *probabilistic jump instructions*:

- $\#\%\mathsf{H}(k)$, having the same effect as $\#j$ with probability $1/k$ for $j \in [1, \bar{k}]$, for $k \in \mathfrak{M}$ with $\mathbb{N}(k) = 0$;
- $\#\%\mathsf{G}(q)(k)$, having the same effect as $\#j$ with probability $\hat{q} \cdot (1 - \hat{q})^{j-1}$ for $j \in [1, \bar{k}]$, for $q \in \mathfrak{M}$ and $k \in \mathfrak{M}$ with $\mathbb{N}(k) = 0$;
- $\#\%\mathsf{G}(q)l$, having the same effect as $\#\bar{l} \cdot j$ with probability $\hat{q} \cdot (1 - \hat{q})^{j-1}$ for $j \in [1, \infty)$, for $q \in \mathfrak{M}$ and $l \in \mathfrak{M}$ with $\mathbb{N}(l) = 0$.

The letter H in $\#\%\mathsf{H}(k)$ indicates a homogeneous probability distribution, and the letter G in $\#\%\mathsf{G}(q)(k)$ and $\#\%\mathsf{G}(q)l$ indicates a geometric probability distribution. Instructions of the forms $\#\%\mathsf{H}(k)$ and $\#\%\mathsf{G}(q)(k)$ are bounded probabilistic jump instructions, whereas instructions of the form $\#\%\mathsf{G}(q)l$ are unbounded probabilistic jump instructions.

Like in the case of the probabilistic basic instructions, we propose in addition the following probabilistic jump instructions:

- $\#\%\mathsf{G}()(k)$ as the special case of $\#\%\mathsf{G}(q)(k)$ where $q = 1/2$;
- $\#\%\mathsf{G}()l$ as the special case of $\#\%\mathsf{G}(q)l$ where $q = 1/2$.

We believe that all probabilistic jump instructions can be eliminated. In particular, we believe that unbounded probabilistic jump instructions can be eliminated. This believe can be understood as the judgement that it is reasonable to expect from a semantic model of probabilistic instruction sequences that the following identity and similar ones hold:

$$
\begin{aligned}
&+\mathtt{a} ; \#\%\mathrm{G}()2 ; (+\mathtt{b} ; ! ; \mathtt{c})^{\omega} = \\
&+\mathtt{a} ; +\%() ; \#8 ; \#10 ; \\
&\quad (+\mathtt{b} ; \#5 ; \#10 ; +\%() ; \#8 ; \#10 ; \\
&\quad\ \ ! ; \#5 ; \#10 ; +\%() ; \#8 ; \#10 ; \\
&\quad\ \ \mathtt{c} ; \#5 ; \#10 ; +\%() ; \#8 ; \#10)^{\omega} .
\end{aligned}
$$

Taking this identity and similar ones as our point of departure, the question arises what is the most simple model that justifies them. A more general question is whether instruction sequences with unbounded probabilistic jump instructions can be translated into ones with only probabilistic test instructions provided it does not bother us that the instruction sequences may become much longer (e.g. expectation of the length bounded, but worst case length unbounded).

8.3.5 *The probabilistic process algebra thesis*

In the preceding chapters, we have seen that, in the absence of probabilistic instructions, threads as considered in BTA can be used to represent the behaviours produced by instruction sequences under execution. Processes as considered in general process algebras such as ACP, CCS and CSP can be used as well, but they give rise to a more complicated representation of the behaviours of instruction sequences under execution.

In the presence of probabilistic instructions, we would need a probabilistic thread algebra, i.e. a variant of thread algebra that covers probabilistic behaviours. It appears that any probabilistic thread algebra is inherently more complicated to such an extent that the advantage of not using a general process algebra evaporates. Moreover, it appears that any probabilistic thread algebra requires justification by means of an appropriate probabilistic process algebra. This leads us to the following thesis:

Thesis 8.1. *Modelling the behaviours produced by probabilistic instruction sequences under execution is a matter of using directly processes as considered in some probabilistic process algebra.*

Notice that once we move from deterministic instructions to probabilistic instructions, instruction sequence becomes an indispensable concept. Instruction sequences cannot be replaced by threads or processes without taking potentially premature design decisions. It is reasonable to claim that, like for deterministic instruction sequence notations, all probabilistic instruction sequence notations can be provided with a probabilistic semantics by translation of the instruction sequences concerned into appropriate single-pass instruction sequences. Thus, the approach of projection semantics works for probabilistic instruction sequence notations as well.

A probabilistic thread algebra has to cover the interaction between instruction sequence under execution and the named services from the service family provided by the execution environment. It appears that the intricacy of a probabilistic thread algebra originates in large part from this kind of interaction, in particular from the facet of it to which the use operator is related.

8.3.6 *Related work*

In [Sharir *et al.* (1984)], a notation for probabilistic programs is introduced in which we can write, for example, $\mathrm{random}(p \cdot \delta_0 + q \cdot \delta_1)$. In general, $\mathrm{random}(\lambda)$ produces a value according to the probability distribution λ. In this case, δ_i is the probability distribution that gives probability 1 to i and probability 0 to other values. Thus, for $p + q = 1$, $p \cdot \delta_0 + q \cdot \delta_1$ is the probability distribution that gives probability p to 0, probability q to 1, and probability 0 to other values. Clearly, $\mathrm{random}(p \cdot \delta_0 + q \cdot \delta_1)$ corresponds to $\%(p)$. Moreover, using this kind of notation, we could write $\#(\frac{1}{k} \cdot (\delta_1 + \cdots + \delta_{\bar{k}}))$ for $\#\%\mathsf{H}(k)$ and $\#(\hat{q} \cdot \delta_1 + \hat{q} \cdot (1 - \hat{q}) \cdot \delta_2 + \cdots + \hat{q} \cdot (1 - \hat{q})^{k-1} \cdot \delta_{\bar{k}})$ for $\#\%\mathsf{G}(q)(k)$.

In much work on probabilistic programming, see e.g. [He Jifeng *et al.* (1997); McIver and Morgan (2001); Morgan *et al.* (1996)], we find the binary probabilistic choice operator ${}_p\oplus$. This operator chooses between its operands, taking its left operand with probability p. Clearly, $\boldsymbol{p} \;{}_p\oplus\; \boldsymbol{q}$ can be taken as an abbreviation for $+\%(p) \;;\; \mathbf{u}(\boldsymbol{p} \;;\; \#2) \;;\; \mathbf{u}(\boldsymbol{q})$, where $\mathbf{u}$ is an operator which turns sequences of instructions into single instructions.[2] This kind of primitives dates back to [Kozen (1985)] at least.

Quite related, but from a different perspective, is the toss primitive introduced in [Chadha *et al.* (2007)]. The intuition is that $\mathsf{toss}(bm, p)$ assigns to the Boolean memory cell bm the value t with probability $\hat{p}$ and the value f with probability $1 - \hat{p}$. This means that $\mathsf{toss}(bm, p)$ has a side-effect on a state, which we understand as making use of a service. In other words, $\mathsf{toss}(bm, p)$ corresponds to a deterministic instruction intended to be processed by a probabilistic service.

[2] In [Ponse (2002)], this operator is provided with a meaning by a translation from closed terms of PGA extended with $\mathbf{u}$ into closed PGA terms.

Common in probabilistic programming are assignments of values randomly chosen from some interval of natural numbers to program variables (see e.g. [Schöning (2002)]). Clearly, such random assignments correspond also to deterministic instructions intended to be processed by probabilistic services. Suppose that $x{=}i$ is a primitive instruction for assigning value i to program variable x. Then we can write: $\#\%\mathsf{H}(k)\ ;\ \mathbf{u}(x{=}1\ ;\ \#k)\ ;\ \mathbf{u}(x{=}2\ ;\ \#k{-}1)\ ; \ldots ;\ \mathbf{u}(x{=}k\ ;\ \#1)$. This is a realistic representation of the assignment to x of a value randomly chosen from $\{1, \ldots, k\}$. However, it is clear that this way of representing random assignments leads to an exponential blow up in the size of any concrete instruction sequence representation, provided the concrete representation of k is its decimal representation.

The refinement oriented theory of programs uses demonic choice, usually written $\sqcap$, as a primitive (see e.g. [McIver and Morgan (2001); Meinicke and Solin (2008)]). A demonic choice can be regarded as a probabilistic choice with unknown probabilities. Demonic choice could be written $+\sqcap$ in a SPISA-like notation. However, a primitive instruction corresponding to demonic choice is not reasonable: no mechanism for the execution of $+\sqcap$ is conceivable. Demonic choice exists in the world of specifications, but not in the world of instruction sequences. This is definitely different with $+\%(p)$, because a mechanism for its execution is conceivable.

It appears that quantum computing has something to offer that cannot be obtained by conventional computing: it makes a stateless generator of random bits available (see e.g. [Gay (2006); Perdrix and Jorrand (2006)]). By that quantum computing indeed provides a justification of $+\%(1/2)$ as a probabilistic instruction.

Appendix A

Five Challenges for Projectionism

In this appendix, we sketch five challenges for the semantic viewpoint that we call projectionism.

Projectionism is the point of view that:

- any instruction sequence p, and more general even any program p, first and for all represents a single-pass instruction sequence as considered in SPISA;
- this single-pass instruction sequence, found by a translation called a projection, represents in a natural and preferred way what is supposed to take place on execution of p;
- SPISA provides the preferred notation for single-pass instruction sequences.

In a rigid form, as in Sect. 2.3, projectionism provides a definition of what constitutes a program.

The fact that projectionism is feasible for some instruction sequence notation, does not imply that it is uncomplicated. To give an idea of the complications that may arise, we will sketch below five challenges for projectionism that we have encountered.

First, we introduce some notational conventions. ISN stands for an arbitrary instruction sequence notation, p stands for an arbitrary ISN instruction sequence, and `isn2spisa` is the projection that translates each ISN instruction sequence into the closed SPISA term that denotes the single-pass instruction sequence producing the same behaviour.

We have encountered the following challenges for projectionism:

- *Explosion of size.* If $\mathtt{isn2spisa}(p)$ is much longer than p, then the requirement that it represents in a natural way what is supposed to take place on execution of p is challenged. For example, if the primitive instructions of ISN include instructions to set and test up to n Boolean registers, then the projection to $\mathtt{isn2spisa}(p)$ may give rise to a combinatorial explosion of size. In such cases, the usual compromise is to permit single-pass instruction sequences to make use of services, i.e. to interact with registers, stacks or whatever is appropriate (see e.g. Sect. 3.3).

- *Degradation of performance.* If isn2spisa(p)'s natural execution is much slower than p's execution, supposing a clear operational understanding of p, then the requirement that it represents in a natural way what is supposed to take place on execution of p is challenged. For example, if the primitive instructions of *ISN* include indirect jump instructions, then the projection to isn2spisa(p) may give rise to a degradation of performance (see e.g. Sect. 6.1).
- *Incompatibility of services.* If isn2spisa(p) has to make use of services that are not deterministic, then the requirement that it represents in a natural way what is supposed to take place on execution of p is challenged. For example, if the primitive instructions of *ISN* include the instructions of the form $+\%(q)$ or $-\%(q)$ introduced in Sect. 8.3, then p cannot be projected to a single-pass instruction sequence without the use of probabilistic services. In this case, either probabilistic services must be permitted or probabilistic instruction sequences must not be considered instruction sequences.
- *Complexity of projection description.* The description of isn2spisa may be so complex that it defeats isn2spisa(p)'s purpose of being a natural explanation of what is supposed to take place on execution of p. For example, the projection semantics given for recursion in [Bergstra and Bethke (2007)] suffers from this kind of complexity when compared with the conventional denotational semantics. In such cases, projectionism may be maintained conceptually, but rejected pragmatically.
- *Aesthetic degradation.* In isn2spisa(p), something elegant may have been replaced by quite nasty details. For example, if *ISN* provides guarded commands, then isn2spisa(p), which will be much more detailed, might be considered to exhibit signs of aesthetic degradation. This challenge is probably the most serious one, provided we accept that such elegant features belong to instruction sequence notations. Of course, it may be decided to ignore aesthetic criteria altogether. However, more often than not, they have both conceptual and pragmatic importance.

One might be of the opinion that conceptual projectionism can accept explosion of size and/or degradation of performance. We do not share this opinion: both challenges require a more drastic response than a mere shift from a pragmatic to a conceptual understanding of projectionism. This drastic response may include viewing certain mechanisms as intrinsically indispensable for either execution performance or instruction sequence compactness. For example, it is reasonable to consider the probabilistic basic instructions of the form

$\%(q)$, where q is a computable real number, indispensable if the expectations of the times to execute their realizations by means of $\%()$ are not all finite.

Appendix B

Natural Number Functional Units

In this appendix, we investigate functional units for natural numbers. The main results concern universal computable functional units for natural numbers. The main consequences of considering the special case where the state space is $\mathbb{N}$ are the following: (i) $\mathbb{N}$ is infinite, (ii) there is a notion of computability known which can be used without further preparations.

B.1 The Unbounded Natural Number Counter

A typical example of a functional unit in $\mathcal{FU}(\mathbb{N})$ is the unbounded natural number counter NNC introduced in Sect. 3.2.5. The following proposition shows that there are infinitely many functional units for natural numbers with mutually different sets of derived method operations whose method operations are derived method operations of a major restriction of the functional unit NNC.

Proposition B.1. *We have that there exist infinitely many functional unit degrees below* $(\{\mathtt{pred}, \mathtt{iszero}\}, \mathit{NNC})$.

Proof. For each $n \in \mathbb{N}^+$, we define a functional unit $U_n \in \mathcal{FU}(\mathbb{N})$ such that $U_n \leq (\{\mathtt{pred}, \mathtt{iszero}\}, \mathit{NNC})$ as follows:

$$U_n = \{(\mathtt{pred}{:}n, \mathit{Pred}{:}n), (\mathtt{iszero}, \mathit{Iszero})\} ,$$

where

$$\mathit{Pred}{:}n(x) = \begin{cases} (\mathsf{t}, x - n) & \text{if } x \geq n \\ (\mathsf{f}, 0) & \text{if } x < n \,. \end{cases}$$

It follows immediately that $U_1 \equiv (\{\mathtt{pred}, \mathtt{iszero}\}, \mathit{NNC})$. Let $n, m \in \mathbb{N}^+$ be such that $n < m$. Then $\mathit{Pred}{:}n(m) = (\mathsf{t}, m - n)$. However, there does not exist a $\boldsymbol{p} \in \mathcal{L}(\mathtt{f}.\mathcal{I}(U_m))$

such that $|\boldsymbol{p}|_{U_m}(m) = (\mathtt{t}, m - n)$ because $\mathit{Pred}{:}m(m) = (\mathtt{t}, 0)$, $\mathit{Pred}{:}m(0) = (\mathtt{f}, 0)$, $\mathit{Iszero}(m) = (\mathtt{f}, 0)$, and $\mathit{Iszero}(0) = (\mathtt{t}, 0)$. Hence, $U_n \not\leq U_m$ for all $n, m \in \mathbb{N}^+$ with $n < m$. □

B.2 Universal Functional Units

Below, we will show that there exists a universal functional unit among the computable functional units in $\mathcal{FU}(\mathbb{N})$. First, we make precise which functional units are computable.

Definition B.1. A method operation $M \in \mathcal{MO}(\mathbb{N})$ is *computable* if there exist computable functions $F, G{:}\mathbb{N} \to \mathbb{N}$ such that $M(n) = (\beta(F(n)), G(n))$ for all $n \in \mathbb{N}$, where $\beta{:}\mathbb{N} \to \mathbb{B}$ is inductively defined by $\beta(0) = \mathtt{t}$ and $\beta(n+1) = \mathtt{f}$. A functional unit $U \in \mathcal{FU}(\mathbb{N})$ is *computable* if, for each $(\boldsymbol{m}, M) \in U$, M is computable.

We have the following result concerning the connection between the relation $\leq$ on $\mathcal{FU}(\mathbb{N})$ and the computability of functional units in $\mathcal{FU}(\mathbb{N})$.

Theorem B.1. *Let $U, U' \in \mathcal{FU}(\mathbb{N})$ be such that $U \leq U'$. Then U is computable if U' is computable.*

Proof. We will show that all derived method operations of U' are computable.

Take an arbitrary $\boldsymbol{p} \in \mathcal{L}(\mathtt{f}.\mathcal{I}(U'))$ such that $|\boldsymbol{p}|_{U'}$ is a derived method operation of U'. It follows immediately from the axioms of the thread extraction operator that $|\boldsymbol{p}|$ denotes a component of the solution of a finite linear recursive specification over BTA. Let $\boldsymbol{E}$ be a finite linear recursive specification over BTA such that $|\boldsymbol{p}|$ denotes the $\boldsymbol{x}_1$-component of the solution of $\boldsymbol{E}$. Because $|\boldsymbol{p}|_{U'}$ is total, it may be assumed without loss of generality that D does not occur as the right-hand side of an equation in $\boldsymbol{E}$. Suppose that

$$\boldsymbol{E} = \{\boldsymbol{x}_i = \boldsymbol{x}_{l(i)} \trianglelefteq \mathtt{f}.\boldsymbol{m}_i \trianglerighteq \boldsymbol{x}_{r(i)} \mid i \in [1, n]\} \cup \{\boldsymbol{x}_{n+1} = \mathsf{S{+}}, \boldsymbol{x}_{n+2} = \mathsf{S{-}}\} .$$

From this set of equations, using the relevant axioms and definitions, we obtain a set of equations for which the $\boldsymbol{F}_1$-component of its solution is $|\boldsymbol{p}|^{\mathsf{e}}_{U'}$:

$$\begin{aligned}&\{\boldsymbol{F}_i(s) = \boldsymbol{F}_{l(i)}(\boldsymbol{m}_i{}^{\mathsf{e}}_{U'}(s)) \cdot \overline{\mathsf{sg}}(\chi_i(s)) + \boldsymbol{F}_{r(i)}(\boldsymbol{m}_i{}^{\mathsf{e}}_{U'}(s)) \cdot \mathsf{sg}(\chi_i(s)) \mid i \in [1, n]\} \\ &\quad \cup \{\boldsymbol{F}_{n+1}(s) = s, \boldsymbol{F}_{n+2}(s) = s\} ,\end{aligned}$$

where, for every $i \in [1, n]$, the function $\chi_i : \mathbb{N} \to \mathbb{N}$ is such that for all $s \in \mathbb{N}$:

$$\chi_i(s) = 0 \Leftrightarrow \boldsymbol{m}_i{}^{\mathsf{r}}_{U'}(s) = \mathtt{t} ,$$

and the functions sg, $\overline{\text{sg}} : \mathbb{N} \to \mathbb{N}$ are defined as usual:

$$\begin{aligned} \text{sg}(0) &= 0\,, & \overline{\text{sg}}(0) &= 1\,, \\ \text{sg}(n+1) &= 1\,, & \overline{\text{sg}}(n+1) &= 0\,. \end{aligned}$$

It follows from the way in which this set of equations is obtained from $\boldsymbol{E}$, the fact that $\boldsymbol{m}_i{}^{\mathrm{e}}_{U'}$ and χ_i are computable for each $i \in [1, n]$, and the fact that sg and $\overline{\text{sg}}$ are computable, that this set of equations is equivalent to a set of equations by which $|\boldsymbol{p}|^{\mathrm{e}}_{U'}$ is defined recursively in the sense of [Kleene (1936)]. This means that $|\boldsymbol{p}|^{\mathrm{e}}_{U'}$ is general recursive, and hence computable.

In a similar way, it is proved that $|\boldsymbol{p}|^{\mathrm{r}}_{U'}$ is computable. □

Definition B.2. A computable $U \in \mathcal{FU}(\mathbb{N})$ is *universal* if for each computable $U' \in \mathcal{FU}(\mathbb{N})$, we have $U' \leq U$.

There exists a universal computable functional unit for natural numbers.

Theorem B.2. *There exists a computable $U \in \mathcal{FU}(\mathbb{N})$ that is universal.*

Proof. We will show that there exists a computable $U \in \mathcal{FU}(\mathbb{N})$ with the property that each computable $M \in \mathcal{MO}(\mathbb{N})$ is a derived method operation of U.

As a corollary of Theorem 10.3 from [Shepherdson and Sturgis (1963)],[1] we have that each computable $M \in \mathcal{MO}(\mathbb{N})$ can be computed by means of a register machine with six registers, say $\mathtt{r0}$, $\mathtt{r1}$, $\mathtt{r2}$, $\mathtt{r3}$, $\mathtt{r4}$, and $\mathtt{r5}$. The registers are used as follows: $\mathtt{r0}$ as input register; $\mathtt{r1}$ as output register for the output in $\mathbb{B}$; $\mathtt{r2}$ as output register for the output in $\mathbb{N}$; $\mathtt{r3}$, $\mathtt{r4}$ and $\mathtt{r5}$ as auxiliary registers. The content of $\mathtt{r1}$ represents the Boolean output as follows: 0 represents t and all other natural numbers represent f. For each $i \in [0, 5]$, register $\mathtt{r}i$ can be incremented by one, decremented by one, and tested for zero by means of instructions $\mathtt{r}i\mathtt{.succ}$, $\mathtt{r}i\mathtt{.pred}$ and $\mathtt{r}i\mathtt{.iszero}$, respectively. We write $\mathcal{L}(\mathcal{RM}_6)$ for the set of all ISNR^{s} instruction sequences, taking $\{\mathtt{r}i.m \mid i \in [0, 5] \wedge m \in \{\mathtt{succ}, \mathtt{pred}, \mathtt{iszero}\}\}$ as the set $\mathfrak{A}$ of basic instructions. Clearly, $\mathcal{L}(\mathcal{RM}_6)$ is adequate to represent all register machine programs using six registers.

We define a computable functional unit $Univ \in \mathcal{FU}(\mathbb{N})$ whose method operations can simulate the effects of the register machine instructions by encoding the register machine states by natural numbers such that the contents of the registers can reconstructed by prime

[1] That theorem can be looked upon as a corollary of Theorem Ia from [Minsky (1961)].

factorization. This functional unit is defined as follows:

$$\begin{aligned} \mathit{Univ} = {} & \{(\mathtt{r}i{:}\mathtt{succ}, Ri{:}\mathit{succ}) \mid i \in [0,5]\} \cup \{(\mathtt{r}i{:}\mathtt{pred}, Ri{:}\mathit{pred}) \mid i \in [0,5]\} \\ \cup \; & \{(\mathtt{r}i{:}\mathtt{iszero}, Ri{:}\mathit{iszero}) \mid i \in [0,5]\} \cup \{(\mathtt{exp2}, \mathit{Exp2}), (\mathtt{fact5}, \mathit{Fact5})\} , \end{aligned}$$

where the method operations are defined as follows:

$$\begin{aligned} Ri{:}\mathit{succ}(x) &= (\mathsf{t}, p_i \cdot x) , \\ Ri{:}\mathit{pred}(x) &= \begin{cases} (\mathsf{t}, x/p_i) & \text{if } p_i \mid x \\ (\mathsf{f}, x) & \text{if } \neg(p_i \mid x) , \end{cases} \\ Ri{:}\mathit{iszero}(x) &= \begin{cases} (\mathsf{t}, x) & \text{if } \neg(p_i \mid x) \\ (\mathsf{f}, x) & \text{if } p_i \mid x , \end{cases} \end{aligned}$$ [2]

for each $i \in [0,5]$, and

$$\begin{aligned} \mathit{Exp2}(x) &= (\mathsf{t}, 2^x) , \\ \mathit{Fact5}(x) &= (\mathsf{t}, \max\{y \mid \exists z \bullet x = 5^y \cdot z\}) , \end{aligned}$$

where p_i is the $(i{+}1)$th prime number, i.e. $p_0 = 2, p_1 = 3, p_2 = 5, \ldots$.

We define a function rml2ful from $\mathcal{L}(\mathcal{RM}_6)$ to $\mathcal{L}(\mathtt{f}.\mathcal{I}(\mathit{Univ}))$, which gives, for each instruction sequence $\boldsymbol{p}$ in $\mathcal{L}(\mathcal{RM}_6)$, the instruction sequence in $\mathcal{L}(\mathtt{f}.\mathcal{I}(\mathit{Univ}))$ by which the effect produced by $\boldsymbol{p}$ on a register machine with six registers can be simulated by means of the method operations of Univ. This function is defined as follows:

$$\begin{aligned} & \mathtt{rml2ful}(\boldsymbol{u}_1 \,;\ldots;\, \boldsymbol{u}_k) \\ & \quad = \mathtt{f.exp2} \,;\, \varphi(\boldsymbol{u}_1) \,;\ldots;\, \varphi(\boldsymbol{u}_k) \,; \\ & \quad\quad -\mathtt{f.r1{:}iszero} \,;\, \#3 \,;\, \mathtt{f.fact5} \,;\, !\mathsf{t} \,;\, \mathtt{f.fact5} \,;\, !\mathsf{f} , \end{aligned}$$

where

$$\begin{aligned} \varphi(\boldsymbol{a}) &= \psi(\boldsymbol{a}) , \\ \varphi(+\boldsymbol{a}) &= +\psi(\boldsymbol{a}) , \\ \varphi(-\boldsymbol{a}) &= -\psi(\boldsymbol{a}) , \\ \varphi(\boldsymbol{u}) &= \boldsymbol{u} \qquad \text{if } \boldsymbol{u} \text{ is a jump or termination instruction} , \end{aligned}$$

where, for each $i \in [0,5]$:

$$\begin{aligned} \psi(\mathtt{r}i.\mathtt{succ}) &= \mathtt{f.r}i{:}\mathtt{succ} , \\ \psi(\mathtt{r}i.\mathtt{pred}) &= \mathtt{f.r}i{:}\mathtt{pred} , \\ \psi(\mathtt{r}i.\mathtt{iszero}) &= \mathtt{f.r}i{:}\mathtt{iszero} . \end{aligned}$$

Take an arbitrary computable $M \in \mathcal{MO}(\mathbb{N})$. Then there exists an instruction sequence in $\mathcal{L}(\mathcal{RM}_6)$ that computes M. Take an arbitrary $\boldsymbol{p} \in \mathcal{L}(\mathcal{RM}_6)$ that computes M. Then $|\mathtt{rml2ful}(\boldsymbol{p})|_{\mathit{Univ}} = M$. Hence, M is a derived method operation of Univ. □

[2] As usual, we write $x \mid y$ for y is divisible by x.

The universal computable functional unit Univ defined in the proof of Theorem B.2 has 20 method operations. However, three method operations suffice.

Theorem B.3. *There exists a computable $U \in \mathcal{FU}(\mathbb{N})$ with only three method operations that is universal.*

Proof. We know from the proof of Theorem B.2 that there exists a universal computable $U \in \mathcal{FU}(\mathbb{N})$ with 20 method operations, say $M_0, \ldots, M_{19}$. We will show that there exists a computable $U' \in \mathcal{FU}(\mathbb{N})$ with only three method operations such that $U \leq U'$.

We define a computable functional unit $\mathit{Univ}' \in \mathcal{FU}(\mathbb{N})$ with only three method operations such that $\mathit{Univ} \leq \mathit{Univ}'$ as follows:

$$\mathit{Univ}' = \{(\mathrm{g1}, G1), (\mathrm{g2}, G2), (\mathrm{g3}, G3)\}\ ,$$

where the method operations are defined as follows:

$$\begin{aligned} G1(x) &= (\mathsf{t}, 2^x)\ , \\ G2(x) &= \begin{cases} (\mathsf{t}, 3 \cdot x) & \text{if } \neg(3^{19} \mid x) \land \exists y, z \bullet x = 3^y \cdot 2^z \\ (\mathsf{t}, x/3^{19}) & \text{if } 3^{19} \mid x \land \neg(3^{20} \mid x) \land \exists y, z \bullet x = 3^y \cdot 2^z \\ (\mathsf{f}, 0) & \text{if } 3^{20} \mid x \lor \neg\exists y, z \bullet x = 3^y \cdot 2^z\ , \end{cases} \\ G3(x) &= M_{\mathit{fact3}(x)}(\mathit{fact2}(x))\ , \end{aligned}$$

where

$$\begin{aligned} \mathit{fact2}(x) &= \max\{y \mid \exists z \bullet x = 2^y \cdot z\}\ , \\ \mathit{fact3}(x) &= \max\{y \mid \exists z \bullet x = 3^y \cdot z\}\ . \end{aligned}$$

We have that $M_i(x) = G3(3^i \cdot 2^x)$ for each $i \in [0, 19]$. Moreover, state $3^i \cdot 2^x$ can be obtained from state x by first applying $G1$ once and next applying $G2$ i times. Hence, for each $i \in [0, 19]$, $|\mathtt{f.g1}\,;\mathtt{f.g2}^i\,;+\mathtt{f.g3}\,;!\mathsf{t}\,;!\mathsf{f}|_{\mathit{Univ}'} = M_i$.[3] Hence, $M_0, \ldots, M_{19}$ are derived method operations of Univ'. □

The universal computable functional unit Univ' defined in the proof of Theorem B.3 has three method operations. We can show that one method operation does not suffice.

Theorem B.4. *There does not exist a computable $U \in \mathcal{FU}(\mathbb{N})$ with only one method operation that is universal.*

Proof. We will show that there does not exist a computable $U \in \mathcal{FU}(\mathbb{N})$ with one method operation such that $\mathit{NNC} \leq U$. Here, NNC is the functional unit introduced in Sect. 3.2.5.

[3] For each primitive instruction u, the instruction sequence u^n is defined by induction on n as follows: $u^0 = \#1$, $u^1 = u$ and $u^{n+2} = u\ ;\ u^{n+1}$.

Assume that there exists a computable $U \in \mathcal{FU}(\mathbb{N})$ with one method operation such that $NNC \leq U$. Let $U' \in \mathcal{FU}(\mathbb{N})$ be such that U' has one method operation and $NNC \leq U'$, and let m be the unique method name such that $\mathcal{I}(U') = \{m\}$. Take arbitrary $p_1, p_2 \in \mathcal{L}(\mathtt{f}.\mathcal{I}(U'))$ such that $|p_1|_{U'} = \mathit{Succ}$ and $|p_2|_{U'} = \mathit{Pred}$. Then $|p_1|_{U'}(0) = (\mathsf{t}, 1)$ and $|p_2|_{U'}(1) = (\mathsf{t}, 0)$. Instruction $\mathtt{f}.m$ is processed at least once if p_1 is applied to $U'(0)$ or p_2 is applied to $U'(1)$. Let k_0 be the number of times that instruction $\mathtt{f}.m$ is processed on application of p_1 to $U'(0)$ and let k_1 be the number of times that instruction $\mathtt{f}.m$ is processed on application of p_2 to $U'(1)$ (irrespective of replies). Then, from state 0, state 0 is reached again after $\mathtt{f}.m$ is processed $k_0 + k_1$ times. Thus, by repeated application of p_1 to $U'(0)$ at most $k_0 + k_1$ different states can be reached. This contradicts with $|p_1|_{U'} = \mathit{Succ}$. Hence, there does not exist a computable $U \in \mathcal{FU}(\mathbb{N})$ with one method operation such that $NNC \leq U$. □

It is an open problem whether two method operations suffice.

To the best of our knowledge, there are no existing results in computability theory directly related to Theorems B.2, B.3 and B.4. We could not even say which existing notion from computability theory corresponds to the universality of a functional unit for natural numbers.

Appendix C

Dynamically Instantiated Instructions

In this appendix, we illustrate the usefulness of dynamically instantiated instructions (introduced in Sect. 3.3.5) by means of an example. Before that, we introduce a concrete notation for basic instructions and basic proto-instructions, for the case where each basic instruction consists of a focus and a method. The resulting concrete notation will be used in the example.

C.1 A Concrete Notation for Basic Proto-instructions

First of all, we distinguish neutral strings and active strings.

A *neutral string* is an empty string or a string of one or more characters of which the first character is a letter or a colon and each of the remaining characters is a letter, a digit or a colon. An *active string* is a string of two or more characters of which the first character is an asterisk and each of the remaining characters is a digit.

A *concrete basic instruction* is a string of the form $f.m$, where f and m are neutral strings of which the first character is a letter. A *concrete basic proto-instruction* is a string of the form $f.m$, where f and m are non-empty strings of characters in which neutral strings and active strings alternate, starting with a neutral string of which the first character is a letter, and at least one active string occurs in the whole.

For example, passw.chk:110 is a concrete basic instruction, because both passw and chk:110 are neutral strings of which the first character is a letter. On the other hand, passw.chk:*1:*2:*3 is a concrete basic proto-instruction, because both passw and chk:*1:*2:*3 are strings in which neutral strings and active strings alternate, starting with a neutral string of which the first character is a letter, and there occur three active strings in passw.chk:*1:*2:*3.

The intention is that instantiation of a concrete basic proto-instruction amounts to simultaneously replacing all active strings occurring in it by strings according to some assignment of strings to active strings. The assignment concerned must be such that concrete basic proto-instructions are turned into concrete basic instructions.

To accomplish the assignment of strings to active strings straightforwardly, we stipulate that all active strings of interest must be of the form $*\delta$, where δ is the decimal representation of some $i \in [1, i_{\mathrm{max}}]$.[1] Moreover, an encoding of the assignable strings by numbers in $[0, n_{\mathrm{max}}]$ must be given.[1] Then each state of the register file being involved in $\mathrm{ISNA}_{\mathrm{dii}}$ induces an assignment as follows: for each active string of interest, say $*\delta$, the string assigned to it is the one that is encoded by the content of the register with the number of which δ is the decimal representation.

The concrete notation for concrete basic proto-instructions introduced above is sufficiently expressive for all applications that we have in mind. The assignable strings are in many cases binary or decimal representations of numbers in the interval $[0, n_{\mathrm{max}}]$. In such cases, it is most natural to encode the representations simply by the numbers that they represent.

C.2 An Example

Consider an instruction sequence that on execution reads digit by digit the binary representation of a password and then performs an action to have the password checked by some service. The binary representation of a password is a character sequence of a fixed length, say n, of which all characters are among the binary digits 0 and 1. The instruction sequence reads in the binary digits which make up the binary representation of the password by performing actions that are processed by some other service. Suppose that the service used for reading in binary digits only accepts methods of the form getb and returns the reply f if the next binary digit is 0 and t if the next binary digit is 1. Moreover, suppose that the service used for checking passwords only accepts methods of the form chk:pw, where pw is the binary representation of a password. The focus stdin is used below as a name of the former service and the focus passw is used below as a name of the latter service.

In $\mathrm{ISNA}_{\mathrm{dii}}$, where proto-instructions are available, the instruction sequence has to distinguish among only $2 \cdot n$ cases. In ISNA, where no proto-instructions are available, the instruction sequence has to distinguish among 2^n cases.

Take $i_{\mathrm{max}} = n$ and $n_{\mathrm{max}} = 1$. Consider the case where $n = 3$. The initial part of the

[1] i_{max} and n_{max} are the parameters of the register file being involved in $\mathrm{ISNA}_{\mathrm{dii}}$ (see Sect. 3.3.5).

most obvious $\mathrm{ISNA}_{\mathrm{dii}}$ instruction sequence looks as follows:

$$+\mathsf{stdin.getb}\ ;\ \#\#5\ ;\ \mathsf{set}{:}1{:}0\ ;\ \#\#6\ ;\ \mathsf{set}{:}1{:}1\ ;$$
$$+\mathsf{stdin.getb}\ ;\ \#\#10\ ;\ \mathsf{set}{:}2{:}0\ ;\ \#\#11\ ;\ \mathsf{set}{:}2{:}1\ ;$$
$$+\mathsf{stdin.getb}\ ;\ \#\#15\ ;\ \mathsf{set}{:}3{:}0\ ;\ \#\#16\ ;\ \mathsf{set}{:}3{:}1\ ;$$
$$+\mathsf{passw.chk}{:}{*}1{:}{*}2{:}{*}3\ ;\ \ldots$$

The initial part of the most obvious ISNA instruction sequence looks as follows:

$$+\mathsf{stdin.getb}\ ;\ \#\#7\ ;\ \#\#4\ ;$$
$$+\mathsf{stdin.getb}\ ;\ \#\#13\ ;\ \#\#10\ ;\ +\mathsf{stdin.getb}\ ;\ \#\#19\ ;\ \#\#16\ ;$$
$$+\mathsf{stdin.getb}\ ;\ \#\#25\ ;\ \#\#22\ ;\ +\mathsf{stdin.getb}\ ;\ \#\#31\ ;\ \#\#28\ ;$$
$$+\mathsf{stdin.getb}\ ;\ \#\#37\ ;\ \#\#34\ ;\ +\mathsf{stdin.getb}\ ;\ \#\#43\ ;\ \#\#40\ ;$$
$$+\mathsf{passw.chk}{:}000\ ;\ \#\#44\ ;\ \#\#45\ ;\ +\mathsf{passw.chk}{:}001\ ;\ \#\#44\ ;\ \#\#45\ ;$$
$$+\mathsf{passw.chk}{:}010\ ;\ \#\#44\ ;\ \#\#45\ ;\ +\mathsf{passw.chk}{:}011\ ;\ \#\#44\ ;\ \#\#45\ ;$$
$$+\mathsf{passw.chk}{:}100\ ;\ \#\#44\ ;\ \#\#45\ ;\ +\mathsf{passw.chk}{:}101\ ;\ \#\#44\ ;\ \#\#45\ ;$$
$$+\mathsf{passw.chk}{:}110\ ;\ \#\#44\ ;\ \#\#45\ ;\ +\mathsf{passw.chk}{:}111\ ;\ \ldots$$

The initial part of the ISNA instruction sequence that results from the translation of the $\mathrm{ISNA}_{\mathrm{dii}}$ instruction sequence by means of `isnadii2isna` (see Sect. 3.3.5) looks as follows:

$$+\mathsf{stdin.getb}\ ;\ \#\#5\ ;\ \mathtt{nnr}{:}1.\mathtt{set}{:}0\ ;\ \#\#6\ ;\ \mathtt{nnr}{:}1.\mathtt{set}{:}1\ ;$$
$$+\mathsf{stdin.getb}\ ;\ \#\#10\ ;\ \mathtt{nnr}{:}2.\mathtt{set}{:}0\ ;\ \#\#11\ ;\ \mathtt{nnr}{:}2.\mathtt{set}{:}1\ ;$$
$$+\mathsf{stdin.getb}\ ;\ \#\#15\ ;\ \mathtt{nnr}{:}3.\mathtt{set}{:}0\ ;\ \#\#16\ ;\ \mathtt{nnr}{:}3.\mathtt{set}{:}1\ ;$$
$$+\mathtt{nnr}{:}1.\mathsf{eq}{:}0\ ;\ \#\#19\ ;\ \#\#22\ ;$$
$$+\mathtt{nnr}{:}2.\mathsf{eq}{:}0\ ;\ \#\#25\ ;\ \#\#28\ ;\ +\mathtt{nnr}{:}2.\mathsf{eq}{:}0\ ;\ \#\#31\ ;\ \#\#34\ ;$$
$$+\mathtt{nnr}{:}3.\mathsf{eq}{:}0\ ;\ \#\#37\ ;\ \#\#40\ ;\ +\mathtt{nnr}{:}3.\mathsf{eq}{:}0\ ;\ \#\#43\ ;\ \#\#46\ ;$$
$$+\mathtt{nnr}{:}3.\mathsf{eq}{:}0\ ;\ \#\#49\ ;\ \#\#52\ ;\ +\mathtt{nnr}{:}3.\mathsf{eq}{:}0\ ;\ \#\#55\ ;\ \#\#58\ ;$$
$$+\mathsf{passw.chk}{:}000\ ;\ \#\#59\ ;\ \#\#60\ ;\ +\mathsf{passw.chk}{:}001\ ;\ \#\#59\ ;\ \#\#60\ ;$$
$$+\mathsf{passw.chk}{:}010\ ;\ \#\#59\ ;\ \#\#60\ ;\ +\mathsf{passw.chk}{:}011\ ;\ \#\#59\ ;\ \#\#60\ ;$$
$$+\mathsf{passw.chk}{:}100\ ;\ \#\#59\ ;\ \#\#60\ ;\ +\mathsf{passw.chk}{:}101\ ;\ \#\#59\ ;\ \#\#60\ ;$$
$$+\mathsf{passw.chk}{:}110\ ;\ \#\#59\ ;\ \#\#60\ ;\ +\mathsf{passw.chk}{:}111\ ;\ \ldots$$

These instruction sequences take 16, 43 and 58 instructions, respectively, up to and including the password-check (proto-)instructions. In general, we have that:

- The most obvious $\mathrm{ISNA}_{\mathrm{dii}}$ instruction sequence takes $5 \cdot n + 1$ instructions up to and including the password-check proto-instruction;

- The most obvious ISNA instruction sequence takes $6 \cdot (2^n - 1) + 1$ instructions up to and including the last password-check instruction;
- The ISNA instruction sequence that results from the translation of the ISNA_{dii} instruction sequence takes $5 \cdot n + 6 \cdot (2^n - 1) + 1$ instructions up to and including the last password-check instruction.

It is clear, that the availability of proto-instructions is very convenient in this example. Notice that the first ISNA instruction sequence can be looked upon as an optimization of the second ISNA instruction sequence.

Appendix D
Analytic Execution Architectures

In this appendix, we discuss the notion of an analytic execution architecture in the setting of SPISA.

D.1 The Notion of an Analytic Execution Architecture

An analytic execution architecture is a model of a hypothetical execution environment for instruction sequences that is designed for the purpose of explaining how an instruction sequence may be executed. An analytic execution architecture makes explicit the interaction of an instruction sequence under execution with the components of its execution environment.

We will discuss the notion of an analytic execution architecture in the setting of SPISA. An analytic execution architecture for SPISA instruction sequences consists of a component containing a SPISA instruction sequence and a number of components which are called *reactors*.[1] The component containing a SPISA instruction sequence is capable of processing instructions one at a time, issuing appropriate requests to reactors and awaiting replies from reactors. Each reactor is capable of processing particular requests from the component containing a SPISA instruction sequence and issuing replies to it. This implies that, for each reactor, there is a channel for communication between the component containing a SPISA instruction sequence and that reactor. Foci are used as names of those channels.

Recall that the threads that represent the behaviours of SPISA instruction sequences under execution can be extracted from the SPISA instruction sequences with the thread extraction operator $|\_|$ introduced in Sect. 2.2.5. In Chap. 7, the behaviours represented by

[1] This term has been chosen because the components in question behave (exclusively or non-exclusively) in response to requests issued by the component containing an instruction sequence.

threads are taken for processes as considered in the algebraic theory of processes known as ACP^τ. The behaviours that are represented by threads can be extracted from the threads with the process extraction operator $|\_|$ introduced in Sect. 7.1.2. The behaviour of the component containing the SPISA instruction sequence denoted by the closed SPISA term t is the process represented by $||t||$. Thus, the obvious way to go is to describe analytic execution architectures using ACP^τ.

We need an extension of ACP^τ with action renaming operators ρ_h, where $h : \mathsf{A}_\tau \to \mathsf{A}_\tau$ such that $h(\tau) = \tau$. The axioms for action renaming are given in [Fokkink (2000)]. Intuitively, $\rho_h(t)$ behaves as t with each atomic action replaced according to h. A and $|$ are taken such that, in addition to the conditions mentioned at the beginning of Sect. 7.1.2, with the exception of the condition $\mathtt{stop}(r) \mid e = \delta$, the following conditions are satisfied:

$$\begin{aligned} \mathsf{A} \supseteq\ & \{\mathtt{s}_{\mathtt{serv}}(r) \mid r \in \mathbb{B}\} \cup \{\mathtt{r}_{\mathtt{serv}}(m) \mid m \in \mathcal{M}\} \\ \cup\ & \{\mathtt{stop}_{i+2}(r) \mid i \in \mathbb{N} \wedge r \in \mathbb{B} \cup \{\mathsf{m}\}\} \end{aligned}$$

and for all $e \in \mathsf{A}$, $m \in \mathcal{M}$, $r \in \mathbb{B}$, $r' \in \mathbb{B} \cup \{\mathsf{m}\}$, and $i, j \in \mathbb{N}$:

$$\begin{aligned} &\mathtt{s}_{\mathtt{serv}}(r) \mid e = \delta \;, \\ &e \mid \mathtt{r}_{\mathtt{serv}}(m) = \delta \;, \\[1ex] &\mathtt{stop}(r') \mid \mathtt{stop}(r') = \mathtt{stop}_2(r') \;, \\ &\mathtt{stop}(r') \mid \mathtt{stop}_{j+2}(r') = \mathtt{stop}_{j+3}(r') \;, \\ &\mathtt{stop}_{i+2}(r') \mid \mathtt{stop}_{j+2}(r') = \mathtt{stop}_{i+j+4}(r') \;, \\ &\mathtt{stop}(r') \mid e = \delta \quad\ \ \text{if } e \neq \mathtt{stop}(r') \wedge \textstyle\bigwedge_{j \in \mathbb{N}} e \neq \mathtt{stop}_{j+2}(r') \;, \\ &\mathtt{stop}_{i+2}(r') \mid e = \delta \ \text{ if } e \neq \mathtt{stop}(r') \wedge \textstyle\bigwedge_{j \in \mathbb{N}} e \neq \mathtt{stop}_{j+2}(r') \;. \end{aligned}$$

We also need to define a set $A_f \subseteq \mathsf{A}$ and a function $h_f : \mathsf{A}_\tau \to \mathsf{A}_\tau$ for each $f \in \mathcal{F}$:

$$A_f = \{\mathtt{s}_f(d) \mid d \in \mathcal{M} \cup \mathbb{B}\} \cup \{\mathtt{r}_f(d) \mid d \in \mathcal{M} \cup \mathbb{B}\} \;;$$

for all $e \in \mathsf{A}_\tau$, $m \in \mathcal{M}$ and $r \in \mathbb{B}$:

$$\begin{aligned} &h_f(\mathtt{s}_{\mathtt{serv}}(r)) = \mathtt{s}_f(r) \;, \\ &h_f(\mathtt{r}_{\mathtt{serv}}(m)) = \mathtt{r}_f(m) \;, \\ &h_f(e) = e \qquad\qquad \text{if } \textstyle\bigwedge_{r \in \mathbb{B}} e \neq \mathtt{s}_{\mathtt{serv}}(r) \wedge \bigwedge_{m \in \mathcal{M}} e \neq \mathtt{r}_{\mathtt{serv}}(m) \;; \end{aligned}$$

and a set $A_{\mathtt{stop},n} \subseteq \mathsf{A}$ and a function $h_{\mathtt{stop},n} : \mathsf{A}_\tau \to \mathsf{A}_\tau$ for each $n > 1$:

$$A_{\mathtt{stop},n} = \{\mathtt{stop}(r) \mid r \in \mathbb{B} \cup \{\mathsf{m}\}\} \cup \{\mathtt{stop}_i(r) \mid 1 < i < n \wedge r \in \mathbb{B} \cup \{\mathsf{m}\}\} \;;$$

for all $e \in \mathsf{A}_\tau$ and $r \in \mathbb{B} \cup \{\mathsf{m}\}$:

$$h_{\mathtt{stop},n}(\mathtt{stop}_n(r)) = \mathtt{stop}(r) \;,$$
$$h_{\mathtt{stop},n}(e) = e \qquad\qquad \text{if } \textstyle\bigwedge_{r \in \mathbb{B} \cup \{\mathsf{m}\}} e \neq \mathtt{stop}_n(r) \;.$$

The behaviours of reactors are also taken for processes as considered in ACP$^\tau$. We assume that, for each reactor R, a closed ACP+REC term $|R|$ representing the behaviour of R has been given. We require that:

- the set of all atomic actions that can be performed by the process represented by $|R|$ includes at least one of the following sets:

$$\{\mathtt{s}_{\mathtt{serv}}(\mathsf{t})\} \cup \{\mathtt{r}_{\mathtt{serv}}(\boldsymbol{m}) \mid \boldsymbol{m} \in \mathcal{M}\} \cup \{\mathtt{stop}(r) \mid r \in \mathbb{B} \cup \{\mathsf{m}\}\} \;,$$
$$\{\mathtt{s}_{\mathtt{serv}}(\mathsf{f})\} \cup \{\mathtt{r}_{\mathtt{serv}}(\boldsymbol{m}) \mid \boldsymbol{m} \in \mathcal{M}\} \cup \{\mathtt{stop}(r) \mid r \in \mathbb{B} \cup \{\mathsf{m}\}\} \;;$$

- in all series of atomic actions that can be performed by the process represented by $|R|$:
  - each occurrence of an atomic action of the form $\mathtt{s}_{\mathtt{serv}}(r)$ is preceded by an occurrence of an atomic action of the form $\mathtt{r}_{\mathtt{serv}}(\boldsymbol{m})$;
  - as long as atomic actions of the form $\mathtt{s}_{\mathtt{serv}}(r)$ occur, they occur alternately with atomic actions of the form $\mathtt{r}_{\mathtt{serv}}(\boldsymbol{m})$;
- in all states of the process represented by $|R|$ in which an atomic action of the form $\mathtt{r}_{\mathtt{serv}}(\boldsymbol{m})$ can be performed, all atomic actions of the forms $\mathtt{r}_{\mathtt{serv}}(\boldsymbol{m})$ and $\mathtt{stop}(r')$ can be performed.

The behaviour of an analytic execution architecture made up of a component containing the SPISA instruction sequence denoted by the closed SPISA term t and reactors $R_1, \ldots, R_n$ with channels named $\boldsymbol{f}_1, \ldots, \boldsymbol{f}_n$, respectively, is represented by

$$\rho_{h_{\mathtt{stop},n+1}}(\partial_{A'}(|\!|t|\!| \parallel \rho_{h_{f_1}}(|R_1|) \parallel \ldots \parallel \rho_{h_{f_n}}(|R_n|))) \;,$$

where

$$A' = A_{f_1} \cup \ldots \cup A_{f_n} \cup A_{\mathtt{stop},n+1} \;.$$

D.2 A Classification of Reactors

In this section, we provide a classification of reactors.

A distinction is made between target reactors and para-target reactors:

- a reactor R is a *para-target reactor* if the set of all atomic actions that can be performed by the process represented by $|R|$ is included in the set

$$\{\mathtt{s_{serv}}(r) \mid r \in \mathbb{B}\} \cup \{\mathtt{r_{serv}}(m) \mid m \in \mathcal{M}\} \cup \{\mathtt{stop}(r) \mid r \in \mathbb{B} \cup \{\mathtt{m}\}\}\ ,$$

- a reactor R is a *target reactor* if it is not a para-target reactor.

A reactor is a para-target reactor if the result of the processing of commands by the reactor is wholly unobservable externally. Storing auxiliary data in internal memory and fetching auxiliary data from internal memory are typical examples of using a para-target reactor.

A reactor is a target reactor if the result of the processing of commands by the reactor is partly observable externally. Reading input data from a keyboard, showing output data on a screen and storing permanent data in external memory are typical examples of using a target reactor.

The overall intuition about instruction sequences under execution, para-target reactors and target reactors is that:

- the behaviour produced by an instruction sequence under execution interacts with reactors provided by the execution environment of the instruction sequence;
- the intentions about the resulting behaviour pertain only to interaction with target reactors;
- interaction with para-target reactors takes place only in as far as it is needed to obtain the intended behaviour in relation to target reactors.

One of the assumptions made in BTA+TSI, is that the behaviours of para-target reactors are deterministic. The exclusion of non-deterministic behaviours is a simplification. We believe however that this simplification is adequate in the cases that we address: para-target reactors that keep data for an instruction sequence under execution. Of course, it is inadequate in cases where reactors such as dice-playing reactors are taken into consideration. In the setting of BTA+TSI, the behaviours of para-target reactors are called *services*. Another assumption made in BTA+TSI is that the behaviours of target reactors are non-deterministic. The reason for this assumption is that the dependence of target reactors on external conditions make it appear to instruction sequences under execution that they behave non-deterministically.

Bibliography

Arnold, K. and Gosling, J. (1996). *The Java Programming Language* (Addison-Wesley, Reading, MA).

Arora, S. and Barak, B. (2009). *Computational Complexity: A Modern Approach* (Cambridge University Press, Cambridge).

Baeten, J. C. M. and Bergstra, J. A. (1992). Process algebra with signals and conditions, in M. Broy (ed.), *Programming and Mathematical Methods, NATO ASI Series*, Vol. F88 (Springer-Verlag), pp. 273–323.

Baeten, J. C. M. and Weijland, W. P. (1990). *Process Algebra, Cambridge Tracts in Theoretical Computer Science*, Vol. 18 (Cambridge University Press, Cambridge).

Baker, H. G. (1991). Precise instruction scheduling without a precise machine model, *SIGARCH Computer Architecture News* **19**, 6, pp. 4–8.

Balcázar, J. L., Díaz, J. and Gabarró, J. (1988). *Structural Complexity I, EATCS Monographs on Theoretical Computer Science*, Vol. 11 (Springer-Verlag, Berlin).

Bergstra, J. A. and Bethke, I. (2007). Predictable and reliable program code: Virtual machine based projection semantics, in J. A. Bergstra and M. Burgess (eds.), *Handbook of Network and Systems Administration* (Elsevier, Amsterdam), pp. 653–685.

Bergstra, J. A. and Bethke, I. (2009). Square root meadows, `arXiv:0901.4664v1 [cs.LO]`.

Bergstra, J. A. and Bethke, I. (2012). On the contribution of backward jumps to instruction sequence expressiveness, *Theory of Computing Systems* **50**, 4, pp. 706–720.

Bergstra, J. A. and Klop, J. W. (1984). Process algebra for synchronous communication, *Information and Control* **60**, 1–3, pp. 109–137.

Bergstra, J. A. and Loots, M. E. (2000). Program algebra for component code, *Formal Aspects of Computing* **12**, 1, pp. 1–17.

Bergstra, J. A. and Loots, M. E. (2002). Program algebra for sequential code, *Journal of Logic and Algebraic Programming* **51**, 2, pp. 125–156.

Bergstra, J. A. and Middelburg, C. A. (2007a). Instruction sequences with indirect jumps, *Scientific Annals of Computer Science* **17**, pp. 19–46.

Bergstra, J. A. and Middelburg, C. A. (2007b). Maurer computers with single-thread control, *Fundamenta Informaticae* **80**, 4, pp. 333–362.

Bergstra, J. A. and Middelburg, C. A. (2007c). Thread algebra for strategic interleaving, *Formal Aspects of Computing* **19**, 4, pp. 445–474.

Bergstra, J. A. and Middelburg, C. A. (2008a). Instruction sequences for the production of processes, `arXiv:0811.0436v2 [cs.PL]`.

Bergstra, J. A. and Middelburg, C. A. (2008b). Program algebra with a jump-shift instruction, *Journal of Applied Logic* **6**, 4, pp. 553–563.

Bergstra, J. A. and Middelburg, C. A. (2009a). Instruction sequence notations with probabilistic instructions, arXiv:0906.3083v1 [cs.PL].

Bergstra, J. A. and Middelburg, C. A. (2009b). Instruction sequences with dynamically instantiated instructions, *Fundamenta Informaticae* **96**, 1–2, pp. 27–48.

Bergstra, J. A. and Middelburg, C. A. (2010a). Instruction sequences and non-uniform complexity theory, arXiv:0809.0352v3 [cs.CC].

Bergstra, J. A. and Middelburg, C. A. (2010b). On the operating unit size of load/store architectures, *Mathematical Structures in Computer Science* **20**, 3, pp. 395–417.

Bergstra, J. A. and Middelburg, C. A. (2010c). A thread calculus with molecular dynamics, *Information and Computation* **208**, 7, pp. 817–844.

Bergstra, J. A. and Middelburg, C. A. (2011a). Indirect jumps improve instruction sequence performance, arXiv:0909.2089v2 [cs.PL].

Bergstra, J. A. and Middelburg, C. A. (2011b). Inversive meadows and divisive meadows, *Journal of Applied Logic* **9**, 3, pp. 203–220.

Bergstra, J. A. and Middelburg, C. A. (2011c). On the behaviours produced by instruction sequences under execution, arXiv:1106.6196v1 [cs.PL].

Bergstra, J. A. and Middelburg, C. A. (2011d). Thread extraction for polyadic instruction sequences, *Scientific Annals of Computer Science* **21**, 2, pp. 283–310.

Bergstra, J. A. and Middelburg, C. A. (2012a). Instruction sequence processing operators, *Acta Informatica* **49**, 3, pp. 139–172.

Bergstra, J. A. and Middelburg, C. A. (2012b). On the expressiveness of single-pass instruction sequences, *Theory of Computing Systems* **50**, 2, pp. 313–328.

Bergstra, J. A. and Ponse, A. (2002). Combining programs and state machines, *Journal of Logic and Algebraic Programming* **51**, 2, pp. 175–192.

Bergstra, J. A. and Ponse, A. (2007). Execution architectures for program algebra, *Journal of Applied Logic* **5**, 1, pp. 170–192.

Bergstra, J. A. and Ponse, A. (2008). A generic basis theorem for cancellation meadows, arXiv:0803.3969v2 [math.RA].

Bergstra, J. A. and Ponse, A. (2009). An instruction sequence semigroup with involutive anti-automorphisms, *Scientific Annals of Computer Science* **19**, pp. 57–92.

Bergstra, J. A. and Tucker, J. V. (2007). The rational numbers as an abstract data type, *Journal of the ACM* **54**, 2, p. Article 7.

Bergstra, J. A. and van der Zwaag, M. B. (2008). Mechanistic behavior of single-pass instruction sequences, arXiv:0809.4635v1 [cs.PL].

Bishop, J. and Horspool, N. (2004). *C# Concisely* (Addison-Wesley, Reading, MA).

Brock, C. and Hunt, W. A. (1997). Formally specifying and mechanically verifying programs for the Motorola complex arithmetic processor DSP, in *ICCD '97*, pp. 31–36.

Brookes, S. D., Hoare, C. A. R. and Roscoe, A. W. (1984). A theory of communicating sequential processes, *Journal of the ACM* **31**, 3, pp. 560–599.

Chadha, R., Cruz-Filipe, L., Mateus, P. and Sernadas, A. (2007). Reasoning about probabilistic sequential programs, *Theoretical Computer Science* **379**, 1–2, pp. 142–165.

Cooper, D. C. (1967). Böhm and Jacopini's reduction of flow charts, *Communications of the ACM* **10**, 8, pp. 463, 473.

Diertens, B. (2003). A toolset for PGA, Electronic Report PRG0302, Programming Research Group, University of Amsterdam, available from http://www.science.uva.nl/research/prog/publications.html.

Fokkink, W. J. (2000). *Introduction to Process Algebra*, Texts in Theoretical Computer Science, An EATCS Series (Springer-Verlag, Berlin).

Gay, S. J. (2006). Quantum programming languages: Survey and bibliography, *Mathematical Structures in Computer Science* **16**, 4, pp. 581–600.

Groote, J. F. and Ponse, A. (1994). Proof theory for μCRL: A language for processes with data, in

D. J. Andrews, J. F. Groote and C. A. Middelburg (eds.), *Semantics of Specification Languages*, Workshops in Computing Series (Springer-Verlag), pp. 232–251.

Groote, J. F. and Ponse, A. (1995). The syntax and semantics of μCRL, in A. Ponse, C. Verhoef and S. F. M. van Vlijmen (eds.), *Algebra of Communicating Processes 1994*, Workshops in Computing Series (Springer-Verlag), pp. 26–62.

He Jifeng, Seidel, K. and McIver, A. K. (1997). Probabilistic models for the guarded command language, *Science of Computer Programming* **28**, 2–3, pp. 171–192.

Hennessy, J., Jouppi, N., Przybylski, S., Rowen, C., Gross, T., Baskett, F. and Gill, J. (1982). MIPS: A microprocessor architecture, in *MICRO '82*, pp. 17–22.

Hennessy, J. L. and Patterson, D. A. (2003). *Computer Architecture: A Quantitative Approach*, 3rd edn. (Morgan Kaufmann, San Francisco).

Hennessy, M. and Milner, R. (1985). Algebraic laws for non-determinism and concurrency, *Journal of the ACM* **32**, 1, pp. 137–161.

Hoare, C. A. R. (1985). *Communicating Sequential Processes* (Prentice-Hall, Englewood Cliffs).

Hodges, W. A. (1993). *Model Theory, Encyclopedia of Mathematics and Its Applications*, Vol. 42 (Cambridge University Press, Cambridge).

Hopcroft, J. E., Motwani, R. and Ullman, J. D. (2001). *Introduction to Automata Theory, Languages and Computation*, 2nd edn. (Addison-Wesley, Reading, MA).

Jonsson, B., Larsen, K. G. and Yi, W. (2001). Probabilistic extensions of process algebras, in J. A. Bergstra, A. Ponse and S. A. Smolka (eds.), *Handbook of Process Algebra* (Elsevier, Amsterdam), pp. 685–710.

Karp, R. M. and Lipton, R. J. (1980). Some connections between nonuniform and uniform complexity classes, in *STOC '80* (ACM Press), pp. 302–309.

Kleene, S. C. (1936). General recursive functions of natural numbers, *Mathematische Annalen* **112**, pp. 727–742.

Kozen, D. (1985). A probabilistic PDL, *Journal of Computer and System Sciences* **30**, 2, pp. 162–178.

Kranakis, E. (1987). Fixed point equations with parameters in the projective model, *Information and Computation* **75**, 3, pp. 264–288.

Lunde, A. (1977). Empirical evaluation of some features of instruction set processor architectures, *Communications of the ACM* **20**, 3, pp. 143–153.

Lynch, N. A. and Blum, E. K. (1981). Relative complexity of algebras, *Mathematical Systems Theory* **14**, 1, pp. 193–214.

Margenstern, M. (1997). Decidability and undecidability of the halting problem on Turing machines, a survey, in S. Adian and A. Nerode (eds.), *LFCS'97, Lecture Notes in Computer Science*, Vol. 1234 (Springer-Verlag), pp. 226–236.

Maurer, W. D. (1966). A theory of computer instructions, *Journal of the ACM* **13**, 2, pp. 226–235.

Maurer, W. D. (2006). A theory of computer instructions, *Science of Computer Programming* **60**, pp. 244–273.

McIver, A. K. and Morgan, C. C. (2001). Demonic, angelic and unbounded probabilistic choices in sequential programs, *Acta Informatica* **37**, 4–5, pp. 329–354.

Meinicke, L. and Solin, K. (2008). Refinement algebra for probabilistic programs, *Electronic Notes in Theoretical Computer Science* **201**, pp. 177–195.

Milner, R. (1989). *Communication and Concurrency* (Prentice-Hall, Englewood Cliffs).

Minsky, M. L. (1961). Recursive unsolvability of Post's problem of "tag" and other topics in theory of Turing machines, *Annals of Mathematics* **74**, 3, pp. 437–455.

Morgan, C. C., McIver, A. K. and Seidel, K. (1996). Probabilistic predicate transformers, *ACM Transactions on Programming Languages and Systems* **18**, 3, pp. 325–353.

Mosses, P. D. (2006). Formal semantics of programming languages — an overview, *Electronic Notes in Theoretical Computer Science* **148**, pp. 41–73.

Nair, R. and Hopkins, M. E. (1997). Exploiting instruction level parallelism in processors by caching scheduled groups, *SIGARCH Computer Architecture News* **25**, 2, pp. 13–25.

Ofelt, D. and Hennessy, J. L. (2000). Efficient performance prediction for modern microprocessors, in *SIGMETRICS '00*, pp. 229–239.

Patterson, D. A. and Ditzel, D. R. (1980). The case for the reduced instruction set computer, *SIGARCH Computer Architecture News* **8**, 6, pp. 25–33.

Pavlotskaya, L. M. (1973). Solvability of the halting problem for certain classes of Turing machines, *Mathematical Notes* **13**, 6, pp. 537–541.

Perdrix, S. and Jorrand, P. (2006). Classically controlled quantum computation, *Mathematical Structures in Computer Science* **16**, 4, pp. 601–620.

Ponse, A. (2002). Program algebra with unit instruction operators, *Journal of Logic and Algebraic Programming* **51**, 2, pp. 157–174.

Ponse, A. and van der Zwaag, M. B. (2006). An introduction to program and thread algebra, in A. Beckmann *et al.* (eds.), *CiE 2006, Lecture Notes in Computer Science*, Vol. 3988 (Springer-Verlag), pp. 445–458.

Sannella, D. and Tarlecki, A. (1999). Algebraic preliminaries, in E. Astesiano, H.-J. Kreowski and B. Krieg-Brückner (eds.), *Algebraic Foundations of Systems Specification* (Springer-Verlag, Berlin), pp. 13–30.

Schmidt, D. A. (1986). *Denotational Semantics: A Methodology for Language Development* (Allyn and Bacon, Boston).

Schöning, U. (2002). A probabilistic algorithm for k-SAT based on limited local search and restart, *Algorithmica* **32**, 4, pp. 615–623.

Sharir, M., Pnueli, A. and Hart, S. (1984). Verification of probabilistic programs, *SIAM Journal of Computing* **13**, 2, pp. 292–314.

Shepherdson, J. C. and Sturgis, H. E. (1963). Computability of recursive functions, *Journal of the ACM* **10**, 2, pp. 217–255.

Skyum, S. and Valiant, L. G. (1985). A complexity theory based on boolean algebra, *Journal of the ACM* **32**, 2, pp. 484–502.

Tennenhouse, D. L. and Wetherall, D. J. (2007). Towards an active network architecture, *SIGCOMM Computer Communication Review* **37**, 5, pp. 81–94.

Thierauf, T. (2000). *The Computational Complexity of Equivalence and Isomorphism Problems, Lecture Notes in Computer Science*, Vol. 1852 (Springer-Verlag, Berlin).

Thornton, J. (1970). *Design of a Computer – The Control Data 6600* (Scott, Foresman and Co., Glenview, IL).

Turing, A. M. (1937). On computable numbers, with an application to the Entscheidungs problem, *Proceedings of the London Mathematical Society, Series 2* **42**, pp. 230–265, correction: *ibid*, 43:544–546, 1937.

van Glabbeek, R. J., Smolka, S. A. and Steffen, B. (1995). Reactive, generative and stratified models of probabilistic processes, *Information and Computation* **121**, 1, pp. 59–80.

Wirsing, M. (1990). Algebraic specification, in J. van Leeuwen (ed.), *Handbook of Theoretical Computer Science*, Vol. B (Elsevier, Amsterdam), pp. 675–788.

Xia, C. and Torrellas, J. (1996). Instruction prefetching of systems codes with layout optimized for reduced cache misses, in *ISCA '96*, pp. 271–282.

Glossary

Instruction Sequence Algebra

Symbol/Notation	*Meaning*	*Sect.*
SPISA	single-pass instruction sequence algebra	2.1.2
SPISA+SC	SPISA with structural congruence predicate	2.1.4
$\mathrm{SPISA}_{\mathrm{g}}$	SPISA with labels and gotos	4.3.1
$\mathrm{SPISA}_{\mathrm{js}}$	SPISA with jump shift instruction	4.4.1
$\mathrm{SPISA}_{\mathrm{iss}}$	SPISA with instruction sequence splitting	5.2.4
$\mathrm{SPISA}_{\mathrm{p}}$	SPISA with polyadic instruction sequences	8.1.1
C	SPISA variant with backward instructions	8.2.1
$\mathfrak{A}$	the set of basic instructions	2.1.1
$\mathfrak{I}$	the set of primitive instructions	2.1.1
$\mathbf{IS}$	instruction sequence	2.1.2
a	plain basic instruction	2.1.2
$+a$	positive test instruction	2.1.2
$-a$	negative test instruction	2.1.2
$\#l$	forward jump instruction	2.1.2
!	plain termination instruction	2.1.2
!t	positive termination instruction	2.1.2
!f	negative termination instruction	2.1.2
;	concatenation	2.1.2
$^{\omega}$	repetition	2.1.2
$\cong_{\mathrm{s}}$	structural congruence	2.1.4
$\equiv_{\mathsf{b}}$	behavioural equivalence	2.2.6
$\cong_{\mathsf{b}}$	behavioural congruence	2.2.6
$[l]$	label instruction	4.3.1
$\#[l]$	goto instruction	4.3.1
$\#'$	jump-shift instruction	4.4.1
$\mathsf{split}(bp)$	splitting instruction	5.2.4
$\mathsf{reply}(bp)$	direct replying instruction	5.2.4

$\#\#\#i$	switch-over instruction	8.1.1
$\$\mathsf{put}{:}i{:}\boldsymbol{u}$	put instruction	8.1.1
$\$\mathsf{get}{:}i$	get instruction	8.1.1
$/\boldsymbol{a}$	forward plain basic instruction	8.2.1
$+/\boldsymbol{a}$	forward positive test instruction	8.2.1
$-/\boldsymbol{a}$	forward negative test instruction	8.2.1
$/\#l$	forward jump instruction	8.2.1
$\backslash\boldsymbol{a}$	backward plain basic instruction	8.2.1
$+\backslash\boldsymbol{a}$	backward positive test instruction	8.2.1
$-\backslash\boldsymbol{a}$	backward negative test instruction	8.2.1
$\backslash\#l$	backward jump instruction	8.2.1
$\#$	abort instruction	8.2.1

Instruction Sequence Notations

Symbol/Notation	*Meaning*	*Sect.*
ISNR	instruction sequence notation with relative jumps	2.3.1
ISNR^{s}	ISNR with strict Boolean termination	2.3.1
ISNRI	ISNR with implicit termination convention	2.3.4
ISNR_{ij}	ISNR with indirect jumps	3.3.2
ISNA	instruction sequence notation with absolute jumps	2.3.2
ISNAI	ISNA with implicit termination convention	2.3.4
ISNA_{ij}	ISNA with indirect jumps	3.3.1
ISNA_{dij}	ISNA with double indirect jumps	3.3.3
ISNA_{rj}	ISNA with returning jumps	3.3.4
ISNA_{dii}	ISNA with dynamic instruction instantiation	3.3.5
$\backslash\#l$	backward jump instruction	2.3.1
$\#\#l$	absolute jump instruction	2.3.2
$\mathsf{set}{:}i{:}n$	register set instruction	3.3.2
$\mathsf{i}\#i$	indirect forward jump instruction	3.3.2
$\mathsf{i}\backslash\#i$	indirect backward jump instruction	3.3.2
$\mathsf{i}\#\#i$	indirect absolute jump instruction	3.3.1
$\mathsf{ii}\#\#i$	double indirect absolute jump instruction	3.3.3
$\mathsf{r}\#\#l$	returning absolute jump instruction	3.3.4
$\#\#\mathsf{r}$	absolute return instruction	3.3.4
$\boldsymbol{e}$	plain basic proto-instruction	3.3.5
$+\boldsymbol{e}$	positive test proto-instruction	3.3.5
$-\boldsymbol{e}$	negative test proto-instruction	3.3.5
$;_{i=1}^{n} \boldsymbol{p}_i$	stands for $\boldsymbol{p}_1 ; \ldots ; \boldsymbol{p}_n$	2.3.1
`isnr2spisa`	projection from ISNR to SPISA	2.3.1
`isna2spisa`	projection from ISNA to SPISA	2.3.2

Thread Algebra

Symbol/Notation	*Meaning*	*Sect.*
BTA	basic thread algebra	2.2.1
BTA+REC	BTA with guarded recursion	2.2.2
BTA+REC+AIP	BTA+REC with approximation induction	2.2.2
SFA	service family algebra	3.1.1
BTA+TSI	BTA with thread-service interaction	3.1.2
BTA+TSI+REC	BTA+TSI with guarded recursion	3.1.3
BTA+TSI+REC+AIP	BTA+TSI+REC with approximation induction	3.1.3
BTA+TSI+ABSTR	BTA+TSI with abstraction	3.1.9
BTA+MTTS	BTA with multi-threading and thread splitting	5.2.4
$\mathcal{A}$	the set of basic actions	2.2.1
$\mathbf{T}$	thread	2.2.1
D	inaction	2.2.1
S	plain termination	2.2.1
$\mathsf{S+}$	positive termination	2.2.1
$\mathsf{S-}$	negative termination	2.2.1
$\unlhd\, \boldsymbol{a} \,\unrhd$	postconditional composition	2.2.1
$\boldsymbol{a} \circ$	action prefixing	2.2.1
$\langle \boldsymbol{x} \vert \boldsymbol{E} \rangle$	solution of guarded recursive specification	2.2.2
π_n	nth projection	2.2.2
$Res(t)$	the set of residual threads of thread t	2.2.3
$\mathcal{I}$(BTA)	the initial model of BTA	2.2.4
$\mathcal{I}^{\infty}$(BTA)	the projective limit model of BTA	2.2.4
$\vert\_\vert$	thread extraction for instruction sequences	2.2.5
$\mathcal{F}$	the set of foci	3.1.1
$\mathcal{M}$	the set of methods	3.1.1
$\mathbf{R}$	reply	3.1.1
$\mathbf{S}$	service	3.1.1
$\mathbf{SF}$	service family	3.1.1
t	true	3.1.1
f	false	3.1.1
d	divergent	3.1.1
m	meaningless	3.1.1
δ	empty service	3.1.1
$\frac{\partial}{\partial m}$	derived service	3.1.1
ϱ_m	service reply	3.1.1
$\emptyset$	empty service family	3.1.1
$\boldsymbol{f}.$	singleton service family	3.1.1
$\oplus$	service family composition	3.1.1
∂_F	service family encapsulation	3.1.1
$\bigoplus_{i=1}^{n} \boldsymbol{t}_i$	stands for $\boldsymbol{t}_1 \oplus \ldots \oplus \boldsymbol{t}_n$	3.1.1

$/$	use	3.1.2
$\bullet$	apply	3.1.2
$!$	reply	3.1.2
$\downarrow$	convergence	3.1.6
$\downarrow_{\mathbb{B}}$	convergence with Boolean reply	3.1.6
$\uparrow$	divergence	3.1.6
$//$	abstracting use	3.1.9
τ_{tau}	abstraction	3.1.9
$\mathbf{TV}$	thread vector	5.2.4
$\Vert$	cyclic interleaving	5.2.4
S_{D}	inaction at termination	5.2.4
I_{b}^{bp}	parameter instantiation	5.2.4
$\trianglelefteq \mathsf{split}(\boldsymbol{bp}) \trianglerighteq$	splitting postconditional composition	5.2.4
$\trianglelefteq \mathsf{reply}(\boldsymbol{bp}) \trianglerighteq$	direct replying postconditional composition	5.2.4

Functional Units

Symbol/Notation	*Meaning*	*Sect.*
$\mathcal{MO}(\Sigma)$	the set of method operations on state space Σ	3.2.1
M^{r}	reply of method operation M	3.2.1
M^{e}	effect of method operation M	3.2.1
$\mathcal{FU}(\Sigma)$	the set of functional units for state space Σ	3.2.1
$\mathcal{I}(U)$	interface of functional unit U	3.2.1
m_U	method operation named m in functional unit U	3.2.1
$U(\sigma)$	functional unit U in state σ	3.2.1
$\leq$	functional unit derivability	3.2.1
$\equiv$	functional unit bi-derivability	3.2.1
U_H	functional unit induced by Maurer machine H	6.2.1

Process Algebra

Symbol/Notation	*Meaning*	*Sect.*
ACP^{τ}	algebra of communicating processes with silent step	7.1.1
A	the set of atomic actions	7.1.1
$\mathbf{P}$	process	7.1.1
$\boldsymbol{a}$	atomic action	7.1.1
τ	silent step	7.1.1
δ	inaction	7.1.1
$+$	alternative composition	7.1.1
$\cdot$	sequential composition	7.1.1
$\Vert$	parallel composition	7.1.1
$\lfloor\!\lfloor$	left merge	7.1.1
$\mid$	communication merge	7.1.1
$\partial_{\boldsymbol{A}}$	encapsulation	7.1.1
$\tau_{\boldsymbol{A}}$	abstraction	7.1.1

$\langle \boldsymbol{x} \vert \boldsymbol{E} \rangle$	solution of guarded recursive specification	7.1.1
π_n	nth projection	7.1.1
$Sub(p)$	the set of subprocesses of process p	7.1.1
$\vert \_ \vert$	process extraction for threads	7.1.2
$:\rightarrow$	non-branching conditional	7.2.1
ρ_h	action renaming	D.1

General Mathematical Notations

The precedence conventions used in logical formulas are as follows: operators bind stronger than predicate symbols, and predicate symbols bind stronger than logical connectives and quantifiers; $\neg$ binds stronger than $\wedge$ and $\vee$, and $\wedge$ and $\vee$ bind stronger than $\Rightarrow$ and $\Leftrightarrow$; quantifiers are given the smallest possible scope.

Symbol/Notation	*Meaning*
$\neg\varphi$	not φ
$\varphi \wedge \varphi'$	φ and φ'
$\varphi \vee \varphi'$	φ or φ'
$\varphi \Rightarrow \varphi'$	φ implies φ'
$\varphi \Leftrightarrow \varphi'$	φ if and only if φ'
$\forall x \bullet \varphi$	for every object x, φ
$\exists x \bullet \varphi$	for some object x, φ
$a \in A$	a is an element of A
$A \subseteq A'$	A is a subset of A'
$\emptyset$	the empty set
$\mathcal{P}(A)$	the set of all subsets of A
$A \cup A'$	the union of A and A'
$A \cap A'$	the intersection of A and A'
$A \setminus A'$	the difference of A and A'
$A \times A'$	the cartesian product of A and A'
$\{x \mid \varphi\}$	the set containing those x for which φ holds
$\{a_1, \ldots, a_n\}$	the set whose elements are $a_1, \ldots, a_n$
$(a_1, \ldots, a_n)$	the ordered n-tuple whose ith element is a_i ($i \in [1, n]$)
$\bigcup_{i \in I} A_i$	the union of an indexed family of sets
$A \rightarrow A'$	the set of all functions from A to A'
$[a \mapsto a']$	the unique function from $\{a\}$ to $\{a'\}$
$f \oplus g$	the override of f by g
$f \restriction A$	the restriction of f to A
$\mathrm{dom}(f)$	the domain of f
$\mathrm{rng}(f)$	the range of f
$f : A \rightarrow A'$	f is a function from A to A'
A^*	the set of all finite sequences over A
ϵ	the empty sequence
a	the sequence containing only a
$\sigma\sigma'$	the concatenation of σ and σ'
$\mathrm{tl}(\sigma)$	the tail of σ
$\mathrm{len}(\sigma)$	the length of σ

$\mathbb{B}$	the set of all boolean values
$\mathbb{N}$	the set of all natural numbers
$\mathbb{N}^+$	the set of all positive natural numbers
$\mathbb{Z}$	the set of all integers
$[i, i']$	the set of all integers j for which $i \leq j \leq i'$
$t\,[t'/x]$	the result of substituting term t' for variable x in term t

Index